This new edition of the successful calendars book is being published at the turn of the millennium and expands the treatment of the previous edition to new calendars and variants. As interest grows in the impact of seemingly arbitrary calendrical systems upon our daily lives, this book frames the calendars of the world in a completely algorithmic form. The book gives a description of twenty-five calendars and how they relate to one another: the Gregorian (current civil), ISO (International Organization for Standardization), Egyptian (and nearly identic

Ethiopic, Islamic (Moslem), modern Persian (
Bahá'í (both present and future forms), Heb
and tzolkin), Balinese Pawukon, French Rev
metic forms), Chinese (and nearly identical Ja
and modern Hindu (solar and lunisolar). Eas
by-product of the approach, as is the determin............ .. ..u .....g.ous holidays.
Calendrical Calculations makes accurate calendrical algorithms readily available for computer use with Lisp, Mathematica, and Java code for all the algorithms included on the CD, and updates are available on the Web.

This book will be a valuable resource for working programmers as well as a fount of useful algorithmic tools for computer scientists. In addition, the lay reader will find the historical setting and general calendar descriptions of great interest.

Edward M. Reingold was born in Chicago, Illinois, in 1945. He has an undergraduate degree in mathematics from the Illinois Institute of Technology and a doctorate in computer science from Cornell University. Reingold was a faculty member in the Department of Computer Science at the University of Illinois at Urbana-Champaign from 1970–2000; he retired as a Professor Emeritus of Computer Science in December 2000 and is now chair of the Department of Computer Science at the Illinois Institute of Technology. His research interests are in theoretical computer science—especially the design and analysis of algorithms and data structures. A Fellow of the Association for Computing Machinery since 1995, Reingold has authored or coauthored more than 50 research papers and 9 books; his papers on backtrack search, generation of combinations, weight-balanced binary trees, and drawing of trees and graphs are considered classics. He has won awards for his undergraduate and graduate teaching. Reingold is intensely interested in calendars and their computer implementation: in addition to *Calendrical Calculations*, he is the author and maintainer of the calendar/diary part of GNU Emacs.

Beyond his expertise in calendars, Nachum Dershowitz is a leading figure in software verification in general and termination of programs in particular; he is an international authority on equational inference and term rewriting. Other areas in which he has made major contributions include program semantics and combinatorial enumeration. Dershowitz has authored or coauthored more than 100 research papers and several books and has held visiting positions at prominent institutions around the globe. He has won numerous awards for his research and teaching. He was born in 1951, and his graduate degrees in applied mathematics are from the Weizmann Institute in Israel. He is currently a professor of computer science at Tel Aviv University.

CALENDRICAL CALCULATIONS
The Millennium Edition

EDWARD M. REINGOLD

University of Illinois at Urbana–Champaign
and
Illinois Institute of Technology

NACHUM DERSHOWITZ

Tel Aviv University

CAMBRIDGE
UNIVERSITY PRESS

PUBLISHED BY THE PRESS SYNDICATE OF THE UNIVERSITY OF CAMBRIDGE
The Pitt Building, Trumpington Street, Cambridge, United Kingdom

CAMBRIDGE UNIVERSITY PRESS
The Edinburgh Building, Cambridge CB2 2RU, UK
40 West 20th Street, New York, NY 10011-4211, USA
477 Williamstown Road, Port Melbourne, VIC 3207, Australia
Ruiz de Alarcón 13, 28014 Madrid, Spain
Dock House, The Waterfront, Cape Town 8001, South Africa

http://www.cambridge.org

© Edward M. Reingold   Nachum Dershowitz 2001

First published 2001
Second Printing 2002 (Corrected)

Printed in the United States of America

Typeface Times 10/13 pt.   *System* Unix   [TB]

A catalog record for this book is available from the British Library.

Library of Congress Cataloging in Publication data
Reingold, Edward M., 1945–
Calendrical calculations / Edward M. Reingold, Nachum Dershowitz.—The millennium ed.
p.   cm.
Includes bibliographical references and index.
ISBN 0-521-77167-6 (hardback)—ISBN 0-521-77752-6 (pbk.)
1. Calendar—Mathematics.   I. Dershowitz, Nachum.   II. Title.
CE12 .R45   2001
529′.3—dc21   00-031263

ISBN 0 521 77167 6 hardback
ISBN 0 521 77752 6 paperback

לקהלות הקדש
שמסרו נפשם על קדשת השם
יהי זכרם ברוך

Contents

List of Frontispieces

List of Figures

List of Tables

Abbreviations

Abbreviation	Meaning	Explanation
a.d.	Ante Diem	Prior day
A.D.	Anno Domini (= C.E.)	In the year of the Lord
A.H.	Anno Hegiræ	In the year of Mohammed's emigration to Medina
A.M.	Anno Mundi	In the year of the world since creation
	Anno Martyrum	Era of the Martyrs
a.m.	Ante meridiem	Before noon
A.P.	Anno Persico Anno Persarum	Persian year
A.U.C.	Ab Urbe Condita	From the founding of the city of Rome
B.C.	Before Christ (= B.C.E.)	
B.C.E.	Before the Common Era (= B.C.)	
B.E.	Bahá'í Era	
C.E.	Common Era (= A.D.)	
E.E.	Ethiopic Era	
JD	Julian Day number	Elapsed days since noon on Monday, January 1, 4713 B.C.E. (Julian); sometimes J.A.D., Julian Astronomical Day
K.Y.	Kali Yuga	"Iron Age" epoch of the traditional Hindu calendar
m	Meters	
MJD	Modified Julian Day number	Julian day number minus 2400000.5
S.E.	Śaka Era	Epoch of the modern Hindu calendar
p.m.	Post meridiem	After noon
R.D.	Rata Die	Fixed date—elapsed days since the onset of Monday, January 1, 1 (Gregorian)
U.T.	Universal Time	Mean solar time at Greenwich, England (0° meridian), reckoned from midnight; sometimes G.M.T., Greenwich Mean Time
V.E.	Vikrama Era	Alternative epoch of the modern Hindu calendar

Notation	Name	Meaning
$\lfloor x \rfloor$	Floor	Largest integer not larger than x
$\lceil x \rceil$	Ceiling	Smallest integer not smaller than x
$\text{round}(x)$	Round	Nearest integer to x, that is, $\lfloor x + 0.5 \rfloor$
$x \bmod y$	Remainder	$x - y\lfloor x/y \rfloor$
$x \text{ amod } y$	Adjusted mod	y if $x \bmod y = 0$, $x \bmod y$ otherwise
$\lvert x \rvert$	Absolute value	Unsigned value of x
$\text{signum}(x)$	Sign	-1 when x is negative, $+1$ when x is positive, 0 when x is 0
$i° j' k''$	Angle	i degrees, j arc minutes, and k arc seconds
π	Pi	Ratio of circumference of circle to diameter
$\sin x$	Sine	Sine of x, given in degrees
$\cos x$	Cosine	Cosine of x, given in degrees
$\tan x$	Tangent	Tangent of x, given in degrees
$\arcsin x$	Arc sine	Inverse sine of x, in degrees
$\arccos x$	Arc cosine	Inverse cosine of x, in degrees
$\arctan x$	Arc tangent	Inverse tangent of x, in degrees
$[l : u]$	Closed interval	All real numbers $x, l \leq x \leq u$
$(l : u)$	Open interval	All real numbers $x, l < x < u$
$[l : u)$	Half open interval	All real numbers $x, l \leq x < u$
$\neg p$	Logical negation	True when p is false and vice versa
$\displaystyle\sum_{i \geq k}^{p(i)} f(i)$	Summation	The sum of $f(i)$ for all integers $i = k, k+1, \ldots$, continuing only as long as the condition $p(i)$ holds
$\displaystyle\text{MAX}_{\xi \geq \mu}\{\psi(\xi)\}$	Maximum integer value	The largest integer $\xi = \mu$, $\mu + 1, \ldots$ such that $\psi(\mu)$, $\psi(\mu + 1), \ldots, \psi(\xi)$ are true
$\displaystyle\text{MIN}_{\xi \geq \mu}\{\psi(\xi)\}$	Minimum integer value	The smallest integer $\xi = \mu$, $\mu + 1, \ldots$ such that $\psi(\xi)$ is true
$\displaystyle\text{MIN}_{\xi \in [\mu:\nu]}^{p(\mu,\nu)}\{\psi(\xi)\}$	Minimum value	The value ξ such that ψ is false in $[\mu : \xi)$ and is true in $[\xi : \nu]$; see equation (1.21) on page 22 for details
$\langle x_0, x_1, x_2, \ldots \rangle$	List formation	The list containing $x_0, x_1, x_2, \ldots$
$\langle \, \rangle$	Empty list	A list with no elements

(Continued)

Notation	Name	Meaning
$L_{[i]}$	List element	The ith element of list L; 0-based
$A \parallel B$	Concatenation	The concatenation of lists A and B
$\tilde{x}$	Vector	Indexed list of elements $\langle x_0, x_1, \ldots \rangle$
$i^{\mathrm{d}} j^{\mathrm{h}} k^{\mathrm{m}} l^{\mathrm{s}}$	Interval of time	i days, j hours, k minutes, and l seconds
bogus	Error	Invalid calendar date

בָּרוּךְ הַגֶּבֶר אֲשֶׁר יִבְטַח בַּה' (ירמיה י"ז:ז') · ترجمه: مبارك باد كسيكه بر خداوند توكل نمايد (ارميا ۱۷ : ۷)

• تذكرانهٔ بازوی توانا •
• بگرفتن دست ناتوانا است •

بادواره حماسه‌آفرین (اسْتِر ومُرْدِخای) و (جشن مذهبی و تاریخی پوریم)را به عموم همكيشان وارجمند مقيم ايران و خارج از كشور نبريك و تهنيت مى‌گوييم.

פורים פורים פורים לַה'. בָּרוּךְ אֲשֶׁר בָּחַר בָּנוּ:

	قمری	شمسی	عبری	
20 میلادی	ذیقعده ۱۴۱۸	اسفند ۱۳۷۶	ادار ۵۷۵۸	**ایام یمیم**

JOURS / DAYS	مارس MARS 1998	NOTE ملاحظات הערות	ذیقعده ZIGHADEH ۱۴۱۸	اسفند ESFAND ۱۳۷۶	ادار ADAR ۵۷۵۸	ایام یمیم
Jeudi THURSDAY	12	POURIM (جشن پوریم)	۱۳	۲۱	۱۴	پنجشنبه חמישי
Vendredi FRIDAY	13	POURIM SHOUSHAN (پوریم شوشن)	۱۴	۲۲	۱۵	آدینه ششی
SAMEDI SATURDAY SHABAT	14	KI TISSA (כי תשא / פר' ۲۱)	۱۵	۲۳	۱۶	شنبه שבת شبات
Dimanche SUNDAY	15		۱۶	۲۴	۱۷	یكشنبه ראשון
Lundi MONDAY	16		۱۷	۲۵	۱۸	دوشنبه שני
Mardi TUESDAY	17		۱۸	۲۶	۱۹	سه‌شنبه שלישי
Mercredi WEDNESDAY	18		۱۹	۲۷	۲۰	چهارشنبه רביעי
Jeudi THURSDAY	19		۲۰	۲۸	۲۱	پنجشنبه חמישי
Vendredi FRIDAY	20		۲۱	۲۹	۲۲	آدینه ششی
SAMEDI SATURDAY SHABAT	21	NOWROOZ (عید نوروز باستانی ۱۳۷۷) VAYAGHEL - PEKUDEH (ויקהל - פקודי) SH. PARAH	۲۲	فروردین FARVARDIN ۲۳	כג ۲۳	شنبه שבת شبات

Page from an Iranian synagogue calendar for mid-March 1998 showing the Gregorian, Hebrew, Persian, and Islamic calendars.

Preface

> You ought to know that no one has the right to speak in public
> before he has rehearsed what he wants to say two, three, and four
> times, and learned it; then he may speak.... But if a man...puts it
> down in writing, he should revise it a thousand times, if possible.
> —Moses Maimonides: *The Epistle on Martyrdom*
> *(circa 1165)*

This book has developed over a 15-year period during which the calendrical algorithms and our presentation of them have continually evolved. Our initial motivation was an effort by one of us (E.M.R.) to create Emacs-Lisp code that would provide calendar and diary features for GNU Emacs [8]; this version of the code included the Gregorian, Islamic, and Hebrew calendars (the Hebrew implemented by N.D.). A deluge of inquiries from around the globe soon made it clear to us that there was keen interest in an explanation that would go beyond the code itself, leading to our article [2] and encouraging us to rewrite the code completely, this time in Common Lisp [9]. The subsequent addition—by popular demand—of the Mayan and French Revolutionary calendars to GNU Emacs prompted a second article [6]. We received many hundreds of reprint requests for these articles. The response engendered far exceeded our expectations and provided the impetus to write a book in which we could more fully address the multifaceted subject of calendars and their implementation.

The subject of calendars has always fascinated us with its cultural, historical, and mathematical wealth, and we have occasionally employed calendars as accessible examples in introductory programming courses. Once the book's plan took shape, our curiosity turned into obsession. We began by extending our programs to include other calendars such as the Chinese, Coptic, modern Hindu, and modern Persian. Then, of course, the code for these newly added calendars needed to be rewritten, in some cases several times, to bring it up to the standards of the earlier material. We have long lost track of the number of revisions, and, needless to say, we could undoubtedly devote another decade to polishing what we have, tracking down minutiæ, and implementing and refining additional interesting calendars. As much as we might be tempted to, circumstances do not allow us to follow Maimonides' dictum quoted above.

In this book we give a unified algorithmic presentation for 25 calendars of current and historical interest: the Gregorian (current civil), ISO (International Organization for Standardization), Egyptian (and nearly identical Armenian), Julian (old civil), Coptic, Ethiopic, Islamic (Moslem), modern Persian (both astronomical and arithmetic forms), Bahá'í (both present and future forms), Hebrew (Jewish), Mayan (long count, haab, and tzolkin), Balinese Pawukon, French Revolutionary (both astronomical and arithmetic forms), Chinese (and nearly identical Japanese), old Hindu (solar and lunisolar), and modern Hindu (solar and lunisolar). Easy conversion among these calendars is a natural outcome of the approach, as is the determination of secular and religious holidays.

Our goal in this book is twofold: to give precise descriptions of each calendar and to make accurate calendrical algorithms readily available for computer use. The complete workings of each calendar are described in prose and in mathematical/algorithmic form. Working computer programs are included in an appendix and an accompanying compact disc.

Calendrical problems are notorious for plaguing software, as shown by the following examples:

1. Since the early days of computers, when storage was at a premium, programmers—especially COBOL programmers—usually allocated only two decimal digits for internal storage of years [4], thus billions of dollars were spent fixing untold numbers of programs to prevent their going awry on New Year's Day of 2000 by interpreting "00" as 1900 instead of 2000. This became known as the "Y2K problem."

2. Many programs err in, or simply ignore, the century rule for leap years on the Gregorian calendar (every 4th year is a leap year, except every 100th year, which is not, except every 400th year, which is):

   (a) According to the *New York Times* of March 1, 1997, the New York City Taxi and Limousine Commission chose March 1, 1996, as the start date for a new, higher fare structure for cabs. Meters programmed by one company in Queens ignored the leap day and charged customers the higher rate on February 29.

   (b) According to the *New Zealand Herald* of January 8, 1997, a computer software error at the Tiwai Point aluminum smelter at midnight on New Year's Eve caused more than A\$1 million of damage. The software error was the failure to consider 1996 a leap year; the same problem occurred 2 hours later at Comalco's Bell Bay smelter in Tasmania (which was 2 hours behind New Zealand). The general manager of operations for New Zealand Aluminum Smelters, David Brewer, said, "It was a complicated problem and it took quite some time to find the cause."

(c) Early releases of the popular spreadsheet program Lotus® 1-2-3® treated 2000 as a nonleap year—a problem eventually fixed. However, all releases of Lotus® 1-2-3® take 1900 as a leap year, which is a serious problem with historical data; by the time this error was recognized, the company deemed it too late to correct: "The decision was made at some point that a change now would disrupt formulas which were written to accommodate this anomaly" [10]. Excel®, part of Microsoft Office®, suffers from the same flaw.

3. The calculation of holidays and special dates is a source of confusion:

(a) According to the *New York Times* of January 12, 1999, for example, Microsoft Windows® 95, 98, and NT get the start of daylight saving time wrong for years, like 2001, in which April 1 is a Sunday; in such cases Windows has daylight saving time starting on April 8. An estimated 40 million to 50 million computers are affected, including some in hotels that are used for wake-up calls.

(b) Microsoft Outlook® 98 has the wrong date for U.S. Memorial Day in 1999, giving it as May 24, 1999, instead of May 31, 1999. It gives wrong dates for U.S. Thanksgiving Day for 1997–2000. Outlook® 2000 corrected the Memorial Day error but compounded the Thanksgiving Day error by giving *two dates* for Thanksgiving for 1998–2000.

(c) Various programs calculate the Hebrew calendar by first determining the date of Passover using Gauss's method [3] (see [7]); this method is correct only when sufficient precision is used, and thus such an approach often leads to errors.

(d) Delrina Technology's 1994 Daily Planner has 3 days for Rosh ha-Shanah.

4. At least one modern, standard source for calendrical matters, Parise [5], has many errors, some of which are presumably not due to sloppy editing, but to the algorithms used to produce the tables. For example, the Mayan date 8.1.19.0.0 is given incorrectly as February 14, 80 (Gregorian) on page 290; the dates given on pages 325–327 for Easter for the years 1116, 1152, and 1582 are not Sundays; the epact for 1986 on page 354 is wrongly given as 20; Chinese New Year is wrong for many years; the epoch is wrong for the Ethiopic calendar, and hence that entire table is flawed.

The algorithms presented also serve to illustrate all the basic features of nonstandard calendars: The Mayan calendar requires dealing with multiple, independent cycles and exemplifies the kind of reasoning often needed for calendrical-historical research. The French and Chinese calendars are examples in which accurate astronomical calculations are paramount. The Hindu calendar is an example of one in which the cycles (days of the month, months of the year) are irregular.

We hope that in the process of reworking classical calendrical calculations and rephrasing them in the algorithmic language of the computer age we have also succeeded in affording the reader a glimpse of the beauty and individuality of diverse cultures past and present.

The Millennium Edition

Obiter dicimus priorem illam editionem huius ævi ingeniorum examen fuisse, ex qua non minus quid non possent, quam quid nollent scire, perspici potuit.
[We say in passing that the first edition was a test for the minds of this age, from which both what they could not, and what they did not want to know could be seen.]
—Joseph Justus Scaliger: *De Emendatione Temporum, dedication to the second edition (1598)*

After the first edition of the book was published in 1997 we continued to gather material, polish the algorithms, and keep track of errors. Because the second edition was to be published in the year 2000, some wag at Cambridge University Press dubbed it "The Millennium Edition," and that title got used in prepublication catalogs, creating a *fait accompli*. This millennium edition is a comprehensive revision of the first edition.

In preparing this second edition we have corrected all known errors (though, fortunately, no truly serious errors were ever reported), added much new material, reworked and rearranged some of the material from the first edition to accommodate the new material, and tried to improve the robustness of the functions.

The most serious error corrected is the epoch of the Ethiopic calendar in which we erred by 1 year, following Parise [5] instead of more reliable sources. Also, the modern Hindu solar calendar did not follow a consistent rule for determining the start of the month. The remaining errors were very minor, except for some bad sample data in Appendix C resulting from the erroneous epoch for the Ethiopic calendar and the misapplication of the solar and lunar longitude functions to R.D. dates instead of JD dates.

Among the new material the reader will find an implementation of the early Egyptian calendar (and several calendars nearly identical to it); some alternative functions for the Gregorian calendar; a discussion of the Roman nomenclature for dates, along with functions to implement it; a chapter on the Balinese calendar; a general discussion of astronomical calendars, including the future Bahá'í calendar, the observational Islamic calendar, and the astronomical rules for the determination of Passover and Easter; the astronomical Persian calendar; and the Japanese calendar.

The Hebrew calendar functions have been rewritten largely to improve their robustness. The Chinese calendar implementation has been completely redesigned so as not to depend on the Gregorian calendar. The modern Hindu calendar computations have been substantially simplified. The astronomical functions, which had been drawn from disparate sources, have been revised to make them consistent.

The Compact Disc

This edition of *Calendrical Calculations* comes with a compact disc for personal computers that contains the following files and directories:

- The Lisp code that appears in Appendix B and that implements the calendar functions in this book.
- Lists of the month names used in the different calendars.
- CALENDRICA, a Java implementation of the Lisp code by Robert C. McNally.
- A Mathematica implementation of the Lisp code by Robert C. McNally.
- A directory of tab-separated tables of dates for all the calendars covered in this book for the years 2000–2005. These are suitable for use in spreadsheet programs.
- A directory containing the tables of sample dates from Appendix C.
- An applet for converting dates based on the algorithms of this book.

Calendrical Tabulations

A man who possessed a calendar and could read it was an
important member of the village community, certain to be widely
consulted and suitably awarded.
—K. Tseng: "Balinese Calendar,"
Myths & Symbols in Indonesian Art (1991)

A companion volume by the authors, *Calendrical Tabulations*, is also available. It contains tables for easy conversion of dates and some holidays on the world's major calendars (Gregorian, Hebrew, Islamic, Hindu, Chinese, Coptic/Ethiopic, and Persian) for the years 1900–2200. These tables were computed using the Lisp functions from Appendix B.

> I determined, therefore, to attempt the reformation; I consulted the best lawyers and the most skilled astronomers, and we cooked up a bill for that purpose. But then my difficulty began: I was to bring in this bill, which was necessarily composed of law jargon and astronomical calculations, to both of which I am an utter stranger. However, it was absolutely necessary to make the House of Lords think that I knew something of the matter; and also to make them believe that they knew something themselves, which they do not. For my own part, I could just as soon have talked Celtic or Sclavonian to them, as astronomy, and could have understood me full as well; so I resolved. . . to please instead of informing them. I gave them, therefore, only an historical account of calendars, from the Egyptian down to the Gregorian, amusing them now and then with little episodes. . . They thought I was informed, because I pleased them; and many of them said, that I had made the whole story very clear to them; when, God knows, I had not even attempted it.
>
> —Letter from Philip Dormer Stanhope (Fourth Earl of Chesterfield, the man who in 1751 introduced the bill in Parliament for reforming the calendar in England) to his son, March 18, 1751 C.E. (Julian), the day of the Second Reading debate

The Web Page

To facilitate electronic communication with our readers, we have established a home page for this book on the World Wide Web:

```
http://www.calendarists.com
```

An errata document for the book is available via that home page. Try as we have, at least one error remains in this book.

> It is traditional for the author to magnanimously accept the blame for whatever deficiencies remain. I don't. Any errors, deficiencies, or problems in this book are somebody else's fault, but I would appreciate knowing about them so as to determine who is to blame.
>
> —Steven Skiena: *The Algorithm Design Manual (1997)*

Acknowledgments

We thank Reza Abdollahy, Liú Băolín, Ahmad Birashk, the late LeRoy E. Doggett, Jacques Dutka, Denis A. Elliott, John S. Justeson, Tzvi Langermann, Denis B. Roegel, Robert H. Stockman, and Robert H. van Gent for their comments on various parts of the first edition of this book, and Srinathan Kadambi and Lynne Yancy for their help. Stewart M. Clamen wrote an early version of the Mayan calendar code. Parts of Section 2.3 are based on suggestions by Michael H. Deckers.

Our preparation of the millennium edition was aided considerably by the help of Helmer Aslaksen, Simon Cassidy, John Cross, Michael Deckers, Scott Deifik, Idan Dershowitz, Stewart Dickson, Zecharia Dor-Shav, Paul Eggert, Robert Fowler, Erich Fussi, Mitchell A. Harris, Thomas Heim, Kees van't Hoff, Saori Ihara, Jeffrey C. Jacobs, Svante Janson, J. Bruce King, Joe Kress, Michael Krieger, Tzvi Langermann, Alan Liu, Liú Băolín, Yaaqov Loewinger, Robert McNally, Arthur L. Reingold, Steven Renshaw, Denis Roegel, Trudi de Ruiter, S. Khalid Shaukat, Bruce D. Sinclair, Robert H. Stockman, Robert Stone, Michael Terry, Robert H. van Gent, Thomas M. Widmann, and Georg Zotti, who pointed out errors, suggested improvements, and helped gather materials.

Gerald M. Browne, Sharat Chandran, Shigang Chen, Jeffrey L. Copeland, Mayer Goldberg, Shiho Inui, Yoshiyasu Ishigami, Subhash Kak, Sakai Kō, Howard Jacobson, Claude Kirchner, Nabeel Naser El-deen, the late Gerhard A. Nothmann, Roman Waupotitsch, Daniel Yaqob, and Afra Zomorodian helped us with various translations and foreign language fonts. Charles Hoot labored hard on the program for automatically transforming Lisp code into arithmetic expressions and provided general expertise in Lisp. Mitchell A. Harris helped with fonts, star names, and the automatic translation; Charles Thompson was our omniscient, tireless system support person; Marla Brownfield helped with various tables. Erga Dershowitz, Idan Dershowitz, Molly Flesner, Schulamith Halevy, Christine Mumm, Deborah Reingold, Eve Reingold, Rachel Reingold, Ruth Reingold, and Joyce Woodworth were invaluable in proofreading tens of thousands of dates, comparing our results with published tables. We are grateful to all of them.

Portions of this book appeared, in a considerably less polished state, in our papers [2] and [6]. We thank John Wiley & Sons for allowing us to use that material here.

THE END.
This work was completed on the 17th or 27th day of May, 1618;
but Book v was reread (while the type was being set) on
the 9th or 19th of February, 1619.
At Linz, the capital of Austria—above the Enns.
—Johannes Kepler: *Harmonies of the World*

R.D. 730,120

Urbana, Illinois   E.M.R.

Tel Aviv, Israel   N.D.

References

[1] A. Birashk, *A Comparative Calendar of the Iranian, Muslim Lunar, and Christian Eras for Three Thousand Years*, Mazda Publishers (in association with Bibliotheca Persica), Costa Mesa, CA, 1993.

[2] N. Dershowitz and E. M. Reingold, "Calendrical Calculations," *Software—Practice and Experience*, volume 20, no. 9, pp. 899–928, September 1990.

[3] C. F. Gauss, "Berechnung des jüdischen Osterfestes," *Monatliche Correspondenz zur Beförderung der Erd- und Himmelskunde*, volume 5 (1802), pp. 435–437. Reprinted in Gauss's *Werke*, Herausgegeben von der Königlichen Gesellschaft der Wissenschaften, Göttingen, volume 6, pp. 80–81, 1874.

[4] P. G. Neumann, "Inside Risks: The Clock Grows at Midnight," *Communications of the ACM*, volume 34, no. 1, p. 170, January 1991.

[5] F. Parise, ed., *The Book of Calendars*, Facts on File, New York, 1982.

[6] E. M. Reingold, N. Dershowitz, and S. M. Clamen, "Calendrical Calculations, Part II: Three Historical Calendars," *Software—Practice and Experience*, volume 23, no. 4, pp. 383–404, April 1993.

[7] I. Rhodes, "Computation of the Dates of the Hebrew New Year and Passover," *Computers & Mathematics with Applications*, volume 3, pp. 183–190, 1977.

[8] R. M. Stallman, *GNU Emacs Manual*, 13th ed., Free Software Foundation, Cambridge, MA, 1997.

[9] G. L. Steele, Jr., *Common Lisp: The Language*, 2nd ed., Digital Press, Bedford, MA, 1990.

[10] Letter to Nachum Dershowitz from Kay Wilkins, Customer Relations Representative, Lotus Development Corporation, Cambridge, MA, April 21, 1992.

Credits

Whoever relates something in the name of its author brings
redemption to the world.
—Midrash Tanḥuma (Numbers, 27)

Quote on page xxiii from *Epistles of Maimonides: Crisis and Leadership*,
A. Halkin, trans., Jewish Publication Society, 1993; used with permission.

Translation of Scaliger's comment on the Roman calendar on page 63 from
*Joseph Scaliger: A Study in the History of Classical Scholarship, volume II,
Historical Chronography*, A. T. Grafton, Oxford University Press, Oxford,
1993; used with permission.

Letter on page 230 reprinted with permission.

License and Limited Warranty and Remedy

The Functions (code, formulas, and calendar data) contained in this book were written by Edward M. Reingold and Nachum Dershowitz (the "Authors"), who retain all rights to them except as granted in the License and subject to the warranty and liability limitations below. These Functions are subject to this book's copyright.

The Authors' public service intent is more liberal than suggested by the License below, as are their licensing policies for otherwise nonallowed uses such as—without limitation—those in commercial, Web site, and large-scale academic contexts. Please see the above-mentioned Web site for all uses not authorized below; in case there is cause for doubt about whether a use you contemplate is authorized, please contact the Authors.

1. LICENSE. The Authors grant you a license for personal use only. This means that for strictly personal use you may copy and use the code and keep a backup or archival copy also. Any other uses, including without limitation, allowing the code or its output to be accessed, used, or available to others, are not permitted.

2. WARRANTY.

    (a) *The Authors and Publisher provide no warranties of any kind, either express or implied, including, without limiting the generality of the foregoing, any implied warranty of merchantability or fitness for a particular purpose.*

    (b) *Neither the Authors nor Publisher shall be liable to you or any third parties for damages of any kind, including without limitation, any lost profits, lost savings, or other incidental or consequential damages arising out of, or related to, the use, inability to use, or accuracy of calculations of the code and functions contained herein, or the breach of any express or implied warranty, even if the Authors or Publisher have been advised of the possibility of those damages.*

    (c) *The foregoing warranty may give you specific legal rights which may vary from state to state in the U.S.A.*

3. LIMITATION OF LICENSEE REMEDIES. You acknowledge and agree that your exclusive remedy (in law or in equity), and Authors' and Publisher's entire liability with respect to the material herein, for any breach of representation or for any inaccuracy shall be a refund of the price of this book. *Some States in the U.S.A. do not allow the exclusion or limitation of liability for incidental or consequential damages, and thus the preceding exclusions or limitation may not apply to you.*

4. DISCLAIMER. Except as expressly set forth above, Authors and Publisher:

    (a) make no other warranties with respect to the material and expressly disclaim any others;

    (b) do not warrant that the functions contained in the code will meet your requirements or that their operation shall be uninterrupted or error free;

    (c) license this material on an "as is" basis, and the entire risk as to the quality, accuracy, and performance herein is yours should the code or functions prove defective (except as expressly warranted herein). You alone assume the entire cost of all necessary corrections.

CALENDRICAL CALCULATIONS

MENSIVM DIVISIO.

MENSES ENNEADECAETERICI.

IVDÆO-RVM	OSYROCHAL-DÆORVM	SYROGRÆ-CORVM	DIVS	HAGARE-NORVM	CALIPPI ET SAXONVM
TISRI	TISRIN prior	DIVS		RABIE prior	Pyanepfion
Marchē-	Tifrialter	Apellaus		Rabie alter	Mem. fterion
febuan	Canum prior	Audynæus		Giumadiprior	Pofideon
Casleu	Canum alter	Peritius		Giumadialter	Gamelion
Tebetb	Achbat	Dyftrus		Regiab	Anthefterion
Selebat	Adar	Xanthicus		Subabonu	Elaphebolion
Adarprior	Nifan	Artemifius		Ramadhan	Munychion
fierit	Ijar	Dafius		Schewal	Thargelion
Nifan	HaZiran	Panemus		Dulkaida	Scurophorion
Iiar	Ab	Loüs		Dulhegia	prior
Siwan	Iiul	Gorpiaus		Moharam	Scurophorio
Tamuz	Tebuthembol	Dioscurus		TZephar	alter
Ab		HYPERRE			HECATOM-BÆON
Elul		RETÆVS			Metaginon
					Boedromion

MENSES ÆQVABILES VAGI

ÆGYPTIO-RVM	ARMENIO-RVM	PERSARVM NOVRM
THOTH	Nawafard	Bchemen
Paophi	Hori	Alphi.mlir
Athyr	Maherak	PHRVADIN
Choeac	SAHAMI	Alarphagfhib
Tybi	Thera	Charidad
Mechir	Cegais	Tyr
Phamenoth	Haraiz	Mardad
Pharmuthi	Mahie	Scheheriz
Pachon	Arach	Mehar
Payni	Aheli	Aban
Epiphi	Marrii	Adar
Mefori	Marcaiis	Di
Epagomenæ	Harwaifo	

MENSES ÆQVABILES TETRAETERICI

ATTICO-RVM	MACEDO-RVM	THERANO-RVM	BVCATIVS
GAMELION	Dyftrus		Hermæus
Anthefterion	Xanthicus		
Elaphebolion	Artemifius		*
Munychion	Dafius prior		*
Thargelion	Dafius pofterior		*
Scurophorion	Panemus		Hippodromius
Hecatombæon	PANEMVS		Pancmus
Metageitnion	Loüs		*
Boedromion	Gorpiaus		Dimatrius
Pyanepfion	Hyperbcretæus		Valcomenos
Mem. fterion	Dius		
Pofideon alter	Audynæus		Embolimus
Apelidæ	Peritius		Anæpædus

MEN-

MENSES IVLIANI.

ROMANO-RVM	ATHENIEN-RVM	SYROGRÆ-CORVM	ANTIOCHE-NORVM	HAGARE-NORVM
LVNARIVS	Pyanepfion	Audynæus	Canum alter	Giumadi alter
Februarius	Mæmacterion	Peritius	Achbat	Regiab
Martius	Pofideon	Dyftrus	Adar	Sababen
Aprilis	Gamelion	Xanthicus	Nifan	Ramadhan
Maius	Anthefterion	Artemifius	Ijar	Schewal
Iunius	Elaphebolion	Dafius	HaZiran	Dulkaida
Iulius	Munychion	Panemus	Tamuz	Dulhegia
Auguftus	Thargelion	Loüs	Ab	Moharam
September	Scurophorion	Gorpiaus	Elul	TZephar
October	HECATOM-	HYPERBE-	TISRIN prior	RABIE prior
November	BÆON	RETÆVS	Tifrin alter	Rabie alter
December	Metaginon	Dius alter	Canum prior	Giumadi prior
	Boedromion	Apellaus		

MISCELA MENSIVM.

MENSES VA-GI LVNA-IGI.	MENSES VI-TIOLI.LY-DIIG.	MENSES SO-LARES FULIANI æquabiles.	MENSES TRO-PICI ÆQVAB-lcs Gelaliæ.	MENSES COE-LESTES INTITIG-buß.
MVHAMETA-NORVM	MARTIVS	THOTH	PERSARVM	PTOLOMÆI PHILADELPH.
MPHARAM	Aprilis	Papa	Aban	Zygon
TZephar	Maius	Hathur	Adar	Scorpion
Rabieprior	Iunius	Chiac	Di	Toxon
Rabie alter	Quintilis	Tuba	Bchemen	Ægon
Giumadiprior	Sextilis	Amfhir	Alphander	Hydion
Giumadialter	September	Parmahath	Mfteraks	Ichthyon
Regiab	October	Parmuda	PHRFADIN	Quadrum diei
Sahaben	November	Pafchnes	Alarphagfhib	KRION
Schewal	December	Pauni	Charidad	Tauron
Dulkaida	Ianuarius	Epip	Thir	Didymon
Dulhegia	Februarius	Mafri	Mardad	Karkinon
	Mercelonius	Nifi	Scheheriz	Leonton
			Mehar	Parthenon

Ii 4

Two pages of Joseph Scaliger's, *De Emendatione Temporum* (Frankfort edition, 1593), giving month names on many calendars. (Courtesy of the University of Illinois, Urbana, IL.)

1

Introduction

A learned man once asked me regarding the eras used by different
nations, and regarding the difference of their roots, that is, the
epochs where they begin, and of their branches, that is, the months
and years, on which they are based; further regarding the causes
which led to such difference, and the famous festivals and
commemoration-days for certain times and events, and regarding
whatever else one nation practices differently from another. He
urged me to give an explanation, the clearest possible, of all this,
so as to be easily intelligible to the mind of the reader, and to free
him from the necessity of wading through widely scattered books,
and of consulting their authors. Now I was quite aware that this
was a task difficult to handle, an object not easily to be attained or
managed by anyone, who wants to treat it as a matter of logical
sequence, regarding which the mind of the student is not agitated
by doubt.

—Abū-Raihān Muḥammad ibn 'Aḥmad al-Bīrūnī:
Al-Āthār al-Bāqiyah 'an al-Qurūn al-Khāliyah (1000)

Calendrical calculations are ubiquitous. Banks need to calculate interest on
a daily basis. Corporations issue paychecks on weekly, biweekly, or monthly
schedules. Bills and statements must be generated periodically. Computer op-
erating systems need to switch to and from daylight saving time. Dates of secular and religious holidays must be computed for consideration in planning
events. Most of these calculations are not difficult because the rules of our
civil calendar (the Gregorian calendar) are straightforward.

Complications begin when we need to know the day of the week on which
a given date falls or when various religious holidays based on other calendars
occur. These complications lead to difficult programming tasks—not often difficult in an algorithmic sense but difficult because it can be extremely tedious

3

to delve, for example, into the complexities of the Hebrew calendar and its relation to the civil calendar.

The purpose of this book is to present, in a unified, completely algorithmic form, a description of 25 calendars and how they relate to one another: the present civil calendar (Gregorian); the recent ISO commercial calendar; the old civil calendar (Julian); the ancient Egyptian calendar (and its Armenian equivalent); the Coptic and the (virtually identical) Ethiopic calendars; the Islamic (Moslem) calendar (both the arithmetical version and one based on calculated observability); the (modern) Persian calendar (both astronomical and arithmetic forms); the Bahá'í calendar (both present Western and future forms); the Hebrew (Jewish) calendar; the three Mayan calendars; the Pawukon calendar from Bali; the French Revolutionary calendar (both astronomical and arithmetic forms); the Chinese calendar and (virtually identical) Japanese; and both the old (mean) and new (true) Hindu (Indian) solar and lunisolar calendars. Information that is sufficiently detailed to allow computer implementation is difficult to find for most of these calendars because the published material is often inaccessible, ecclesiastically oriented, incomplete, inaccurate, based on extensive tables, overburdened with extraneous material, focused on shortcuts for hand calculation to avoid complicated arithmetic or to check results, or difficult to find in English. Most existing computer programs are proprietary, incomplete, or inaccurate.

The need for such a secular, widely available presentation was made clear to us when we (primarily E.M.R. with contributions by N.D.), in implementing a calendar/diary feature for GNU Emacs [25], found difficulty in gathering and interpreting appropriate source materials that describe the interrelationships among the various calendars and the determination of the dates of holidays. Some of the calendars (Chinese, Japanese, and Hindu) never had full algorithmic descriptions published in English.

The calendar algorithms in this book are presented as mathematical function definitions in standard mathematical format; Appendix A gives the types (ranges and domains) of all functions and constants we use. To ensure correctness, all calendar functions were automatically typeset[1] directly from the working Common Lisp [27] functions listed in Appendix B.[2] Appendix C tabulates results of the calendar calculations for 33 sample dates.

---

[1] This has meant some sacrifice in the typography of the book; we hope readers sympathize with our decision.

[2] We provide these Lisp functions on the compact disc accompanying this book under the terms of the License Agreements and Limited Warranty on page xxxii. Any errata are available over the World Wide Web at http://www.calendarists.com

We chose mathematical notation as the vehicle for presentation because of its universality and easy convertibility to any programming language. We have endeavored to simplify the calculations as much as possible without obscuring the intuition. Many of the algorithms we provide are considerably more concise than previously published ones; this is particularly true of the arithmetic Persian, Hebrew, and old Hindu calendars.

We chose Lisp as the vehicle for implementation because it encourages functional programming and has a trivial syntax, nearly self-evident semantics, historical durability, and wide distribution; moreover, Lisp was amenable to translation into ordinary mathematical notation. Except for a few short macros, the code uses only a very simple, side-effect-free subset of Lisp. We emphasize that our choice of Lisp should be considered largely irrelevant to readers, whom we expect to follow the mathematical notation used in the text, not to delve into Appendix B.

It is not the purpose of this book to give a detailed historical treatment of the material, nor, for that matter, a mathematical one; our goal is to give a logical, thorough *computational* treatment. Thus, although we give much historical, religious, mathematical, and astronomical data to leaven the discussion, the focus of the presentation is algorithmic. Full historical/religious details and mathematical/astronomical underpinnings of the calendars can be pursued in the references.

In the remainder of this chapter, we describe the underlying unifying theme of all the calculations along with some useful mathematical facts. The details of specific calendars are presented in subsequent chapters. Historically, the oldest of the calendars that we consider is the Egyptian (more than 3000 years old). The Chinese and Mayan calendars also derive from millennia-old calendars. Next are the Julian (the roots of which date back to the ancient Roman empire), the Coptic and Ethiopic (third century), the current Hebrew (fourth century) and the old Hindu (fifth century), followed by the Islamic calendar (seventh century), the newer Hindu calendars (tenth century), the Persian calendar (eleventh century), the Gregorian modification to the Julian calendar (sixteenth century), the French Revolutionary calendar (eighteenth century), and the Bahá'í calendar (nineteenth century). Finally, the International Organization for Standardization's ISO calendar and the arithmetic Persian calendar are of twentieth-century origin.

For expository purposes, however, we present the Gregorian calendar first, in Part I, because it is the most popular calendar currently in use. Because the Julian calendar is so close in substance to the Gregorian, we present it next, followed by the very similar Coptic and Ethiopic calendars. Then we give the ISO calendar, which is trivial to implement and depends wholly on the Gregorian. The arithmetic Islamic calendar, which because of its simplicity is easy to implement, follows. Next, we present the Hebrew calendar, one of the more complicated and difficult calendars to implement, followed by a chapter on the computation of Easter, which is lunisolar like the Hebrew calendar. The ancient Hindu solar and lunisolar calendars are described next; these are simple versions of the modern Hindu solar and lunisolar calendars described in Part II. Next, the Mayan calendar (actually three calendars), of historical interest, has several unique computational aspects. We conclude Part I with the Balinese Pawukon calendar. All of the calendars described in Part I are "arithmetical" in that they operate by straightforward integer-based rules.

In Part II we present calendars that are controlled by irregular astronomical events (or close approximations to them), although these calendars may have an arithmetical component as well. We use the (future) Bahá'í New Year as a simple example and also describe the proposed astronomical calculation of Easter. Calculation of observability of the new moon allows an approximation of the real Islamic calendar and the classical determination of Passover. We then give the modern Persian calendar in its astronomical and arithmetic forms followed by the Bahá'í calendar, also in two versions: the Western, which depends wholly on the Gregorian, and the future version, which is astronomical. Next we describe the original (astronomical) and modified (arithmetic) forms of the French Revolutionary calendar. All of these calendars are computationally simple, provided certain astronomical values are available. Next is the Chinese lunisolar calendar and its Japanese version. Finally, we describe the modern Hindu calendars, which are by far the most complicated of the calendars in this book. Because the calendars in Part II require some understanding of astronomical events such as solstices and new moons, we begin Part II with a chapter introducing the needed topics and algorithms.

As each calendar is discussed, we also provide algorithms for computing holidays based on it. In this regard we take the ethnocentric view that our task is to compute the dates of holidays in a given *Gregorian year*; there is clearly little difficulty in finding the dates of, say, Islamic New Year in a given Islamic year! In general we have tried to mention all significant holidays on the calendars we cover, but have not attempted to be exhaustive and include all variations. The interested reader can find extensive holiday definitions in [11], [12], and [13].

The selection of calendars we present was chosen with two purposes: to include all common modern calendars and to cover all calendrical techniques. We do not give all variants of the calendars we discuss, but we have given enough details to make any calendar easy to implement.

1.1 Calendar Units and Taxonomy

Teach us to number our days, that we may attain a wise heart.
—Psalms 90:12

The sun moves from east to west, and night follows day with predictable regularity. This apparent motion of the sun as viewed by an earthbound observer provided the earliest time-keeping standard for humankind. The day is, accordingly, the basic unit of time underlying all calendars, but various calendars use different conventions to structure days into larger units: weeks, months, years, and cycles of years. Different calendars also begin their day at different times: the French Revolutionary day, for example, begins at true (apparent) midnight; the Islamic, Bahá'í, and Hebrew days begin at sunset; the Hindu day begins at sunrise. The various definitions of *day* are surveyed in Section 12.3.

The purpose of a calendar is to give a name to each day. The mathematically simplest naming convention would be to assign an integer to each day; fixing day 1 would determine the whole calendar. The Babylonians had such a day count (in base 60). Such *diurnal* calendars are used by astronomers (see Section 12.3) and by calendarists (see, for example, Section 9.1); we use a day numbering in this book as an intermediate device for converting from one calendar to another (see the following section). Day-numbering schemes can be complicated by using a mixed-radix system in which the day number is given as a sequence of numbers or names. The Mayans, for example, utilized such a method (see Section 10.1).

Calendar day names are generally distinct, but this is not always the case. For example, the day of the week is a calendar, in a trivial sense, with infinitely many days having the same day name (see Section 1.10). A 7-day week is almost universal today. In many cultures, the days of the week were named after the 7 "wandering stars" (or after the gods associated with those heavenly bodies), namely, the Sun, the Moon, and the five planets visible to the naked eye—Mercury, Venus, Mars, Jupiter, and Saturn. In some languages—Arabic, Lithuanian, Portuguese, and Hebrew are examples—some or all of the days of the week are numbered, not named. In the Armenian calendar, for example, the days of the week are named as follows:

Sunday	Miashabathi
Monday	Erkoushabathi
Tuesday	Erekhshabathi
Wednesday	Chorekhshabathi
Thursday	Hingshabathi
Friday	Urbath
Saturday	Shabath

Other cycles of days have also been used, including 4-day weeks (in the Congo), 5-day weeks (in Africa, in Bali, and in Russia in 1929), 8-day weeks (in Africa and in the Roman Republic), and 10-day weeks (in ancient Egypt and in France at the end of the eighteenth century; see page 234). The mathematics of cycles of days are described in Section 1.10. Many calendars repeat after one or more years. In one of the Mayan calendars (see Section 10.2), and in many preliterate societies, day names are recycled every year. The Chinese calendar uses a repeating 60-name scheme for days and years, and at one time used it to name months.

An interesting variation in some calendars is the use of two or more cycles running simultaneously. For example, the Mayan tzolkin calendar (Section 10.2) combines a cycle of 13 names with a cycle of 20 numbers. The Chinese cycle of 60 names for years is actually composed of cycles of length 10 and 12 (see Section 16.4). The Balinese calendar takes this idea to an extreme; see Chapter 11. The mathematics of simultaneous cycles are described in Section 1.11.

The notions of "month" and "year," like the day, were originally based on observations of heavenly phenomena, namely the waxing and waning of the moon, and the cycle of seasons, respectively. Some calendars begin each month with the new moon, when the crescent moon first becomes visible (as in the Hebrew calendar of classical times and in the religious calendar of the Moslems today—see Sections 12.8 and 12.9); others begin the month at full moon (in northern India, for example)—see page 132. For calendars in which the month begins with the observed new moon, beginning the day at sunset is natural.

Over the course of history, many different schemes have been devised for determining the start of the year. Some are astronomical, beginning at the autumnal or spring equinox, or at the winter or summer solstice. Solstices are more readily observable, either by observing when the shadow of a gnomon is longest (winter solstice in the northern hemisphere) or shortest (summer), or by noting the point in time when the sun rises or sets as far south at it does during the course of the year (which is winter in the northern hemisphere) or maximally north (summer). The ancient Egyptians began their year with the *heliacal rising* of Sirius—that is, on the day that the Dog Star Sirius (the brightest fixed star in the sky) can first be seen in the morning after a period during which the sun's proximity to Sirius makes the latter invisible to the naked eye. The Pleiades ("Seven Sisters") were used by the Maoris and other peoples for the same purpose. Various other natural phenomena have been used among North American tribes [3] to establish the onset of a new year such as harvests or the rutting seasons of certain animals.

Calendars have an integral number of days in a month and an integral number of months in a year. However, these astronomical periods—day, month, and year—are incommensurate: their periods do not form integral multiples of one another. The lunar month is about $29\frac{1}{2}$ days long, and the solar year is about $365\frac{1}{4}$ days long. (See Chapter 12 for precise definitions and values.) How exactly one coordinates these time periods and the accuracy with which they approximate their astronomical values are what differentiate one calendar from another.

Broadly speaking, solar calendars—including the Egyptian, Armenian, Persian, Gregorian, Julian, Coptic, Ethiopic, ISO, French Revolutionary, and Bahá'í—are based on the yearly solar cycle, whereas lunar and lunisolar calendars—such as the Islamic, Hebrew, Hindu, and Chinese—take the monthly lunar cycle as their basic building block. Most solar calendars are divided into months, but these months are divorced from the lunar events; they are sometimes related to the movement of the sun through the 12 signs of the zodiac, notably in the Hindu solar calendars (see Chapter 17).

Because observational methods suffer from vagaries of weather and chance, they have for the most part been supplanted by calculations. The simplest option is to approximate the length of the year, of the month, or of both. Originally, the Babylonian solar calendar was based on 12 months of 30 days each, overestimating the length of the month and underestimating the year. Such a calendar is easy to calculate, but each month begins at a slightly later lunar phase than the previous, and the seasons move forward slowly through the year. The ancient Egyptian calendar achieved greater accuracy by having 12 months of 30 days plus 5 extra days. Conversions for this calendar are illustrated in Section 1.9. To achieve better correlation with the motion of the moon, one can instead alternate months of 29 and 30 days. Twelve such months, however, amount to 354 days—more than 11 days short of the solar year.

Almost every calendar in this book, and virtually all other calendars, incorporate a notion of "leap" year to deal with the cumulative error caused by approximating a year by an integral number of days and months. Solar calendars add a day every few years to keep up with the astronomical year. Calculations are simplest when the leap years are evenly distributed; the Julian, Coptic, and Ethiopic calendars add 1 day every 4 years. To get a more precise mean year, one needs somewhat fewer leap years. Formulas for the evenly distributed case, such as when one has a leap year every fourth or fifth year, are derived in Section 1.12. The old Hindu solar calendar (Chapter 9) follows such a pattern; the arithmetical Persian calendar almost does (see Chapter 13). The Gregorian calendar, however, uses an uneven distribution of leap years

Table 1.1 *Length of mean year on solar and lunisolar calendars and length of mean lunar month on lunar and lunisolar calendars. Year length is given in italics when the sidereal, rather than tropical, value is intended. These may be compared with the astronomical values given for various millennial points—in solar days current at the indicated time. No values are given here for the Chinese, astronomical Persian, observational Islamic, future Bahá'í, Japanese, and (original) French Revolutionary calendars because they are self-adjusting.*

Calendar	Mean Year	Mean Month
Egyptian	365	
Mayan (haab)	365	
Julian/Coptic/Ethiopic	365.25	
Hebrew	365.2468	29.530594
Easter (Orthodox)	365.25	29.530851
Islamic (Arithmetic)		29.530556
Hindu (Arya)	*365.25868*	29.530582
Hindu (Sūrya)	*365.25876*	29.530588
Gregorian	365.2425	
Easter (Gregorian)	365.2425	29.530587
French (Arithmetic)	365.24225	
Persian (Arithmetic)	365.24220	
Year −1000	365.242569	29.530598
Year 0	365.242441	29.530595
Year 1000	365.242310	29.530591
Year 2000	365.242177	29.530588
Year 3000	365.242044	29.530584

but a relatively easy-to-remember rule (see Chapter 2). The modified French Revolutionary calendar (Chapter 15) included an even more accurate but uneven rule.

Most lunar calendars incorporate the notion of a year. Purely lunar calendars may approximate the solar year with 12 lunar months (as does the Islamic), though this is about 11 days short of the astronomical year. Lunisolar calendars invariably alternate 12- and 13-month years, either according to some fixed rule (as in the Hebrew calendar) or astronomically determined pattern (Chinese and modern Hindu). The so-called *Metonic cycle* is based on the observation that 19 solar years contain almost exactly 235 lunar months. This correspondence, named after the Athenian astronomer Meton (who published it in 432 B.C.E.) and known much earlier to ancient Babylonian and Chinese astronomers, makes a relatively simple and accurate fixed solar/lunar calendar feasible. The $235 = 12 \times 12 + 7 \times 13$ months in the cycle are divided into 12 years of 12 months and 7 leap years of 13 months. The Metonic cycle is used in the Hebrew calendar (Chapter 7) and for the ecclesiastical calculation of Easter (Chapter 8).

The Metonic cycle is currently accurate to within 6.5 minutes a year. Other lunisolar cycles are conceivable: 3 solar years are approximately 37 lunar months with an error of 1 day per year; 8 years are approximately 99 months with an error of 5 hours per year; 11 years are approximately 136 months with an error of 3 hours per year; 84 years are approximately 1039 months with an error of 33 minutes per year; and 334 years are 4131 months with an error of 3 minutes per year. The old Hindu calendar is even more accurate, comprising 2,226,389 months in a cycle of 180,000 years (see Chapter 9) to which the leap-year formulas of Section 1.12 apply, and errs by fewer than 8 seconds per year.

Table 1.1 compares the values for the mean length of the year and month as implemented by the various solar, lunar, and lunisolar calendars in this book. The true values change over time, as explained in Chapter 12.

1.2 Fixed Day Numbers

> May those who calculate a fixed date...perish.
>
> —Morris Braude: *Conscience on Trial: Three Public Religious Disputations between Christians and Jews in the Thirteenth and Fifteenth Centuries* (1952)

Over the centuries, human beings have devised an enormous variety of methods for specifying dates.[3] None are ideal computationally, however, because all

---

[3] The best reference is still Ginzel's monumental three-volume work [6]. An exceptional survey can be found in the *Encyclopædia of Religion and Ethics* [11, vol. III, pp. 61–141 and vol. V, pp. 835–894]. Useful, modern summaries are [2], [4], [22], and [26]; [2] and [22] have an extensive bibliographies. The incomparable tables of Schram [23] are the best available for converting dates by hand, whereas those of Parise [18] are best avoided because of the embarassingly large numbers of errors.

have idiosyncrasies resulting from attempts to coordinate a convenient human labeling with lunar and solar phenomena.

For a computer implementation, the easiest way to reckon time is simply to count days: Fix an arbitrary starting point as day 1 and specify a date by giving a day number relative to that starting point; a single 32-bit integer allows the representation of more than 11.7 million years. Such a reckoning of time is, evidently, extremely awkward for human beings and is not in common use, except among astronomers, who use *julian day numbers* to specify dates (see Section 1.5) and calendarists, who use them to facilitate conversion among calendars (see equation 9.1 for the ancient Indian method; for a more modern example, see [23]).

We have chosen midnight at the onset of Monday, January 1, 1 (Gregorian) as our fixed date 1, which we abbreviate as R.D.[4] 1, and count forward day-by-day from there. Of course, this is anachronistic because there was no year 1 on the Gregorian calendar—the Gregorian calendar was devised only in the sixteenth century—thus by January 1, 1 (Gregorian) we mean the day we get if we extrapolate backwards from the present; this day turns out to be Monday, January 3, 1 C.E.[5] (Julian); this too is anachronistic.

We should thus think of the passage of time as a sequence of days numbered $\ldots, -2, -1, 0, 1, 2, 3, \ldots$, which the various human-oriented calendars label differently. For example, R.D. 710,347 is called

- Monday, November 12, 1945, on the Gregorian calendar.
- October 30, 1945 C.E., on the Julian calendar, which would be called *ante diem III Kalendas Novembris* in the Roman nomenclature.
- Julian day number 2,431,772 (at noon).
- Modified julian day number 31,771.
- Month 7, day 10, 2694, on the ancient Egyptian calendar.
- Trê 5, 1395, on the Armenian calendar.
- Day 1 of week 46 of year 1945, on the ISO calendar.
- Hatur 3, 1662, Era of the Martyrs, on the Coptic calendar (until sunset).
- Khedār 3, 1938, on the Ethiopic calendar (until sunset).
- Dhu al-Ḥijja 6, 1364, on the arithmetic Islamic calendar (until sunset).
- Kislev 7, 5706, on the Hebrew calendar (until sunset).
- 12.16.11.16.9 in the Mayan long count.
- 7 Zac on the Mayan haab calendar.
- 11 Muluc on the Mayan tzolkin calendar.

---

[4] *Rata Die*, or fixed date. We are indebted to Howard Jacobson for this coinage.
[5] Common Era, or A.D.

- Luang, Pepet, Pasah, Sri, Pon, Tungleh, Coma of Gumbreg, Ludra, Urungan, Pati on the Balinese Pawukon calendar.
- Tulā 29, 5046, Kali Yuga Era (elapsed) on the old Hindu solar calendar (after sunrise).
- Day 8 in the bright half of Kārtika, 5046, Kali Yuga Era (elapsed) on the old Hindu lunisolar calendar (after sunrise).
- Abān 21, 1324, on the modern Persian calendar.
- The day of Asmā', of the month of Qudrat, of the year Abad, of the sixth Vahid, of the first Kull-i-Shay on the Bahá'í calendar (until sunset).
- Décade III, Primidi de Brumaire de l'Année 154 de la Révolution on the French Revolutionary calendar.
- Day 8 of the tenth month in the year Yǐyǒu of the seventy-seventh sexagesimal cycle on the Chinese calendar.
- Tulā 27, 1867, Śaka Era (elapsed) on the modern Hindu solar calendar (after sunrise).
- Day 7 in the bright half of Kārtika, 2002, Vikrama Era (elapsed) on the modern Hindu lunisolar calendar (after sunrise).

All that is required for calendrical conversion is to be able to convert each calendar to and from this fixed calendar. Because some calendars begin their day at midnight and others at sunrise or sunset, *we fix the time of day at which conversions are performed to be noon*; see Figure 1.1.

We give, in subsequent chapters, functions to do the conversions for the 25 calendars. For each calendar x, we write a function **fixed-from-x**(x-*date*) to convert a given date x-*date* on that calendar to the corresponding R.D. date, and a function x-**from-fixed**(*date*) to do the inverse operation, taking the R.D. *date* and computing its representation in calendar x. One direction is often much simpler to calculate than the other, and occasionally we resort to considering a range of possible dates on calendar x, searching for the one that converts to the given R.D. date (see Section 1.7). To convert from calendar x to calendar y, one need only compose the two functions:

$$y\text{-from-}x(x\text{-}date) \;\; \overset{\text{def}}{=}$$

$$y\text{-from-fixed}(\text{fixed-from-}x(x\text{-}date))$$

Each calendar has an *epoch*, the first day of the first year of that calendar (see Section 1.4). We assign an integer R.D. date to an epoch, even if the calendar in question begins its days at a time other than midnight. Such assignment is done as per Figure 1.1. All of the algorithms given in this book give mathematically sensible results for dates prior to the calendar's epoch.

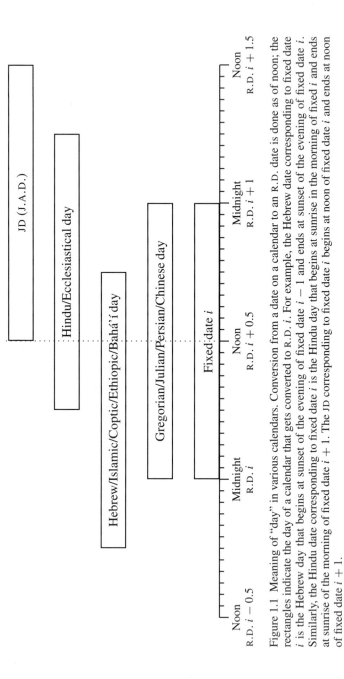

Figure 1.1 Meaning of "day" in various calendars. Conversion from a date on a calendar to an R.D. date is done as of noon; the rectangles indicate the day of a calendar that gets converted to R.D. i. For example, the Hebrew date corresponding to fixed date i is the Hebrew day that begins at sunset of the evening of fixed date $i - 1$ and ends at sunset of the evening of fixed date i. Similarly, the Hindu date corresponding to fixed date i is the Hindu day that begins at sunrise in the morning of fixed i and ends at sunrise of the morning of fixed date $i + 1$. The JD corresponding to fixed date i begins at noon of fixed date i and ends at noon of fixed date $i + 1$.

1.3 Negative Years

The date Monday, January 1, 1 (Gregorian), though arbitrarily chosen as our starting point, has a desirable characteristic: It is early enough that almost all dates of interest are represented by positive integers of moderate size. However, we cannot avoid dealing with dates before the common era. For example, the Hebrew calendar begins at sunset on Sunday, September 6, −3760 (Gregorian); scholarly literature is replete with such statements. Thus, to aid the reader, we now explain how years before the common era are conventionally handled. This convention is often a source of confusion, even among professional historians.

It is computationally convenient, and mathematically sensible, to label years with the sequence of integers . . . , −3, −2, −1, 0, 1, 2, 3, . . . so that year 0 precedes year 1; we do this when extrapolating backward on the Gregorian calendar so that the same leap-year rule will apply based on divisibility by 4, 100, and 400 (see Chapter 2). However, on the Julian calendar it is customary to refer to the year preceding 1 C.E. as 1 B.C.E.,[6] counting it as a leap year in accordance with the every-fourth-year leap-year rule of the Julian calendar. Thus, the beginning of the Hebrew calendar can alternatively be referred to as sunset October 6, 3761 B.C.E. (Julian). To highlight this asymmetry, in the *prose* of this book we append "B.C.E." *only* to Julian calendar years, reserving the minus sign for Gregorian calendar years. Care must therefore be taken when doing arithmetic with year numbers. For $n \geq 0$, the rough present-day alignment of the Julian and Gregorian calendars gives

$$\text{year } -n \text{ (Gregorian)} \approx \text{year } (n+1) \text{ B.C.E. (Julian)},$$

and, for $n \geq 1$,

$$\text{year } n \text{ (Gregorian)} \approx \text{year } n \text{ C.E. (Julian)}.$$

However, as an internal computer representation of B.C.E. Julian years in the Lisp functions in Appendix B and sample data in Appendix C, we also use negative numbers with the convention that year n B.C.E. (Julian) is represented as $-n$.

1.4 Epochs

Epochæ celebriores, astronomis, historicis, chronologis,
Chataiorvm, Syro-Græcorvm Arabvm, Persarvm, Chorasmiorvm,
usitatæ

---

[6] Before the Common Era, or B.C.

[Famous epochs customarily in use by astronomers, historians,
chronologists, Hittites, Syrian-Greeks, Arabs, Persians, and
Chorasmians]
—Title of John Greaves' Latin/Persian edition (1650) of a work by
the fourteenth-century Persian astronomer Ulugh Beg,
grandson of Tamerlane

Every calendar has an *epoch* or starting date. This date is virtually never the date the calendar was adopted but rather a hypothetical starting point for the first day. For example, the Gregorian calendar was devised and adopted in the sixteenth century, but its epoch is January 1, 1. Because days begin at different hours on different calendars, we adopt the convention that a calendar's epoch is the onset of the (civil) day containing the first noon (see Figure 1.1). For example, we take midnight at the onset of September 7, −3760 (Gregorian) as the epoch of the Hebrew calendar, which was codified in the fourth century, though the first Hebrew day began at sunset the preceding evening. For calendars like the Balinese Pawukon, in which cycles are unnumbered, the choice of epoch is arbitrary; the first day of any cycle can be used.

Table 1.2 gives the epochs of the calendars discussed in this book. With the exception of Julian day number, we express the epochs of all the calendars as integer R.D. dates, that is, the integer R.D. day number at *noon* of the first day of the calendar (again, see Figure 1.1). Thus, the epoch for the Gregorian calendar is R.D. 1, and that for the Hebrew calendar is R.D. −1, 373, 427. Using this form of calendar epochs is convenient because

$$\text{R.D. } d \;=\; (d - \text{calendar epoch}) \text{ days since the start of that calendar.}$$

For example,

$$
\begin{aligned}
710{,}347 - (\text{Hebrew calendar epoch}) \;&=\; 710{,}347 - (-1{,}373{,}427) \\
&=\; 2{,}083{,}774,
\end{aligned}
$$

and hence

$$\text{R.D. } 710{,}347 = 2{,}083{,}774 \text{ days since the start of the Hebrew calendar.}$$

Because, for the most part, our formulas depend on the number of days elapsed on some calendar, we often use the expression $(d - \text{epoch})$ in our calendar formulas.

For many calendars, including the Gregorian, the same calendar rules were used with different eras and different month names at different times and in different places. In Taiwan, for instance, the Gregorian calendar is used with an era beginning with the founding of the republic in 1911. An often-encountered era from the second century B.C.E. until recent times—used with

Table 1.2 *Epochs for the calendars.*

Calendar	Epoch (R.D.)	Equivalents
Julian day number	−1,721,424.5	Noon, November 24, −4713 (Gregorian) Noon, January 1, 4713 B.C.E. (Julian)
Hebrew	−1,373,427	September 7, −3760 (Gregorian) October 7, 3761 B.C.E. (Julian)
Mayan	−1,137,142	August 11, −3113 (Gregorian) September 6, 3114 B.C.E. (Julian)
Hindu (Kali Yuga)	−1,132,959	January 23, −3101 (Gregorian) February 18, 3102 B.C.E. (Julian)
Chinese	−963,099	February 15, −2636 (Gregorian) March 8, 2637 B.C.E. (Julian)
Egyptian	−272,787	February 18, −746 (Gregorian) February 26, 747 B.C.E. (Julian)
Julian	−1	December 30, 0 (Gregorian) January 1, 1 C.E. (Julian)
Gregorian	1	January 1, 1 (Gregorian) January 3, 1 C.E. (Julian)
ISO	1	January 1, 1 (Gregorian) January 3, 1 C.E. (Julian)
Ethiopic	2796	August 27, 8 (Gregorian) August 29, 8 C.E. (Julian)
Coptic	103,605	August 29, 284 (Gregorian) August 29, 284 C.E. (Julian)
Zoroastrian	141,412	March 4, 388 (Gregorian) March 3, 388 C.E. (Julian)
Armenian	201,443	July 13, 552 (Gregorian) July 11, 552 C.E. (Julian)
Persian	226,896	March 22, 622 (Gregorian) March 19, 622 C.E. (Julian)
Islamic	227,015	July 19, 622 (Gregorian) July 16, 622 C.E. (Julian)
Yazdegerd	230,638	June 19, 632 (Gregorian) June 16, 632 C.E. (Julian)
French Revolutionary	654,415	September 22, 1792 (Gregorian) September 11, 1792 C.E. (Julian)
Bahá'í	673,222	March 21, 1844 (Gregorian) March 9, 1844 C.E. (Julian)
Modified julian day number	678,576	November 17, 1858 (Gregorian) November 5, 1858 C.E. (Julian)

many calendars—was the Era of Alexander, or the Seleucid Era, in which year 1 corresponds to 312 B.C.E. In general, we avoid describing the details of such trivial variants of calendars.

1.5 Julian Day Numbers

Iulianam vocauimus: quia ad annum Iulianum dumtaxat accommodata est.
[I have called this the Julian period because it is fitted to the Julian year.]
—Joseph Justus Scaliger: *De Emendatione Temporum,* end of introduction to Book V (1583)

Astronomers in recent centuries have avoided the confusing situation of date references on different calendars, each with its idiosyncrasies, by specifying moments in time by giving them in "julian days" or JD (sometimes "julian astronomical days" or J.A.D.). The "Julian period," published in 1583 by Joseph Justus Scaliger, was originally a counting of *years* in a repeating pattern 7980 years long, starting from 4713 B.C.E. (Julian). It is often claimed ([1, page 431], for example) that Scaliger named the period after his father, the Renaissance physician Julius Cæsar Scaliger, but this claim is not borne out by examination of Scaliger's great work, *De Emendatione Temporum,* from which the section quote above is taken. Grafton [7] gives a full history of *De Emendatione Temporum.* The details of the derivation for the value 7980 are given in [20]; the roots of the 7980-year cycle are much earlier than Scaliger, however, dating back to the twelfth century [19]. In the mid-nineteenth century, Herschel [14, page 532] adapted the system into a strict counting of *days* backward and forward from

$$\text{JD } 0 \;=\; \text{Noon on Monday, January 1, 4713 B.C.E. (Julian)}$$
$$=\; \text{Noon on Monday, November 24, } -4713 \text{ (Gregorian)}.$$

A fractional part of a julian[7] date gives the fraction of a day beyond noon; switching dates at noon makes sense for astronomers who work through the night. In this system, for example, the first day of the Hebrew calendar begins at JD 347,997.25 (which is mean sunset). The literature on the Mayan calendar commonly specifies the beginning of the calendar in julian days. Because noon of R.D. 0 is JD 1,721,425, it follows that

$$\text{JD } n = \text{Noon on R.D. } (n - 1,721,425).$$

---

[7] We use lowercase here to avoid any confusion between a julian day number and a date on the Julian calendar.

In other words,

$$\text{Midnight at the onset of R.D. } d = \text{JD}\,(d + 1{,}721{,}424.5). \tag{1.1}$$

We do not use julian days directly, as suggested in [10], because we want our days to begin at civil midnight. *We also use fractional days when we need to calculate with time but begin each day at midnight.*

To distinguish clearly between the Julian calendar and julian days in our functions, we use the abbreviation "jd" instead of "julian." We have

$$\textbf{jd-epoch} \;\stackrel{\text{def}}{=}\; -1721424.5 \tag{1.2}$$

$$\textbf{moment-from-jd}\,(jd) \;\stackrel{\text{def}}{=}\; jd + \textbf{jd-epoch} \tag{1.3}$$

$$\textbf{jd-from-moment}\,(t) \;\stackrel{\text{def}}{=}\; t - \textbf{jd-epoch} \tag{1.4}$$

where *jd* can be a fraction representing time as well as date. We use the term "moment" to mean an R.D. date with a fractional part giving, as a decimal fraction, the time of day.

For dates near the present, the julian day number is inconvenient because at least 7-digit accuracy is needed. Astronomers occasionally use *modified julian day numbers*, or MJD defined as

$$\text{Modified julian day number} = \text{julian day number} - 2400000.5,$$

which counts days from midnight, Wednesday, November 17, 1858 (Gregorian). This is equivalent to defining

$$\textbf{mjd-epoch} \;\stackrel{\text{def}}{=}\; 678576 \tag{1.5}$$

$$\textbf{fixed-from-mjd}\,(mjd) \;\stackrel{\text{def}}{=}\; mjd + \textbf{mjd-epoch} \tag{1.6}$$

$$\textbf{mjd-from-fixed}\,(date) \;\stackrel{\text{def}}{=}\; date - \textbf{mjd-epoch} \tag{1.7}$$

We do not use modified julian days directly because we want positive numbers for dates within recent history.

1.6 Mathematical Notation

The best notation is no notation.
—Paul Halmos: *How to Write Mathematics* (1970)

We use the following mathematical notation (see [8]) when describing the calendar calculations: The *floor function*, $\lfloor x \rfloor$, gives the largest integer less than or equal to x. For example, $\lfloor \pi \rfloor = 3$ and $\lfloor -\pi \rfloor = -4$. The similar *ceiling function*, $\lceil x \rceil$, gives the smallest integer greater than or equal to x. For example, $\lceil \pi \rceil = 4$ and $\lceil -\pi \rceil = -3$. For integers n, $\lfloor n \rfloor = \lceil n \rceil = n$. Using the floor function, we can convert a moment given in julian days to an R.D. date, with no fractional part, with

$$\textbf{fixed-from-jd}\,(jd) \overset{\text{def}}{=} \lfloor \textbf{moment-from-jd}\,(jd) \rfloor \tag{1.8}$$

The inverse is simply the same as **jd-from-moment**:

$$\textbf{jd-from-fixed}\,(date) \overset{\text{def}}{=} \textbf{jd-from-moment}\,(date) \tag{1.9}$$

Occasionally we need to *round* values to the nearest integer. We can express this using the floor function as

$$\text{round}(x) \overset{\text{def}}{=} \lfloor x + 0.5 \rfloor. \tag{1.10}$$

The *remainder*, or *modulus, function*, $x \bmod y$, is defined for $y \neq 0$ as

$$x \bmod y \overset{\text{def}}{=} x - y\lfloor x/y \rfloor, \tag{1.11}$$

which is the remainder when x is divided by y (x and y need not be integers). For example, $9 \bmod 5 = 4$, $-9 \bmod 5 = 1$, $9 \bmod -5 = -1$, and $-9 \bmod -5 = -4$. Definition (1.11) makes sense for any nonzero value of y; for example, $5/3 \bmod 3/4 = 1/6$. In particular, when $y = 1$, $x \bmod 1$ is the *fractional part* of x. Thus, in programming languages (including C, C++, and Pascal) without a built-in remainder function that works for nonintegers, the above definition must be used instead.

There are five important consequences of definition (1.11). First,

$$\text{if } y > 0, \text{ then } x \bmod y \geq 0,$$

for all x, even for negative values of x; we use this property throughout our calculations. Care must thus be exercised in implementing our algorithms in computer languages like C and C++ in which the mod operator % may have $(x \text{ \% } y) < 0$ for $x < 0$, $y > 0$. It follows from (1.11) that

$$(-x) \bmod y = y - (x \bmod y)$$

for $y > 0$. The third consequence is that the definition of the mod function implies that for $y \neq 0$ and $z \neq 0$,

$$a = (x \bmod y) \text{ if and only if } az = (xz \bmod yz). \tag{1.12}$$

Fourth,

$$x - (x \bmod y) \text{ is always a multiple of } y. \tag{1.13}$$

Finally, for $y \neq 0$,

$$0 \leq \text{signum}(y) \times (x \bmod y) < |y|, \qquad (1.14)$$

where

$$\text{signum}(y) \stackrel{\text{def}}{=} \begin{cases} -1 & \text{if } y < 0, \\ 0 & \text{if } y = 0, \\ 1 & \text{if } y > 0. \end{cases} \qquad (1.15)$$

We also find it convenient to use an *adjusted remainder function*, x amod y, defined for $y \neq 0$ as

$$x \text{ amod } y \stackrel{\text{def}}{=} \begin{cases} y & \text{if } x \bmod y = 0, \\ x \bmod y & \text{otherwise.} \end{cases} \qquad (1.16)$$

The amod function can also be described as

$$x \text{ amod } y = y + x \bmod (-y). \qquad (1.17)$$

Lastly, we use a special summation operator,

$$\sum_{i \geq k}^{p(i)} f(i) = f(k) + f(k+1) + \cdots \qquad (1.18)$$

whose value is that obtained when $f(i)$ is summed for all $i = k, k+1, \ldots$, continuing only as long as the condition $p(i)$ holds. The sum is 0 if $p(k)$ is false.

1.7 Search

> ... as two grains of wheat hid in two bushels of chaff: you shall
> seek all day ere you find them, and when you have them, they are
> not worth the search.
> —William Shakespeare: *Merchant of Venice*,
> Act I, scene i (1600)

In many calendar computations, it is easy to compute an approximate date, and easy to check whether a date in question is correct, but difficult to compute the correct date directly. In such cases, we compute a lower bound d_0 on the possible date and then perform a linear search, day by day, until the correct date d is reached. For that purpose we use the operator

$$\underset{d \geq d_0}{\text{MIN}} \{\psi(d)\}, \qquad (1.19)$$

which searches for the smallest d in the sequence $d_0, d_0 + 1, d_0 + 2, \ldots$ such that the condition ψ holds true for d. In other words, using the symbol "¬" for logical negation, we have $\neg\psi(d_0)$, $\neg\psi(d_0+1)$, $\neg\psi(d_0+2)$, ..., $\neg\psi(d-1)$, but $\psi(d)$. Occasionally, we search the sequence for the day prior to the first d' such that $\neg\psi(d')$ and use instead

$$\mathop{\text{MAX}}_{d \ge d_0} \{\psi(d)\}. \tag{1.20}$$

With this operator, we have $\psi(d_0)$, $\psi(d_0+1)$, $\psi(d_0+2)$, ..., $\psi(d)$, but $\neg\psi(d+1)$.

To determine the precise time of astronomical events, such as an equinox or solstice, we will need a special operator to express a bisection search [24, section 3.2]. We define

$$y \approx \mathop{\mathrm{MIN}}_{\xi \in [\mu:\nu]}^{\phi(l,u)} \{\psi(\xi)\} \quad \text{means that} \quad \begin{array}{l} \mu \le l < y < u \le \nu, \\ \phi(l,u),\ \neg\psi(l),\ \text{and}\ \psi(u) \end{array} \tag{1.21}$$

That is, we search for a y satisfying the definiens under the assumption that the region $[\mu:\nu]$ can be split into two intervals $[\mu:x)$ and $[x:\nu]$, such that ψ is false throughout the former and true in the latter. Then y must be close enough to x so that it lies in an interval $(l:u)$, sandwiching x, small enough to satisfy the test $\phi(l,u)$. We implement the definition using a straightforward bisection search of the interval $[\mu:\nu]$:

$$\mathrm{MIN}(\mu,\nu,\phi,\psi) \overset{\text{def}}{=} \tag{1.22}$$

$$\begin{cases} x & \textbf{if } \phi(\mu,\nu) \\ \mathrm{MIN}(\mu,x,\phi,\psi) \\ & \textbf{if not } \phi(\mu,\nu) \textbf{ and } \psi(x) \\ \mathrm{MIN}(x,\nu,\phi,\psi) & \textbf{otherwise} \end{cases}$$

where

$$x = \frac{1}{2} \times (\nu + \mu)$$

If ψ is true of the midpoint x, then we "go left" and let the new upper bound ν be x. On the other hand, if ψ is false, we "go right" and let the new lower bound μ be x. This process continues until the interval $[\mu:\nu]$ is small enough that ϕ is true, at which point the midpoint is returned. At each stage of the search, $\psi(\mu)$ is false and $\psi(\nu)$ is true.

1.8 Dates and Lists

> The list could surely go on, and there is nothing more wonderful
> than a list, instrument of wondrous hypotyposis.
> —Umberto Eco: *The Name of the Rose* (1983)

We represent calendar dates by lists of components—in descending order of significance—usually having the form

year	month	day

in which *year*, *month*, and *day* are all integers. We use subscripts to select components; for example, if $d = $ | 1945 | 11 | 12 |, then $d_{\mathbf{day}} = 12$. The components of dates differ for some calendars; we explain those particular forms in the individual discussions and use analogously named indices for extracting individual components.

We also have occasion to use lists of dates or of other items. Our use of lists requires manipulations such as forming lists, selecting elements from a list, or concatenating lists. We use the following notation in our calendar functions:

- Angle brackets indicate list construction, that is, the formation of a list from individual components. For example, $\langle 1945, 11, 12 \rangle$ is a list of the three components 1945, 11, and 12, respectively.
- Subscripts in square brackets indicate list element selection, with the indices of the elements being 0-based. Thus if $b = \langle 1945, 11, 12 \rangle$, then $b_{[0]}$ is 1945, $b_{[1]}$ is 11, and $b_{[2]}$ is 12.
- Empty angle brackets, $\langle\ \rangle$, indicate the list with no elements.
- Double bars indicate concatenation of lists, and thus

$$\langle 1945 \rangle \| \langle 11, 12 \rangle = \langle 1945, 11, 12 \rangle.$$

The identity under concatenation is $\langle\ \rangle$; that is, the concatenation of $\langle\ \rangle$ with any list leaves the list unchanged.

When referring to intervals of time, we will have occasion to use the notation

$$i^{\mathrm{d}} j^{\mathrm{h}} k^{\mathrm{m}} l^{\mathrm{s}} = i + \frac{j + \dfrac{k + \frac{l}{60}}{60}}{24} \text{days} \tag{1.23}$$

for i days, j hours, k minutes, and l seconds. For example, a fifth of a day is $0^{\mathrm{d}} 4^{\mathrm{h}} 48^{\mathrm{m}} 0^{\mathrm{s}}$, or $4^{\mathrm{h}} 48^{\mathrm{m}}$, for short, and $10^{\mathrm{d}} - 4^{\mathrm{h}} 48^{\mathrm{m}} = 9.8^{\mathrm{d}} = 9^{\mathrm{d}} 19^{\mathrm{h}} 12^{\mathrm{m}}$. The following function converts the fractional part of R.D. moment t into hours, minutes, and seconds on a 24-hour clock (as used in most parts of the world), taking midnight as 0:00:00 hours:

$$\textbf{time-from-moment}\,(t) \;\overset{\text{def}}{=}\; \tag{1.24}$$

$$hour : minute : second$$

where

$$
\begin{aligned}
hour &= \lfloor t \times 24 \;\;\mathrm{mod}\;\; 24 \rfloor \\
minute &= \lfloor t \times 24 \times 60 \;\;\mathrm{mod}\;\; 60 \rfloor \\
second &= t \times 24 \times 60 \times 60 \;\;\mathrm{mod}\;\; 60
\end{aligned}
$$

To round to the nearest second, let

$$second = \textbf{round}(t \times 24 \times 60 \times 60)\;\mathrm{mod}\;\;60$$

instead.

Similarly, angles may be described in terms of a list of degrees, arc minutes, and arc seconds:

$$i^{\circ}\,j'\,k'' = i + \frac{j + \frac{k}{60}}{60} \text{ degrees.} \tag{1.25}$$

1.9 A Simple Calendar

> This calendar is, indeed, the only intelligent calendar which ever
> existed in human history.
> —Otto Neugebauer: *The Exact Sciences in Antiquity* (1952)

A simple solar calendar with 365 days each year and no leap-year rule was in use in Egypt for millennia before the adoption of the Julian calendar in the third century C.E. and was also used in Babylon and Persia. It served as the canonical calendar for astronomers until the sixteenth century, and it is to this calendar that Neugebauer refers in the preceding quote. Each month had 30 days, except for the last 5 days of the year, called *epagomenæ*, which were considered an unlucky period and which we can treat as a short thirteenth month. Days began at noon. We use that calendar as a simple example of calendar conversion functions. Our calendar functions always use numbers to represent months; we provide tables of names, when known, for each calendar.

The epoch for this calendar chosen by the famous Alexandrian astronomer Ptolemy, author of the *Almagest*, and called the *Nabonassar era* after the Chaldean king Nabonassar, is given by [16] as JD 1,448,638:

$$\textbf{egyptian-epoch} \;\overset{\text{def}}{=}\; \textbf{fixed-from-jd}\,(1448638) \tag{1.26}$$

which corresponds to R.D. $-272, 787$, or February 26, 747 B.C.E. (Julian). Because all years have fixed length, converting Egyptian dates into fixed dates is trivial:

$$\textbf{fixed-from-egyptian}\left(\boxed{\begin{array}{c|c|c} year & month & day \end{array}}\right) \overset{\text{def}}{=} \tag{1.27}$$

$$\textbf{egyptian-epoch} + 365 \times (year - 1) + 30 \times (month - 1) + day - 1$$

The short last month causes no problem, because we only count the number of days in prior months.

For the inverse, converting fixed dates to Egyptian dates, we make straight-forward use of the floor and mod functions:

$$\textbf{egyptian-from-fixed}\,(date) \overset{\text{def}}{=} \boxed{\begin{array}{c|c|c} year & month & day \end{array}} \tag{1.28}$$

where

$$
\begin{aligned}
days &= date - \textbf{egyptian-epoch} \\[2mm]
year &= \left\lfloor \frac{days}{365} \right\rfloor + 1 \\[2mm]
month &= \left\lfloor \frac{days \bmod 365}{30} \right\rfloor + 1 \\[2mm]
day &= days - 365 \times (year - 1) - 30 \times (month - 1) + 1
\end{aligned}
$$

The rules of the Armenian calendar were identical to those of the Egyptian; the only difference is the epoch (see [15]):

$$\textbf{armenian-epoch} \overset{\text{def}}{=} 201443 \tag{1.29}$$

which corresponds to July 11, 552 C.E. (Julian). To convert R.D. dates to and from the Armenian calendar, we simply adjust by the difference in epochs:

$$\textbf{fixed-from-armenian}\left(\boxed{\begin{array}{c|c|c} year & month & day \end{array}}\right) \overset{\text{def}}{=} \tag{1.30}$$

$$\textbf{armenian-epoch} +$$

$$\textbf{fixed-from-egyptian}\left(\boxed{\begin{array}{c|c|c} year & month & day \end{array}}\right) -$$

$$\textbf{egyptian-epoch}$$

$$\textbf{armenian-from-fixed}\,(date) \overset{\text{def}}{=} \tag{1.31}$$

$$\textbf{egyptian-from-fixed}$$

$$(date + \textbf{egyptian-epoch} - \textbf{armenian-epoch})$$

The 12 Armenian months were called

(1) Nawasardi	(7) Mehekani
(2) Hoṟi	(8) Areg
(3) Sahmi	(9) Ahekani
(4) Trē	(10) Mareri
(5) K'aloch	(11) Margach
(6) Arach	(12) Hrotich

and the epagomenæ were called *aweleach*.

The Zoroastrian and Yazdegerd calendars also had identical structure to that of the Egyptian calendar but with different epochs (see Table 1.2) and month names. In the past, the Persians used individual names for each of the days of the month; the Persian names were

(1) Hormuz	هرمز	(16) Mehr	مهر
(2) Bahman	بهمن	(17) Sorūsh	سروش
(3) Ordībehesht	ارديبهشت	(18) Rashn	رشن
(4) Shahrīvar	شهريور	(19) Farvardīn	فروردين
(5) Esfandārmud	اسفندارمذ	(20) Bahrām	بهرام
(6) Xordād	خرداذ	(21) Rām	رام
(7) Mordād	مرداذ	(22) Bād	باد
(8) Diy be Āzar	دى باذر	(23) Diy be Dīn	دى بدين
(9) Āzar	آزر	(24) Dīn	دين
(10) Ābān	آبان	(25) Ard	ارد
(11) Xor	خور	(26) Ashtād	اشتاذ
(12) Māh	ماه	(27) Asmān	اسمان
(13) Tīr	تير	(28) Zāmyād	زامياد
(14) Goosh	گوش	(29) Māresfand	مارسفند
(15) Diy be Mehr	دى بمهر	(30) Anīrān	انيران

and the epagomenæ were sometimes named:

(1) Ahnad	اهند
(2) Ashnad	اشند
(3) Esfandārmud	اسفندارمد
(4) Axshatar	اخشتر
(5) Behesht	بهشت

1.10 Cycles of Days

And day by day I'll do this heavy task.
—Shakespeare: *Titus Andronicus*, Act V, scene ii (1594)

Because R.D. 1 is a Monday, determining the day of the week amounts to taking the R.D. date modulo 7: 0 is Sunday, 1 is Monday, and so forth. We define the seven constants

$$\textbf{sunday} \stackrel{\text{def}}{=} 0 \tag{1.32}$$

$$\textbf{monday} \stackrel{\text{def}}{=} \textbf{sunday} + 1 \tag{1.33}$$

$$\textbf{tuesday} \stackrel{\text{def}}{=} \textbf{sunday} + 2 \tag{1.34}$$

$$\textbf{wednesday} \stackrel{\text{def}}{=} \textbf{sunday} + 3 \tag{1.35}$$

$$\textbf{thursday} \stackrel{\text{def}}{=} \textbf{sunday} + 4 \tag{1.36}$$

$$\textbf{friday} \stackrel{\text{def}}{=} \textbf{sunday} + 5 \tag{1.37}$$

$$\textbf{saturday} \stackrel{\text{def}}{=} \textbf{sunday} + 6 \tag{1.38}$$

and determine the day of the week with

$$\textbf{day-of-week-from-fixed}\,(\textit{date}) \stackrel{\text{def}}{=} \textit{date} \bmod 7 \tag{1.39}$$

Many holidays are on the nth occurrence of a given day of the week, counted forward or backward from some date. For example, Thanksgiving in the United States is the fourth Thursday in November, that is, the fourth Thursday on or after November 1. We handle such specifications by writing a function that encapsulates the formula, derived below,

$$d - [(d - k) \bmod 7], \tag{1.40}$$

to find the kth day of the week ($k = 0$ for Sunday, and so on) that falls in the 7-day period ending on R.D. *date*:

$$\textbf{kday-on-or-before}\,(\textit{date}, k) \stackrel{\text{def}}{=} \tag{1.41}$$

$$\textit{date} - \textbf{day-of-week-from-fixed}\,(\textit{date} - k)$$

In our functions (and programs) we will generally use the parameter *date* for R.D. dates.

Formula (1.40) is an instance of a more general principle for finding the occurrence of the kth day of a repeating m-day cycle that is closest to but not past day number d, where day number 0 is day Δ of the cycle:

$$\boxed{d - [(d + \Delta - k) \bmod m]} \tag{1.42}$$

Before proving formula (1.42), let us note that it works equally well for negative and nonintegral dates d (that is, for a time of day) and for nonintegral positions k, shifts Δ, and periods m. We use such computations extensively for the Hindu calendars (Chapter 9), the Mayan calendars (Chapter 10), and the Balinese Pawukon calendar (Chapter 11).

The derivation for formula (1.42) is as follows: We have days numbered $\dots, -2, -1, 0, 1, 2, \dots$. Suppose we also have a cycle of labels $0, 1, 2, \dots,$ $m - 1$ for the days, in which day 0 has label Δ. We must determine the last k-label day on or before the start of day number d. (In spite of appearances, there is no assumption that m, k, or Δ are integers. The labels can be continuous over the range 0 up to, but not including, m; in the continuous case, moments are labeled rather than days.)

Because day number 0 is a Δ-label day, day number $-\Delta$ is a 0-label day. Thus, the k-label days are the days numbered $k - \Delta + xm$ for any integer x. We want the day number D such that

$$D = k - \Delta + xm \le d \tag{1.43}$$

(because D is to be a k-label day on or before day d) and

$$d < D + m = k - \Delta + (x + 1)m \tag{1.44}$$

(because D is to be the last such k-label day). Inequality (1.43) tells us that

$$x \le (d - k + \Delta)/m,$$

and inequality (1.44) tells us that

$$x + 1 > (d - k + \Delta)/m.$$

That is,

$$x \le (d - k + \Delta)/m < x + 1,$$

and thus

$$x = \lfloor (d - k + \Delta)/m \rfloor.$$

But, because $D = k - \Delta + xm$ by (1.43),

$$D = k - \Delta + \lfloor (d - k + \Delta)/m \rfloor \times m,$$

which we can rewrite as

$$
\begin{aligned}
D &= d - (d - k + \Delta - \lfloor (d - k + \Delta)/m \rfloor \times m) \\
&= d - ((d - k + \Delta) \bmod m),
\end{aligned}
$$

by definition (1.11). Thus, formula (1.42) is verified.

Note that if the cycle of labels is $1, 2, \ldots, m$ (that is, based at 1 instead of 0), the corresponding formula for the last k-label day on or before day number d is found by simply shifting the label sought by -1:

$$d - ((d + \Delta - 1 - k) \bmod m). \tag{1.45}$$

We use this in the Chinese calendar (Chapter 16).

Applying our function **kday-on-or-before** above to $d + 6$ gives us the **kday-on-or-after** R.D. d. Similarly, applying it to $d + 3$ gives the **kday-nearest** to R.D. d, applying it to $d - 1$ gives the **kday-before** R.D. d, and applying it to $d + 7$ gives the **kday-after** R.D. d:

$$\textbf{kday-on-or-after}\,(\textit{date}, k) \quad \overset{\text{def}}{=} \tag{1.46}$$

$$\qquad \textbf{kday-on-or-before}\,(\textit{date} + 6, k)$$

$$\textbf{kday-nearest}\,(\textit{date}, k) \quad \overset{\text{def}}{=} \tag{1.47}$$

$$\qquad \textbf{kday-on-or-before}\,(\textit{date} + 3, k)$$

$$\textbf{kday-before}\,(\textit{date}, k) \quad \overset{\text{def}}{=} \tag{1.48}$$

$$\qquad \textbf{kday-on-or-before}\,(\textit{date} - 1, k)$$

$$\textbf{kday-after}\,(\textit{date}, k) \quad \overset{\text{def}}{=} \tag{1.49}$$

$$\qquad \textbf{kday-on-or-before}\,(\textit{date} + 7, k)$$

1.11 Simultaneous Cycles

> In the year 4-House of the eighth sheaf of years of the Mexican era
> the Emperor Monteçuçuma the Younger had a great fright. We
> know this year as 1509. The Mexicans counted their time in
> "sheafs" of fifty-two years, and in order to designate them without
> error or ambiguity, a system had been adopted which can be best
> understood by reference to a pack of cards: as if we were to call
> our years one of spades, two of hearts, three of diamonds, four of
> clubs, five of spades, six of hearts, seven of diamonds, eight of
> clubs, etc. It is clear that the series or "sheaf" would begin again
> every fifty-two years. The Mexican calendar divided the fifty-two
> years of a "sheaf" into four sets or "colours" of thirteen years, i.e.,
> rabbits, reeds, flints and houses.
> —Salvador de Madariaga: *Hernán Cortés: Conqueror of Mexico*
> (1942)

Some calendars employ two cycles running simultaneously. Each day is labeled by a pair of numbers $\langle a, b \rangle$, beginning with $\langle 0, 0 \rangle$, followed by $\langle 1, 1 \rangle$, $\langle 2, 2 \rangle$, and so on. Suppose the first component repeats after c days and the second after d days, with $c < d < 2c$, then after day $\langle c - 1, c - 1 \rangle$ come days $\langle 0, c \rangle$, $\langle 1, c + 1 \rangle$, and so on, until $\langle d - c - 1, d - 1 \rangle$, which is followed by $\langle d - c, 0 \rangle$. If day 0 of the calendar is labeled $\langle 0, 0 \rangle$, then day n is $\langle n \bmod c, n \bmod d \rangle$. The Chinese use such pairs to identify years (see Section 16.4), with cycles of length $c = 10$ and $d = 12$, but because the first component ranges from 1 to 10, inclusive, and the second from 1 to 12, we would use the adjusted mod function: $\langle n \text{ amod } 10, n \text{ amod } 12 \rangle$.

More generally, if the label of day 0 is $\langle \Gamma, \Delta \rangle$, then day n is labeled

$$\boxed{\langle (n + \Gamma) \bmod c, (n + \Delta) \bmod d \rangle} \qquad (1.50)$$

For the Mayan tzolkin calendar, with $c = 13$, $d = 20$, $\Gamma = 3$, $\Delta = 19$, and beginning the cycles with 1 instead of 0, this is $\langle (n + 3) \text{ amod } 13, (n + 19) \text{ amod } 20 \rangle$. It follows that day 1 of the Mayan calendar is labeled $\langle 4, 20 \rangle$ (see Section 10.2).

How many distinct day names does such a scheme provide? If m is the least common multiple (lcm) of c and d, then such a calendar repeats after m days. If the cycle lengths c and d are relatively prime (that is, no integer greater than 1 divides both c and d without remainder), then $m = c \times d$ days. Thus, for the Mayan tzolkin calendar, with $c = 13$ and $d = 20$, m is 260. For the Chinese year names lcm$(10, 12) = 60$, yielding a sexagesimal cycle.

Inverting this representation is harder. Suppose first that $\Gamma = \Delta = 0$. Given a pair $\langle a, b \rangle$, where a is an integer in the range $0 \ldots c - 1$ and b is an integer in the range $0 \dots d - 1$, we are looking for an n, $0 \leq n < m$, such that $a = n \bmod c$ and $b = n \bmod d$. This requires the solution to a pair of simultaneous linear congruences:

$$n \equiv a \pmod{c}$$
$$n \equiv b \pmod{d}.$$

The first congruence means that

$$n = a + ic \tag{1.51}$$

for some integer i. Substituting this for n in the second congruence and transposing, we get

$$ic \equiv b - a \pmod{d}.$$

Let g be the greatest common divisor (gcd) of c and d, and let k be the multiplicative inverse of c/g modulo d/g, which is obtained using the Euclidean algorithm (see [17] for details). That is,

$$(ck) \bmod d = g.$$

Then,

$$i \equiv ik\frac{c}{g} \equiv k\frac{b-a}{g} \left(\bmod \frac{d}{g}\right).$$

Using this value of i in equation (1.51), we get day number

$$a + c\left[k\frac{b-a}{g} \bmod \frac{d}{g}\right] = a + \left[\frac{ck}{g}(b-a) \bmod \frac{cd}{g}\right].$$

When day 0 is labeled $\langle \Gamma, \Delta \rangle$, we must subtract Γ from a and Δ from b. To make sure that n is in the range $0 \dots m - 1$, we use

$$\boxed{n = \left(a - \Gamma + \frac{ck[b - a + \Gamma - \Delta]}{\gcd(c, d)}\right) \bmod \operatorname{lcm}(c, d)} \tag{1.52}$$

where k is the multiplicative inverse of $c/\gcd(c, d)$ modulo $d/\gcd(c, d)$.

For example, if $c = 10$ and $d = 12$, as in the Chinese calendar, then $\gcd(10, 12) = 2$, $\operatorname{lcm}(10, 12) = 60$, and $k = 5$ because $(5 \times 10) \bmod 12 = 2$. Using $\Gamma = \Delta = 0$, but counting from 1 instead of 0, we find that Chinese year name $\langle a, b \rangle$ corresponds to year number

$$(a - 1 + 25(b - a)) \bmod 60 + 1 \tag{1.53}$$

of the sexagesimal cycle; we use this formula in Section 16.4. We use other derivations of this sort for the Mayan calendars in Section 10.2 and for the Balinese calendar in Chapter 11.

Note that some combinations $\langle a, b \rangle$ are impossible. In general, there is no solution unless

$$\boxed{\gcd(c, d) \text{ divides } (b - a + \Gamma - \Delta)} \tag{1.54}$$

or, equivalently,

$$(b - a + \Gamma - \Delta) \bmod \gcd(c, d) = 0.$$

For example, with the Chinese scheme, the odd-even parity of the two components must be the same because c and d are both even, and only 60 of the 120 conceivable pairs are possible.

1.12 Cycles of Years

At the expiration of the years, come challenge me.
—Shakespeare: *Love's Labour's Lost*, Act V, scene ii (1598)

We now derive some general formulas that are useful in calendar conversions for the Julian, Islamic, Coptic, Hebrew, arithmetic Persian, and old Hindu lunisolar calendars (although not in the same way for the Gregorian calendar, unfortunately). These calendars have in common that they follow a simple type of leap-year rule in which leap years are spread as evenly as possible over a cycle of years; the particular constants that define these leap-year rules are given in Table 1.3. The formulas in this section are closely related to Bresenham's "midpoint line algorithm" for drawing lines in two dimensions on a discrete raster [9], [28].

Suppose we have a sequence of years $\ldots, -2, -1, 0, 1, 2, \ldots$, and we want to place l leap years in a cycle of c years, with year 0 as the first year of the cycle. How can we spread the leap years evenly over the cycle? If l is a divisor of c, our problem is easy: Have year numbers that are multiples of c/l be leap years. If l is not a divisor of c, however, the best we can do is have year numbers that are *roughly* multiples of c/l be leap years—specifically, we have a leap year whenever the year number has reached or just passed a multiple of c/l. Let y be a year number; then it is a leap year if

$$y - 1 < k\frac{c}{l} \leq y$$

for some integer k. Rearranging this inequality, we get

$$k\frac{c}{l} \leq y < k\frac{c}{l} + 1, \tag{1.55}$$

Table 1.3 *Constants describing the simple leap-year structure of various calendars. c is the length of the leap-year cycle, l is the number of leap years in that cycle of c years, Δ is the position in the cycle of year 0, L is the length of an ordinary year (hence L + 1 is the length of a leap year), $\bar{L} = (cL + l)/c$ is the average length of a year, and $\delta = (\Delta l)/c$ mod 1 is the time of day (as a fraction of a day) when mean year 0 begins. This cyclic pattern also applies to Islamic months, and approximately to the Gregorian/Julian months.*

Calendar	Section	c	l	Δ	L	$\bar{L} = \frac{cL+l}{c}$	δ
Julian years C.E.	3.1	4	1	0	365 days	$\frac{1{,}461}{4}$ days	0 days
Julian years B.C.E.	3.1	4	1	1	365 days	$\frac{1{,}461}{4}$ days	$\frac{1}{4}$ day
Coptic years	4.1	4	1	1	365 days	$\frac{1{,}461}{4}$ days	$\frac{1}{4}$ day
Islamic years	6.1	30	11	4	354 days	$\frac{10{,}631}{30}$ days	$\frac{7}{15}$ day
Islamic years (variant)	6.1	30	11	15	354 days	$\frac{10{,}631}{30}$ days	$\frac{1}{2}$ day
Hebrew years	7.1	19	7	11	12 months	$\frac{235}{19}$ months	$\frac{1}{19}$ month
Ecclesiastical years	8.1	19	7	13	12 months	$\frac{235}{19}$ months	$\frac{1}{19}$ month
Old Hindu lunisolar years	9.3				12 months	$\frac{2{,}226{,}389}{180{,}000}$ months	$\frac{2{,}093{,}611}{2{,}160{,}000}$ month
Persian years (Jalālī)	13.3	128	31	38	365 days	$\frac{46751}{128}$ days	$\frac{13}{64}$ day
Persian years (partial)	13.3	2816	682	38	365 days		
Gregorian/Julian months (approximate)	2.1	12	7	11	30 days	$\frac{367}{12}$ days	$\frac{5}{12}$ day
Gregorian/Julian months (approximate)	2.3	7	4	6	30 days	$\frac{214}{7}$ days	$\frac{3}{7}$ day
Gregorian/Julian months (from March)	2.3	5	3	4	30 days	$\frac{153}{5}$ days	$\frac{2}{5}$ day
Islamic months	6.1	11	6	10	29 days	$\frac{325}{11}$ days	$\frac{5}{11}$ day

which is the same as saying that

$$0 \le \left(y \bmod \frac{c}{l}\right) < 1.$$

Multiplying by l and using equation (1.12), we obtain

$$0 \le (yl \bmod c) < l.$$

Because our cycles always have length $c > 0$, the definition of the mod function guarantees that $(yl \bmod c) \ge 0$, so we can drop that part of the inequality to get

$$(yl \bmod c) < l. \tag{1.56}$$

For example, on the Julian calendar for years C.E. (see Chapter 3) we want $l = 1$ leap year in the cycle of $c = 4$ years; then year $y > 0$ is a leap year if

$$(y \bmod 4) < 1,$$

or, in other words, if

$$(y \bmod 4) = 0.$$

We can complicate the leap-year situation by insisting year 0 be in position Δ in the cycle of c years. In this case, we have the same analysis but pretend that the cycle begins at year 0 and ask about year $y + \Delta$. Inequality (1.56) becomes,

$$\boxed{[(y + \Delta)l \bmod c] < l} \tag{1.57}$$

For example, the Julian calendar for years B.C.E. (Chapter 3) and the Coptic calendar (Chapter 4) have a cycle of $c = 4$ years containing $l = 1$ leap years with $\Delta = 1$. Inequality (1.57) becomes

$$[(y + 1) \bmod 4] < 1;$$

this is equivalent to

$$(y \bmod 4) = 3.$$

The Islamic calendar (Chapter 6) has a cycle of $c = 30$ years containing $l = 11$ leap years with $\Delta = 4$ (some Moslems have a different leap-year structure that corresponds to $\Delta = 15$; see page 89), so the test for an Islamic leap year is

$$[(11y + 14) \bmod 30] < 11.$$

Spreading 11 leap years evenly over 30 years implies gaps of 2 or 3 years between leap years. Because $\frac{30}{11} = 2\frac{8}{11}$, 3 of the 11 leap years occur after only

2 years. These three short gaps are also placed at regular intervals within the 30-year cycle, to which formula (1.57) could also be applied (with $c = 11$, $l = 8$, and $\Delta = 8$).

If $\Delta = 0$, inequality (1.55) implies that

$$k = \left\lfloor \frac{y}{c/l} \right\rfloor \tag{1.58}$$

is the number of leap years in the range of years $1 \ldots y$. When $\Delta \neq 0$, we again pretend that the cycle begins at year 0 and ask about year $y + \Delta$ instead of year y. Thus, the number of leap years in the range $1 \ldots y - 1$ for $\Delta \neq 0$ is the same as the number of leap years in the unshifted range of years $\Delta + 1 \ldots y + \Delta - 1$ (whether y is positive or negative), namely,

$$\left\lfloor \left\lfloor \frac{y + \Delta - 1}{c/l} \right\rfloor - \left\lfloor \frac{\Delta}{c/l} \right\rfloor = \left\lfloor \frac{ly - l + (\Delta l \bmod c)}{c} \right\rfloor \right\rfloor \tag{1.59}$$

the number of years in the unshifted range $1 \ldots y + \Delta - 1$ minus the number in the unshifted range $1 \ldots \Delta$. For example, $\lfloor (y - 1)/4 \rfloor$ is the number of leap years before year y on the Julian calendar (counting from the Julian epoch), $\lfloor (11y + 3)/30 \rfloor$ is the number of leap years prior to year y on the Islamic calendar, and $\lfloor y/4 \rfloor$ is the number of leap years prior to year y on the Coptic calendar.

Using formula (1.59), we immediately get the following formula for the number of days in the years before year y—that is, the number of days in the years $1, 2, 3, \ldots, y - 1$, assuming there are L days in an ordinary year and $L + 1$ days in a leap year:

$$n = \left\lfloor \left\lfloor \frac{ly - l + (\Delta l \bmod c)}{c} \right\rfloor + L(y - 1) \right\rfloor \tag{1.60}$$

For example, for the Julian calendar this yields $\lfloor (y - 1)/4 \rfloor + 365(y - 1)$, for the Coptic calendar this yields $\lfloor y/4 \rfloor + 365(y - 1)$, and for the Islamic calendar it yields $\lfloor (11y + 3)/30 \rfloor + 354(y - 1)$. Because the Hebrew calendar (and lunisolar calendars in general) adds leap months, formula (1.60) does not apply to days, but it does apply to *months*: The number of months prior to year y on the Hebrew calendar is $\lfloor (7y - 6)/19 \rfloor + 12(y - 1)$.

Formula (1.60) works for $y \leq 0$. In this case it computes the number of days in years $y \ldots 0$ as a negative number.

Finally, we can derive an inverse to formula (1.60) to find the year at day n, counting day $n = 0$ as the first day of year 1 (the epoch). Because there are L

days in an ordinary year and $L + 1$ days in a leap year, the average year length is

$$\bar{L} = \frac{cL + l}{c}.$$

In the simple case that $\Delta = 0$, year y begins on day

$$
\begin{aligned}
n &= (y - 1)L + (\text{number of leap years in } 1 \ldots y - 1) \\
&= (y - 1)L + \left\lfloor \frac{y - 1}{c/l} \right\rfloor \\
&= \lfloor (y - 1)\bar{L} \rfloor
\end{aligned}
\tag{1.61}
$$

by using formula (1.58) and simplifying. Day n is in year y provided that it is on or after the first day of year y and before the first day of year $y + 1$; that is,

$$\lfloor (y - 1)\bar{L} \rfloor \le n < \lfloor y\bar{L} \rfloor. \tag{1.62}$$

The sequence $\lfloor \bar{L} \rfloor, \lfloor 2\bar{L} \rfloor, \lfloor 3\bar{L} \rfloor, \ldots$ is called the *spectrum* of $\bar{L}$ (see [8, Section 3.2]); in our case, they are the initial day numbers of successive years. Inequality (1.62) is equivalent to

$$(y - 1)\bar{L} - 1 < n \le y\bar{L} - 1,$$

from which it follows that

$$y = \left\lceil \frac{n + 1}{\bar{L}} \right\rceil. \tag{1.63}$$

In general, when $\Delta \neq 0$, we must shift Δ years backward; that is, shift the first day of year 1 to the first day of year $-\Delta + 1$. The number of days in the shifted years $-\Delta + 1, \ldots, 0$ is the same as the number of days in the unshifted years $1, \ldots, \Delta$, which is computed by adding the L ordinary days in each of those Δ years, plus the $\lfloor \Delta/(c/l) \rfloor$ leap days in those years as given by (1.58). The shift of Δ years thus corresponds to a shift of $\Delta L + \lfloor \Delta/(c/l) \rfloor$ days. So the shifted form of (1.63) is

$$y + \Delta = \left\lceil \frac{n + 1 + \Delta L + \lfloor \frac{\Delta}{c/l} \rfloor}{\bar{L}} \right\rceil,$$

which is the same as

$$
\begin{aligned}
y &= \left\lceil \frac{cn + c - (l\Delta \bmod c)}{cL + l} \right\rceil \\
&= \left\lfloor \frac{cn + cL + l - 1 + c - (l\Delta \bmod c)}{cL + l} \right\rfloor
\end{aligned}
\tag{1.64}
$$

We usually prefer the latter form because the floor function is more readily available than the ceiling function in computer languages.

For the Julian calendar, formula (1.64) gives day n occurring in year

$$\left\lceil \frac{4n + 4}{1461} \right\rceil = \left\lfloor \frac{4n + 1464}{1461} \right\rfloor,$$

for the Coptic calendar it gives year

$$\left\lceil \frac{4n + 3}{1461} \right\rceil = \left\lfloor \frac{4n + 1463}{1461} \right\rfloor,$$

and for the Islamic calendar it gives year

$$\left\lceil \frac{30n + 16}{10,631} \right\rceil = \left\lfloor \frac{30n + 10,646}{10,631} \right\rfloor.$$

Formula (1.64) does not apply to days on the Hebrew calendar but rather to months, giving the formula

$$\left\lceil \frac{19n + 18}{235} \right\rceil = \left\lfloor \frac{19n + 252}{235} \right\rfloor$$

for the year in which month n occurs; we have no use for this formula, however.

Formula (1.64) makes sense when $n < 0$, too. In this case it gives the correct year as a negative number (but, as discussed earlier, this is off by one for Julian B.C.E. years).

A more general approach to leap-year distribution is to imagine a sequence of *mean years* of (noninteger) length $\bar{L}$, with year 1 starting on day 0 at time δ, $0 \leq \delta < 1$, where δ expresses time as a fraction of a day. We define a *calendar year* y to begin at the start of the day on which mean year y begins; that is, mean year y begins at moment $\delta + (y - 1)\bar{L}$, and thus calendar year y begins on day

$$\boxed{n = \lfloor (y - 1)\bar{L} + \delta \rfloor} \tag{1.65}$$

Calendar year y is an ordinary year if

$$\lfloor y\bar{L} + \delta \rfloor - \lfloor (y - 1)\bar{L} + \delta \rfloor = \lfloor \bar{L} \rfloor$$

and a leap year if

$$\lfloor y\bar{L} + \delta \rfloor - \lfloor (y - 1)\bar{L} + \delta \rfloor = \lfloor \bar{L} \rfloor + 1.$$

By definition (1.11), this latter equation tells us that calendar year y is a leap year if

$$\left(\delta + (y - 1)(\bar{L} \bmod 1) \right) \bmod 1 \geq 1 - \left(\bar{L} \bmod 1 \right),$$

or, equivalently, if

$$\boxed{\left(\delta + (y-1)\bar{L}\right) \bmod 1 \geq 1 - \left(\bar{L} \bmod 1\right)} \tag{1.66}$$

For the old Hindu lunisolar calendar, with the year count beginning at 0 (not 1), average year length of

$$\bar{L} = \frac{2{,}226{,}389}{180{,}000} \approx 12.368828$$

months, and

$$\delta = \frac{2{,}093{,}611}{2{,}160{,}000},$$

inequality (1.66) means that y is a leap year if

$$\left(\frac{2{,}093{,}611}{2{,}160{,}000} + y\,\frac{2{,}226{,}389}{180{,}000}\right) \bmod 1 \geq 1 - \frac{66{,}389}{180{,}000} = \frac{113{,}611}{180{,}000},$$

or, equivalently,

$$(2{,}093{,}611 + 796{,}668\,y) \bmod 2{,}160{,}000 \geq 1{,}363{,}332.$$

(See page 135.) This test is not, however, needed for other old-Hindu-calendar calculations.

When $\delta = 0$, mean year 1 and calendar year 1 both begin at the same moment, and equation (1.65) tells us that leap years follow the same pattern as for $\Delta = 0$ in our earlier discussion. More generally, given any Δ, if we choose

$$\delta = \frac{\Delta l}{c} \bmod 1, \tag{1.67}$$

the leap-year test (1.66) simplifies to (1.57), and thus we have the same leap-year structure. For example, the Coptic calendar has $\delta = [(1 \times 1)/4] \bmod 1 = 1/4$.

Our δ formulas generalize our Δ formulas because formula (1.67) gives a corresponding value of δ for each Δ. However, there need not be a value of Δ for arbitrary $\bar{L}$ and δ; indeed, there is no such Δ for calendars in which the mean and calendar years never begin at exactly the same moment. Given $\bar{L}$ and δ, we have $l/c = \bar{L} \bmod 1$, and (1.67) means that Δ exists only if δ is an integer multiple, modulo 1, of $\bar{L}$. In the old Hindu lunisolar calendar, for example, formula (1.57) cannot be used directly: $\bar{L} \bmod 1 = 66{,}389/180{,}000$, and we must have an integer Δ such that

$$\frac{2{,}093{,}611}{2{,}160{,}000} = \left(\Delta\,\frac{66{,}389}{180{,}000}\right) \bmod 1,$$

or

$$2{,}093{,}611 = (796{,}668\,\Delta) \bmod 2{,}160{,}000.$$

No such Δ exists because 796,668 and 2,160,000 are both even, but 2,093,611 is odd.

The generalization of formula (1.64) in terms of δ follows by solving equation (1.65) for y, to yield

$$y = \left\lceil \frac{n+1-\delta}{\bar{L}} \right\rceil$$

(1.68)

For the Coptic calendar, this becomes

$$y = \left\lceil \frac{n+1-1/4}{1461/4} \right\rceil = \left\lceil \frac{4n+3}{1461} \right\rceil,$$

as we knew before.

For the old Hindu lunisolar calendar, in every 180,000-year cycle there are 66,389 evenly distributed leap years of 13 months. Because the year count begins with year 0, month m falls in year

$$y = \left\lceil \frac{m+1-\frac{2,093,611}{2,160,000}}{\frac{2,226,389}{180,000}} \right\rceil - 1.$$

The application of these formulas to the old Hindu lunisolar calendar is discussed in Chapter 9.

In the foregoing discussion we have counted days beginning with the epoch of the calendars, and thus when formulas (1.60) and (1.64) are used in our calendrical functions, the epoch must be added or subtracted to refer to R.D. dates. For example, to compute the Islamic year of R.D. d, we must write

$$\left\lfloor \frac{30(d - \text{Islamic epoch}) + 10,646}{10,631} \right\rfloor,$$

because R.D. d is (d − Islamic epoch) elapsed days on the Islamic calendar.

1.13 Warnings about the Calculations

Caveat emptor. [Let the buyer beware.]
—Latin motto

We have been careful to insure that our conversion functions work for at least ±10,000 years from the present, if not forever. We have worked hard to insure that our conversion algorithms do not suffer from a Y10K problem!

Many holiday calculations assume that the Gregorian year and the true solar year, and/or the mean year length of a specific calendar, maintain the same alignment, which will not remain the case over millennia. We have endeavored to make these calculations robust for at least ±2000 years from the present. Of course, the dates of most holidays will not be historically correct over that range.

The astronomical code we use is not the best available, but it works quite well in practice, especially for dates near the present time, around which its approximations are centered. More precise code would be more time-consuming and complex and would not necessarily yield more accurate results for those calendars that depended on observations, tables, or less accurate calculations. Thus, the correctness of a date on any of the astronomical calendars is contingent on the historical accuracy of the astronomical code used in its calculation.

We have chosen not to optimize the algorithms at the expense of clarity; consequently, considerable improvements in economy are possible, some of which are pointed out. In particular, our algorithms are designed to convert individual dates from one calendar to another, thus preparation of monthly or yearly calendars would benefit enormously from storing intermediate results and using them for subsequent days. This standard algorithmic technique (called "caching" or "memoization") is ignored in this book.

The functions given in the text are mechanically derived from the working Lisp code in Appendix B. In case of any ambiguity in the functions or discrepancy between the functions and the code, the code should be considered authoritative.

We do not do any error checking in the code. If one asks for the R.D. date corresponding to a date in Julian year 0, or to February 29, 1990, an answer will be forthcoming despite the nonexistence of such dates. Similarly, the code will not object to the absurdity of asking for the R.D. date corresponding to December 39, or even the thirty-ninth day of the thirteenth month. For each calendar x, validity of a date x-*date* on that calendar can be checked by a function

$$\textbf{valid-}x\textbf{-date}(x\text{-}date) \quad \overset{\text{def}}{=}$$

$$x\text{-}date = \textbf{\textit{x}-from-fixed}(\textbf{fixed-from-}\textbf{\textit{x}}(x\text{-}date))$$

All of our functions give "correct" (mathematically sensible) results for negative years and for dates prior to the epoch of a calendar. However, these results may be *culturally* wrong in the sense that, say, the Copts may not refer to a year 0 or −1. It may be considered heretical on some calendars to refer to years before the creation of the world. Year 0 is assumed to exist for all calendars *except* the Julian (Chapter 3) and the Persian (Chapter 13).

Except for our summation operator (page 21) and search functions (page 21), we avoid iteration and instead use recursion, which is natural because we use functional notation. The use of recursion, however, is not essential: it is invariably "tail" recursion and can easily be replaced by iteration.

Our algorithms assume that if $y > 0$, then $(x \bmod y) \geq 0$ for all x, even for negative values of x. Thus, as we stated in Section 1.6, care must thus be exercised in implementing our algorithms in computer languages like C or C++, in which the built-in mod function (often the % operator) may give $(x \bmod y) < 0$ for $x < 0$, $y > 0$. We also assume, in some of the functions, that $x \bmod y$ works for real numbers x and y, as well as for integers.

Checking the results of conversions against the historical record is sometimes misleading because the different calendars begin their days at different times. For example, a person who died in the evening will have a different Hebrew date of death than if he or she had died in the morning of the same Gregorian calendar date; gravestone inscriptions often err in this. All of our conversions are as of noon.

Some of our calculations require extremely large numbers; other calculations depend on numerically accurate approximations to lunar or solar events. All of the calendars in Part I, except the old Hindu, work properly (for dates within thousands of years from the present) in 32-bit integer arithmetic; the Hebrew and arithmetic Persian calendars approach this limit, so we have indicated how to rephrase the calculations to use only small numbers. On the other hand, 64-bit arithmetic is needed to reproduce accurately the results of the astronomical calculations done in Part II. We use exact rational arithmetic, with very large numbers, for the Hindu calendars; 64-bit arithmetic can be used to approximate their calculation.

References

I have, however, read enough in the field to know that many of these treatments of the calendar are sound, some of them brilliant, and some purely fantastic. I also know that practically every theory about the calendar which could conceivably have been devised has been proposed by somebody, and that many have been re-invented several times. I know that very little of what I have to say has not been anticipated....

—Agnes K. Michels: *The Calendar of the Roman Republic* (1967)

[1] *Explanatory Supplement to the Astronomical Ephemeris and the American Ephemeris and Nautical Almanac*, Her Majesty's Stationery Office, London, 1961.

[2] B. Blackburn and L. Holford-Strevens, *The Oxford Companion to the Year*, Oxford University Press, Oxford, 1999.

[3] L. Cope, "Calendars of the Indians North of Mexico," *American Archaeology and Ethnology*, volume 16, pp. 119–176, 1919.

[4] L. E. Doggett, "Calendars," *Explanatory Supplement to the Astronomical Almanac*, P. K. Seidelmann, ed., University Science Books, Mill Valley, CA, pp. 575–608, 1992.

[5] T. Galloway and W. S. B. Woolhouse, "Calendar," *The Encyclopædia Britannica*, 11th ed., volume 4, pp. 987–1004, The Encyclopædia Britannica Co., New York, 1910. The same article also appears in the 8th (1860) through the 13th (1926) editions.

[6] F. K. Ginzel, *Handbuch der mathematischen und technischen Chronologie*, J. C. Hinrichs'sche Buchhandlung, Leipzig, 1906 (volume 1), 1911 (volume 2), and 1914 (volume 3). Reprinted by F. Ullmann Verlag, Zwickau, 1958.

[7] A. T. Grafton, *Joseph Scaliger: A Study in the History of Classical Scholarship, volume II, Historical Chronography*, Oxford University Press, Oxford, 1993.

[8] R. L. Graham, D. E. Knuth, and O. Patashnik, *Concrete Mathematics*, 2nd ed., Addison-Wesley Publishing Company, Reading, MA, 1994.

[9] M. A. Harris, and E. M. Reingold, "Line Drawing and Leap Years," manuscript, 1999.

[10] O. L. Harvey, *Calendar Conversions by Way of the Julian Day Number*, American Philosophical Society, Philadelphia, 1983.

[11] J. Hastings, ed., *Encyclopædia of Religion and Ethics*, Charles Scribner's Sons, New York, 1908–1922.

[12] H. Henderson and B. Puckett, *Holidays & Festivals Index*, Omnigraphics, Inc., Detroit, MI, 1995.

[13] H. Henderson and S. E. Thompson, *Holidays, Festivals & Celebrations of the World Dictionary*, 2nd ed., Omnigraphics, Inc., Detroit, MI, 1997.

[14] J. F. W. Herschel, *Outlines of Astronomy*, 3rd ed., Longman, Brown, Green, Longmans, and Roberts, London, 1849.

[15] F. Macler, "Calendar (Armenian)" in *Encyclopædia of Religion and Ethics*, J. Hastings, ed., Charles Scribner's Sons, New York, 1908–1922.

[16] O. Neugebauer, *A History of Ancient Mathematical Astronomy*, Springer-Verlag, Berlin, 1975 (volume 1, pp. 1–555, volume 2, pp. 556–1058, volume 3, pp. 1059–1457).

[17] Ø. Ore, *Number Theory and Its History*, McGraw-Hill Book Co., Inc., New York, 1948. Reprinted by Dover Publications, Inc., Mineola, NY, 1987.

[18] F. Parise, ed., *The Book of Calendars*, Facts on File, New York, 1982.

[19] R. L. Reese, E. D. Craun, and C. W. Mason, "Twelfth-Century Origins of the 7980-Year Julian Period," *Amer. J. Physics*, volume 51, p. 73, 1983.

[20] R. L. Reese, S. M. Everett, and E. D. Craun, "The Origin of the Year Julian Period: An Application of Congruences and the Chinese Remainder Theorem," *Amer. J. Physics*, volume 49, pp. 658–661, 1981.

[21] E. M. Reingold, J. Nievergelt, and N. Deo, *Combinatorial Algorithms: Theory and Practice*, Prentice-Hall, Englewood Cliffs, NJ, 1977.

[22] E. G. Richards, *Mapping Time: The Calendar and its History*, Oxford University Press, Oxford, 1998.

[23] R. G. Schram, *Kalendariographische und chronologische Tafeln*, J. C. Hinrichs'sche Buchhandlung, Leipzig, 1908.

[24] R. D. Skeel and J. B. Keiper, *Elementary Numerical Computing with Mathematica*, McGraw-Hill, New York, 1993.

[25] R. M. Stallman, *GNU Emacs Manual*, 13th ed., Free Software Foundation, Cambridge, MA, 1997.

[26] D. Steel, *Marking Time: The Epic Quest to Invent the Perfect Calendar*, John Wiley & Sons, New York, 2000.

[27] G. L. Steele, Jr., COMMON LISP: *The Language*, 2nd ed., Digital Press, Bedford, MA, 1990.

[28] A. Troesch, "Interprétation géométrique de l'algorithme d'Euclide et reconnaissance de segments," *Theoret. Comp. Sci.*, volume 115, pp. 291–319, 1993.

[29] B. L. van der Waerden, "Tables for the Egyptian and Alexandrian Calendar," *ISIS*, volume 47, pp. 387–390, 1956.

Part I

Arithmetical Calendars

Lithograph of Pope Gregory XIII from *Compendio delle Heroiche, et Gloriose Attioni, et Santa Vita di Papa Greg. XIII* by M. A. Ciappi, Rome, 1596. (Courtesy of the University of Illinois, Urbana, IL.)

2

The Gregorian Calendar

For some ridiculous reason, to which, however, I've no desire
to be disloyal,
Some person in authority, I don't know who, very likely the
Astronomer Royal,
Has decided that, although for such a beastly month as
February, twenty-eight as a rule are plenty.
One year in every four his days shall be reckoned as
nine-and-twenty.
—Gilbert and Sullivan: *Pirates of Penzance*, Act II (1879)

2.1 Structure

The calendar in use today in most countries is the Gregorian or *new-style* calendar designed by a commission assembled by Pope Gregory XIII in the sixteenth century. The main author of the new system was the Naples astronomer Aloysius Lilius; see [4], [6], [15], and [18] for mathematical and historical details. This strictly solar calendar is based on a 365-day common year divided into 12 months of lengths 31, 28, 31, 30, 31, 30, 31, 31, 30, 31, 30, and 31 days, and on 366 days in leap years, the extra day being added to make the second month 29 days long:

(1) January	31 days	(7) July	31 days
(2) February	28 {29} days	(8) August	31 days
(3) March	31 days	(9) September	30 days
(4) April	30 days	(10) October	31 days
(5) May	31 days	(11) November	30 days
(6) June	30 days	(12) December	31 days

The leap-year structure is given in curly brackets. A year is a leap year if it is divisible by 4 and is not a century year (multiple of 100) or if it is divisible by 400. For example, 1900 is not a leap year; 2000 is. The Gregorian calendar differs from its predecessor, the old-style or Julian calendar, only in that the Julian calendar did not include the century rule for leap years—all century years were leap years. It is the century rule that causes the leap year structure to fall outside the cycle-of-years paradigm of Section 1.12 (but Gregorian-like leap year rules have their own interesting mathematical properties; see [19]). Days on both calendars begin at midnight.

Although the month lengths seem arbitrarily arranged, they would precisely satisfy the cyclic formulas of Section 1.12 with $c = 12$, $l = 7$, $\Delta = 11$, and $L = 30$, if February always had 30 days. In other words, if we assume February has 30 days, formula (1.60) tells us that there are

$$\left\lfloor \frac{7m - 2}{12} \right\rfloor + 30(m - 1) = \left\lfloor \frac{367m - 362}{12} \right\rfloor \tag{2.1}$$

days in the months $1, \ldots, m - 1$, and formula (1.64) tells us that day n of the year falls in month number

$$\left\lfloor \frac{12n + 373}{367} \right\rfloor. \tag{2.2}$$

It is a simple matter to use these formulas and correct for the mistaken assumption that February has 30 days (see the next section).

The Julian calendar was instituted on January 1, 709 A.U.C.[1] (45 B.C.E.) by Julius Cæsar, with the help of Alexandrian astronomer Sosigenes; it was a modification of the Roman Republican (see [14]) and ancient Egyptian calendars. Because every fourth year was a leap year, a cycle of 4 years contained $4 \times 365 + 1 = 1461$ days, giving an average length of year of 365.25 days. This is somewhat more than the mean length of the tropical year, and over the centuries the calendar slipped with respect to the seasons. By the sixteenth century, the true date of the vernal (spring) equinox had shifted from around March 21 in the fourth century when the date of Easter was fixed (see Chapter 8) to around March 11. If this error were not corrected, gradually Easter, whose

---

[1] *Ab Urbe Condita*; from the founding of the city (of Rome). Varro gives the year of the founding of Rome as 753 B.C.E. which gives 709 A.U.C. = 45 B.C.E. as the year of institution of the Julian calendar; it is commonly, but not universally, accepted. The counting of years according to the Christian era was instituted by the Roman monk and scholar Dionysius Exiguus in the sixth century but only became commonplace a few centuries later; Dionysius erred by a few years in his determination of the year of Jesus's birth. Much of the Christian world used "Anno Diocletiani" for many years (the Julian calendar with Diocletian's reign as the origin—the same origin as the Coptic calendar discussed in Chapter 4); Dionysius's innovation was to substitute his estimate of Jesus's natal year for the origin. Dionysius did not invent the notion of "B.C."—his system started at 1. The "1 B.C.E. is the year before 1 C.E." problem was a result of the system introduced and popularized by the Venerable Bede around 731; Bede did not know about 0, so he did not use it. The use of a year 0 preceding year 1 on the Gregorian calendar is due to Cassini in 1740 [5]; see also Dick Teresi, "Zero," *The Atlantic Monthly*, volume 280, no. 1, pp. 88–94, July 1997.

date depends on the ecclesiastical approximation of March 21 for the vernal equinox, would migrate through the seasons, eventually to become a summer holiday.

Pope Gregory XIII instituted only a minor change in the calendar—century years not divisible by 400 would no longer be leap years. (He also improved the rules for Easter; see Chapter 8.) Thus, 3 out of 4 century years are common years, giving a cycle of 400 years containing $400 \times 365 + 97 = 146,097$ days and an average year length of $146097/400 = 365.2425$ days. He also corrected the accumulated 10-day error in the date of the equinox by proclaiming that Thursday, October 4, 1582 C.E. according to the calendar still in use (Julian) would be followed by Friday, October 15, 1582, the first day of the new-style (Gregorian) calendar. Catholic countries followed his rule: Spain, Portugal, and Italy adopted it immediately, as did the Catholic states in Germany. However, Protestant countries resisted. The Protestant parts of Germany waited until 1700 to adopt it. The various cantons of Switzerland changed at different times. Sweden began a gradual changeover in 1699, omitting February 29 in 1700. At that point the plan was abandoned, leaving the Swedish calendar one day off from the Julian. This was only rectified in 1712 by adding a February 30 to that year! The Swedish calendar stayed in tune with the Julian until 1753, when the Gregorian was adopted.[2] Great Britain and her colonies (including the United States) waited until 1752; Russia held out until 1918, after the Bolshevik Revolution, which is also known as the October Revolution because it occurred October 25–26, 1917 C.E. (Julian) = November 7–8, 1917 (Gregorian).[3] Different parts of what is now the United States changed over at different dates; Alaska, for example, changed only when it was purchased by the United States in 1867.[4] Turkey did not change to the Gregorian calendar until 1927. An extensive list of dates of adoption of the Gregorian calendar can be found in [2].

---

[2] See [8, page 275]. We are indebted to Tapani Tarvainen and Donald Knuth for pointing out this anomaly.

[3] In 1923 the Congress of the Orthodox Oriental Churches adopted a slightly more accurate leap-year rule: Century years are leap years only if they leave a remainder of 2 or 6 when divided by 9; this "Revised Julian" rule agrees with the usual Gregorian rule for 1700–2700 (see M. Milankovitch, "Das Ende des julianischen Kalenders und der neue Kalender der orientalischen Kirche," *Astronomische Nachrichten*, volume 220, pp. 379–384, 1924). The Soviet Union adopted this rule at that time. Like the rest of the world, we ignore this "improvement."

[4] Alaska skipped only 11 days instead of 12 (as we might expect) but with a repeated weekday because it also jumped the International Date Line when it became United States territory in 1867: Friday, October 6, 1867 C.E. (Julian) was followed by Friday, October 18, 1867 (Gregorian)! Even without the change from the Julian to the Gregorian calendar, jumping the date line causes bizarre situations. In 1892 Samoa jumped the date line and also switched from "Asian Time" to "American Time," causing the Fourth of July to be celebrated for 2 consecutive days; the reverse happened when the Philippines jumped the date line in the other direction in 1844: Monday, December 30, 1844, was followed by Wednesday, January 1, 1845.

By universal current custom, the new Gregorian year number begins on January 1. There have, however, been other beginnings—parts of Europe began the New Year variously on March 1, Easter, September 1, Christmas, and March 25 (see, for example, [10]). This is no small matter in interpreting dates between January 1 and the point at which the number of the year changed. For example, in England the commencement of the ecclesiastical year on March 25 in the sixteenth and seventeenth centuries means that a date like February 1, 1660, leaves the meaning of the year in doubt. Such confusion led to the practice of writing a hyphenated year giving both the legal year first and the calendar year number second: February 1, 1660-1. The same ambiguity occurs even today when we speak of the "fiscal year," which can run from July to July or from October to October, but we would always give the calendar year number, not the fiscal year number in specifying dates.

Although the Gregorian calendar did not exist prior to the sixteenth century, we can extrapolate backwards using its rules to obtain what is sometimes called the "proleptic Gregorian calendar,"[5] which we implement in the next section. Unlike the Julian calendar, this proleptic calendar *does* have a year 0. (See footnote on page 48.) By our choice of the starting point of our fixed counting of days, we define

$$\textbf{gregorian-epoch} \overset{\text{def}}{=} 1 \tag{2.3}$$

2.2 Implementation

For convenience, we define 12 numerical constants by which we will refer to the 12 months of the Gregorian and Julian calendars:

$$\textbf{january} \overset{\text{def}}{=} 1 \tag{2.4}$$

$$\textbf{february} \overset{\text{def}}{=} \textbf{january} + 1 \tag{2.5}$$

$$\textbf{march} \overset{\text{def}}{=} \textbf{january} + 2 \tag{2.6}$$

$$\textbf{april} \overset{\text{def}}{=} \textbf{january} + 3 \tag{2.7}$$

$$\textbf{may} \overset{\text{def}}{=} \textbf{january} + 4 \tag{2.8}$$

$$\textbf{june} \overset{\text{def}}{=} \textbf{january} + 5 \tag{2.9}$$

$$\textbf{july} \overset{\text{def}}{=} \textbf{january} + 6 \tag{2.10}$$

---

[5] The name is really a misnomer because "proleptic" refers to the future, not the past.

$$\textbf{august} \overset{\text{def}}{=} \textbf{january} + 7 \tag{2.11}$$

$$\textbf{september} \overset{\text{def}}{=} \textbf{january} + 8 \tag{2.12}$$

$$\textbf{october} \overset{\text{def}}{=} \textbf{january} + 9 \tag{2.13}$$

$$\textbf{november} \overset{\text{def}}{=} \textbf{january} + 10 \tag{2.14}$$

$$\textbf{december} \overset{\text{def}}{=} \textbf{january} + 11 \tag{2.15}$$

To convert from a Gregorian date to an R.D. date, we first need a function that tells us when a year is a leap year. We write

$$\textbf{gregorian-leap-year?}\,(g\text{-}year) \overset{\text{def}}{=} \tag{2.16}$$

$$(g\text{-}year \bmod 4) = 0 \text{ and } (g\text{-}year \bmod 400) \notin \{100, 200, 300\}$$

The calculation of the R.D. date from the Gregorian date (which was described in [11] as "impractical") can now be done by counting the number of days in prior years (both common and leap years), the number of days in prior months of the current year, and the number of days in the current month:

$$\textbf{fixed-from-gregorian}\left(\begin{array}{|c|c|c|} year & month & day \end{array}\right) \overset{\text{def}}{=} \tag{2.17}$$

$$\textbf{gregorian-epoch} - 1 + 365 \times (year - 1) + \left\lfloor \frac{year - 1}{4} \right\rfloor -$$

$$\left\lfloor \frac{year - 1}{100} \right\rfloor + \left\lfloor \frac{year - 1}{400} \right\rfloor + \left\lfloor \frac{367 \times month - 362}{12} \right\rfloor +$$

$$\begin{cases} 0 & \text{if } month \leq 2 \\ -1 & \text{if } month > 2 \text{ and } \textbf{gregorian-leap-year?}\,(year) \\ -2 & \text{otherwise} \end{cases} + day$$

The explanation of this function is as follows. We add together the number of days *before* the epoch of the calendar (0, but we do it explicitly so that the dependence on our arbitrary starting date is clear), the number of nonleap days since the epoch, the number of leap days since the epoch, the number of days in prior months of the given date, and the number of days in the given month up to and including the given date. The number of leap days since the epoch is determined by the mathematical principle of "inclusion and exclusion"

[12, chapter 4]: add all Julian-leap-year-rule leap days (multiples of 4), subtract all the century years (multiples of 100), and then add back all multiples of 400. The number of days in prior months of the given year is determined by formula (2.1), corrected by 0, -1, or -2 for the assumption that February always has 30 days.

For example, to compute the R.D. date of November 12, 1945 (Gregorian), we compute $365 \times (1945 - 1) = 709{,}560$ prior nonleap days, $\lfloor(1945 - 1)/4\rfloor = 486$ prior Julian-rule leap days (multiples of 4), $-\lfloor(1945 - 1)/100\rfloor = -19$ prior century years, $\lfloor(1945 - 1)/400\rfloor = 4$ prior 400-multiple years, $\lfloor(367 \times 11 - 362)/12\rfloor = 306$ prior days, corrected by -2 because November is beyond February and 1945 is not a Gregorian leap year. Adding these values and the day 12 together gives $709{,}560 + 486 - 19 + 4 + 306 - 2 + 12 = 710{,}347$.

Calculating the Gregorian date from the R.D. *date* involves sequentially determining the year, month, and day of the month. Because of the century rule for Gregorian leap years allowing an occasional 7-year gap between leap years, we cannot use the methods of Section 1.12—in particular, formula (1.64)—to determine the Gregorian year. Rather, the exact determination of the Gregorian year from the R.D. *date* is an example of base conversion in a mixed-radix system [17]:

$$\textbf{gregorian-year-from-fixed}\,(date) \overset{\text{def}}{=} \qquad\qquad (2.18)$$

$$\begin{cases} year & \textbf{if } n_{100} = 4 \textbf{ or } n_1 = 4 \\ year + 1 & \textbf{otherwise} \end{cases}$$

where

$$d_0 \quad = \quad date - \textbf{gregorian-epoch}$$

$$n_{400} \quad = \quad \left\lfloor \frac{d_0}{146097} \right\rfloor \quad .$$

$$d_1 \quad = \quad d_0 \bmod 146097$$

$$n_{100} \quad = \quad \left\lfloor \frac{d_1}{36524} \right\rfloor$$

$$d_2 \quad = \quad d_1 \bmod 36524$$

$$n_4 \quad = \quad \left\lfloor \frac{d_2}{1461} \right\rfloor$$

$$d_3 \quad = \quad d_2 \bmod 1461$$

$$n_1 \quad = \quad \left\lfloor \frac{d_3}{365} \right\rfloor$$

$$year \quad = \quad 400 \times n_{400} + 100 \times n_{100} + 4 \times n_4 + n_1$$

This function can be extended to compute the ordinal day of *date* in its Gregorian year:

$$\text{Ordinal day of } date \text{ in its Gregorian year} \qquad\qquad (2.19)$$

$$= \begin{cases} (d_3 \bmod 365) + 1 & \text{if } n_1 \neq 4 \text{ and } n_{100} \neq 4, \\ 366 & \text{otherwise.} \end{cases}$$

That is, if $n_{100} = 4$ or $n_1 = 4$, then *date* is the last day of a leap year (day 146,097 of the 400-year cycle or day 1461 of a 4-year cycle); in other words, *date* is December 31 of *year*. Otherwise, *date* is ordinal day $(d_3 \bmod 365) + 1$ in *year* + 1.

This calculation of the Gregorian year of R.D. *date* is also correct for nonpositive years. In that case, n_{400} gives the number of 400-year cycles from *date* until the start of the Gregorian calendar—*including* the current cycle—as a *negative* number because the floor function always gives the largest integer smaller than its argument. Then the rest of the calculation yields the number of years from the *beginning* of that cycle, as a *positive* integer, because the modulus is always nonnegative for positive divisor—see equations (1.13) and (1.14).

Now that we can determine the year of an R.D. date, we can find the month by formula (2.2) corrected by 0, 1, or 2 for the assumption that February always has 30 days. Knowing the year and month, we determine the day of the month by subtraction. Putting these pieces together, we have

$$\textbf{gregorian-from-fixed}\,(date) \quad \overset{\text{def}}{=} \qquad\qquad (2.20)$$

year	*month*	*day*

where

$$year \qquad = \qquad \textbf{gregorian-year-from-fixed}\,(date)$$

$$prior\text{-}days \quad = \quad date - \textbf{fixed-from-gregorian}$$

$$\left(\begin{array}{|c|c|c|} \hline \textit{year} & \textbf{january} & 1 \\ \hline \end{array} \right)$$

$$
correction \quad = \quad
\begin{cases}
0 & \textbf{if } date < \textbf{fixed-from-gregorian} \\
& \left(\boxed{\begin{array}{c|c|c} year & \textbf{march} & 1 \end{array}} \right) \\[4pt]
1 & \textbf{if } date \geq \textbf{fixed-from-gregorian} \\
& \left(\boxed{\begin{array}{c|c|c} year & \textbf{march} & 1 \end{array}} \right) \textbf{ and} \\
& \textbf{gregorian-leap-year?} \\
& (year) \\[4pt]
2 & \textbf{otherwise}
\end{cases}
$$

$$
month \quad = \quad \left\lfloor \frac{12 \times (prior\text{-}days + correction) + 373}{367} \right\rfloor
$$

$$
day \quad = \quad date - \textbf{fixed-from-gregorian} \left(\boxed{\begin{array}{c|c|c} year & month & 1 \end{array}} \right) + 1
$$

We can use our fixed numbering of days to facilitate the calculation of the number of days difference between two Gregorian dates:

$$
\textbf{gregorian-date-difference}\,(g\text{-}date_1, g\text{-}date_2) \quad \overset{\text{def}}{=} \tag{2.21}
$$

$$
\textbf{fixed-from-gregorian}\,(g\text{-}date_2) \; -
$$
$$
\textbf{fixed-from-gregorian}\,(g\text{-}date_1)
$$

This function can then be used to compute the ordinal day number of a date on the Gregorian calendar within its year:

$$
\textbf{day-number}\,(g\text{-}date) \quad \overset{\text{def}}{=} \tag{2.22}
$$

$$
\textbf{gregorian-date-difference}
$$
$$
\left(\boxed{\begin{array}{c|c|c} g\text{-}date_{\textbf{year}} - 1 & \textbf{december} & 31 \end{array}} , g\text{-}date \right)
$$

The ordinal day number could also be computed directly using equation (2.19) in a modified version of **gregorian-year-from-fixed**. It is easy to determine the number of days remaining after a given date in the Gregorian year:

$$
\textbf{days-remaining}\,(g\text{-}date) \quad \overset{\text{def}}{=} \tag{2.23}
$$

$$
\textbf{gregorian-date-difference}
$$
$$
\left(g\text{-}date, \boxed{\begin{array}{c|c|c} g\text{-}date_{\textbf{year}} & \textbf{december} & 31 \end{array}} \right)
$$

2.3 Alternative Formulas

We noted in Section 2.1 that if we pretend that February always has 30 days, the month lengths satisfy the cycle-of-years formulas of Section 1.12 with $c = 12$, $l = 7$, $\Delta = 11$, and $L = 30$; we used the resulting formulas (2.1) and (2.2) to convert Gregorian dates to and from fixed dates. Because these formulas are only applied to month numbers $1 \ldots 12$, the fraction $7/12$ used in the left-hand side of (2.1) is not critical—any value in the open range $(1/2, 3/5)$ works as well (these lower and upper bounds come from considering each of the twelve month numbers)—and the fraction $4/7$ has the smallest denominator in the acceptable range. This leads us to see that $c = 7$, $l = 4$, $\Delta = 6$, and $L = 30$ also work, and thus we could substitute

$$\left\lfloor \frac{4m - 1}{7} \right\rfloor + 30(m - 1) = \left\lfloor \frac{214m - 211}{7} \right\rfloor$$

and

$$\left\lfloor \frac{7n + 217}{214} \right\rfloor,$$

respectively, for (2.1) and (2.2) in **fixed-from-gregorian** and **gregorian-from-fixed**.

More significant use of the cycle-of-years formulas is also possible. Instead of pretending that February has 30 days and correcting for the pretense, we could instead consider the annual period from March 1 to the end of February of the following year (see, for example, [3] and [21]). For this shifted year, the cycle-of-years formulas with $c = 12, l = 7, \Delta = 1$, and $L = 30$ work perfectly because the formulas are never applied in cases in which the length of February matters. Again, as above, the fraction $7/12$ can be replaced by any fraction in the open range $(4/7, 5/8)$; the fraction of smallest denominator in the allowable range, $3/5$, leads to $c = 5, l = 3, \Delta = 4$, and $L = 30$. The well-known "Zeller's congruence" [22], [23] (see [16] or [21]) for determining the day of the week of a given date is based on this idea as are calendar formulas such as [20] (see [13, pp. 61–63]), and many others.

The shifted-year formulas are then applied as follows. The number of days in months starting in March prior to month m (where March is $m = 1$, April is $m = 2, \ldots,$ February is $m = 12$) is

$$\left\lfloor \frac{3m - 1}{5} \right\rfloor + 30(m - 1) = \left\lfloor \frac{153m - 151}{5} \right\rfloor$$

To consider March (*month* = 3) of *year* to be month $m = 1$ of year $y = year + 1$, April (*month* = 4) of *year* to be month $m = 2$ of year $y = year + 1, \ldots,$ February (*month* = 2) of *year* + 1 to be month $m = 12$ of year $y = year + 1$, we shift the month numbers with

$$m = (month - 2) \text{ amod } 12$$

and adjust the year with

$$y = year + \left\lfloor \frac{month + 9}{12} \right\rfloor.$$

Because there are 306 days in March–December, we can write

alt-fixed-from-gregorian   (2.24)

$$\left(\begin{array}{|c|c|c|} \hline year & month & day \\ \hline \end{array} \right) \stackrel{\text{def}}{=}$$

$$\textbf{gregorian-epoch} - 1 - 306 + 365 \times (y - 1) + \left\lfloor \frac{y - 1}{4} \right\rfloor -$$

$$\left\lfloor \frac{y - 1}{100} \right\rfloor + \left\lfloor \frac{y - 1}{400} \right\rfloor + \left\lfloor \frac{3 \times m - 1}{5} \right\rfloor + 30 \times (m - 1) + day$$

where

$$m = (month - 2) \text{ amod } 12$$

$$y = year + \left\lfloor \frac{month + 9}{12} \right\rfloor$$

In the reverse direction, the same idea leads to

alt-gregorian-from-fixed (*date*) $\stackrel{\text{def}}{=}$ (2.25)

$$\begin{array}{|c|c|c|} \hline year & month & day \\ \hline \end{array}$$

where

$$y = \textbf{gregorian-year-from-fixed}$$
$$(\textbf{gregorian-epoch} - 1 + date + 306)$$

$$prior\text{-}days = date - \textbf{fixed-from-gregorian}$$
$$\left(\begin{array}{|c|c|c|} \hline y - 1 & 3 & 1 \\ \hline \end{array} \right)$$

$$month = \left(\left\lfloor \frac{5 \times prior\text{-}days + 155}{153} \right\rfloor + 2 \right) \text{ amod } 12$$

$$year \quad = \quad y - \left\lfloor \frac{month + 9}{12} \right\rfloor$$

$$day \quad = \quad date - \textbf{fixed-from-gregorian} \quad + 1$$
$$\left(\boxed{\begin{array}{c|c|c} year & month & 1 \end{array}} \right)$$

These functions are slightly simpler in appearance than our original functions to convert Gregorian dates to and from fixed dates, but the intuition has been lost with no gain in efficiency. Versions of these alternative functions are the basis for the conversion algorithms in [7] (see [5, p. 604]) and many others because by using formulas (1.11) and (1.17) to eliminate the mod and amod operators, **alt-fixed-from-gregorian** and **alt-gregorian-from-fixed** can be written as single arithmetic expressions over the integer operations of addition, subtraction, multiplication, and division with no conditionals.

Finally, we can give an alternative version of **gregorian-year-from-fixed** by doing a simple but approximate calculation and correcting it when needed. The approximate year is found by dividing the number of days from the epoch until 2 days after the given fixed date by the average Gregorian year length. The fixed date of the start of the next year is then found; if the given date is before the start of that next year, the approximation is correct, and otherwise the correct year is the year after the approximation:

$$\textbf{alt-gregorian-year-from-fixed}\,(date) \quad \overset{\text{def}}{=} \quad \hspace{3cm} (2.26)$$

$$\begin{cases} approx & \textbf{if } date < start \\ approx + 1 & \textbf{otherwise} \end{cases}$$

where

$$approx \quad = \quad \left\lfloor \frac{date - \textbf{gregorian-epoch} + 2}{\frac{146097}{400}} \right\rfloor$$

$$start \quad = \quad \textbf{gregorian-epoch} + 365 \times approx + \left\lfloor \frac{approx}{4} \right\rfloor$$
$$- \left\lfloor \frac{approx}{100} \right\rfloor + \left\lfloor \frac{approx}{400} \right\rfloor$$

2.4 Holidays

> The information in this book has been gathered from many
> sources. Every effort has been made to insure its accuracy.
> Holidays sometimes are subject to change, however, and Morgan
> Guaranty cannot accept responsibility should any date or
> statement included prove to be incorrect.
> —Morgan Guaranty: *World Calendar* (1978)

Secular holidays on the Gregorian calendar are either on fixed days or on a particular day of the week relative to the beginning or end of a month. (An extensive list of secular holidays can be found in [9].) Fixed holidays are trivial to deal with; for example, to determine the R.D. date of United States Independence Day in a given Gregorian year we would use

$$\textbf{independence-day} \ (g\text{-}year) \ \overset{\text{def}}{=} \tag{2.27}$$

$$\textbf{fixed-from-gregorian} \left(\ \boxed{g\text{-}year \ \big| \ \textbf{july} \ \big| \ 4} \ \right)$$

Other holidays are on the nth occurrence of a given day of the week, counting from either the beginning or the end of the month. U. S. Labor Day, for example, is the first Monday in September, and U. S. Memorial Day is the last Monday in May. To find the R.D. date of the nth k-day (k is the day of the week) on or after/before a given Gregorian date (counting backward when $n < 0$), we write

$$\textbf{nth-kday} \ (n, k, g\text{-}date) \ \overset{\text{def}}{=} \tag{2.28}$$

$$
\begin{cases}
7 \times n + \textbf{kday-before} \\
\qquad (\ \textbf{fixed-from-gregorian} \ (g\text{-}date) \ , \ k \ ) \\
\qquad\qquad\qquad\qquad\qquad\qquad \textbf{if } n > 0 \\
7 \times n + \textbf{kday-after} \\
\qquad (\ \textbf{fixed-from-gregorian} \ (g\text{-}date) \ , \ k \ ) \\
\qquad\qquad\qquad\qquad\qquad\qquad \textbf{otherwise}
\end{cases}
$$

using the functions of Section 1.10 (page 29). It is also convenient to define two special cases for use with this function:

$$\textbf{first-kday} \ (k, g\text{-}date) \ \overset{\text{def}}{=} \ \textbf{nth-kday} \ (1, k, g\text{-}date) \tag{2.29}$$

gives the fixed date of the first k-day on or after a Gregorian date;

$$\textbf{last-kday} \ (k, g\text{-}date) \ \overset{\text{def}}{=} \ \textbf{nth-kday} \ (-1, k, g\text{-}date) \tag{2.30}$$

gives the fixed date of the k-day on or before a Gregorian date.

Now we can define holiday dates, such as U. S. Labor Day,

$$\textbf{labor-day} \, (g\text{-}year) \quad \overset{\text{def}}{=} \tag{2.31}$$

$$\textbf{first-kday} \left(\textbf{monday}, \; \boxed{g\text{-}year \;\mid\; \textbf{september} \;\mid\; 1} \right)$$

U. S. Memorial Day,

$$\textbf{memorial-day} \, (g\text{-}year) \quad \overset{\text{def}}{=} \tag{2.32}$$

$$\textbf{last-kday} \left(\textbf{monday}, \; \boxed{g\text{-}year \;\mid\; \textbf{may} \;\mid\; 31} \right)$$

U. S. Election Day (the Tuesday after the first Monday in November, which is the first Tuesday on or after November 2),

$$\textbf{election-day} \, (g\text{-}year) \quad \overset{\text{def}}{=} \tag{2.33}$$

$$\textbf{first-kday} \left(\textbf{tuesday}, \; \boxed{g\text{-}year \;\mid\; \textbf{november} \;\mid\; 2} \right)$$

or determine the starting and ending dates of U. S. daylight saving time (the first Sunday in April and the last Sunday in October, respectively):

$$\textbf{daylight-saving-start} \, (g\text{-}year) \quad \overset{\text{def}}{=} \tag{2.34}$$

$$\textbf{first-kday} \left(\textbf{sunday}, \; \boxed{g\text{-}year \;\mid\; \textbf{april} \;\mid\; 1} \right)$$

$$\textbf{daylight-saving-end} \, (g\text{-}year) \quad \overset{\text{def}}{=} \tag{2.35}$$

$$\textbf{last-kday} \left(\textbf{sunday}, \; \boxed{g\text{-}year \;\mid\; \textbf{october} \;\mid\; 31} \right)$$

The main Christian holidays are Christmas, Easter, and various days connected with them (Advent Sunday, Ash Wednesday, Good Friday, and others; see [10, vol. V, pp. 844–853]). The date of Christmas on the Gregorian calendar is fixed and hence easily computed:

$$\textbf{christmas} \, (g\text{-}year) \quad \overset{\text{def}}{=} \tag{2.36}$$

$$\textbf{fixed-from-gregorian} \left(\boxed{g\text{-}year \;\mid\; \textbf{december} \;\mid\; 25} \right)$$

The related dates of Advent Sunday (the Sunday closest to November 30) and Epiphany (the first Sunday after January 1)[6] are computed by

$$\textbf{advent}\,(g\text{-}year) \;\overset{\text{def}}{=} \tag{2.37}$$

kday-nearest

$$\left(\;\textbf{fixed-from-gregorian}\right.$$

$$\left(\;\boxed{\;\boxed{g\text{-}year}\;\boxed{\textbf{november}}\;\boxed{30}\;}\;\right),$$

$$\left.\textbf{sunday}\;\right)$$

$$\textbf{epiphany}\,(g\text{-}year) \;\overset{\text{def}}{=} \tag{2.38}$$

$$\textbf{first-kday}\left(\;\textbf{sunday},\;\boxed{\;\boxed{g\text{-}year}\;\boxed{\textbf{january}}\;\boxed{2}\;}\;\right)$$

The date of Assumption (August 15), celebrated in Catholic countries, is fixed and presents no problem.

We defer the calculation of Easter and related "movable" Christian holidays, which depend on lunar events, until Chapter 8.

References

[1] *The Nautical Almanac and Astronomical Ephemeris for the Year 1938*, His Majesty's Stationery Office, London, 1937.

[2] *Explanatory Supplement to the Astronomical Ephemeris and the American Ephemeris and Nautical Almanac*, Her Majesty's Stationery Office, London, 1961.

[3] J. A. Ball, *Algorithms for RPN Calculators*, John Wiley & Sons, Inc., New York, 1978.

[4] G. V. Coyne, M. A. Hoskin, and O. Pedersen, *Gregorian Reform of the Calendar: Proceedings of the Vatican Conference to Commemorate Its 400th Anniversary, 1582–1982*, Pontifica Academica Scientiarum, Specola Vaticana, Vatican, 1983.

[5] L. E. Doggett, "Calendars," *Explanatory Supplement to the Astronomical Almanac*, P. K. Seidelmann, ed., University Science Books, Mill Valley, CA, pp. 575–608, 1992.

[6] J. Dutka, "On the Gregorian Revision of the Julian Calendar," *Mathematical Intelligencer*, volume 10, pp. 56–64, 1988.

[7] H. F. Fliegel and T. C. van Flandern, "A Machine Algorithm for Processing Calendar Dates," *Communications of the ACM*, volume 11, p. 657, 1968.

[8] F. K. Ginzel, *Handbuch der mathematischen und technischen Chronologie*, volume 3, J. C. Hinrichs'sche Buchhandlung, Leipzig, 1914. Reprinted by F. Ullmann Verlag, Zwickau, 1958.

[9] R. W. Gregory, *Special Days*, Citadel, Secaucus, NJ, 1975. Previous editions appeared under the title *Anniversaries and Holidays*.

---

[6] Outside the United States, Epiphany is celebrated on January 6.

[10] J. Hastings, ed., *Encyclopædia of Religion and Ethics*, Charles Scribner's Sons, New York, 1911.

[11] L. Lamport, "On the Proof of Correctness of a Calendar Program," *Communications of the ACM*, volume 22, pp. 554–556, 1979.

[12] C. L. Liu, *Introduction to Combinatorial Mathematics*, McGraw-Hill Book Co., New York, 1968.

[13] J. Meeus, *Astronomical Algorithms*, 2nd ed., Willmann-Bell, Inc., Richmond, VA, 1998.

[14] A. K. Michels, *The Calendar of the Roman Republic*, Princeton University Press, Princeton, NJ, 1967.

[15] G. Moyer, "The Gregorian Calendar," *Scientific American*, volume 246, no. 5, pp. 144–152, May 1982.

[16] Ø. Ore, *Number Theory and Its History*, McGraw-Hill Book Co., Inc., New York, 1948. Reprinted by Dover Publications, Inc., Mineola, NY, 1988.

[17] E. M. Reingold, J. Nievergelt, and N. Deo, *Combinatorial Algorithms: Theory and Practice*, Prentice-Hall, Englewood Cliffs, NJ, 1977.

[18] V. F. Rickey, "Mathematics of the Gregorian Calendar," *Mathematical Intelligencer*, volume 7, pp. 53–56, 1985.

[19] J. Shallit, "Pierce Expansions and Rules for the Determination of Leap Years," *Fibonacci Quarterly*, volume 32, pp. 416–423, 1994.

[20] R. G. Tantzen, "Algorithm 199: Conversions Between Calendar Date and Julian Day Number," *Communications of the ACM*, volume 6, p. 444, 1963.

[21] J. V. Uspensky and M. A. Heaslet, *Elementary Number Theory*, McGraw-Hill, New York, 1939.

[22] C. Zeller, "Problema duplex Calendarii fundamentale," *Bull. Société Mathématique*, volume 11, pp. 59–61, March 1883.

[23] C. Zeller, "Kalender-Formeln," *Acta Mathematica*, volume 9, pp. 131–136, 1887.

Profile of Julius Cæsar from *C. Ivlii Cæsaris Quæ Extant*, with emendations of Joseph Scaliger (1635). (Courtesy of the University of Chicago, Chicago, IL.)

3

The Julian Calendar

Cæsar set out the problem before the best philosophers and
mathematicians and, from the methods available, he concocted his
own correction that was more precise.
—Plutarch: *Life of Cæsar* (75 C.E.)

3.1 Structure and Implementation

Atque hic erat anni Romani status cum C. Cæsar ei manum
admovit: qui ex lunari non malo in pessimum a Numa aut alio
rupice et rustico depravatus, vitio intercalationis veteres fines suos
tamen tueri non potuit. Vt non semel miratus sim, orbis terrarum
dominam gentem, quæ generi humano leges dabat, sibi unam
legem anni ordinati statuere non potuisse, ut post hominum
memoriam nulla gens in terris ineptiore anni forma usa sit.
[Such was the condition of the Roman calendar when Julius Cæsar
went about his work on it. Numa or some other rustic clod took a
lunar calendar that was not too bad and made it appalling. Thanks
to his faulty system of intercalation it could not stay in its original
bounds. I have been amazed more than once that the people who
ruled the entire world and gave laws to the entire human race could
not make one law for itself for an orderly calendar. As a result, no
nation in human memory has used a worse calendar than theirs.]
—Joseph Justus Scaliger: *De Emendatione Temporum*
(1583)[1]

The calculations for the Julian calendar, which we described in introducing the
Gregorian calendar in Chapter 2, are nearly identical to those for the Gregorian
calendar, but we must change the leap-year rule to

$$\textbf{julian-leap-year?} \; (j\text{-}year) \quad \overset{\text{def}}{=} \tag{3.1}$$

---

[1] *Lectores ne credant huius libri auctores his sententiis subscribere.*

$$(j\text{-}year \bmod 4) = \begin{cases} 0 & \textbf{if } j\text{-}year > 0 \\ 3 & \textbf{otherwise} \end{cases}$$

The upper part is formula (1.56); the lower part is formula (1.57) with $\Delta = 1$ because there is no year 0 on the Julian calendar. Note that the Julian leap-year rule was applied inconsistently for some years prior to 8 C.E. (see [6, pp. 156–158]).

The months of the Julian calendar are the same as on the Gregorian calendar (see page 47).

Converting from a Julian date to an R.D. date requires a calculation similar to that in the Gregorian case but with two minor adjustments: We no longer need consider century-year leap days, and we must define the epoch of the Julian calendar in terms of our fixed dating. For the epoch, we know that R.D. 1 is January 3, 1 C.E. (Julian), and thus the first day of the Julian calendar, January 1, 1 C.E. (Julian) must be December 30, 0 (Gregorian), that is, R.D. -1:

$$\textbf{julian-epoch} \overset{\text{def}}{=} \tag{3.2}$$

$$\textbf{fixed-from-gregorian}\left(\begin{array}{|c|c|c|} \hline 0 & \textbf{december} & 30 \\ \hline \end{array} \right)$$

Now we can write

$$\textbf{fixed-from-julian}\left(\begin{array}{|c|c|c|} \hline year & month & day \\ \hline \end{array} \right) \overset{\text{def}}{=} \tag{3.3}$$

$$\textbf{julian-epoch} - 1 + 365 \times (y - 1) + \left\lfloor \frac{y-1}{4} \right\rfloor +$$

$$\left\lfloor \frac{367 \times month - 362}{12} \right\rfloor +$$

$$\begin{cases} 0 & \textbf{if } month \leq 2 \\ -1 & \textbf{if } month > 2 \text{ and } \textbf{julian-leap-year?}\,(year) \\ -2 & \textbf{otherwise} \end{cases} +$$

$$day$$

where

$$y = \begin{cases} year + 1 & \textbf{if } year < 0 \\ year & \textbf{otherwise} \end{cases}$$

This function is similar in structure to that of **fixed-from-gregorian**. We add together the number of days before the epoch of the calendar, the number of nonleap days since the epoch, the number of leap days since the epoch, the number of days in prior months of the given date, and the number of days in the given month up to and including the given date. For nonpositive years, we adjust the year to accommodate the lack of year 0.

For the inverse function, we handle the missing year 0 by subtracting 1 from the year as determined by formula (1.64) for dates before the epoch:

$$\textbf{julian-from-fixed}\ (\textit{date}) \overset{\text{def}}{=} \boxed{\ \textit{year}\ |\ \textit{month}\ |\ \textit{day}\ } \tag{3.4}$$

where

$$\textit{approx} = \left\lfloor \frac{4 \times (\textit{date} - \textbf{julian-epoch}) + 1464}{1461} \right\rfloor$$

$$\textit{year} = \begin{cases} \textit{approx} - 1 & \textbf{if } \textit{approx} \leq 0 \\ \textit{approx} & \textbf{otherwise} \end{cases}$$

$$\textit{prior-days} = \textit{date} - \textbf{fixed-from-julian} \left(\boxed{\ \textit{year}\ |\ \textbf{january}\ |\ 1\ } \right)$$

$$\textit{correction} = \begin{cases} 0 & \textbf{if } \textit{date} < \textbf{fixed-from-julian} \\ & \qquad \left(\boxed{\ \textit{year}\ |\ \textbf{march}\ |\ 1\ } \right) \\ 1 & \textbf{if } \textit{date} \geq \textbf{fixed-from-julian} \\ & \qquad \left(\boxed{\ \textit{year}\ |\ \textbf{march}\ |\ 1\ } \right) \textbf{ and} \\ & \quad \textbf{julian-leap-year?} \ (\textit{year}) \\ 2 & \textbf{otherwise} \end{cases}$$

$$\textit{month} = \left\lfloor \frac{12 \times (\textit{prior-days} + \textit{correction}) + 373}{367} \right\rfloor$$

$$\textit{day} = \textit{date} - \textbf{fixed-from-julian} \left(\boxed{\ \textit{year}\ |\ \textit{month}\ |\ 1\ } \right) + 1$$

Alternative functions in the style of **alt-fixed-from-gregorian** and **alt-gregorian-from-fixed** can be constructed for **fixed-from-julian** and **julian-from-fixed**. See Section 2.3.

3.2 Roman Nomenclature

> Brutus: Is not tomorrow, boy, the ides of March?
> Lucius: I know not, sir.
> Brutus: Look in the calendar and bring me word.
> —Shakespeare: *Julius Cæsar*, Act II, scene i (1623)

In ancient Rome it was customary to refer to days of the month by counting down to certain key events in the month: the *kalends*, the *nones*, and the *ides*. This custom, in popular use well past the middle ages, is evidently quite ancient, coming from a time in which the month was still synchronized with the lunar cycle: the kalends were the new moon, the nones the first quarter moon, and the ides the full moon. (Indeed, the word *calendar* is derived from *kalendæ*, meaning "account book," for loans were due on the first of the month.) We define three special constants

$$\textbf{kalends} \overset{\text{def}}{=} 1 \tag{3.5}$$

$$\textbf{nones} \overset{\text{def}}{=} 2 \tag{3.6}$$

$$\textbf{ides} \overset{\text{def}}{=} 3 \tag{3.7}$$

to identify these events.

The kalends are always the first of the month. The ides are near the middle of the month—the thirteenth of the month, except in March, May, July, and October when they fall on the fifteenth; hence,

$$\textbf{ides-of-month}\ (\textit{month}) \overset{\text{def}}{=} \tag{3.8}$$

$$\begin{cases} 15 & \textbf{if } \textit{month} \in \{\textbf{march, may, july, october}\} \\ 13 & \textbf{otherwise} \end{cases}$$

The nones are always 8 days before the ides:

$$\textbf{nones-of-month}\ (\textit{month}) \overset{\text{def}}{=} \tag{3.9}$$

$$\textbf{ides-of-month}\ (\textit{month}) - 8$$

Dates that fall on the kalends, the nones, or the ides are referred to as such. Thus, March 15 is called "the ides of March," for example, whereas January 1 and 5 are, respectively, the kalends and nones of January. Dates that fall on the day before one of these special days are called *pridie* ("day before" in Latin); for example, July 6, the day before the nones of July, is *pridie Non. Jul.* in Latin. All dates other than the kalends, nones, or ides, or days immediately preceding them are described by the number of days (inclusive) until the next upcoming event: The Roman name for October 30 is *ante diem III Kal. Nov.*, meaning 3 days (inclusive) before the kalends of November; the idiomatic English usage would describe this as "2 days before the first of November," but the Roman idiom uses the inclusive count.

In a leap year, February has an extra day, and modern authorities understand the Roman custom as intercalating that day after February 24, before February 25 (but see [6] for another possibility). Because February 24 was *ante diem VI Kal. Mar.*, the extra day was called *ante diem bis VI Kal. Mar.* or "the second sixth day before the kalends of March." The phrase *bis VI* was read *bis sextum* which gave rise to the English words *bissextus* for leap day and *bissextile* as an adjective to describe a leap year [1, p. 795].

Table 3.1 gives abbreviated names for all the days according to the Roman system. Full spellings of all the names can be found day by day in [2]; details of the Latin grammar of those names can also be found there [2, pp. 672–673].

We represent the Roman method of referring to a day of the month by a list containing the year number, the month, the next event, a count (inclusive) of days until that event, and a **true/false** leap-day indicator:

year	*month*	*event*	*count*	*leap*

Although the Roman method of referring to days of the month is sometimes used in the context of Gregorian calendar dates, such use is anachronistic, and it is more sensible to tie the Roman nomenclature to the Julian calendar, as we do here.

Determining the fixed date corresponding to a given Roman form involves subtracting the count from the date of the event in the specified month and year, adjusting for the leap day if the event is the kalends of March in a leap year:

fixed-from-roman (3.10)

$$\left(\begin{array}{|c|c|c|c|c|} \hline year & month & event & count & leap \\ \hline \end{array}\right) \stackrel{\text{def}}{=}$$

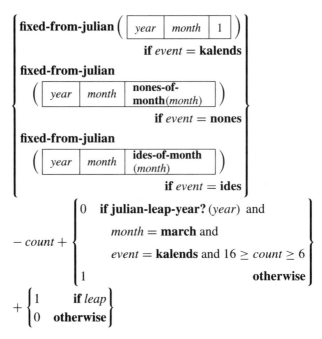

Converting a fixed date to the Roman form thus requires converting that fixed date to a Julian year-month-day and then determining the next event. If the month is February of a leap year, the special cases must be handled separately:

$$\textbf{roman-from-fixed} \, (\mathit{date}) \quad \overset{\text{def}}{=} \qquad\qquad\qquad\qquad (3.11)$$

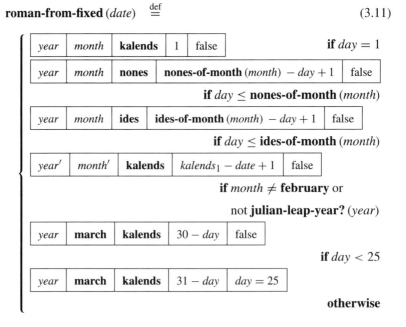

Table 3.1 *Roman nomenclature for days of the month on the Julian calendar. The abbreviation "a.d." stands for the Latin* ante diem. *In dates after the ides of a month, "Kal." means the kalends of the coming month; "Non." and "Id." mean the nones and ides, respectively, of the current month. Adapted from [3] and [5].*

Day	January August December	February (ordinary)	February (leap)	March May July October	April June September November
1	**Kalends**	**Kalends**	**Kalends**	**Kalends**	**Kalends**
2	a.d. iv Non.	a.d. iv Non.	a.d. iv Non.	a.d. vi Non.	a.d. iv Non.
3	a.d. iii Non.	a.d. iii Non.	a.d. iii Non.	a.d. v Non.	a.d. iii Non.
4	pridie Non.	pridie Non.	pridie Non.	a.d. iv Non.	pridie Non.
5	**Nones**	**Nones**	**Nones**	a.d. iii Non.	**Nones**
6	a.d. viii Id.	a.d. viii Id.	a.d. viii Id.	pridie Non.	a.d. viii Id.
7	a.d. vii Id.	a.d. vii Id.	a.d. vii Id.	**Nones**	a.d. vii Id.
8	a.d. vi Id.	a.d. vi Id.	a.d. vi Id.	a.d. viii Id.	a.d. vi Id.
9	a.d. v Id.	a.d. v Id.	a.d. v Id.	a.d. vii Id.	a.d. v Id.
10	a.d. iv Id.	a.d. iv Id.	a.d. iv Id.	a.d. vi Id.	a.d. iv Id.
11	a.d. iii Id.	a.d. iii Id.	a.d. iii Id.	a.d. v Id.	a.d. iii Id.
12	pridie Id.	pridie Id.	pridie Id.	a.d. iv Id.	pridie Id.
13	**Ides**	**Ides**	**Ides**	a.d. iii Id.	**Ides**
14	a.d. xix Kal.	a.d. xvi Kal.	a.d. xvi Kal.	pridie Id.	a.d. xviii Kal.
15	a.d. xviii Kal.	a.d. xv Kal.	a.d. xv Kal.	**Ides**	a.d. xvii Kal.
16	a.d. xvii Kal.	a.d. xiv Kal.	a.d. xiv Kal.	a.d. xvii Kal.	a.d. xvi Kal.
17	a.d. xvi Kal.	a.d. xiii Kal.	a.d. xiii Kal.	a.d. xvi Kal.	a.d. xv Kal.
18	a.d. xv Kal.	a.d. xii Kal.	a.d. xii Kal.	a.d. xv Kal.	a.d. xiv Kal.
19	a.d. xiv Kal.	a.d. xi Kal.	a.d. xi Kal.	a.d. xiv Kal.	a.d. xiii Kal.
20	a.d. xiii Kal.	a.d. x Kal.	a.d. x Kal.	a.d. xiii Kal.	a.d. xii Kal.
21	a.d. xii Kal.	a.d. ix Kal.	a.d. ix Kal.	a.d. xii Kal.	a.d. xi Kal.
22	a.d. xi Kal.	a.d. viii Kal.	a.d. viii Kal.	a.d. xi Kal.	a.d. x Kal.
23	a.d. x Kal.	a.d. vii Kal.	a.d. vii Kal.	a.d. x Kal.	a.d. ix Kal.
24	a.d. ix Kal.	a.d. vi Kal.	a.d. vi Kal.	a.d. ix Kal.	a.d. viii Kal.
25	a.d. viii Kal.	a.d. v Kal.	a.d. bis vi Kal.	a.d. viii Kal.	a.d. vii Kal.
26	a.d. vii Kal.	a.d. iv Kal.	a.d. v Kal.	a.d. vii Kal.	a.d. vi Kal.
27	a.d. vi Kal.	a.d. iii Kal.	a.d. iv Kal.	a.d. vi Kal.	a.d. v Kal.
28	a.d. v Kal.	pridie Kal.	a.d. iii Kal.	a.d. v Kal.	a.d. iv Kal.
29	a.d. iv Kal.		pridie Kal.	a.d. iv Kal.	a.d. iii Kal.
30	a.d. iii Kal.			a.d. iii Kal.	pridie Kal.
31	pridie Kal.			pridie Kal.	

where

$$j = \textbf{julian-from-fixed}\ (date)$$
$$month = j_{\textbf{month}}$$
$$day = j_{\textbf{day}}$$

$$year \quad = \quad j_{\mathbf{year}}$$

$$month' \quad = \quad (month + 1) \ \mathrm{amod} \ 12$$

$$year' \quad = \quad \begin{cases} year + 1 & \textbf{if } month' = 1 \\ year & \textbf{otherwise} \end{cases}$$

$$kalends_1 \quad = \quad \textbf{fixed-from-roman}$$

$$\left(\begin{array}{|c|c|c|c|c|} \hline year' & month' & \textbf{kalends} & 1 & \text{false} \\ \hline \end{array} \right)$$

Note that when the upcoming event is the kalends, it is the kalends of the *next* month, not the present month; thus, dates following the ides of a month carry the name of the next month, and after the ides of December dates carry the following year number.

3.3 Holidays

> It is related that once a Roman asked a question to Rabbi Yoḥanan
> ben Zakkai: We have festivals and you have festivals; we have the
> Kalends, Saturnalia, and Kratesis, and you have Passover, Shavuot,
> and Sukkot; which is the day whereon we and you rejoice alike?
> Rabbi Yoḥanan ben Zakkai replied: "It is the day when rain falls."
> —*Deuteronomy Rabbah*, VII, 7

Until 1923 Eastern Orthodox Christmas depended on the Julian calendar. At that time, the Ecumenical Patriarch, Meletios IV, convened a congress at which it was decided to use the Gregorian date instead.[2] By 1968 all but the churches of Jerusalem, Russia, and Serbia adopted the new date, December 25 on the Gregorian calendar. There remain, however, *Palaioemerologitai* groups, especially in Greece, who continue to use the old calendar. Virtually all Orthodox churches continue to celebrate Easter according to the Julian calendar (see Chapter 8).

The occurrence of the old Eastern Orthodox Christmas in a given Gregorian year is somewhat involved. Because the Julian year is always at least as long as the corresponding Gregorian year (it will take some 50,000 years for them to be a full year out of alignment), Eastern Orthodox Christmas can occur at most once in a given Gregorian year, but it can occur either at the beginning or the end; in some years (for example, 1100) it does not occur at all. We write a general function that gives a list of the corresponding R.D. dates of

---

[2] The Congress of the Orthodox Oriental Churches actually adopted a "revised" Gregorian leap-year rule; see footnote on page 49.

occurrence, within a specified Gregorian year, of a given month and day on the Julian calendar:

$$\textbf{julian-in-gregorian}\,(j\text{-}month, j\text{-}day, g\text{-}year) \overset{\text{def}}{=} \tag{3.12}$$

$$\begin{cases} \langle date_1 \rangle & \textbf{if } jan_1 \le date_1 \le dec_{31} \\ \langle \, \rangle & \textbf{otherwise} \end{cases}$$

$$\| \begin{cases} \langle date_2 \rangle & \textbf{if } jan_1 \le date_2 \le dec_{31} \\ \langle \, \rangle & \textbf{otherwise} \end{cases}$$

where

$$jan_1 \quad = \quad \textbf{fixed-from-gregorian}$$

$$\left(\boxed{\quad g\text{-}year \quad | \quad \textbf{january} \quad | \quad 1 \quad} \right)$$

$$dec_{31} \quad = \quad \textbf{fixed-from-gregorian}$$

$$\left(\boxed{\quad g\text{-}year \quad | \quad \textbf{december} \quad | \quad 31 \quad} \right)$$

$$y \quad = \quad \textbf{julian-from-fixed}\,\big(jan_1\big)_{\textbf{year}}$$

$$y' \quad = \quad \begin{cases} 1 & \textbf{if } y = -1 \\ y + 1 & \textbf{otherwise} \end{cases}$$

$$date_1 \quad = \quad \textbf{fixed-from-julian}\left(\boxed{\quad y \quad | \quad j\text{-}month \quad | \quad j\text{-}day \quad} \right)$$

$$date_2 \quad = \quad \textbf{fixed-from-julian}\left(\boxed{\quad y' \quad | \quad j\text{-}month \quad | \quad j\text{-}day \quad} \right)$$

Recall that $\|$ is our notation for list concatenation (see Section 1.8).

For example, we use this function to determine a list of zero or one R.D. dates of December 25 (Julian) for a given year of the Gregorian calendar:

$$\textbf{eastern-orthodox-christmas}\,(g\text{-}year) \overset{\text{def}}{=} \tag{3.13}$$

$$\textbf{julian-in-gregorian}\,(\textbf{december}, 25, g\text{-}year)$$

Other fixed Orthodox holidays are the Nativity of the Virgin Mary (September 8), the Elevation of the Life-Giving Cross (September 14), the Presentation of the Virgin Mary in the Temple (November 21), Epiphany (January 6), the Presentation of Christ in the Temple (February 2), the Annunciation (March 25), the Transfiguration (August 6), and the Repose of the Virgin Mary

(August 15). Orthodox periods of fasting include the Fast of the Repose of the Virgin Mary (August 1–14) and the 40-day Christmas Fast (November 15–December 24).

Orthodox movable holidays and fasts are explained in Chapter 8.

References

[1] *The Nautical Almanac and Astronomical Ephemeris for the Year 1938*, His Majesty's Stationery Office, London, 1937.

[2] B. Blackburn and L. Holford-Strevens, *The Oxford Companion to the Year*, Oxford University Press, Oxford, 1999.

[3] L. E. Doggett, "Calendars," *Explanatory Supplement to the Astronomical Almanac*, P. K. Seidelmann, ed., University Science Books, Mill Valley, CA, pp. 575–608, 1992.

[4] A. K. Michels, *The Calendar of the Roman Republic*, Princeton University Press, Princeton, NJ, 1967.

[5] E. G. Richards, *Mapping Time: The Calendar and its History*, Oxford University Press, Oxford, 1998.

[6] A. E. Samuel, *Greek and Roman Chronology: Calendars and Years in Classical Antiquity*, C. H. Beck'sche Verlagsbuchhandlung, Munich, 1972.

The calendar monument at Medinet Habu, Thebes, including dates of celebrations and sacrifices. From the reign of Ramses III (twelfth century B.C.E.). (Courtesy of the Oriental Institute, University of Chicago, Chicago, IL.)

4

The Coptic and Ethiopic Calendars

Kiyahk: ṣabāḥak misāk
[In Kiyahk, your morning is your evening.]
—Coptic rhyme about the short days of winter

4.1 The Coptic Calendar

The Christian Copts, modern descendants of the Pharaonic Egyptians, use a calendar based on the ancient Egyptian solar calendar (see Section 1.9) but with leap years. The year starts in late summer. Days begin at sunset, and the calendar consists of 12 months of 30 days each, followed by an extra 5-day period. Once every fourth year a leap day is added to this extra period to make it 6 days, making the average year $365\frac{1}{4}$ days long like the Julian calendar of Chapter 3. The months are called by coptized forms of their ancient Egyptian names; in Coptic (Sahidic) they are:

(1) Thoout	Ɵⲟⲟⲩⲧ	30 days
(2) Paope	Ⲡⲁⲟⲡⲉ	30 days
(3) Athôr	Ϩⲁⲑⲱⲣ	30 days
(4) Koiak	Ⲕⲟⲓⲁⲕ	30 days
(5) Tôbe	Ⲧⲱⲃⲉ	30 days
(6) Meshir	Ⲙϣⲓⲣ	30 days
(7) Paremotep	Ⲡⲁⲣⲙⲟⲧⲡ	30 days
(8) Parmoute	Ⲡⲁⲣⲙⲟⲩⲧⲉ	30 days
(9) Pashons	Ⲡⲁϣⲟⲛⲥ	30 days
(10) Paône	Ⲡⲁⲱⲛⲉ	30 days
(11) Epêp	Ⲉⲡⲏⲡ	30 days
(12) Mesorê	Ⲙⲉⲥⲟⲣⲏ	30 days
(13) Epagomenê	Ⲉⲡⲁⲅⲟⲙⲉⲛⲏ	5 {6} days

75

(The leap-year structure is given in curly brackets.) We treat epagomenê, the extra 5 or 6 days, as a short thirteenth month. Indeed, they are called "the small month" (*p abot n kouji*) in Coptic.

The day names are

Sunday	Tkyriakê	Ⲧⲕⲩⲣⲓⲁⲕⲏ
Monday	Pesnau	Ⲡⲉⲥⲛⲁⲩ
Tuesday	Pshoment	Ⲡϣⲟⲙⲉⲛ̄ⲧ
Wednesday	Peftoou	Ⲡⲉϥⲧⲟⲟⲩ
Thursday	Ptiou	Ⲡⲧⲟⲩ
Friday	Psoou	Ⲡⲥⲟⲟⲩ
Saturday	Psabbaton	Ⲡⲥⲁⲃⲃⲁⲧⲟⲛ

The Copts count their years from August 29, 284 C.E. (Julian), R.D. 103,605, the beginning of year 1 A.M.[1] Thus, we define

$$\textbf{coptic-epoch} \;\overset{\text{def}}{=}\; \tag{4.1}$$

$$\textbf{fixed-from-julian} \left(\;\boxed{\;284\text{ C.E.} \;\mid\; \textbf{august} \;\mid\; 29\;}\; \right)$$

Leap years occur whenever the Coptic year number leaves a remainder of 3 when divided by 4; this is $c = 4$, $l = 1$, $\Delta = 1$ in formula (1.57). We express this rule by

$$\textbf{coptic-leap-year?} \; (c\text{-}year) \;\overset{\text{def}}{=}\; (c\text{-}year \bmod 4) = 3 \tag{4.2}$$

but we do not ever need this function.

Considering the epagomenê as a month, to convert a Coptic date

$$\boxed{\;year \;\mid\; month \;\mid\; day\;}$$

to an R.D. date, we do as with the corresponding Gregorian and Julian functions: Add together the days before the start of the Coptic calendar, the number of days since the epoch aside from leap days, the number of leap days, the number of days in prior months in *year*, and the number of days in *month*:

$$\textbf{fixed-from-coptic} \left(\;\boxed{\;year \;\mid\; month \;\mid\; day\;}\; \right) \;\overset{\text{def}}{=}\; \tag{4.3}$$

$$\textbf{coptic-epoch} - 1 + 365 \times (year - 1) + \left\lfloor \frac{year}{4} \right\rfloor +$$

$$30 \times (month - 1) + day$$

---

[1] *Anno Martyrum* or "Era of the Martyrs"; this is the year Diocletian ascended the emperorship of Rome.

To convert an R.D. date to a Coptic date, we use formula (1.64) to determine the year. Then, unlike the Gregorian or Julian calendars, the simple month-length structure of the Coptic calendar allows us to determine the month by dividing by 30. As in the other calendars, we determine the day by subtraction:

$$\textbf{coptic-from-fixed}\,(date) \stackrel{\text{def}}{=} \boxed{\;year\;|\;month\;|\;day\;} \tag{4.4}$$

where

$$year = \left\lfloor \frac{4 \times (date - \textbf{coptic-epoch}) + 1463}{1461} \right\rfloor$$

$$month = \left\lfloor \frac{date - \textbf{fixed-from-coptic}\left(\boxed{\;year\;|\;1\;|\;1\;}\right)}{30} \right\rfloor + 1$$

$$day = date + 1 - \textbf{fixed-from-coptic} \left(\boxed{\;year\;|\;month\;|\;1\;}\right)$$

4.2 The Ethiopic Calendar

The Ethiopic calendar is identical to the Coptic calendar except for the epoch, the month names, and the day names. Many calendars in this book have similar variants, differing only in month names and year numbers, and can be treated analogously.

The Amharic Ethiopic months are

(1)	Maskaram	መስከረም	30 days
(2)	Teqemt	ጥቅምት	30 days
(3)	Ḥedār	ኅዳር	30 days
(4)	Tākhśāś	ታሕሣሥ	30 days
(5)	Ṭer	ጥር	30 days
(6)	Yakātit	የካቲት	30 days
(7)	Magābit	መጋቢት	30 days
(8)	Miyāzyā	ሚያዝያ	30 days
(9)	Genbot	ግንቦት	30 days
(10)	Sanē	ሰኔ	30 days
(11)	Ḥamlē	ሐምሌ	30 days
(12)	Naḥasē	ነሐሴ	30 days
(13)	Pāguemēn	ጳጉሜን	5 {6} days

and the day names are

Sunday	Iḥud	እሑ·ድ
Monday	Sanyo	ሰኞ
Tuesday	Maksanyo	ማክሰኞ
Wednesday	Rob/Rabu'e	ር·ብ/ረቡ·ዕ
Thursday	Ḥamus	ኃሙ·ስ
Friday	Arb	ዓር·ብ
Saturday	Kidāmmē	ቅዳሜ

Ethiopic year 1 E.E.[2] starts on August 29, 8 C.E. (Julian), our R.D. 2796:

$$\textbf{ethiopic-epoch} \overset{\text{def}}{=} \tag{4.5}$$

$$\textbf{fixed-from-julian}\left(\boxed{\begin{array}{c|c|c} 8 \text{ C.E.} & \textbf{august} & 29 \end{array}}\right)$$

To convert Ethiopic dates to and from R.D. dates, we just use our Coptic functions above but adjust for the different epoch:

$$\textbf{fixed-from-ethiopic}\left(\boxed{\begin{array}{c|c|c} \textit{year} & \textit{month} & \textit{day} \end{array}}\right) \overset{\text{def}}{=} \tag{4.6}$$

$$\textbf{ethiopic-epoch} +$$
$$\textbf{fixed-from-coptic}\left(\boxed{\begin{array}{c|c|c} \textit{year} & \textit{month} & \textit{day} \end{array}}\right) -$$
$$\textbf{coptic-epoch}$$

$$\textbf{ethiopic-from-fixed}\,(\textit{date}) \overset{\text{def}}{=} \tag{4.7}$$

$$\textbf{coptic-from-fixed}$$
$$(\textit{date} + \textbf{coptic-epoch} - \textbf{ethiopic-epoch})$$

4.3 Holidays

Determining the corresponding Gregorian date of a date on the Coptic or Ethiopic calendars is similar to the corresponding determination for the Julian calendar. Indeed, the Coptic and Julian are consistently aligned, except for a fluctuation of one day caused by the difference in leap-year rule and the absence of year 0 on the Julian calendar. For the Coptic calendar, which spans two Gregorian years, to determine the R.D. dates of a given Coptic month/day

---

[2] Ethiopic Era (of Mercy).

during a Gregorian year, we use

$$\textbf{coptic-in-gregorian}\,(c\text{-}month,\,c\text{-}day,\,g\text{-}year) \;\stackrel{\text{def}}{=} \qquad (4.8)$$

$$\begin{cases} \langle date_1 \rangle & \textbf{if } jan_1 \leq date_1 \leq dec_{31} \\ \langle\,\rangle & \textbf{otherwise} \end{cases}$$

$$\| \begin{cases} \langle date_2 \rangle & \textbf{if } jan_1 \leq date_2 \leq dec_{31} \\ \langle\,\rangle & \textbf{otherwise} \end{cases}$$

where

$$jan_1 \;=\; \textbf{fixed-from-gregorian} \left(\boxed{\;g\text{-}year\;|\;\textbf{january}\;|\;1\;} \right)$$

$$dec_{31} \;=\; \textbf{fixed-from-gregorian} \left(\boxed{\;g\text{-}year\;|\;\textbf{december}\;|\;31\;} \right)$$

$$y \;=\; \textbf{coptic-from-fixed}\,(jan_1)_{\,\textbf{year}}$$

$$date_1 \;=\; \textbf{fixed-from-coptic} \left(\boxed{\;y\;|\;c\text{-}month\;|\;c\text{-}day\;} \right)$$

$$date_2 \;=\; \textbf{fixed-from-coptic} \left(\boxed{\;y+1\;|\;c\text{-}month\;|\;c\text{-}day\;} \right)$$

For example, the Copts celebrate Christmas on Koiak 29 (which is always either December 25 or 26 on the Julian calendar) and thus we can write

$$\textbf{coptic-christmas}\,(g\text{-}year) \;\stackrel{\text{def}}{=} \qquad (4.9)$$

$$\textbf{coptic-in-gregorian}\,(4,\,29,\,g\text{-}year)$$

to give us a list of R.D. dates of Coptic Christmas during a given Gregorian year.

Other Coptic holidays include the Building of the Cross (Thoout 17), Jesus's Circumcision (Ṭôbe 6), Epiphany (Ṭôbe 11), Mary's Announcement (Paremotep 29), and Jesus's Transfiguration (Mesorê 13). The date of Easter may be determined by the Orthodox rule (page 119) and converted to the Coptic calendar.

Ethiopic holidays have the same fixed dates as the Coptic ones, and thus nothing more is needed for their computation. Locating arbitrary Ethiopic dates requires only a straightforward modification of **coptic-in-gregorian**, changing all references from the Coptic calendar to the Ethiopic.

References

[1] M. Chaîne, *La chronologie des temps Chrétiens de l'Égypte et de l'Éthiopie*, Paul Geuthner, Paris, 1925.

[2] A. Cody, "Coptic Calendar," *The Coptic Encyclopedia*, volume 2, pp. 433–436, Macmillan, New York, 1991.

[3] F. K. Ginzel, *Handbuch der mathematischen und technischen Chronologie*, volume 3, J. C. Hinrichs'sche Buchhandlung, Leipzig, section 262, 1914. Reprinted by F. Ullmann Verlag, Zwickau, 1958.

[4] C. W. Wassef, *Pratiques rituelles et alimentaires des Coptes*, Publications de L'Institut Français d'Archéologie Orientale du Caire, Bibliothèque d'Études Coptes, Cairo, 1971.

Banker's calendar, arranged by weeks and including day numbers. From *The Banker's Almanac and Register* (1881). (Courtesy of the publisher.)

5

The ISO Calendar

O tempora! O mores!
[Oh what times! Oh what standards!]
—Cicero: *In Catilinam* (63 B.C.E.)

The International Organization for Standardization (ISO) calendar, popular in Sweden and other European countries, specifies a date by giving the ordinal day in the week and the "calendar week" in a Gregorian year. The ISO standard [1, section 3.17] defines a *calendar week* as

a seven day period within a calendar year, starting on a Monday and identified by its ordinal number within the year; the first calendar week of the year is the one that includes the first Thursday of that year. In the Gregorian calendar, this is equivalent to the week which includes 4 January.

This does not define a new calendar per se but rather a representation of dates on the Gregorian calendar; still, it is convenient for us to treat it as a separate calendar, because the representation depends on weeks and the day of the week.

It follows from the ISO standard that an ISO year begins with the Monday between December 29 and January 4 and ends with a Sunday between December 28 and January 3. Accordingly, a year on the ISO calendar consists of 52 or 53 whole weeks, making the year either 364 or 371 days long. The epoch is the same as the Gregorian calendar, namely R.D. 1, because January 1, 1 (Gregorian) was a Monday.

The week number of a given ISO date gives the number of weeks after the first Sunday on or after December 28 of the preceding year. Hence the determination of the R.D. date corresponding to an ISO date is easy using **nth-kday** (page 58). The ISO calendar counts Sunday as the seventh day of the week, and thus we implement this calendar as follows:

$$\textbf{fixed-from-iso}\left(\boxed{\;year\;|\;week\;|\;day\;}\right) \stackrel{\text{def}}{=} \tag{5.1}$$

$$\textbf{nth-kday}\left(week, \textbf{sunday}, \boxed{\;year-1\;|\;\textbf{december}\;|\;28\;}\right) + day$$

$$\textbf{iso-from-fixed}\,(date) \stackrel{\text{def}}{=} \boxed{\;year\;|\;week\;|\;day\;} \tag{5.2}$$

where

$$approx = \textbf{gregorian-year-from-fixed}\,(date - 3)$$

$$year = \begin{cases} approx + 1 & \textbf{if } date \geq \textbf{fixed-from-iso} \\ & \left(\boxed{\;approx+1\;|\;1\;|\;1\;}\right) \\ approx & \textbf{otherwise} \end{cases}$$

$$week = \left\lfloor \frac{date - \textbf{fixed-from-iso}\left(\boxed{\;year\;|\;1\;|\;1\;}\right)}{7} \right\rfloor + 1$$

$$day = date \text{ amod } 7$$

We use the amod function defined on page 21, to assign 7 to *day* for Sundays.

The calculation of the ISO day and week numbers from the fixed date is clear once the ISO year has been found. Because the ISO year can extend as much as 3 days into the following Gregorian year, we find the Gregorian year for *date* − 3; this approximation is guaranteed to be either the desired ISO year or the prior ISO year. We determine which is the case by comparing the *date* to the R.D. date of the start of the approximate ISO year.

Reference

Cave ab homine unius libri.
[Beware the man of one book.]
—Latin motto

[1] *Data Elements and Interchange Formats—Information Interchange— Representation of Dates*, ISO 8601, International Organization for Standardization, 1988. This standard replaced ISO 2015, the original document describing the ISO calendar.

Page containing a discussion of months in the pre-Islamic Arab, Hebrew, Islamic, and Hindu calendars, along with an illustration of Mohammed instituting the purely lunar calendar. From a seventeenth-century copy of an illuminated fourteenth-century manuscript of the eleventh-century work *Al-Āthār al-Bāqiyah ʿan al-Qurūn al-Khāliyah* by the great Persian scholar and scientist Abū-Raihān Muhammad ibn ʾAhmad al-Bīrūnī. (Courtesy of Bibliothèque Nationale de France, Paris.)

6

The Islamic Calendar

> The number of months with God is twelve in accordance with
> God's law since the day he created the heavens and the Earth....
> Intercalating a month is adding to unbelief.
>
> —*Koran* (IX, 36–37)

6.1 Structure and Implementation

The Islamic calendar is a straightforward, strictly lunar calendar, with no inter-calation of months (unlike lunisolar calendars). Its independence of the solar cycle means that its months do not occur in fixed seasons but migrate through the solar year. Days begin at sunset. In this chapter, we describe the arithmetic Islamic calendar in which months follow a set pattern; for religious purposes, virtually all Moslems (except the Ismāʿīlīs) follow an observation-based calendar (discussed in Chapter 12) and use the arithmetic calendar only for estimation.

The week begins on Sunday; the days Sunday–Thursday are numbered, not named:

Sunday	yaum al-aḥad (the first day)	يَوْم الأَحد
Monday	yaum al-ithnayna (the second day)	يَوْم الإِثْنين
Tuesday	yaum ath-thalāthā' (the third day)	يَوْم الثَلَاثَاء
Wednesday	yaum al-arbaʿā' (the fourth day)	يَوْم الأَربَعَاء
Thursday	yaum al-ḥamīs (the fifth day)	يَوْم الخَميس
Friday	yaum al-jumʿa (the day of assembly)	يَوْم الجُمعة
Saturday	yaum as-sabt (the sabbath day)	يَوْم السَبْت

The calendar is computed, by the majority of the Moslem world, starting at sunset of Thursday, July 15, 622 C.E. (Julian), the year of Mohammed's

87

emigration[1] to Medina. The introduction of the calendar is often attributed to the Caliph 'Umar in 639 C.E., but there is evidence that it was in use before his succession. In essence, Moslems count R.D. 227,015 = Friday, July 16, 622 C.E. (Julian) as the beginning of the Islamic year 1, that is, as Muḥarram 1, A.H.[2] 1, and thus we define

$$\textbf{islamic-epoch} \stackrel{\text{def}}{=} \tag{6.1}$$

$$\textbf{fixed-from-julian}\left(\boxed{\;622\text{ C.E.}\;\;\vert\;\;\text{july}\;\vert\;\;16\;} \right)$$

There are 12 Islamic months, which contain, alternately, 29 or 30 days:

(1) Muḥarram	مُحَرَّم	30 days
(2) Ṣafar	صَفَر	29 days
(3) Rabī' I (Rabī' al-Awwal)	رَبيع الأَوَّل	30 days
(4) Rabī' II (Rabī' al-Āhir)	رَبيع الآخِر	29 days
(5) Jumādā I (Jumādā al-Ūlā)	جُمَادَى الأُولَى	30 days
(6) Jumādā II (Jumādā al-Āhira)	جُمَادَى الآخِرة	29 days
(7) Rajab	رَجَب	30 days
(8) Sha'bān	شَعبَان	29 days
(9) Ramaḍān	رَمَضَان	30 days
(10) Shawwāl	شَوَّال	29 days
(11) Dhu al-Qa'da	ذو القَعدة	30 days
(12) Dhu al-Ḥijja	ذو الحِجَّة	29 {30} days

The leap-year structure is given in curly brackets—the last month, Dhu al-Ḥijja, contains 30 days in years 2, 5, 7, 10, 13, 16, 18, 21, 24, 26, and 29 of a 30-year cycle. This gives an average month of $29.5305555\cdots$ days and an average year of $354.3666\cdots = 354\frac{11}{30}$ days. The cycle of common and leap years can be expressed concisely by observing that an Islamic year y is a leap year if and only if $(11y + 14)$ mod 30 is less than 11; this is an instance of

---

[1] The term "flight," though commonly used in English to describe the beginning of the Islamic epoch, does not accurately reflect the meaning of the Arabic term *hijra*, which has more a connotation of "breaking of ties" than of "running away."

[2] *Anno Hegiræ*; in the year of the Hegira (Mohammed's emigration to Medina)—see the previous footnote.

formula (1.57) with $c = 30$, $l = 11$, and $\Delta = 4$:

$$\textbf{islamic-leap-year?} \ (\textit{i-year}) \ \overset{\text{def}}{=} \tag{6.2}$$

$$((14 + 11 \times \textit{i-year}) \ \text{mod} \ 30) < 11$$

We never need this function, however. Some Moslems take year 15 of the 30-year cycle as a leap year instead of year 16. This variant structure, which is used by Birashk [1], corresponds to $L = 354$, $c = 30$, $l = 11$, and $\Delta = 15$ in the cycle formulas from Section 1.12; our functions thus require only minor modification for this variant leap-year rule.[3]

Converting from an Islamic date to an R.D. date is done by summing the days so far in the current month, the days so far in prior months of the current Islamic year, the days in prior Islamic years [by formula (1.60)], and the days prior to the Islamic calendar. The days in months prior to month m of the current Islamic year are also computed by (1.60) with $\lfloor (6m - 1)/11 \rfloor + 29(m - 1)$ because the pattern of Islamic month lengths satisfies the cycle formulas of Section 1.12 with $c = 11$, $l = 6$, $\Delta = 10$, and $L = 29$:

$$\textbf{fixed-from-islamic}\left(\begin{array}{|c|c|c|} \hline \textit{year} & \textit{month} & \textit{day} \\ \hline \end{array}\right) \ \overset{\text{def}}{=} \tag{6.3}$$

$$\textit{day} + 29 \times (\textit{month} - 1) + \left\lfloor \frac{6 \times \textit{month} - 1}{11} \right\rfloor + (\textit{year} - 1) \times 354 \ +$$

$$\left\lfloor \frac{3 + 11 \times \textit{year}}{30} \right\rfloor + \textbf{islamic-epoch} - 1$$

Computing the Islamic date equivalent to a given R.D. date is more straightforward than the computations for the Gregorian calendar or the Julian: We calculate the exact value of the year using formula (1.64). The month is determined in the same way, and the day of the month is determined by subtraction:

$$\textbf{islamic-from-fixed} \ (\textit{date}) \ \overset{\text{def}}{=} \begin{array}{|c|c|c|} \hline \textit{year} & \textit{month} & \textit{day} \\ \hline \end{array} \tag{6.4}$$

where

$$\textit{year} \ = \ \left\lfloor \frac{30 \times (\textit{date} - \textbf{islamic-epoch}) + 10646}{10631} \right\rfloor$$

[3] Specifically, the following three changes are needed: replacing 14 by 15 in **islamic-leap-year?**, replacing the numerator $3 + 11 \times \textit{year}$ by $4 + 11 \times \textit{year}$ in **fixed-from-islamic**, and replacing the 10,646 by 10,645 in the numerator of the value for *year* in **islamic-from-fixed**.

$$prior\text{-}days \;=\; date \;-\; \textbf{fixed-from-islamic}\left(\;\boxed{year}\;\boxed{1}\;\boxed{1}\;\right)$$

$$month \quad=\; \left\lfloor \frac{11 \times prior\text{-}days + 330}{325} \right\rfloor$$

$$day \qquad =\; date \;-\; \textbf{fixed-from-islamic} \qquad +1 \\ \left(\;\boxed{year}\;\boxed{month}\;\boxed{1}\;\right)$$

It is important to realize that, to a great extent, the foregoing calculations are merely hypothetical because there are many disparate forms of the Islamic calendar [6]. Furthermore, much of the Islamic world relies not on the calculations of this *arithmetical* calendar at all but on proclamation of the new moon by religious authorities based on visibility of the lunar crescent. Consequently, the dates given by the functions here can be in error by a day or two from what will actually be observed in various parts of the Islamic world; this is unavoidable.

One could use astronomical functions (see Chapter 12) to determine the likely date of visibility of a new moon (see [5]). The calculation of such an astronomical Islamic calendar—sketched in Section 12.8—is quite intricate and not generally accepted.

6.2 Holidays

> Only approximate positions have been used for predicting the commencement of a Hijri month, as accurate places cannot be computed without a great amount of labour.... Users of this Diglott Calendar must, therefore, at the commencement of each year correct the dates with those in the official Block Calendar issued by the Nizamiah Observatory.
> —Director of Nizamiah Observatory,
> quoted by Mazhar Husain: *Diglott Calendar,* volume II, p. iii
> (1961)

Determining the R.D. dates of holidays occurring in a given Gregorian year is complicated, because an Islamic year is always shorter than the Gregorian year, and thus each Gregorian year contains parts of at least 2 and sometimes 3 successive Islamic years. Hence, any given Islamic date occurs at least once and possibly twice in any given Gregorian year. For example, Islamic New Year (Muḥarram 1) occurred twice in 1943: on January 8 and again on December 28. Accordingly, we approach the problem of the Islamic holidays by writing a general function to return a list of the R.D. dates of a given Islamic date occurring in a given Gregorian year:

$$\textbf{islamic-in-gregorian}\,(\textit{i-month},\,\textit{i-day},\,\textit{g-year}) \quad \overset{\text{def}}{=} \quad (6.5)$$

$$\left\{ \begin{array}{ll} \langle date_1 \rangle & \textbf{if } jan_1 \le date_1 \le dec_{31} \\ \langle \, \rangle & \textbf{otherwise} \end{array} \right\}$$

$$\parallel \left\{ \begin{array}{ll} \langle date_2 \rangle & \textbf{if } jan_1 \le date_2 \le dec_{31} \\ \langle \, \rangle & \textbf{otherwise} \end{array} \right\}$$

$$\parallel \left\{ \begin{array}{ll} \langle date_3 \rangle & \textbf{if } jan_1 \le date_3 \le dec_{31} \\ \langle \, \rangle & \textbf{otherwise} \end{array} \right\}$$

where

$$jan_1 \quad = \quad \textbf{fixed-from-gregorian}$$
$$\left(\boxed{\;\textit{g-year}\;\mid\;\textbf{january}\;\mid\;1\;} \right)$$

$$dec_{31} \quad = \quad \textbf{fixed-from-gregorian}$$
$$\left(\boxed{\;\textit{g-year}\;\mid\;\textbf{december}\;\mid\;31\;} \right)$$

$$y \quad = \quad \textbf{islamic-from-fixed}\,(jan_1)_{\textbf{year}}$$

$$date_1 \quad = \quad \textbf{fixed-from-islamic}\left(\boxed{\;y\;\mid\;\textit{i-month}\;\mid\;\textit{i-day}\;} \right)$$

$$date_2 \quad = \quad \textbf{fixed-from-islamic}\left(\boxed{\;y+1\;\mid\;\textit{i-month}\;\mid\;\textit{i-day}\;} \right)$$

$$date_3 \quad = \quad \textbf{fixed-from-islamic}$$
$$\left(\boxed{\;y+2\;\mid\;\textit{i-month}\;\mid\;\textit{i-day}\;} \right)$$

There is little uniformity among the Islamic sects and countries as to holidays. In general, the principal holidays of the Islamic year are Islamic New Year (Muḥarram 1), 'Ashūrā' (Muḥarram 10), Mawlid an-Nabī (Rabī' I 12), Lailat-al-Miʿrāj (Rajab 27), Lailat-al-Barāʾa (Shaʿbān 15), Ramaḍān (Ramaḍān 1), Lailat-al-Kadr (Ramaḍān 27), ʿĪd-al-Fiṭr (Shawwāl 1), and ʿĪd-al-ʾAdḥā (Dhu al-Ḥijja 10). Other days, too, have religious significance—for example, the entire month of Ramaḍān. Like all Islamic days, an Islamic holiday begins at sunset the prior evening. We can determine a list of the

corresponding R.D. dates of occurrence in a given Gregorian year by using
islamic-in-gregorian above, as in

$$\textbf{mawlid-an-nabi}\,(g\text{-}year) \;\overset{\text{def}}{=}\; \tag{6.6}$$

islamic-in-gregorian $(3, 12, g\text{-}year)$

It bears reiterating that the determination of the Islamic holidays cannot be
fully accurate because the actual day of their occurrence depends on proclamation by religious authorities.

References

[1] A. Birashk, *A Comparative Calendar of the Iranian, Muslim Lunar, and Christian Eras for Three Thousand Years*, Mazda Publishers (in association with Bibliotheca Persica), Costa Mesa, CA, 1993.

[2] F. C. de Blois and B. van Dalen, "Ta'rikh" (Part I) *The Encyclopaedia of Islam*, 2nd ed., volume 10, pp. 257–271, E. J. Brill, Leiden, 1998.

[3] S. B. Burnaby, *Elements of the Jewish and Muhammadan Calendars, with Rules and Tables and Explanatory Notes on the Julian and Gregorian Calendars*, George Bell and Sons, London, 1901.

[4] G. S. P. Freeman-Grenville, *The Muslim and Christian Calendars*, 2nd ed., Rex Collings, London, 1977. A new edition has been published as *The Islamic and Christian Calendars* A.D. 622–2222 (A.H. 1–1650): *A Complete Guide for Converting Christian and Islamic Dates and Dates of Festivals*, Garnet Publications, Reading, MA, 1995.

[5] M. Ilyas, *A Modern Guide to Astronomical Calculations of Islamic Calendar, Times & Qibla*, Berita Publishing, Kuala Lumpur, 1984.

[6] V. V. Tsybulsky, *Calendars of Middle East Countries*, Institute of Oriental Studies, USSR Academy of Sciences, Moscow, 1979.

[7] W. S. B. Woolhouse, *Measures, Weights, & Moneys of All Nations: and an Analysis of the Christian, Hebrew, and Mahometan Calendars*, 7th ed., Crosby Lockwood, London, 1890. Reprinted by Ares Publishers, Chicago, 1979.

[8] F. Wüstenfeld and E. Mahler, *Wüstenfeld-Mahler'sche Vergleichungs-Tabellen zur muslimischen und iranischen Zeitrechnung mit Tafeln zur Umrechnung orient-christlicher Ären*, 3rd ed. revised by J. Mayr and B. Spuler, Deutsche Morgenländische Gesellschaft, Wiesbaden, 1961.

Sixteenth-century astrolabe, with zodiac and star names inscribed in Hebrew. (Courtesy of Adler Planetarium & Astronomy Museum, Chicago, IL.)

7

The Hebrew Calendar

Do not take these [visibility] calculations lightly... for they are
deep and difficult and constitute the "secret of intercalation" that
was [only] known to the great sages.... On the other hand, this
computation that is calculated nowadays... even school children
can master in three or four days.

—Moses Maimonides: *Mishneh Torah,*
Book of Seasons (1178)

The Hebrew calendar, promulgated by the patriarch Hillel II in the mid-fourth
century[1] and attributed by Sa'adia Gaon to Mosaic revelation, is more complicated than the other calendars we have considered so far. Its complexity is
inherent in the requirement that calendar months be strictly lunar, whereas
Passover must always occur in the spring. Because the seasons depend on
the solar year, the Hebrew calendar must harmonize simultaneously with both
lunar and solar events, as do all lunisolar calendars, including the Hindu and
Chinese calendars described in Chapters 9, 16, and 17. The earliest extant description of the Hebrew calendar is by the famous al-Khowārizmī [11], after
whom the words *algebra* and *algorithm* were coined. The most comprehensive
early work is by Savasorda of the eleventh century [16].

As in the Islamic calendar, days begin at sunset, the week begins on Sunday,
and the days Sunday–Friday are numbered, not named, as follows:

Sunday	yom rishon (first day)	יום ראשון
Monday	yom sheni (second day)	יום שני
Tuesday	yom shelishi (third day)	יום שלישי
Wednesday	yom revi'i (fourth day)	יום רביעי

---

[1] Bornstein [3] and others dispute the assertion of the tenth-century Hai Gaon that the current
calendar was formulated in 359 C.E. (year 670 of the Seleucid Era); see also [14, p. 118].

Thursday	yom ḥamishi (fifth day)	יום חמישי
Friday	yom shishi (sixth day)	יום ששי
Saturday	yom shabbat (sabbath day)	יום שבת

7.1 Structure and History

Iudaicus computus, omnium qui hodie extant antiquissimus,
articiosissimus, et elegantissimus.
[Of all methods of intercalation which exist today the Jewish
calculation is the oldest, the most skillful, and the most elegant.]
—Joseph Justus Scaliger: *De Emendatione Temporum*
(1593)[2]

The Hebrew year consists of 12 months in a common year and 13 in a leap ("gravid" or "embolismic") year:

(1) Nisan	30 days	ניסן
(2) Iyyar	29 days	אייר
(3) Sivan	30 days	סיון
(4) Tammuz	29 days	תמוז
(5) Av	30 days	אב
(6) Elul	29 days	אלול
(7) Tishri	30 days	תשרי
(8) Marḥeshvan	29 or 30 days	חשון or מרחשון
(9) Kislev	29 or 30 days	כסלו
(10) Tevet	29 days	טבת
(11) Shevat	30 days	שבט
{(12) Adar I	30 days	{אדר ראשון
(12) {(13)} Adar {II}	29 days	אדר {שני}

The leap-year structure is given in curly brackets—in a leap year there is an interpolated twelfth month of 30 days called Adar I to distinguish it from the final month, Adar II. The length of the eighth and ninth months varies from year to year according to criteria that will be explained below. Our ordering of the Hebrew months follows biblical convention (Leviticus 23:5) in which (what is now called) Nisan is the first month. This numbering causes the Hebrew New Year (Rosh ha-Shanah) to begin on the first of Tishri, which by our ordering is the seventh month—but this too agrees with biblical usage (Leviticus 23:24). It will be convenient to have the following constants defined for these two months:

$$\textbf{tishri} \stackrel{\text{def}}{=} 7 \tag{7.1}$$

[2] המובאות אינן מיצגות בהכרח את דעות המחברים.

$$\textbf{nisan} \stackrel{\text{def}}{=} 1 \qquad\qquad (7.2)$$

Adding up the lengths of the months, we see that a normal year has 353–355 days, whereas a leap year has 383–385 days. (These are the same year lengths as would be possible with an astronomical lunisolar calendar; see Section 12.9.)

In the Hebrew calendar, leap years occur in years 3, 6, 8, 11, 14, 17, and 19 of the 19-year Metonic cycle. This sequence can be computed concisely by noting that Hebrew year y is a leap year if and only if $(7y + 1)$ mod 19 is less than 7—another instance of formula (1.57).[3] Thus, we determine whether a year is a Hebrew leap year by

$$\textbf{hebrew-leap-year?}\ (h\text{-}year) \stackrel{\text{def}}{=} \qquad\qquad (7.3)$$

$$((7 \times h\text{-}year + 1)\ \ \text{mod}\ \ 19) < 7$$

and the number of months in a Hebrew year by

$$\textbf{last-month-of-hebrew-year}\ (h\text{-}year) \stackrel{\text{def}}{=} \qquad\qquad (7.4)$$

$$\begin{cases} 13 & \textbf{if hebrew-leap-year?}\ (h\text{-}year) \\ 12 & \textbf{otherwise} \end{cases}$$

The number of days in a Hebrew month is a more complex issue. The twelfth month, Adar or Adar I, has 29 days in a common year and 30 days in a leap year, but the number of days in the eighth month (Marḥeshvan) and ninth month (Kislev) depends on the overall length of the year, which in turn depends on factors discussed later in this section.

The beginning of the Hebrew New Year is determined by the occurrence of the mean new moon (conjunction) of the seventh month (Tishri), subject to possible postponements of 1 or 2 days. The new moon of Tishri A.M.[4] 1, the first day of the first year for the Hebrew calendar, is fixed at Sunday night at 11:11:20 p.m. Because Hebrew days begin at sunset, whereas our fixed dates begin at midnight, we define the epoch of the Hebrew calendar (that is, Tishri 1, A.M. 1) to be Monday, September 7, −3760 (Gregorian) or October 7, 3761 B.C.E. (Julian).

The Hebrew day is traditionally divided into 24 hours, and the hour is divided into 1080 *parts* (*ḥalaqim*), and thus a day has 25,920 parts of $3\frac{1}{3}$ seconds duration each. These divisions are of Babylonian origin. The new moon of

---

[3] An equivalent formula appears in Slonimski [17, p. 21].
[4] *Anno Mundi*; in the (traditional) year of the world (since creation).

Tishri A.M. 1, which occurred 5 hours and 204 parts after sunset (6 p.m.) on Sunday night, is called *molad beharad*, because the numerical value of the letter *beth* is 2, signifying the second day of the week; *heh* is 5 (hours); *resh* = 200 parts; *daleth* = 4 parts. Other epochs and leap-year distributions appear in classical and medieval literature. In particular, the initial conjunction of the epoch starting 1 year later, called *weyad* (signifying 6 days, 14 hours), occurred on Friday at exactly 8 a.m. the morning Adam and Eve were created according to the traditional chronology.[5]

The length of a mean lunar period in this representation is 29 days, 12 hours, and 793 parts, or $29\frac{13,753}{25,920} \approx 29.530594$ days. This is a classical value for the lunar (synodic) month, attributed to Cidenas in about 383 B.C.E. and used by Ptolemy in his *Almagest*.[6] With $354^d8^h48^m40^s$ for an ordinary year and $383^d21^h32^m43\frac{1}{3}^s$ for a leap year, this value gives an average Hebrew year length of about 365.2468 days. The start of each New Year, Rosh ha-Shanah (Tishri 1), coincides with the calculated day of the mean conjunction of Tishri—12 months after the previous New Year conjunction in ordinary years, and 13 in leap years—unless one of 4 delays is mandated:

1. If the time of mean conjunction is at midday or after, then the New Year is delayed.[7]
2. In no event may the New Year (Rosh ha-Shanah) be on Sunday, Wednesday, or Friday. (This rule is called *lo iddo rosh*.)[8] If the conjunction is on Saturday, Tuesday, or Thursday afternoon, then this rule combines with the previous rule and results in a 2-day delay.

---

[5] The ambiguities in the Hebrew epoch have led to some confusion. For example, M. Kantor's *The Jewish Time Line Encyclopedia*, Jason Aronson, Inc., Northvale, NJ (1989), and A. Spier [18] erroneously give 69 C.E., rather than 70 C.E., as the date Titus captured Jerusalem. Similarly, Sephardim, every Tishah be-Av (see page 109) in the synagogue, announce the wrong number of elapsed years since the fall of Jerusalem.

[6] The astronomer/mathematician Abraham bar Ḥiyya Savasorda (eleventh century) suggested that the reason for the choice of 1080 parts per hour is that it is the smallest number that allows this particular value of the length of a month to be expressed with an integral number of parts (in other words, 793/1080 is irreducible).

[7] According to Maimonides [13, 6:2] (cf. al-Bīrūnī [2, p. 149]), seasonal time is used in which "daylight hours" and "nighttime hours" have different lengths that vary according to the seasons (see Section 12.6). Postponement occurs if the conjunction is 18 variable-length hours or more after sunset. Others use fixed-length hours, but the computation is unaffected, because true noon is 18 temporal (seasonal) hours after true sunset just as mean local noon is 18 civil hours after mean local sunset (6 p.m. local mean time).

[8] Excluding Wednesday and Friday serves the ritual purpose of preventing Yom Kippur (Tishri 10) from falling on Friday or Sunday; excluding Sunday prevents Hoshana Rabba (Tishri 21) from falling on Saturday. Maimonides [13, 7:8] ascribes this correction in the calendar of approximately half a day, on the average, to the need to better match the mean date of appearance of the new moon of the month of Tishri; al-Bīrūnī [2] attributes it to astrological considerations. The real purpose of the delay is moot.

3. In some cases (about once in 30 years) an additional delaying factor may need to be employed to keep the length of a year within the allowable ranges. (It is the irregular effect of the second delay that makes this necessary.) If Rosh ha-Shanah were before noon on Tuesday of a common year and the conjunction of the following year at midday or later, then applying the previous two rules would result in delaying the *following* Rosh ha-Shanah from Saturday or Sunday—the day of the next conjunction for a common year—until Monday. This would require an unacceptable year length of 356 days, and thus instead the *current* Rosh ha-Shanah is delayed (skipping Wednesday) until Thursday, giving a 354-day year. For the following year's conjunction to fall on Saturday afternoon, the current year's must have occurred after 3:11:20 a.m. The prior year cannot become too long because of this delay, for its New Year conjunction must have been on Friday (in a common year) or Wednesday (in a leap year) and would have been delayed a day by the second rule.

4. In rare cases (about once in 186 years), Rosh ha-Shanah on Monday after a leap year can pose a similar problem by causing the year just ending to be too short—when the *prior* New Year conjunction was after midday on Tuesday and was, therefore, delayed until Thursday. If the conjunction were after midday Tuesday the previous year, then in the current year it would be after $9{:}32{:}43\frac{1}{3}$ a.m. on Monday. In this case, Rosh ha-Shanah is postponed from Monday to Tuesday, extending the leap year just ending from 382 days to 383.

The precise rules for delays were the subject of a short-lived dispute (921–923 C.E.) between Palestinian and Babylonian Jewish authorities. In 923 C.E. the calculated conjunction fell just after midday, but the Palestinian authority, Aaron ben Meir, insisted that the first delaying rule applied only when the conjunction was at 12:35:40 p.m. or later presumably because they (the Palestinians) did their calculations from Nisan, instead of Tishri, and rounded the time of the epochal new moon differently. Because of the retroactive effect of the third delay, this already affected dates in 921 (see the sample calculation beginning on page 105). In the end, the Babylonian gaon, Sa'adia ben Joseph al-Fayyūmi, prevailed, and the rules have since been fixed as given above. (Some scant details can be found in [14, vol. III, p. 119] and [9, col. 539–540]; [3] is a full discussion of the controversy; see also [10].) Interestingly, according to Maimonides [13, 5:13], the final authority in calendrical matters is vested in the residents of the Holy Land, and their decision—even if erroneous—should be followed worldwide:

Our own calculations are solely for the purpose of making the matter available to public knowledge. Since we know that residents of the Land of Israel use the same method of calculation, we perform the same operations in order to find out and ascertain what day it is that has been determined by the people of Israel.

One fairly common misconception regarding the Hebrew calendar is that the correspondence with the Gregorian calendar repeats every 19 years. This, however, is usually not the case because of the irregular Gregorian leap-year rule and the irregular applicability of the delays. Nor does the Hebrew calendar repeat its pattern every 247 years. In the seventeenth century, Hezekiah ben David da Silva of Jerusalem complained about published tables for the Hebrew calendar:[9]

I have seen disaster and scandal [on the part] of some intercalators who are of the [erroneous] opinion that the character [of years] repeats every thirteen cycles [247 years]. For the sake of God, do not rely and do not lean on them. "Far be it from thee to do after this manner," which will—perish the thought—cause the holy and awesome fast to be nullified, leaven to be eaten on Passover, and the holidays to be desecrated. Therefore, you the reader, "Hearken now unto my voice, I will give thee counsel, and God be with thee." Be cautious and careful lest you forget... what I am writing regarding this matter, since it is done according to exact arithmetic, "divided well," and is precise on all counts... from the 278th cycle [1521 C.E.] until the end of time. "Anyone who separates from it, it is as if he separates [himself] from life [itself]."

By the "character" of a year da Silva means the day of the week of New Year and the length of the year. In fact, the Hebrew calendar repeats only after 689,472 years (as was pointed out by the celebrated Persian Moslem writer, al-Bīrūnī [2, p. 154] in 1000 C.E.): The 19-year cycle contains exactly

> 991 weeks, 2 days, 16 hours, and 595 parts
>
> = 991 weeks, 69, 715 parts.

A week has 181,440 parts, so it takes

$$\mathrm{lcm}(69715, 181440)/69715 \;=\; 2{,}529{,}817{,}920 / 69{,}715 \text{ parts}$$
$$= \; 36{,}288 \text{ cycles}$$
$$= \; 689{,}472 \text{ years}$$

for the excess parts to accumulate into an even number of weeks, and for the calendar to return to the same pattern of delays. Thus, the exact correspondence of Hebrew dates (which has a mean year length of $365\frac{24311}{98496}$ days) and dates on the Gregorian calendar (which has a 400 year cycle) repeats only after

---

[9] *Peri Ḥadash, Oraḥ Ḥayyim*, 428.

$$\text{lcm}\left(689472 \times 365\frac{24311}{98496}, 400 \times 365\frac{97}{400}\right)$$

$$= \quad 5{,}255{,}890{,}855{,}047 \text{ days}$$
$$= \quad 14{,}390{,}140{,}400 \text{ Gregorian years}$$
$$= \quad 14{,}389{,}970{,}112 \text{ Hebrew years}$$

Similar astronomically long periods are needed for other pairs of calendars to match up exactly.

7.2 Implementation

The epoch of the Hebrew calendar is R.D. $-1{,}373{,}427$:

$$\textbf{hebrew-epoch} \;\overset{\text{def}}{=} \tag{7.5}$$

$$\textbf{fixed-from-julian}\left(\;\boxed{\;\text{3761 B.C.E.}\;\big|\;\text{october}\;\big|\;7\;}\;\right)$$

We can calculate the time elapsed on the Hebrew calendar from the Hebrew epoch until the new moon of Tishri for Hebrew year y by computing

$$m \times \left(29^{\text{d}}12^{\text{h}}44^{\text{m}}3\tfrac{1}{3}^{\text{s}}\right) - (48^{\text{m}}40^{\text{s}}) \tag{7.6}$$

where m is the number of months before year y, because the first mean conjunction was $48^{\text{m}}40^{\text{s}}$ before midnight on the epoch (see page 98). To compute the total number of months, leap and regular, we just apply formula (1.60):[10]

$$\lfloor(7y - 6)/19\rfloor + 12(y - 1) = \lfloor(235y - 234)/19\rfloor.$$

More generally, the fixed moment of the mean conjunction, called the *molad*, of any month of the Hebrew calendar is computed by

$$\textbf{molad}\,(h\text{-}month,\,h\text{-}year) \;\overset{\text{def}}{=} \tag{7.7}$$

$$\textbf{hebrew-epoch} - \tfrac{876}{25920} +$$
$$months\text{-}elapsed \times \left(29 + 12^{\text{h}} + \tfrac{793}{25920}\right)$$

where

$$y \quad = \quad \begin{cases} h\text{-}year + 1 & \textbf{if } h\text{-}month < \textbf{tishri} \\ h\text{-}year & \textbf{otherwise} \end{cases}$$

$$months\text{-}elapsed \quad = \quad h\text{-}month - \textbf{tishri} + \left\lfloor \frac{235 \times y - 234}{19} \right\rfloor$$

readjusting for the year starting with Tishri.

---

[10] An analogous formula for the number of nonleap years was used by Gauss [8].

To implement the first of the four delays (putting off the New Year if the calculated conjunction is in the afternoon), all we need to do is add 12 hours to the time of the epochal conjunction and let the day be the integer part (the floor) of the value obtained. This is analogous to equation (1.65), except that we are counting days in months of average length $29\frac{13,753}{25,920}$ days, rather than in years. The initial conjunction is $11^{\mathrm{h}}11^{\mathrm{m}}20^{\mathrm{s}}$—that is, 12,084 parts—into the determining period, which began at noon on the day before the epoch.

To test for Sunday, Wednesday, and Friday as required by the second delay, we can use $(3d \bmod 7) < 3$, as in equation (1.56), to determine whether d is one of the three evenly spaced excluded days. These two delays are incorporated in the following function:

$$\textbf{hebrew-calendar-elapsed-days}\,(h\text{-}year) \quad \overset{\mathrm{def}}{=} \tag{7.8}$$

$$\begin{cases} day + 1 & \textbf{if } (3 \times (day + 1) \bmod 7) < 3 \\ day & \textbf{otherwise} \end{cases}$$

where

$$months\text{-}elapsed \quad = \quad \left\lfloor \frac{235 \times h\text{-}year - 234}{19} \right\rfloor$$

$$parts\text{-}elapsed \quad = \quad 12084 + 13753 \times months\text{-}elapsed$$

$$day \quad = \quad 29 \times months\text{-}elapsed + \left\lfloor \frac{parts\text{-}elapsed}{25920} \right\rfloor$$

So that 32 bits suffice for dates in the foreseeable future, whole days and fractional days (parts) are computed separately.[11] When one can work directly with rational numbers, just let

$$day \quad = \quad \left\lfloor \textbf{molad}(\textbf{tishri}, h\text{-}year) - \textbf{hebrew-epoch} + 12^{\mathrm{h}} \right\rfloor$$

using the **molad** function.

The two remaining delays depend on the length of the prior and current years that would result from the putative New Year dates suggested by the previous function. If the current year were 356 days, then it would be too long, and we would delay its start 2 days. If the prior year were 382 days long, then we delay its end by 1 day. Rather than check the day of the week, the time of conjunction, and the leap-year status of the prior and current year as in the

---

[11] The foregoing calculation comes close to the 32-bit limit; to avoid such large numbers one can compute days, hours, and parts separately, as detailed on page 338.

traditional formulation of these delays, we just check for the unacceptable year lengths:

hebrew-new-year-delay (*h-year*) $\overset{\text{def}}{=}$ (7.9)

$$\begin{cases} 2 & \textbf{if } ny_2 - ny_1 = 356 \\ 1 & \textbf{if } ny_1 - ny_0 = 382 \\ 0 & \textbf{otherwise} \end{cases}$$

where

ny_0 $=$ **hebrew-calendar-elapsed-days** (*h-year* $-$ 1)

ny_1 $=$ **hebrew-calendar-elapsed-days** (*h-year*)

ny_2 $=$ **hebrew-calendar-elapsed-days** (*h-year* $+$ 1)

Adding the value of this function to the number of elapsed days determines the day the year begins. To get the R.D. date of the New Year, we have to add the (negative) epoch:

hebrew-new-year (*h-year*) $\overset{\text{def}}{=}$ (7.10)

hebrew-epoch $+$

hebrew-calendar-elapsed-days (*h-year*) $+$

hebrew-new-year-delay (*h-year*)

As already mentioned, the length of the year determines the length of the two varying months: Marḥeshvan and Kislev. Marḥeshvan is long (30 days) if the year has 355 or 385 days; Kislev is short (29 days) if the year has 353 or 383 days. The length of the year, in turn, is determined by the dates of the Hebrew New Years (Tishri 1) preceding and following the year in question:

last-day-of-hebrew-month (*h-month, h-year*) $\overset{\text{def}}{=}$ (7.11)

$$\begin{cases} 29 & \textbf{if } \textit{h-month} \in \{2, 4, 6, 10, 13\} \text{ or} \\ & \quad \big\{ \textit{h-month} = 12 \text{ and} \\ & \quad \text{ not } \textbf{hebrew-leap-year?} \,(\textit{h-year}) \big\} \text{ or} \\ & \quad \big\{ \textit{h-month} = 8 \text{ and} \\ & \quad \text{ not } \textbf{long-marheshvan?} \,(\textit{h-year}) \big\} \text{ or} \\ & \quad \{\textit{h-month} = 9 \text{ and } \textbf{short-kislev?} \,(\textit{h-year})\} \\ 30 & \textbf{otherwise} \end{cases}$$

$$\textbf{long-marheshvan?}\,(\textit{h-year}) \overset{\text{def}}{=} \tag{7.12}$$

$$\textbf{days-in-hebrew-year}\,(\textit{h-year}) \in \{355, 385\}$$

$$\textbf{short-kislev?}\,(\textit{h-year}) \overset{\text{def}}{=} \tag{7.13}$$

$$\textbf{days-in-hebrew-year}\,(\textit{h-year}) \in \{353, 383\}$$

$$\textbf{days-in-hebrew-year}\,(\textit{h-year}) \overset{\text{def}}{=} \tag{7.14}$$

$$\textbf{hebrew-new-year}\,(\textit{h-year} + 1) \ -$$

$$\textbf{hebrew-new-year}\,(\textit{h-year})$$

With all the foregoing machinery, we are now ready to convert from any Hebrew date to an R.D. date:

$$\textbf{fixed-from-hebrew}\left(\ \boxed{\ \textit{year} \ | \ \textit{month} \ | \ \textit{day}\ }\ \right) \overset{\text{def}}{=} \tag{7.15}$$

$$\textbf{hebrew-new-year}\,(\textit{year}) + \textit{day} - 1 +$$

$$\begin{cases} \left(\displaystyle\sum_{m \geq \textbf{tishri}}^{p(m)} \textbf{last-day-of-hebrew-month}\,(m,\,\textit{year}) \right) \\ \quad + \left(\displaystyle\sum_{m \geq \textbf{nisan}}^{m < \textit{month}} \textbf{last-day-of-hebrew-month}\,(m,\,\textit{year}) \right) \\ \hfill \textbf{if } \textit{month} < \textbf{tishri} \\ \displaystyle\sum_{m \geq \textbf{tishri}}^{m < \textit{month}} \textbf{last-day-of-hebrew-month}\,(m,\,\textit{year}) \\ \hfill \textbf{otherwise} \end{cases}$$

where

$$p\,(m) \quad = \quad m \leq \textbf{last-month-of-hebrew-year}\,(\textit{year})$$

To the fixed date of the start of the given year we add the number of elapsed days in the given month and the length of each elapsed month. We distinguish between months before and after Tishri, which is the seventh month, though the New Year begins with its new moon. For dates in the second half of the year (months 1 . . . 6) we need to include the lengths of all months from Tishri until **last-month-of-hebrew-year** (month 12 or 13).

Conversion to Hebrew dates is done as follows:

$$\textbf{hebrew-from-fixed}\,(\textit{date}) \overset{\text{def}}{=} \boxed{\ \textit{year} \ | \ \textit{month} \ | \ \textit{day}\ } \tag{7.16}$$

where

$$approx = \left\lfloor \frac{date - \textbf{hebrew-epoch}}{\frac{35975351}{98496}} \right\rfloor + 1$$

$$year = \underset{y \geq approx-1}{\text{MAX}} \left\{ \textbf{hebrew-new-year}\,(y) \leq date \right\}$$

$$start = \begin{cases} \textbf{tishri} & \text{if } date < \textbf{fixed-from-hebrew} \\ & \left(\boxed{\; year \;|\; \textbf{nisan} \;|\; 1 \;} \right) \\ \textbf{nisan} & \text{otherwise} \end{cases}$$

$$month = \underset{m \geq start}{\text{MIN}} \left\{ \begin{array}{l} date \leq \textbf{fixed-from-hebrew} \\ \left(\boxed{\; year \;|\; m \;|\; \begin{array}{l}\textbf{last-day-of-}\\\textbf{hebrew-month}\\(m,\,year)\end{array} \;} \right) \end{array} \right\}$$

$$day = date - \textbf{fixed-from-hebrew} + 1$$
$$\left(\boxed{\; year \;|\; month \;|\; 1 \;} \right)$$

We first approximate the Hebrew year by dividing the number of elapsed days by the average year length, $\frac{35975351}{98496}$ days. (A simpler value—even 365.25— can be used instead.) The irregularity of year lengths means that the estimate *approx* can be off by 1 in either direction. Thus we search for the right year, adding 1 to *approx* − 1 for each year y whose New Year is not after *date*. To determine the Hebrew month, we search forward from Nisan or Tishri until the first month that begins after *date*.

Consider, as an example, the calculation of the date of Passover in 922 C.E.—that is, Nisan 15, A.M. 4682 (see page 99 for the historical significance of this year). The mean conjunction of the preceding Tishri fell on Wednesday, September 5, 921 C.E. (Julian), R.D. 336,276, at 5:51:46$\frac{2}{3}$ a.m. The mean conjunction of the following Tishri fell on Tuesday, September 29, 922 C.E. (Julian), at 3:24:30 a.m. At the latter time, $57,909 = (235 \times 4683 - 234)/19$ months of mean length $29\frac{13,753}{25,920}$ had elapsed since the primeval conjunction, to which we add $12,084/25,920$ to count from noon on the Sunday before the epoch. By the traditional reckoning, that is Tuesday, 9 hours and 441 parts since sunset the preceding evening. Hebrew year 4683 was year 9 of the 247th 19-year cycle, which is not a leap year, making 4683 an instance of the third delay. Because this conjunction was later than 9 hours and 204 parts, the conjunction of the following year, 4684, fell on Saturday afternoon, just

237 parts (13.167 minutes) after midday, for which time the first two delays apply. Specifically, equation (7.8) yields

$$\textbf{hebrew-calendar-elapsed-days}(4682) = 1{,}709{,}704,$$
$$\textbf{hebrew-calendar-elapsed-days}(4683) = 1{,}710{,}087,$$
$$\textbf{hebrew-calendar-elapsed-days}(4684) = 1{,}710{,}443.$$

With the first two delays, but without the third delay, year 4683 would be of $1{,}710{,}443 - 1{,}710{,}087 = 356$ days duration, which is unacceptably long. Thus, the first of Tishri 4683 is put off 2 days to Thursday, September 26, R.D. 336,662. The start of year 4682 is delayed until Thursday, making 4682 a "long" leap year with a total of 385 days. Tishri (month 7) and Shevat (month 11) are always 30 days long, Tevet (month 10) is 29 days, Marḥeshvan (month 8) and Kislev (month 9) both have 30 days in a long year, and in a leap year Adar I (month 12) has 30 days and Adar II (month 13) has 29. Adding these ($5 \times 30 + 2 \times 29 = 208$), plus 14 days of Nisan (month 1), to the R.D. date of Rosh ha-Shanah of 4682, we arrive at R.D. $336{,}277 + 208 + 14 = 336{,}499$ as the starting date of Passover.[12] That date is Tuesday, April 16, 922 C.E. (Julian) and April 21, 922 (Gregorian). Were the first delay not applied in 4684, there would have been no need for the third delay in 4683. Were it not for the third delay, Hebrew year 4682 would have been "short," and Passover in 922—as well as all other dates between Tevet 1 in late 921 and Elul 29 in the summer of 922—would have occurred 2 days earlier. Dates in Kislev would have been 1 day earlier.

7.3 Holidays and Fast Days

> In the days of wicked Trajan, a son was born to him on Tishah be-Av and they fasted; his daughter died on Ḥanukkah and they lit candles. His wife sent to him and said, rather than conquer the Barbarians, come and conquer the Jews who have revolted.... He came... and the blood flowed in the sea until Cyprus.
> —*Jerusalem Talmud* (Succah 5:1)

As throughout this book, we consider our problem to be the determination of holidays that occur in a specified Gregorian year. Because the Hebrew year

---

[12] Dates during the second half of the Hebrew year (from Nisan through Elul) depend *only* on the date of the following Rosh ha-Shanah, because the intervening months are all of fixed length, and thus in hand calculations it is easier to count backwards from the following Rosh ha-Shanah, subtracting 30 days for Sivan and Av, 29 days for Iyyar, Tammuz, and Elul, and 16 for the remainder of Nisan rather than always starting with the preceding Rosh ha-Shanah, as in our algorithm.

is, on the average, consistently aligned with the Gregorian year, each Jewish holiday occurs just once in a given Gregorian year (with a minor exception noted below). The major holidays of the Hebrew year occur on fixed days on the Hebrew calendar but only in fixed seasons on the Gregorian calendar. They are easy to determine on the Gregorian calendar with the machinery developed above provided we observe that the Hebrew year beginning in the Gregorian year y is given by

Hebrew New Year occurring in the fall of Gregorian year y

$= y + 1 - $ **gregorian-year-from-fixed(hebrew-epoch)**.

The Hebrew year that began in the fall of 1 (Gregorian) was A.M. 3762. This means that holidays occurring in the fall and early winter of the Gregorian year y occur in the Hebrew year $y + 3761$, but holidays in the late winter, spring, and summer occur in Hebrew year $y + 3760$. For example, to find the R.D. date of Yom Kippur (Tishri 10) in a Gregorian year, we would use

$$\textbf{yom-kippur}\ (\textit{g-year})\ \overset{\text{def}}{=} \tag{7.17}$$

$$\textbf{fixed-from-hebrew}\left(\boxed{\ \textit{hebrew-year}\ \mid\ \textbf{tishri}\ \mid\ 10\ } \right)$$

where

$$\textit{hebrew-year}\ =\ \textit{g-year} - \textbf{gregorian-year-from-fixed}\ +\ 1$$
$$(\textbf{hebrew-epoch})$$

The R.D. dates of Rosh ha-Shanah (Tishri 1), Sukkot (Tishri 15), Hoshana Rabba (Tishri 21), Shemini Aẓeret (Tishri 22), and Simḥat Torah (Tishri 23, outside Israel) are identically determined.[13] As on the Islamic calendar, all Hebrew holidays begin at sunset the prior evening.

The dates of the other major holidays—Passover (Nisan 15), ending of Passover (Nisan 21), and Shavuot (Sivan 6)—are determined similarly, but because these holidays occur in the spring, the year corresponding to Gregorian year y is $y + 3760$. Conservative and Orthodox Jews observe 2 days of Rosh ha-Shanah—Tishri 1 and 2. Outside Israel, they also observe Tishri 16, Nisan 16, Nisan 22, and Sivan 7 as holidays.

Thus, for example, we determine the R.D. date of Passover by

$$\textbf{passover}\ (\textit{g-year})\ \overset{\text{def}}{=} \tag{7.18}$$

$$\textbf{fixed-from-hebrew}\left(\boxed{\ \textit{hebrew-year}\ \mid\ \textbf{nisan}\ \mid\ 15\ } \right)$$

---

[13] See *Winning Ways, Volume 2: Games in Particular* [1, p. 800] for another way to determine the date of Rosh ha-Shanah.

where

$$hebrew\text{-}year \quad = \quad g\text{-}year - \textbf{gregorian-year-from-fixed}$$
$$(\textbf{hebrew-epoch})$$

Gauss [8] developed an interesting alternative formula to determine the Gregorian date of Passover in a given year.

The 7-week period beginning on the second day of Passover is called the *omer* (sheave offering); the days of the omer are counted from 1 to 49, and the count is expressed in completed weeks and excess days. The following function tells the omer count for an R.D. date, returning a list of weeks (an integer 0–7) and days (an integer 0–6) if the date is within the omer period, and returning the special constant **bogus**, signifying a nonexistent value, if not:

$$\textbf{omer}\,(date) \quad \overset{\text{def}}{=} \quad \begin{cases} \left\langle \left\lfloor \dfrac{c}{7} \right\rfloor, c \bmod 7 \right\rangle & \textbf{if } 1 \le c \le 49 \\[2ex] \textbf{bogus} & \textbf{otherwise} \end{cases} \quad (7.19)$$

where

$$c \quad = \quad date - \textbf{passover}$$
$$(\textbf{gregorian-year-from-fixed}\,(date))$$

The minor holidays of the Hebrew year are the "intermediate" days of Sukkot (Tishri 16–21) and of Passover (Nisan 16–20); Ḥanukkah (8 days, beginning on Kislev 25); Tu-B'Shevat (Shevat 15); and Purim (Adar 14 in normal years, Adar II 14 in leap years). Ḥanukkah occurs in late fall or early winter, and thus Ḥanukkah of Gregorian year y occurs in the Hebrew year $y + 3761$, whereas Tu-B'Shevat occurs in late winter or early spring, and hence Tu-B'Shevat of Gregorian year y occurs in Hebrew year $y + 3760$; thus, these two holidays are handled as were Yom Kippur and Passover, respectively. Purim also always occurs in late winter or early spring, in the last month of the Hebrew year (Adar or Adar II), hence its R.D. date is computed by

$$\textbf{purim}\,(g\text{-}year) \quad \overset{\text{def}}{=} \quad (7.20)$$

$$\textbf{fixed-from-hebrew}\left(\begin{array}{|c|c|c|} \hline hebrew\text{-}year & last\text{-}month & 14 \\ \hline \end{array} \right)$$

where

$$hebrew\text{-}year \quad = \quad g\text{-}year - \textbf{gregorian-year-from-fixed}$$
$$(\textbf{hebrew-epoch})$$

$$\textit{last-month} \quad = \quad \textbf{last-month-of-hebrew-year}$$

$$(\textit{hebrew-year})$$

The Hebrew year contains several fast days that, though specified by particular Hebrew calendar dates, are shifted when those days occur on Saturday. The fast days are Tzom Gedaliah (Tishri 3), Tzom Tevet (Tevet 10), Ta'anit Esther (the day before Purim), Tzom Tammuz (Tammuz 17), and Tishah be-Av (Av 9). When Purim is on Sunday, Ta'anit Esther occurs on the preceding Thursday, and thus we can write

$$\textbf{ta-anit-esther}\,(\textit{g-year}) \quad \overset{\text{def}}{=} \quad \tag{7.21}$$

$$\begin{cases} \textit{purim-date} - 3 \\ \qquad \textbf{if day-of-week-from-fixed}\,(\textit{purim-date}) \\ \qquad = \textbf{sunday} \\ \textit{purim-date} - 1 \qquad\qquad\qquad \textbf{otherwise} \end{cases}$$

where

$$\textit{purim-date} \quad = \quad \textbf{purim}\,(\textit{g-year})$$

Each of the other fast days, as well as Shushan Purim (the day after Purim, celebrated in Jerusalem), is postponed to the following day (Sunday) when it occurs on Saturday. Because Tzom Gedaliah is always in the fall and Tzom Tammuz and Tishah be-Av are always in the summer, their determination is easy. For example,

$$\textbf{tishah-be-av}\,(\textit{g-year}) \quad \overset{\text{def}}{=} \quad \tag{7.22}$$

$$\begin{cases} av_9 + 1 & \textbf{if day-of-week-from-fixed}\,(av_9) = \textbf{saturday} \\ av_9 & \textbf{otherwise} \end{cases}$$

where

$$\textit{hebrew-year} \quad = \quad \textit{g-year} - \textbf{gregorian-year-from-fixed}$$

$$(\textbf{hebrew-epoch})$$

$$av_9 \quad = \quad \textbf{fixed-from-hebrew}$$

$$\left(\begin{array}{|c|c|c|} \hline \textit{hebrew-year} & 5 & 9 \\ \hline \end{array} \right)$$

Tzom Tevet, which can never occur on Saturday, should be handled like Islamic holidays (Section 6.2), because Tevet 10 can fall on either side of January 1, and thus a single Gregorian calendar year can have 0, 1, or 2 occurrences of Tzom Tevet. For example, Tzom Tevet occurred twice in 1982 but not at all in 1984. We leave it to the reader to work out the details. For the foreseeable future, other Jewish holidays and fasts occur exactly once in each Gregorian year, because the Hebrew leap months and Gregorian leap days keep the two calendars closely aligned.

Yom ha-Shoah (Holocaust Memorial Day) is Nisan 27, unless that day is Sunday (it cannot be Saturday), in which case it is postponed 1 day.[14] Yom ha-Zikkaron (Israel Memorial Day), normally on Iyyar 4, is advanced to Wednesday if it falls on Thursday or Friday. The first delay precludes that date's being a Saturday (or Monday or Wednesday). Thus, we can write

$$\textbf{yom-ha-zikkaron} \, (g\text{-}year) \quad \overset{\text{def}}{=} \tag{7.23}$$

$$\begin{cases} \textbf{kday-before} \, (iyyar_4, \textbf{wednesday}) \\ \quad \textbf{if wednesday} \\ \quad\quad < \textbf{day-of-week-from-fixed} \, (iyyar_4) \\ iyyar_4 \quad\quad\quad\quad\quad\quad\quad\quad \textbf{otherwise} \end{cases}$$

where

$$hebrew\text{-}year \quad = \quad g\text{-}year - \textbf{gregorian-year-from-fixed} \\ (\textbf{hebrew-epoch})$$

$$iyyar_4 \quad\quad = \quad \textbf{fixed-from-hebrew} \\ \left(\boxed{\; hebrew\text{-}year \;\;|\; 2 \;|\; 4 \;} \right)$$

On the Hebrew calendar, the first day of each month is called Rosh Ḥodesh and has minor ritual significance. When the preceding month has 30 days, Rosh Ḥodesh includes also the last day of the preceding month. The determination of these days is elementary (except for the months of Kislev and Tevet, because of the varying length of the months that precede those two).

Some other dates of significance depend on the Julian/Coptic approximation of the tropical year (equinox to equinox), in which each of the four seasons is taken to be $91\frac{5}{16}$ days long: The beginning of *sh'ela* (request for rain) outside Israel, meant to correspond to the start of the sixtieth Hebrew day after the autumnal equinox, corresponds to Athôr 26 on the Coptic calendar and follows the same leap-year structure. (See Chapter 4.) Hence, we write

$$\textbf{sh-ela} \, (g\text{-}year) \quad \overset{\text{def}}{=} \tag{7.24}$$

$$\textbf{coptic-in-gregorian} \, (3, 26, g\text{-}year)$$

[14] This exception was introduced by the Israeli Knesset in May 1997.

which is either December 5 or 6 (Gregorian) during the twentieth and twenty-first centuries (see [18]). As with most other Jewish holidays and events, sh'ela actually begins the prior evening.

By one traditional Hebrew reckoning, the vernal equinox of A.M. 5685 was at 6 p.m. on the eve of Wednesday, Paremotep 30, 1641, on the Coptic calendar, which is March 26, 1925 C.E. (Julian). It recurs on that day of the Coptic and Julian calendars and at that hour of the week every 28 years in what is called the *solar cycle* and is celebrated as *birkath haḥama*. Because 1641 mod 28 = 17, we can write

$$\textbf{birkath-ha-hama}\,(g\text{-}year) \overset{\text{def}}{=} \tag{7.25}$$

$$\begin{cases} dates & \textbf{if } dates \neq \langle\,\rangle \text{ and} \\ & \Big(\textbf{coptic-from-fixed} \\ & \quad (dates_{[0]})_{\textbf{year}} \text{ mod } 28 \Big) = 17 \\ \langle\,\rangle & \textbf{otherwise} \end{cases}$$

where

$$dates \quad = \quad \textbf{coptic-in-gregorian}\,(7,\,30,\,g\text{-}year)$$

(The bracketed subscript 0 extracts the first element of a list.) This function returns an empty list for the 27 out of 28 years in which this event does not occur.

7.4 Personal Days

Finally, the Hebrew calendar contains what we might term "personal" days: One's birthday according to the Hebrew calendar determines the day of one's *Bat* (for girls) or *Bar* (for boys) *Mitzvah* (the twelfth or thirteenth birthday). Dates of death determine when *Kaddish* is recited (*yahrzeit, naḥala*) for parents (and sometimes for other relatives). These are ordinarily just anniversary dates, but the leap-year structure and the varying number of days in some months require that alternative days be used in certain years, just as someone born February 29 on the Gregorian calendar has to celebrate on an alternative day in common years.

The birthday of someone born in Adar of an ordinary year or Adar II of a leap year is also always in the last month of the year, be that Adar or Adar II. Someone born on the thirtieth day of Marḥeshvan, Kislev, or Adar I has his or her birthday postponed until the first of the following month in years when that day does not occur. First, we write a function to determine the anniversary date in a given Hebrew year:

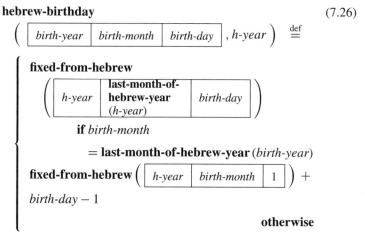

$$
\textbf{hebrew-birthday} \quad\quad (7.26)
$$

$$
\left(\;\boxed{\begin{array}{c|c|c} \textit{birth-year} & \textit{birth-month} & \textit{birth-day} \end{array}}\;,\textit{h-year}\;\right) \;\overset{\text{def}}{=}
$$

$$
\begin{cases}
\textbf{fixed-from-hebrew} \\
\quad \left(\boxed{\begin{array}{c|c|c} \textit{h-year} & \begin{array}{c}\textbf{last-month-of-}\\\textbf{hebrew-year}\\(\textit{h-year})\end{array} & \textit{birth-day} \end{array}}\right) \\
\quad\quad \textbf{if } \textit{birth-month} \\
\quad\quad\quad = \textbf{last-month-of-hebrew-year}\,(\textit{birth-year}) \\[4pt]
\textbf{fixed-from-hebrew}\left(\boxed{\begin{array}{c|c|c} \textit{h-year} & \textit{birth-month} & 1 \end{array}}\right) + \\
\textit{birth-day} - 1 \\
\quad\quad\quad\quad\quad\quad\quad\quad\quad\quad\quad\quad\quad\quad \textbf{otherwise}
\end{cases}
$$

Unlike the Islamic calendar, it will be many millennia before the Hebrew and Gregorian New Years can coincide. Hence, a Gregorian year always comprises part of two Hebrew years. We use this fact to collect a list of the anniversaries in the two possible Hebrew years (compare this with Section 6.2):

$$
\textbf{hebrew-birthday-in-gregorian} \quad\quad (7.27)
$$

$$
(\textit{birthdate}, \textit{g-year}) \;\overset{\text{def}}{=}
$$

$$
\begin{Bmatrix} \langle \textit{date}_1 \rangle & \textbf{if } \textit{jan}_1 \le \textit{date}_1 \\ \langle\,\rangle & \textbf{otherwise} \end{Bmatrix} \;\|\; \begin{Bmatrix} \langle \textit{date}_2 \rangle & \textbf{if } \textit{date}_2 \le \textit{dec}_{31} \\ \langle\,\rangle & \textbf{otherwise} \end{Bmatrix}
$$

where

$$
\textit{jan}_1 \;=\; \textbf{fixed-from-gregorian}\left(\boxed{\begin{array}{c|c|c} \textit{g-year} & \textbf{january} & 1 \end{array}}\right)
$$

$$
\textit{dec}_{31} \;=\; \textbf{fixed-from-gregorian}\left(\boxed{\begin{array}{c|c|c} \textit{g-year} & \textbf{december} & 31 \end{array}}\right)
$$

$$
y \;=\; \textbf{hebrew-from-fixed}\,(\textit{jan}_1)_{\textbf{year}}
$$

$$
\textit{date}_1 \;=\; \textbf{hebrew-birthday}\,(\textit{birthdate}, y)
$$

$$
\textit{date}_2 \;=\; \textbf{hebrew-birthday}\,(\textit{birthdate}, y+1)
$$

Similar functions for birthdays can be written for other calendars with variable-length years.

The customary anniversary date of a death is more complicated and depends also on the character of the year in which the first anniversary occurs. There are several cases:

- If the date of death is Marḥeshvan 30, the anniversary in general depends on the *first* anniversary; if that first anniversary was not Marḥeshvan 30, use the day before Kislev 1.
- If the date of death is Kislev 30, the anniversary in general again depends on the first anniversary—if that was not Kislev 30, use the day before Tevet 1.
- If the date of death is Adar II, the anniversary is the same day in the last month of the Hebrew year (Adar or Adar II).
- If the date of death is Adar I 30, the anniversary in a Hebrew year that is not a leap year (in which Adar has only 29 days) is the last day in Shevat.
- In all other cases, use the normal anniversary of the date of death.

Perhaps these rules are best expressed algorithmically:

yahrzeit (7.28)

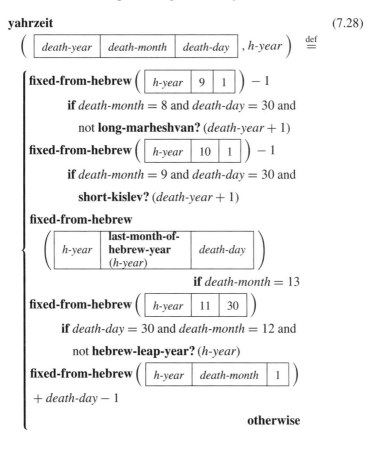

There are minor variations in custom regarding the anniversary date in some of these cases.[15] For example, Spanish and Portuguese Jews never observe the anniversary in Adar I.

As with birthdays, anniversaries in a given Gregorian year must be collected:

$$\textbf{yahrzeit-in-gregorian}\,(\textit{death-date},\,\textit{g-year})\quad\overset{\text{def}}{=}\qquad(7.29)$$

$$\left\{\begin{array}{ll} \langle date_1\rangle & \textbf{if } jan_1 \le date_1 \\ \langle\,\rangle & \textbf{otherwise} \end{array}\right\} \parallel \left\{\begin{array}{ll} \langle date_2\rangle & \textbf{if } date_2 \le dec_{31} \\ \langle\,\rangle & \textbf{otherwise} \end{array}\right\}$$

where

$$jan_1 \;=\; \textbf{fixed-from-gregorian}\left(\boxed{\;\boxed{\textit{g-year}}\;\boxed{\textbf{january}}\;\boxed{1}\;}\right)$$

$$dec_{31} \;=\; \textbf{fixed-from-gregorian}\left(\boxed{\;\boxed{\textit{g-year}}\;\boxed{\textbf{december}}\;\boxed{31}\;}\right)$$

$$y \;=\; \textbf{hebrew-from-fixed}\,\big(jan_1\big)_{\textbf{year}}$$

$$date_1 \;=\; \textbf{yahrzeit}\,(\textit{death-date},\,y)$$

$$date_2 \;=\; \textbf{yahrzeit}\,(\textit{death-date},\,y+1)$$

References

[1] E. R. Berlekamp, J. H. Conway, and R. K. Guy, *Winning Ways: Volume 2, Games in Particular*, Academic Press, New York, 1982.

[2] al-Bīrūnī (= Abū-Raiḥān Muḥammad ibn 'Aḥmad al-Bīrūnī), *Al-Āthār al-Bāqiyah 'an al-Qurūn al-Khāliyah*, 1000. Translated and annotated by C. E. Sachau as *The Chronology of Ancient Nations*, William H. Allen and Co., London, 1879; reprinted by Hijra International Publishers, Lahore, Pakistan, 1983.

[3] H. Y. Bornstein, *Maḥloket Rav Sa'adyah Ga'on u-Ven Me'ir bi-Kevi'at Shenot 4672–4674 (= The Dispute Between Sa'adia Gaon and Ben-Meir Regarding the Character of Years 4672–4674)*, Warsaw, 1904.

[4] S. B. Burnaby, *Elements of the Jewish and Muhammadan Calendars, with Rules and Tables and Explanatory Notes on the Julian and Gregorian Calendars*, George Bell and Sons, London, 1901.

---

[15] The rules described accord with Ashkenazic practice as given in [18] and in the *Talmudic Encyclopedia: A Digest of Halachic Literature from the Tannaitic Period to the Present Time Alphabetically Arranged*, Talmudic Encyclopedia Publishing Ltd., Jerusalem, vol. I (1951), p. 93; vol. XXIII (1997), cols. 153-154. M. Feinstein (*Iggerot Moshe*, vol. 6, *Yoreh Deah*, part 3, p. 426), on the other hand, rules that *yahrzeit* anniversaries of the last day of a month follow the rules for birthdays.

[5] N. Bushwick, *Understanding the Jewish Calendar*, Moznaim Publishing Corp., New York, 1989.

[6] W. M. Feldman, *Rabbinical Mathematics and Astronomy*, M. L. Cailingold, London, 1931; 3rd corrected ed., Sepher-Hermon Press, New York, 1978.

[7] M. Friedländer, "Calendar," in *The Jewish Encyclopedia*, I. Singer, ed., Funk and Wagnalls, New York, 1906.

[8] C. F. Gauss, "Berechnung des jüdischen Osterfestes," *Monatliche Correspondenz zur Beförderung der Erd- und Himmels-Kunde*, Herausgegeben vom Freiherrn von Zach (May 1802). Reprinted in Gauss's *Werke*, Herausgegeben von der Königlichen Gesellschaft der Wissenschaften, Göttingen, volume 6, pp. 80–81, 1874.

[9] N. Golb, "Ben-Meir, Aaron," in *Encyclopædia Judaica*, C. Roth, ed., volume 4, Macmillan, New York, 1971. Translated from *Encyclopædia Hebraica*, Jerusalem, 1960.

[10] M. M. Kasher, Appendix to "Exodus," *Torah Shelemah* (= *Complete Torah*): *Talmudic-Midrashic Encyclopedia of the Pentateuch*, volume 13, American Biblical Encyclopedia Society, Inc., New York, 1949.

[11] al-Khowārizmī (= Abu Ja'far Mohammed ibn Mūsā al-Khowārizmī), *Fi istikhraj ta'rikh al-yahud*. Translated by T. Langermann, *Assufoth*, Jerusalem, pp. 159–168, 1987.

[12] L. Levi, *Jewish Chrononomy: The Calendar and Times of Day in Jewish Law*, Gur Aryeh Institute for Advanced Jewish Scholarship, Brooklyn, NY, 1967. Revised edition published under the title *Halachic Times for Home and Travel*, Rubin Mass, Ltd., Jerusalem, 1992; expanded 3rd ed., 2000.

[13] Maimonides (= Moshe ben Maimon), *Mishneh Torah: Sefer Zemanim—Hilḥot Kiddush HaḤodesh*, 1178. Translated by S. Gandz (with commentary by J. Obermann and O. Neugebauer), as *Code of Maimonides, Book Three, Treatise Eight, Sanctification of the New Moon*, Yale Judaica Series, volume XI, Yale University Press, New Haven, CT, 1956. Addenda and corrigenda by E. J. Wiesenberg appear at the end of *Code of Maimonides, Book Three, The Book of Seasons*, translated by S. Gandz and H. Klein, Yale Judaica Series, volume XIV, Yale University Press, New Haven, CT, 1961.

[14] S. A. Poznański, "Calendar (Jewish)," in *Encyclopædia of Religion and Ethics*, J. Hastings, ed., volume III, pp. 117–124, Charles Scribner's Sons, New York, 1911.

[15] L. A. Resnikoff, "Jewish Calendar Calculations," *Scripta Mathematica*, volume 9, pp. 191–195, 274–277, 1943.

[16] Savasorda (= Abraham bar Ḥiyya al-Bargeloní), *Sefer ha-'Ibbūr*, 1122. Edited and printed by H. Filipowski, Longman, Brown, Green, and Longmans, London, 1851.

[17] H. S. Slonimski, *Yesōde ha-'Ibbūr* (= *Basic Intercalation*), H. N. Schriftgisser, Warsaw, 1852.

[18] A. Spier, *The Comprehensive Hebrew Calendar*, 3rd ed., Feldheim Publishers, New York, 1986.

[19] E. J. Wiesenberg, "Calendar," in *Encyclopædia Judaica*, C. Roth, ed., Macmillan, New York, 1971.

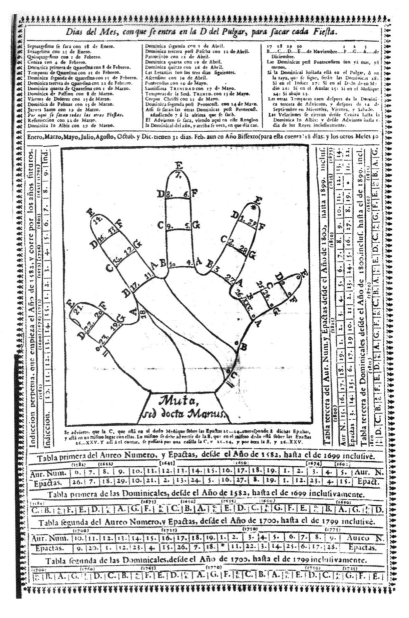

Finger calculation for the date of Easter, according the Gregorian rule, from page 14 of *Astronómica y Harmoniosa Mano* by Buenaventura Francisco de Ossorio, Bibliotheca Mexicana, Mexico, 1757. For an explanation of the calculation, see Florian Cajori's "A Notable Case of Finger-Reckoning in America," *ISIS* **8** (1926), pp. 325–327. Courtesy of the Bancroft Library, University of California, Berkeley.

8

The Ecclesiastical Calendars

> We send you the good news concerning the unanimous consent of
> all in reference to the celebration of the most solemn feast of
> Easter, for this difference also has been made up by the assistance
> of your prayers, so that all the brethren in the East, who formerly
> celebrated this festival at the same time as the Jews, will in future
> conform to the Romans and to us and to all who have from of old
> kept Easter with us.
> —Letter of the Council of Nicæa to the Church of Alexandria
> (325 C.E.)

The calculation of the date of Easter has a fascinating history, and algorithms and computer programs abound (for example, [3], [7], [8], and [12]). The discussion in O'Beirne's *Puzzles and Paradoxes* [11] is especially nice. These computations rely on the formulas of Gauss [4], [5] (see also [6]).[1] Our fixed-date approach allows considerable simplification of "classical" algorithms.

The date of Easter was fixed in 325 C.E. by the Council of Nicæa, convened by Constantine the Great, to be

The first Sunday after the first full moon occurring on or after the vernal equinox.

Easter is thus delayed 1 week if the full moon is on Sunday, which lessens the likelihood of its being on the same day as the Jewish Passover. This ruling was contrary to the practice of the Quartodecimans, who celebrated Easter on the day of the full moon, 14 days into the month, regardless of the day of the week.

The preceding definition seems precise, but accurate determination of the full moon and the vernal equinox is quite complex in reality, and simpler approximations are used in practice.

---

[1] Gauss's original paper contained an error that affects the date of Easter first in 4200 C.E.; see [11].

117

8.1 Orthodox Easter

As implemented by Dionysius Exiguus in 525 C.E., the date of Easter is based on the presumption that the vernal equinox is always March 21 and on ecclesiastical approximations to the lunar phases called *epacts*. Epacts are computed based on the fact that new moons occur on about the same day of the solar year (adjusted for leap years) in a cycle of 19 years, called the *Metonic cycle*, comprising 235 lunations (see page 11).

Before the Gregorian reform of the Julian calendar, the approximations were fairly crude. If the Metonic cycle were perfectly accurate, the phase of the moon on January 1 would be the same every 19 years. Hence, the epact can be approximated by multiplying the number of years since the start of the current Metonic cycle (the so-called golden number) by the 11-day difference between a common year of 365 days and 12 lunar months of $29\frac{1}{2}$ days and adjusting by the epact of January 1, 1 C.E. (Julian)—all this done modulo 30. To find the last full moon (that is, day 14 of the monthly cycle) prior to April 19, we subtract the phase of the moon on April 5 (14 days earlier) from the fixed date of April 19. (The number of days between full moon and April 19 is equal to the days between new moon and April 5.) The moon's phase (in days) on April 5, called the *shifted-epact* in the function below, increases by 11 days each year, modulo 30, taking on the values $14, 25, 6, 17, 28, 9, 20, 1, 12, 23, 4, 15, 26, 7, 18, 29, 10, 21, 2$ in sequence. Going back that number of days from April 19 gives a date between March 21 and April 18, inclusive, for the (ecclesiastical) "Paschal full moon."

Thus, the equivalent of the following calculation was used to determine Easter from the end of the eighth century until the adoption of the Gregorian calendar, and it is still used by all Orthodox churches except those in Finland:

$$\textbf{orthodox-easter}\,(\textit{g-year}) \;\stackrel{\text{def}}{=}\; \tag{8.1}$$

$$\textbf{kday-after}\,(\textit{paschal-moon}, \textbf{sunday})$$

where

$$\textit{shifted-epact} \;=\; (14 + 11 \times (\textit{g-year} \bmod 19)) \bmod 30$$

$$\textit{j-year} \;=\; \begin{cases} \textit{g-year} & \textbf{if } \textit{g-year} > 0 \\ \textit{g-year} - 1 & \textbf{otherwise} \end{cases}$$

$$\textit{paschal-moon} \;=\; \textbf{fixed-from-julian}\left(\boxed{\;\textit{j-year}\;\mid\;\textbf{april}\;\mid\;19\;} \right)$$
$$- \,\textit{shifted-epact}$$

Because the shifted epact is never 0, the calculated full moon is never on April 19. The earliest date for Easter Sunday is therefore March 22, and the latest is April 25. By this rule, Easter and Passover never coincided during 783–1600 C.E.

The Julian leap-year cycle of 4 years contains 208 weeks and 5 days. Only after 28 years do all dates on the Julian calender return to the same day of the week. The combination of this "solar" cycle and the 19-year lunar cycle gives rise to the 532-year "Victorian" or "Dionysian" cycle for the date of Orthodox Easter. The average length of a lunar month according to this method is

$$\frac{19 \times 365\frac{1}{4}}{235} \approx 29.530851 \text{ days.}$$

The number of full moons between April 19 of 2 successive years can be either 12 or 13. The distribution of leap years of 13 lunar cycles and ordinary years of 12 follows a regular pattern describable by formula (1.59) with $\Delta = 13$, namely

$$\left\lfloor \frac{7 \times g\text{-}year + 8}{19} \right\rfloor.$$

This observation leads to an alternative formula for the fixed date of the paschal moon:

$$\textbf{alt-orthodox-easter} \, (g\text{-}year) \overset{\text{def}}{=} \tag{8.2}$$

$$\textbf{kday-after} \, (paschal\text{-}moon, \textbf{sunday})$$

where

$$paschal\text{-}moon \;=\; 354 \times g\text{-}year + 30 \times \left\lfloor \frac{7 \times g\text{-}year + 8}{19} \right\rfloor +$$

$$\left\lfloor \frac{g\text{-}year}{4} \right\rfloor - \left\lfloor \frac{g\text{-}year}{19} \right\rfloor - 272$$

The minimum 12 lunar months per year contribute 354 days; 7 out of 19 years include a thirteenth lunar month of 30 days; each leap year contributes an extra day to the total number of elapsed days; but every 19 years the lunar cycle is reset to begin 1 day earlier. Subtracting 272 accounts for the fixed date of the Paschal full moon in 1 C.E., when $g\text{-}year = 1$.

8.2 Gregorian Easter

> If yet your Lordship think it necessary that the seat of Easter
> should be rectified, that may easily be done, without altering the
> Civil Year. For if in the Rule of Easter, instead of saying, next after
> the one & twentieth of March, you say, next after the Vernal
> Equinox, the work is done. For then every Almanack will tell you
> when it is Equinox and when it is Full Moon for the present Year
> without disturbing the Civil Account, and this Pope Gregory might
> as well have done without troubling the Civil Account of
> Christendom.
> —John Wallis: Letter to the Bishop of Worcester
> (June 30, 1699)

The Gregorian reform of 1582 C.E. included a more accurate approximation to the lunar phases for the calculation of Easter developed by the German Jesuit astronomer Christopher Clavius and based on the suggestions of Naples astronomer Aloysius Lilius. Two corrections and two adjustments are employed in the Gregorian rule for Easter:

- In 3 out of 4 century years, the Gregorian leap-year rule causes a shift of 1 day forward in the date of the full moon. This is taken into account in the calculation of epacts by subtracting 1 for each nonleap century year.
- The first correction keeps the lunar cycle synchronized with the Julian calendar. But 19 Julian years of 365.25 days are a fraction longer than 235 mean lunations. Thus, a corrective factor of 1 day in 8 out of 25 century years is added to the epact. The epacts of centuries 3, 6, 9, 12, 15, 19, 22, and 25 are affected by this correction. A 1-day bias is said to have been introduced deliberately in its initial sixteenth-century value of 5 to minimize coincidences of Easter and Passover (also based on the 19-year Metonic cycle; see Section 7.3) as often as possible [11].
- The old limits on the dates of the ecclesiastical full moon were preserved in the reformed calendar. Unfortunately, with the new century-year rule a shifted epact of 0 becomes possible, which, if used, would place the full moon on April 19. Whenever that occurs, the epact is, therefore, adjusted to 1, which pushes the full moon date back to April 18.
- Clavius also strived to retain the property that the date of the Easter moon never repeats within a single 19-year cycle. The problem is that when the previous adjustment is made and the shifted epact is set to 1 instead of 0, the same shifted epact may also occur 11 years later. The solution is also to increase any shifted epact of 1 occurring in the second half of a cycle.

This is the method now used by Catholic and Protestant churches:

$$\textbf{easter}\,(g\text{-}year) \overset{\text{def}}{=} \tag{8.3}$$

$$\textbf{kday-after}\,(paschal\text{-}moon, \textbf{sunday})$$

where

$$century \quad = \quad \left\lfloor \frac{g\text{-}year}{100} \right\rfloor + 1$$

$$shifted\text{-}epact \quad = \quad \left(14 + 11 \times (g\text{-}year \bmod 19) - \right.$$

$$\left\lfloor \frac{3 \times century}{4} \right\rfloor +$$

$$\left. \left\lfloor \frac{5 + 8 \times century}{25} \right\rfloor \right) \bmod 30$$

$$adjusted\text{-}epact \quad = \quad \begin{cases} shifted\text{-}epact + 1 \\ \quad \textbf{if}\ shifted\text{-}epact = 0\ \text{or} \\ \quad\quad \{\ shifted\text{-}epact = 1\ \text{and} \\ \quad\quad\quad 10 < (g\text{-}year \bmod 19)\ \} \\ shifted\text{-}epact \quad\quad\quad\quad \textbf{otherwise} \end{cases}$$

$$paschal\text{-}moon \quad = \quad \textbf{fixed-from-gregorian}\left(\ \boxed{g\text{-}year \mid \textbf{april} \mid 19}\ \right)$$

$$- adjusted\text{-}epact$$

With the new method, the most likely date of Easter is April 19 (almost 4% of the years); the least likely date is March 22 (less than 0.5%). By this rule, Easter and Passover coincided once in the seventeenth century (in 1609), twice in the nineteenth (1805 and 1825), and 5 times in the twentieth century, but not again until 2123.

The dates of Easter repeat only after 5,700,000 years, the least common multiple of the 19-year Metonic cycle, the 400 years it takes for the Gregorian calendar to return to the same pattern of days of the week, the 4000 years it takes for the Gregorian leap-year corrections to add up to 30 days, and the 9375 years it takes for the correction to the Metonic cycle to amount to 30 days. This cycle comprises 2,081,882,250 days and 70,499,183 months for an average lunar month of approximately 29.530587 days.

8.3 Astronomical Easter

> Easter is a feast, not a planet.
> —Johannes Kepler

As an alternative to the arithmetic calculation of Easter which is based on the mean motions of the sun and moon, astronomical calculations are possible. One needs only to determine the actual time of the first full moon after the vernal equinox. Indeed, Kepler's Rudolphine astronomical tables were used to fix the date of Easter by Protestants in Germany between 1700 and 1776, and Sweden used astronomical rules from 1740 to 1844.

In 1997, the World Council of Churches [13] proposed a uniform date for Easter for both Eastern and Western churches, reverting to astronomical calculations of the equinox and full moon. These calculations are discussed in Section 12.9.

Table 8.1 compares the different dates for the Easter full moon (not for Easter itself, which is on the following Sunday) on the basis of Western and Eastern practice and the proposed astronomical rule, with the dates of Passover Eve, according to the Hebrew calendar of Chapter 7 and the classical, observation-based Hebrew calendar described in Section 12.9.

8.4 Movable Christian Holidays

Many Christian holidays depend on the date of Easter: Septuagesima Sunday (63 days before), Sexagesima Sunday (56 days before), Shrove Sunday (49 days before), Shrove Monday (48 days before), Shrove Tuesday or Mardi Gras, (47 days before), Ash Wednesday (46 days before), Passion Sunday (14 days before), Palm Sunday (7 days before), Holy or Maundy Thursday (3 days before), Good Friday (2 days before), Rogation Sunday (35 days after), Ascension Day (39 days after), Pentecost (also called Whitsunday—49 days after), Whitmundy (50 days after), Trinity Sunday (56 days after), and Corpus Christi (60 days after, or 63 days after, in the Catholic Church in the United States.).[2] All these are easily computed; for example

$$\textbf{pentecost}\,(g\text{-}year) \overset{\text{def}}{=} \textbf{easter}\,(g\text{-}year) + 49 \tag{8.4}$$

---

[2] Because of the extensive liturgical changes after the Second Vatican Council, the Catholic Church no longer observes Septuagesima, Sexagesima, and Shrove Sunday through Tuesday.

Table 8.1 *Julian dates of Passover Eve (Nisan 14), for the years 9–40 C.E., according to the Hebrew arithmetic and observational calendars, and of the Easter full moon preceding Easter Sunday, according to the Orthodox, Gregorian, and proposed astronomical rules. (For the futility of attempting to determine the date of the crucifixion from such data, see [2, Chapter 9].)*

| Julian Year | Passover Eve (Nisan 14) | | Easter Full Moon | | |
	Classical	Arithmetic	Orthodox	Gregorian	Proposed
9 C.E.	Saturday, March 30	Friday, March 29	Wednesday, March 27	Friday, March 29	Friday, March 29
10 C.E.	Friday, April 18	Wednesday, April 16	Tuesday, April 15	Thursday, April 17	Thursday, April 17
11 C.E.	Tuesday, April 7	Monday, April 6	Saturday, April 4	Monday, April 6	Monday, April 6
12 C.E.	Saturday, March 26	Friday, March 25	Thursday, March 24	Saturday, March 26	Saturday, March 26
13 C.E.	Friday, April 14	Friday, April 14	Wednesday, April 12	Friday, April 14	Friday, April 14
14 C.E.	Tuesday, April 3	Monday, April 2	Sunday, April 1	Tuesday, April 3	Wednesday, April 4
15 C.E.	Sunday, March 24	Friday, March 22	Thursday, March 21	Saturday, March 23	Sunday, March 24
16 C.E.	Saturday, April 11	Friday, April 10	Thursday, April 9	Saturday, April 11	Saturday, April 11
17 C.E.	Wednesday, March 31	Wednesday, March 31	Monday, March 29	Wednesday, March 31	Wednesday, March 31
18 C.E.	Tuesday, April 19	Saturday, March 19	Sunday, April 17	Tuesday, April 19	Monday, April 18
19 C.E.	Sunday, April 9	Friday, April 7	Wednesday, April 5	Friday, April 7	Saturday, April 8
20 C.E.	Thursday, March 28	Wednesday, March 27	Monday, March 25	Wednesday, March 27	Wednesday, March 27
21 C.E.	Wednesday, April 16	Monday, April 14	Sunday, April 13	Tuesday, April 15	Tuesday, April 15
22 C.E.	Sunday, April 5	Saturday, April 4	Thursday, April 2	Saturday, April 4	Sunday, April 5
23 C.E.	Thursday, March 25	Wednesday, March 24	Monday, March 22	Wednesday, March 24	Friday, March 26
24 C.E.	Wednesday, April 12	Wednesday, April 12	Monday, April 10	Wednesday, April 12	Wednesday, April 12
25 C.E.	Monday, April 2	Monday, April 2	Friday, March 30	Sunday, April 1	Sunday, April 1
26 C.E.	Friday, March 22	Friday, March 22	Thursday, April 18	Saturday, April 20	Saturday, April 20
27 C.E.	Thursday, April 10	Wednesday, April 9	Monday, April 7	Wednesday, April 9	Wednesday, April 9
28 C.E.	Tuesday, March 30	Monday, March 29	Saturday, March 27	Monday, March 29	Monday, March 29
29 C.E.	Sunday, April 17	Saturday, April 16	Friday, April 15	Sunday, April 17	Sunday, April 17
30 C.E.	Thursday, April 6	Wednesday, April 5	Tuesday, April 4	Thursday, April 6	Thursday, April 6
31 C.E.	Tuesday, March 27	Monday, March 26	Saturday, March 24	Monday, March 26	Tuesday, March 27
32 C.E.	Sunday, April 13	Monday, April 14	Saturday, April 12	Monday, April 14	Monday, April 14
33 C.E.	Friday, April 3	Friday, April 3	Wednesday, April 1	Friday, April 3	Friday, April 3
34 C.E.	Wednesday, March 24	Monday, March 22	Sunday, March 21	Tuesday, March 23	Tuesday, March 23
35 C.E.	Tuesday, April 12	Monday, April 11	Saturday, April 9	Monday, April 11	Monday, April 11
36 C.E.	Saturday, March 31	Friday, March 30	Thursday, March 29	Saturday, March 31	Friday, March 30
37 C.E.	Thursday, March 21	Wednesday, March 20	Wednesday, April 17	Friday, April 19	Thursday, April 18
38 C.E.	Tuesday, April 8	Monday, April 7	Saturday, April 5	Monday, April 7	Tuesday, April 8
39 C.E.	Saturday, March 28	Friday, March 27	Wednesday, March 25	Friday, March 27	Saturday, March 28
40 C.E.	Friday, April 15	Friday, April 15	Wednesday, April 13	Friday, April 15	Friday, April 15

The 40 days of Lent, or *Quadragesima*, begin on Ash Wednesday. Orthodox Christians begin Lent 7 weeks (48 days) before Eastern Orthodox Easter, on Monday. The Eastern Orthodox Church celebrates the Feast of Orthodoxy on the following Sunday (42 days before Eastern Orthodox Easter). The Orthodox Fast of the Apostles begins 8 days after Orthodox Pentecost and ends on June 28 on the Julian calendar.

The ecclesiastical year begins with Advent Sunday (see page 60).

References

[1] *The Nautical Almanac and Astronomical Ephemeris for the Year 1938*, His Majesty's Stationery Office, London, 1937.

[2] R. T. Beckwith, *Calendar and Chronology, Jewish and Christian: Biblical, Intertestamental and Patristic Studies*, E. J. Brill, Leiden, 1996.

[3] E. R. Berlekamp, J. H. Conway, and R. K. Guy, *Winning Ways: Volume 2, Games in Particular*, Academic Press, New York, 1982.

[4] C. F. Gauss, "Berechnung des Osterfestes," *Monatliche Correspondenz zur Beförderung der Erd- und Himmels-Kunde*, Herausgegeben vom Freiherrn von Zach (August 1800). Reprinted in Gauss's *Werke*, Herausgegeben von der Königlichen Gesellschaft der Wissenschaften, Göttingen, volume 6, pp. 73–79, 1874.

[5] C. F. Gauss, "Noch etwas über die Bestimmung des Osterfestes," *Braunschweigisches Magazin* (September 12, 1807). Reprinted in Gauss's *Werke*, Herausgegeben von der Königlichen Gesellschaft der Wissenschaften, Göttingen, volume 6, pp. 82–86, 1874.

[6] H. Kinkelin, "Die Berechnung des christlichen Osterfestes," *Zeitschrift für Mathematik und Physik,* volume 15, pp. 217–228, 1870.

[7] D. E. Knuth, "The Calculation of Easter," *Communications of the ACM*, volume 5, pp. 209–210, 1962.

[8] D. E. Knuth, *The Art of Computer Programming, Volume 1*: *Fundamental Algorithms*, 3rd ed., Addison-Wesley Publishing Company, Reading, MA, 1997.

[9] J. Meeus, *Mathematical Astronomy Morsels*, Willmann-Bell, Inc., Richmond, VA, 1997.

[10] G. Moyer, "The Gregorian Calendar," *Scientific American*, volume 246, no. 5, pp. 144–152, May 1982.

[11] T. H. O'Beirne, *Puzzles and Paradoxes*, Oxford University Press, Oxford, 1965. Reprinted by Dover Publications, New York, 1984.

[12] J. V. Uspensky and M. A. Heaslet, *Elementary Number Theory*, McGraw-Hill, New York, 1939.

[13] World Council of Churches, "The Date of Easter: Science Offers Solution to Ancient Religious Problem," Press release, March 24, 1997.

Stone astrolabe from India. (Courtesy of Adler Planetarium & Astronomy Museum, Chicago, IL.)

9

The Old Hindu Calendars

I sincerely hope that leading Indian pañcāṅg-makers, astronomers
and mathematicians will keep their
Siddhāntic reckoning as pure as possible and not use the old works
for purposes they can never be able to serve, mindful of the sage
word: no man putteth a piece of undressed cloth upon an old
garment; for that which should fill it up taketh from the garment,
and a worse rent is made.
—Walther E. van Wijk: "On Hindu Chronology IV,"
Acta Orientalia, volume IV (1926)

9.1 Structure and History

The Hindus have both solar and lunisolar calendars. In the Hindu lunisolar
system, as in other lunisolar calendars, months follow the lunar cycle and are
synchronized with the solar year by introducing occasional leap months. Unlike the Hebrew lunisolar calendar (described in Chapter 7), Hindu intercalated
months do not follow a short cyclical pattern. Moreover, unlike other calendars,
a day can be *omitted* any time in a lunar month.

Modern Hindu calendars are based on close approximations to the *true* times
of the sun's entrance into the signs of the zodiac and of lunar conjunctions
(new moons). Before about 1100 C.E., however, Hindu calendars used *mean*
times. Though the basic structure of the calendar is similar for both systems,
the mean (*madhyama*) and true (*spaṣṭa*) calendars can differ by a few days or
can be shifted by a month. In this chapter we implement the mean system, as
described in [4, pp. 360–446], which is arithmetical; Chapter 17 is devoted
to the more recent astronomical version. For an ancient description of Hindu

astronomy, calendars, and holidays, see the book on India by al-Bīrūnī [1];[1] a more modern reference is [3].

There are various epochs that are, or have been, used as starting points for the enumeration of years in India. For a list of eras, see [5, pp. 39–47, civ–cvi]. In this chapter, we use the expired Kali Yuga ("Iron Age") epoch. The *expired* year number is the number of years that have *elapsed* since the onset of the Kali Yuga.[2] As van Wijk [6] explains:

> We count the years of human life in expired years. A child of seven years has already lived more than seven years; but on the famous *18 Brumaire de l'An VIII de la République Française une et indivisible* only 7 years and 47 days of the French Era had elapsed.

The first day of year 0 K.Y.[3] is Friday, January 23, −3101 (Gregorian) or February 18, 3102 B.C.E. (Julian), that is, R.D. −1,132,959:

$$\textbf{hindu-epoch} \overset{\text{def}}{=} \tag{9.1}$$

$$\textbf{fixed-from-julian}\left(\begin{array}{|c|c|c|} \hline 3102 \text{ B.C.E.} & \textbf{february} & 18 \\ \hline \end{array} \right)$$

Time is measured in days and fractions since this epoch.

The Kali Yuga epoch marks—in Hindu chronology—the onset of the fourth and final stage (lasting 432,000 years) of the 4,320,000-year era beginning with the last recreation of the world. Civil days begin at mean sunrise reckoned as one quarter of a day past midnight; that is, at 6:00 a.m. The midnight just prior to day 1 of the Hindu calendar is considered to have been the start of a new lunar month; indeed, in Hindu astronomy it was the time of the most recent *mean* conjunction of all the visible planets (the Sun, Moon, Mercury, Venus, Mars, Jupiter, and Saturn).

The Hindus also have a day count beginning with the first day of the Kali Yuga. To compute it we simply add the R.D. date to the number of days from the onset of the Kali Yuga until R.D. 0; that is, we subtract the epoch:

$$\textbf{hindu-day-count}\,(date) \overset{\text{def}}{=} date - \textbf{hindu-epoch} \tag{9.2}$$

The day number is called its *ahargaṇa* ("heap of days") and is traditionally

---

[1] There is some confusion of dates in the note (on page 358) attributed to Schram in Sachau's translation of this book where the following equivalences are given: Thursday, February 25, 1031 C.E. (Julian) = 1 Caitra 953 Śaka Era = 28 Ṣafar 422 A.H. = 19 Ispandârmadh-Mâh 399 Anno Persarum, and New Year 400 Anno Persarum = March 9, 1031 C.E. (Julian) = JD 2,097,686. In fact, February 25, 1031 C.E. (Julian) = 29 Ṣafar 422 A.H. = JD 2,097,686.

[2] For each epoch, there is also a *current* year number, beginning with year 1.

[3] Kali Yuga (Iron Age).

used to determine the day of the week by casting off sevens just as we have done with our R.D. numbering.

The names of the days of the week (dated to the third or fourth century C.E.) are

Sunday	Ravivāra or Ādityavāra
Monday	Chandravāra or Somavāra
Tuesday	Maṅgalavāra or Bhaumavāra
Wednesday	Buddhavāra or Saumyavāra
Thursday	Bṛihaspatvāra or Guruvāra
Friday	Śukravāra
Saturday	Śanivāra

The Hindu value for the (sidereal) year (the mean number of days it takes for the sun to return to the same point vis-à-vis the celestial globe—see Section 12.4) is

$$\textbf{arya-solar-year} \ \overset{\text{def}}{=} \ \frac{1577917500}{4320000} \tag{9.3}$$

or $365\frac{149}{576} = 365.258680555\cdots$ (civil) days.

A Jovian cycle is also employed. It takes Jupiter about 12 years to circle the sun; the Hindu value is

$$\textbf{arya-jovian-period} \ \overset{\text{def}}{=} \ \frac{1577917500}{364224} \tag{9.4}$$

days. The Jovian period is divided into 12 equal periods of time, one for each sign of the zodiac. Five revolutions of Jupiter suggest a 60-year cycle of year names, called *samvatsaras*, listed in Table 9.1. The Jovian year number corresponding to the start of a solar year is computed from a fixed date as follows:

$$\textbf{jovian-year}\,(\textit{date}) \ \overset{\text{def}}{=} \tag{9.5}$$

$$\left(\left\lfloor \frac{\left\lfloor \dfrac{\textbf{hindu-day-count}\,(\textit{date})}{\textbf{arya-jovian-period}} \right\rfloor}{12} \right\rfloor \bmod 60 \right) + 1$$

Because a Jovian "year" is somewhat shorter than a solar year, consecutive solar years do not necessarily carry consecutive Jovian names. In that case, every 86 years or so the samvatsara is said to be "expunged."

The Jovian cycle and all other figures are given in traditional Hindu astronomy as rational numbers. Accordingly, we use rational arithmetic in our calendar functions as well as in the Lisp code given in Appendix B. The numerators and denominators of the rational numbers obtained during the intermediate

Table 9.1 *The names of the samvatsaras of the Hindu*
Jovian cycle of 60 years.

(1) Vijaya	(31) Rudhirodgārin
(2) Jaya	(32) Raktāksha
(3) Manmatha	(33) Krodhana
(4) Durmukha	(34) Kshaya
(5) Hemalamba	(35) Prabhava
(6) Vilamba	(36) Vibhava
(7) Vikārin	(37) Śukla
(8) Śarvari	(38) Pramoda
(9) Plava	(39) Prajāpati
(10) Śubhakṛit	(40) Aṅgiras
(11) Śobhana	(41) Śrīmukha
(12) Krodhin	(42) Bhāva
(13) Viśvāvasu	(43) Yuvan
(14) Parābhava	(44) Dhātṛi
(15) Plavaṅga	(45) Īśvara
(16) Kīlaka	(46) Bahudhānya
(17) Saumya	(47) Pramāthin
(18) Sādhāraṇa	(48) Vikrama
(19) Virodhakṛit	(49) Vṛisha
(20) Paridhāvin	(50) Chitrabhānu
(21) Pramādin	(51) Subhānu
(22) Ānanda	(52) Tāraṇa
(23) Rākshasa	(53) Pārthiva
(24) Anala	(54) Vyaya
(25) Piṅgala	(55) Sarvajit
(26) Kālayukta	(56) Sarvadhārin
(27) Siddhārthin	(57) Virodhin
(28) Rāudra	(58) Vikṛita
(29) Durmati	(59) Khara
(30) Dundubhi	(60) Nandana

calculations exceed 32 binary digits but remain below 2^{63}; thus, they can be reformulated as integer calculations on 64-bit computers.

Different Indian astronomical treatises give slightly varying astronomical constants; in this chapter we follow the (First) *Ārya Siddhānta* of Āryabhaṭa (499 C.E.), as amended by Lalla. There are also many variations in details of the calendars; we describe only one version.

9.2 The Solar Calendar

> Sometimes I cannot help regretting that only so very few readers
> can rejoice with me in the simplicity of the method and the
> exactness of its results.
> —Walther E. van Wijk: "On Hindu Chronology III,"
> *Acta Orientalia* (1924)

A solar month is one twelfth of a year:

$$\textbf{arya-solar-month} \stackrel{\text{def}}{=} \frac{1}{12} \times \textbf{arya-solar-year} \tag{9.6}$$

or 30.438 · · · days. The solar (*saura*) months are sometimes named in Sanskrit after the signs of the zodiac corresponding to the position of the mean sun:

(1) Mesha	(Aries)	मेष
(2) Vrishabha	(Taurus)	व्रषभ
(3) Mithuna	(Gemini)	मिथुन
(4) Karka	(Cancer)	कर्क
(5) Siṁha	(Leo)	सिंह
(6) Kanyā	(Virgo)	कन्या
(7) Tulā	(Libra)	तुळ
(8) Vṛiśchika	(Scorpio)	वृशिचक
(9) Dhanu	(Sagittarius)	धनु
(10) Makara	(Capricorn)	मकर
(11) Kumbha	(Aquarius)	कुंभ
(12) Mīna	(Pisces)	मीन

In most locations, however, the same names are used as in the lunisolar scheme. See page 134.

The solar New Year is called Mesha saṁkrānti. Each solar month is 30 or 31 days long and begins on the day of the first sunrise after the calculated time of the mean sun's entry into the next zodiacal sign. If that calculated time is after midnight but before (or at) sunrise, then the day of entry is the first day of the new month; otherwise, it is the last day of the previous month. Hence, even though the (mean) month is a constant, months vary in length. Our R.D. 0 is Makara 19, 3101 K.Y. on the mean solar calendar.

Converting a solar date according to this old Hindu calendar into an R.D. date is straightforward:

$$\textbf{fixed-from-old-hindu-solar} \tag{9.7}$$

$$\left(\boxed{\begin{array}{c|c|c} year & month & day \end{array}} \right) \stackrel{\text{def}}{=}$$

$$\left\lceil \textbf{hindu-epoch} + year \times \textbf{arya-solar-year} + \right.$$
$$\left. (month - 1) \times \textbf{arya-solar-month} + day - \tfrac{5}{4} \right\rceil$$

Because *year* is the number of years that have *elapsed* since the epoch, we multiply it by the average length of a year, which is a fraction, and add the number of days (and fractions of a day) in the elapsed months of the current year. That gives the time at which the current month began, to which is added the fixed date of the epoch and the number of days up to and including the given *day*. If the resultant moment is after mean sunrise (6 a.m.), then we have the right fixed date; if it is before sunrise, we need to subtract 1. Subtracting 5/4 of a day from the resultant moment and taking the ceiling has this effect.

Inverting the process is not much harder:

$$\textbf{old-hindu-solar-from-fixed}\,(date) \ \overset{\text{def}}{=} \tag{9.8}$$

year	month	day

where

$$sun \quad = \quad \textbf{hindu-day-count}\,(date) + \frac{1}{4}$$

$$year \quad = \quad \left\lfloor \frac{sun}{\textbf{arya-solar-year}} \right\rfloor$$

$$month \quad = \quad \left(\left\lfloor \frac{sun}{\textbf{arya-solar-month}} \right\rfloor \bmod 12 \right) + 1$$

$$day \quad = \quad \lfloor sun \bmod \textbf{arya-solar-month} \rfloor + 1$$

Here, *sun* is the number of days and the fraction (1/4) of days that have elapsed since the Hindu epoch at mean sunrise—the decisive moment—on fixed *date*; *year* is the number of mean years that have elapsed at that moment; *month* is the current solar month, counting mean months from the beginning of that solar year; and *day* is the number of the civil day, counting from the beginning of the solar month.

9.3 The Lunisolar Calendar

We follow the south-India method which months begin and end at new moons (the *amânta* scheme); in the north, months go from full moon to full moon (the *pûrnimânta* scheme). The name of a lunar month depends on the solar month that begins during that lunar month. A month is leap and takes the following month's name when no solar month begins within it. See Figure 9.1.

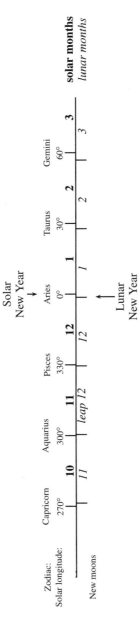

Figure 9.1 The old Hindu lunisolar calendar. Solar events (entry in zodiac constellations) are shown above the time line; lunar events (lunar conjunctions) are shown below; longitudes are sidereal. The solar months are shown in boldface numbers; the lunar months, in italic numbers.

133

The Sanskrit names themselves are based on the longitudinal position of the moon at midmonth:

(1) Chaitra	चैत्र	(7) Āśvina	आश्विन
(2) Vaiśākha	वैशाख	(8) Kārtika	कार्तिक
(3) Jyaishtha	ज्यैष्ठ	(9) Mārgaśīrsha	मार्गशीर्ष
(4) Āshādha	आषाढ	(10) Pausha	पौष
(5) Śrāvana	श्रावण	(11) Māgha	माघ
(6) Bhādrapada	भाद्रपद	(12) Phālguna	फाल्गुन

Some regions of India begin the year with Kārtika and use different or shifted month names.

Because a solar month (see Section 12.5) is longer than a lunar month, a lunar month is intercalated whenever the latter is wholly contained within the former. That lunar month and the following take the same name except that the first is leap, called *adhika* ("added," or *prathama*, first), and the second is *nija* ("regular," or *dvitīya*, second).[4] In the rare event (at the onset of K.Y. 0, and every 360,000 years later) that both the lunar and solar month end at the same moment and, hence, that the following lunar and solar months both begin at the same moment, we follow the explicit statement of al-Bīrūnī [1, vol. 2, pp. 20–21] that the former lunar month is the intercalated one.

Two constants play a major rôle in lunar computations: the length of a solar month **arya-solar-month** (page 131) and that of the lunar month:

$$\textbf{arya-lunar-month} \stackrel{\text{def}}{=} \frac{1577917500}{53433336} \tag{9.9}$$

that is, 29.53058181 ⋯ days. Though a month on the lunisolar calendar can consist of 29 or 30 civil days, it is always divided into 30 "lunar days,"[5] called *tithis*:

$$\textbf{arya-lunar-day} \stackrel{\text{def}}{=} \frac{1}{30} \times \textbf{arya-lunar-month} \tag{9.10}$$

Because a mean lunar month is less than 30 (civil) days long, a lunar day is about 0.98435 days or is somewhat shorter than a day.

Days within a lunar month are numbered by the lunar day current at sunrise, which usually referred to by ordinal number within one fortnight or the other; we use ordinal numbers from 1 to 30. The first 15 lunar days belong to the *suddha* ("bright," waxing; also *śukla*) fortnight and the second 15, to the *bahula* ("dark," waning; also *krishna*) fortnight. Just as there are leap months, there are also "lost" days whenever a lunar day begins and ends between one sunrise

---

[4] In the northern, full-moon scheme, the intercalated month is inserted between the two halves of the ordinary month [2, p. 405].

[5] This should not be confused with what astronomers call a "lunar day."

and the next. The date R.D. 0 is Pausha 19 (that is, dark 4), 3101 K.Y. on the lunisolar calendar.

To determine the number of the month, we look at the next occurrence of a new moon—the second, if it is a leap month—see where the sun is at that moment, and then give the lunar month the number of that solar month. For the lunar year number, we use the solar year of that solar month. The previous mean new moon is found using formula (1.42); the next new moon is 1 month later.

We can apply our leap year formulas (1.65) and (1.68) to the calculation of the old Hindu calendar subject to a few complications:

1. The K.Y. year count begins at 0, not 1.
2. The first lunar year began 1 month before the onset of the Kali Yuga.
3. The determining time is mean sunrise, not midnight.
4. The relevant solar event—the start of solar month Mīna—occurs in the last month of a lunisolar year rather than in the first.

Accordingly, we need to adjust the year numbers by 1, the month enumeration by 1, and the day count by 1/4. The first month of a lunar year is that in which the moment "Mīna plus 1 (lunar) month" occurs. That moment in year 0 was the fraction

$$\delta = 2 - \frac{\text{arya-solar-month}}{\text{arya-lunar-month}}$$

into the first month because the first lunar year began exactly 1 month before the solar New Year. The average year length is

$$\bar{L} = \frac{\text{arya-solar-year}}{\text{arya-lunar-month}} \text{ months.}$$

By inequality (1.66), Hindu year y is leap if

$$\left(2 - \frac{\text{arya-solar-month}}{\text{arya-lunar-month}} + y\frac{\text{arya-solar-year}}{\text{arya-lunar-month}} \right) \bmod 1$$

$$\geq 1 - \frac{\text{arya-solar-year}}{\text{arya-lunar-month}} \bmod 1.$$

Multiplying by **arya-lunar-month** and simplifying, we get the following test:

old-hindu-lunar-leap-year? (*l-year*) $\overset{\text{def}}{=}$ (9.11)

$$\big((l\text{-}year \times \textbf{arya-solar-year} - \textbf{arya-solar-month})$$

$$\bmod \textbf{arya-lunar-month} \big)$$

$$\geq \frac{23902504679}{1282400064}$$

We do not, however, require this test for the conversion functions that follow.

Let $sun = n + 1/4$ be the moment of sunrise on day n since the onset of the Kali Yuga. The number of months m that have elapsed since the first lunar year is

$$m = \lfloor sun/\textbf{arya-lunar-month} \rfloor + 1,$$

which amounts to

$$sun - (sun \bmod \textbf{arya-lunar-month}) + \textbf{arya-lunar-month}$$

days. By equation (1.68), the year number (starting from 0) is

$$\left\lceil \frac{m + 1 - \delta}{\bar{L}} \right\rceil - 1.$$

Using the preceding values for m, δ, and $\bar{L}$ yields

$$
\begin{aligned}
y &= \left\lceil \frac{m + 1 - \left(2 - \dfrac{\textbf{arya-solar-month}}{\textbf{arya-lunar-month}}\right)}{\dfrac{\textbf{arya-solar-year}}{\textbf{arya-lunar-month}}} \right\rceil - 1 \\[2em]
&= \left\lceil \frac{(m - 1) \times \textbf{arya-lunar-month} + \textbf{arya-solar-month}}{\textbf{arya-solar-year}} \right\rceil - 1 \\[2em]
&= \left\lceil \frac{\textit{new-moon} + \textbf{arya-solar-month}}{\textbf{arya-solar-year}} \right\rceil - 1
\end{aligned}
$$

where

$$
\begin{aligned}
\textit{new-moon} &= (m - 1) \times \textbf{arya-lunar-month} \\[1em]
&= \left\lfloor \frac{sun}{\textbf{arya-lunar-month}} \right\rfloor \times \textbf{arya-lunar-month}
\end{aligned}
$$

Intuitively, the lunisolar year number y is the solar year number in effect at the end of the current month.

The same leap-year formula can be used to determine the lunar month name. For this purpose, however, we consider "years" to be a period of either 1- or 2-month duration: 1 for ordinary months and 2 when the month name is shared by a leap month. The average length, A, in lunar months of such periods is **arya-solar-month/arya-lunar-month**. Formula (1.68) tells us that after m

lunar months the number of elapsed periods is

$$
\left\lceil \frac{m + 1 - \delta}{A} \right\rceil - 1 \;=\; \left\lceil \frac{new\text{-}moon + \textbf{arya-solar-month}}{\textbf{arya-solar-month}} \right\rceil - 1
$$

$$
=\; \left\lceil \frac{new\text{-}moon}{\textbf{arya-solar-month}} \right\rceil \qquad (9.12)
$$

The inverse, deriving the fixed date from the Hindu lunar date, is a bit more complicated. By equation (1.65), there are $\lfloor 12yA + \delta \rfloor$ months from the beginning of year 0 until the end of elapsed year $y - 1$. Accordingly, the number of months since the Kali Yuga (which began 1 month after lunar year 0) is

$$
\lfloor 12 \times y \times A + \delta \rfloor - 1 \;=\; \left\lfloor 12 \times y \times \frac{\textbf{arya-solar-month}}{\textbf{arya-lunar-month}} \right.
$$

$$
\left. + \left(2 - \frac{\textbf{arya-solar-month}}{\textbf{arya-lunar-month}} \right) \right\rfloor - 1
$$

$$
=\; \left\lfloor \frac{(12 \times y - 1) \times \textbf{arya-solar-month}}{\textbf{arya-lunar-month}} \right\rfloor + 1
$$

$$
=\; \left\lfloor \frac{mina}{\textbf{arya-lunar-month}} \right\rfloor + 1
$$

where

$$
mina \;=\; (12 \times y - 1) \times \textbf{arya-solar-month}
$$

$$
=\; y \times \textbf{arya-solar-year} - \textbf{arya-solar-month}
$$

is the moment of the determining solar event.

We use a boolean (true/false) value to indicate whether a month is leap. A date is represented as

year	month	leapmonth	day

where *year* is an integer, *month* is an integer in the range 1 through 12, *leapmonth* is either true or false, and *day* is an integer in the range 1 through 30.

old-hindu-lunar-from-fixed (*date*) $\overset{\text{def}}{=}$ (9.13)

year	month	leap	day

where

$$
sun \;=\; \textbf{hindu-day-count} (date) + \frac{1}{4}
$$

$$
new\text{-}moon \;=\; sun - (sun \bmod \textbf{arya-lunar-month})
$$

$$leap \quad = \quad \textbf{arya-solar-month} - \textbf{arya-lunar-month} \geq$$
$$(\textit{new-moon} \bmod \textbf{arya-solar-month}) > 0$$

$$month \quad = \quad \left(\left\lceil \frac{\textit{new-moon}}{\textbf{arya-solar-month}} \right\rceil \bmod 12 \right) + 1$$

$$day \quad = \quad \left(\left\lfloor \frac{\textit{sun}}{\textbf{arya-lunar-day}} \right\rfloor \bmod 30 \right) + 1$$

$$year \quad = \quad \left\lceil \frac{\textit{new-moon} + \textbf{arya-solar-month}}{\textbf{arya-solar-year}} \right\rceil - 1$$

To determine the lunar month, we use equation (9.12) and cast off twelves. A month is leap when it begins closer to the solar month's beginning than the excess of a solar month over a lunar month.

The lunar New Year is the first lunar month to begin in the last solar month (*Mīna*) of the prior solar year. To compute the R.D. date from an old Hindu lunar date, we count lunar months and elapsed lunar days, taking care to check if there was a leap month in the interim. This value is added to the moment of the New Year, as determined above:

fixed-from-old-hindu-lunar $\hspace{6cm}$ (9.14)

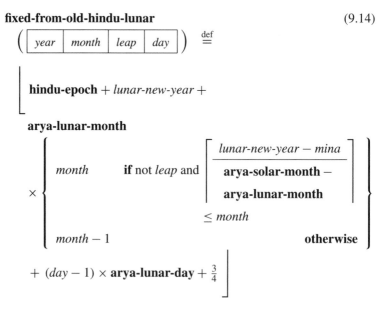

where

$$mina \quad = \quad (12 \times year - 1) \times \textbf{arya-solar-month}$$

$$lunar\text{-}new\text{-}year \quad = \quad \textbf{arya-lunar-month}$$
$$\times \left(\left\lfloor \frac{mina}{\textbf{arya-lunar-month}} \right\rfloor + 1 \right)$$

We add 3/4 before taking the floor because the date at midnight is determined by the lunar day that was current at the prior sunrise.

References

[1] al-Bīrūnī (= Abū-Raihān Muhammad ibn 'Ahmad al-Bīrūnī), *India: An Accurate Description of all Categories of Hindu Thought, as Well those Which are Admissible as those Which Must be Rejected*, circa 1030. Translated and annotated by C. E. Sachau, *Albêrûnî's India: An Account of the Religion, Philosophy, Literature, Geography, Chronology, Astronomy, Customs, Laws and Astrology of India*, William H. Allen and Co., London, 1910; reprinted under the Authority of the Government of West Pakistan, Lahore, 1962, and by S. Chand & Co., New Delhi, 1964.

[2] H. G. Jacobi, "The Computation of Hindu Dates in Inscriptions, &c.," *Epigraphia Indica: A Collection of Inscriptions Supplementary to the Corpus Inscriptionum Indicarum of the Archæological Survey of India*, J. Burgess, ed., Calcutta, pp. 403–460, p. 481, 1892.

[3] D. Pingree, "History of Mathematical Astronomy in India," *Dictionary of Scientific Biography*, C. C. Gillispie, ed., volume XV, supplement I, pp. 533–633, 1978.

[4] R. Sewell, *The Siddhantas and the Indian Calendar, Being a Continuation of the Author's "Indian Chronography," with an Article by the Late Dr. J. F. Fleet on the Mean Place of the Planet Saturn*, Government of India Central Publication Branch, Calcutta, 1924. This is a reprint of a series of articles in *Epigraphica Indica*.

[5] R. Sewell and S. B. Dîkshit, *The Indian Calendar, with Tables for the Conversion of Hindu and Muhammadan into* A.D. *Dates, and Vice Versa, with Tables of Eclipses Visible in India by R. Schram*, Motilal Banarsidass Publishers, Delhi, 1995. Originally published in 1896.

[6] W. E. van Wijk, *Decimal Tables for the Reduction of Hindu Dates from the Data of the Sūrya-Siddhānta*, Martinus Nijhoff, The Hague, 1938.

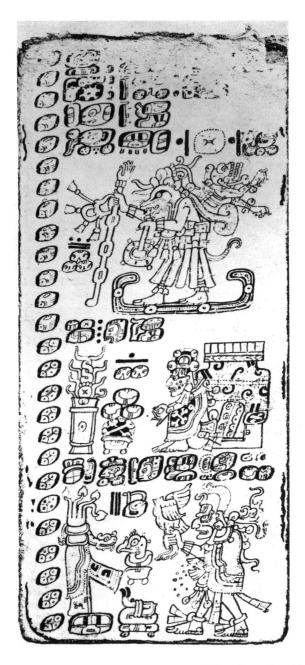

Mayan new year ceremonies. Reproduced, with permission, from Plate 28 in *A Commentary on the Dresden Codex: A Maya Hieroglyphic Book*, by J. E. S. Thompson, American Philosophical Society, Philadelphia, PA, 1972.

10

The Mayan Calendars

The invention of the Central American calendar in the Seventh
century before Christ may be described with all propriety as one of
the outstanding intellectual achievements in the history of man.
This calendar solved with conspicuous success the great problem
of measuring and defining time which confronts all civilized
nations. Moreover it required the elaboration of one of the four or
five original systems of writing the parts of speech in graphic
symbols, and it conjoined with this supplementary invention of
hieroglyphs the earliest discovery of the device of figures with
place values in the notation of numbers. This time machine of
ancient America was distinctly a scientific construction, the
product of critical scrutiny of various natural phenomena by a
master mind among the Mayas. It permitted a school of
astronomer-priests to keep accurate records of celestial occurrences
over a range of many centuries, with the ultimate reduction of the
accumulated data through logical inferences to patterns of truth.
—Herbert J. Spinden: *The Reduction of Mayan Dates* (1924)

The Mayans, developers of an ancient Amerindian civilization in Central
America, employed three separate, overlapping calendrical systems called by
scholars the *long count*, the *haab*, and the *tzolkin*. Their civilization reached
its zenith during the period 250–900 C.E., and the Mayans survive to this
day in Guatemala and in the Yucatan peninsula of Mexico and Belize; some
groups have preserved parts of the calendar systems. What is known today
has been recovered through astroarcheological and epigraphic research. There
is general agreement on the Mayan calendrical rules and the correspondence
between the three Mayan calendars; however, the exact correspondence between the Mayan calendars and Western calendars is still a matter of some
slight dispute. Correspondences are proposed by date equivalences in Spanish

141

sources and by interpreting Mayan recordings of astronomical phenomena, such as new moons. In this book, we give the details for the most popular (and nearly universally accepted) of the correspondences, the *Goodman-Martinez-Thompson correlation* [12]. Another correlation was used by Spinden [9], [10], [11].[1] A superb discussion of Mayan mathematics, astronomy, and calendrical matters is given by Lounsbury [5] (see also [4]). The Aztecs had analogous calendars.

10.1 The Long Count

The long count is a strict counting of days from the beginning of the current cycle, each cycle containing 2,880,000 days (about 7885 solar years); the Mayans believed that the universe is destroyed and recreated at the start of every cycle. The units of the long count are

1 kin	=	1 day	
1 uinal	=	20 kin	(20 days)
1 tun	=	18 uinal	(360 days)
1 katun	=	20 tun	(7200 days)
1 baktun	=	20 katun	(144,000 days)

Thus, the long count date 12.16.11.16.6 means 12 baktun, 16 katun, 11 tun, 16 uinal, and 6 kin, for a total of 1,847,486 days from the start of the Mayan calendar epoch. (It is uncertain when the Mayan day began; there is evidence that the tzolkin day began at sunset and the haab day at sunrise, or in any case that they began at different times of day.)

Although not relevant here, the Mayans used the following larger units for longer time periods:

1 pictun	=	20 baktun	(2,880,000 days)
1 calabtun	=	20 pictun	(57,600,000 days)
1 kinchiltun	=	20 calabtun	(1,152,000,000 days)
1 alautun	=	20 kinchiltun	(23,040,000,000 days)

An alautun is about 63,081,377 solar years!

The starting epoch of the long count, according to the Goodman-Martinez-Thompson correlation, is taken as Wednesday, August 11, −3113 (Gregorian).

---

[1] Some of Spinden's date calculations are wrong. Here are three examples: on page 46 of "Maya Dates and What They Reveal" [11], he gives the equivalence JD 1,785,384 = February 10, 176 (Gregorian), but it should be February 11, 176 (Gregorian); on top of page 55 several Gregorian dates are off by 1 day; on page 57 he gives the equivalence JD 2,104,772 = August 30, 1050 (Gregorian), but it should be July 27, 1050 (Gregorian).

This date equals September 6, 3114 B.C.E. (Julian),[2] which was (at noon) JD 584,283, that is, R.D. $-1,137,142$:[3]

$$\textbf{mayan-epoch} \;\overset{\text{def}}{=}\; \textbf{fixed-from-jd}\,(584283) \tag{10.1}$$

In other words, our R.D. 0 is long count 7.17.18.13.2.

Thus, to convert from a Mayan long count date to an R.D. date we need only compute the total number of days given by the long count and subtract the number of days before R.D. 0 by adding the epoch:

fixed-from-mayan-long-count (10.2)

$$\left(\;\boxed{\begin{array}{c|c|c|c|c} baktun & katun & tun & uinal & kin \end{array}}\; \right) \;\overset{\text{def}}{=}$$

$$\textbf{mayan-epoch} + baktun \times 144000 + katun \times 7200 +$$

$$tun \times 360 + uinal \times 20 + kin$$

In the opposite direction, converting an R.D. date to a Mayan long count date, we need to add the number of days in the long count before R.D. 0 and then divide the result into baktun, katun, tun, uinal, and kin:

$$\textbf{mayan-long-count-from-fixed}\,(date) \;\overset{\text{def}}{=} \tag{10.3}$$

$$\boxed{\begin{array}{c|c|c|c|c} baktun & katun & tun & uinal & kin \end{array}}$$

where

$$
\begin{aligned}
\textit{long-count} \;&=\; \textit{date} - \textbf{mayan-epoch} \\[2mm]
\textit{baktun} \;&=\; \left\lfloor \frac{\textit{long-count}}{144000} \right\rfloor \\[2mm]
\textit{day-of-baktun} \;&=\; \textit{long-count} \bmod 144000 \\[2mm]
\textit{katun} \;&=\; \left\lfloor \frac{\textit{day-of-baktun}}{7200} \right\rfloor \\[2mm]
\textit{day-of-katun} \;&=\; \textit{day-of-baktun} \bmod 7200
\end{aligned}
$$

---

[2] Thompson [12] errs in referring to this date as "3113 B.C.," confusing the two systems of dealing with years before the common era (see page 15). His error has been reproduced by many scholars.

[3] Almost all experts believe this correlation, or possibly JD 584,285, is correct. Spinden's value, now no longer used, is JD 489,384.

$$tun = \left\lfloor \frac{day\text{-}of\text{-}katun}{360} \right\rfloor$$

$$day\text{-}of\text{-}tun = day\text{-}of\text{-}katun \bmod 360$$

$$uinal = \left\lfloor \frac{day\text{-}of\text{-}tun}{20} \right\rfloor$$

$$kin = day\text{-}of\text{-}tun \bmod 20$$

10.2 The Haab and Tzolkin Calendars

> They made a clay image of the demon of evil Uuayayab, that is
> u-uayab-haab, "He by whom the year is poisoned," confronted it
> with the deity who had supreme power over the coming year, and
> then carried it out of the village in the direction of that cardinal
> point to which, on the system of the Mayan calendar, the particular
> year was supposed to belong.
> —Sir James George Frazer: *The Golden Bough* (1890)

The Mayans used a civil calendar, the haab, based approximately on the solar year and consisting of 18 "months" of 20 days each together with 5 additional days at the end. Because the haab calendar accounts for only 365 days (as compared with the mean length of the solar tropical year, 365.2422 days), the civil calendar slowly drifted with respect to the seasons, as did the Egyptian calendar (see Section 1.9). The months were called[4]

(1) Pop	(7) Yaxkin	(13) Mac
(2) Uo	(8) Mol	(14) Kankin
(3) Zip	(9) Chen	(15) Muan
(4) Zotz	(10) Yax	(16) Pax
(5) Tzec	(11) Zac	(17) Kayab
(6) Xul	(12) Ceh	(18) Cumku
		(19) Uayeb

The last of these, Uayeb, was not really a month, but a 5-day unlucky period. The pictographs for the haab names are shown in Figure 10.1. Unlike Gregorian months, the days of the haab months begin at 0 and indicate the number of *elapsed days* in the current month. Thus, 0 Uo follows 19 Pop, and

---

[4] The haab month names and tzolkin day names are transliterated from the Yucatan (Yucatec) Mayan language. The Guatemalan (Quiché) Mayans used slightly different names.

	Carving	Codex		Carving	Codex
Pop			Yax		
Uo			Zac		
Zip			Ceh		
Zotz			Mac		
Tzec			Kankin		
Xul			Muan		
Yaxkin			Pax		
Mol			Kayab		
Chen			Cumku		
			Uayeb		

Figure 10.1 The haab month signs. Adapted from Spinden [10, Fig. 3].

the fifth monthless day is followed by 0 Pop. This method of counting is also used for years in the Hindu calendar discussed in Chapters 9 and 17.

We represent haab dates as pairs

$$\boxed{\quad month \quad | \quad day \quad},$$

where *month* and *day* are integers in the ranges 1 to 19 and 0 to 19, respectively; thus, we treat Uayeb as a defective nineteenth month. We can count how many days after the first day of a cycle any given haab date is as follows:

$$\textbf{mayan-haab-ordinal}\left(\boxed{month \mid day} \right) \overset{\text{def}}{=} \qquad (10.4)$$

$$(month - 1) \times 20 + day$$

The long count date 0.0.0.0.0 is considered to be haab date 8 Cumku (there is no disagreement here between the various correlations), which we specify by giving the starting R.D. date of the haab cycle preceding the start of the long count:

$$\textbf{mayan-haab-epoch} \overset{\text{def}}{=} \qquad (10.5)$$

$$\textbf{mayan-epoch} - \textbf{mayan-haab-ordinal}\left(\boxed{18 \mid 8} \right)$$

We can convert an R.D. date to a haab date by

$$\textbf{mayan-haab-from-fixed}\,(date) \overset{\text{def}}{=} \boxed{month \mid day} \qquad (10.6)$$

where

$$count \quad = \quad (date - \textbf{mayan-haab-epoch}) \bmod 365$$

$$day \quad = \quad count \bmod 20$$

$$month \quad = \quad \left\lfloor \frac{count}{20} \right\rfloor + 1$$

It is not possible to convert a haab date to an R.D. date because without a "year" there is no unique corresponding R.D. date. We can ask, though, for the R.D. date of the Mayan haab date on or before a given R.D. date:

$$\textbf{mayan-haab-on-or-before}\,(haab, date) \overset{\text{def}}{=} \qquad (10.7)$$

$$date - \Big(\big(date - \textbf{mayan-haab-epoch} -$$

$$\textbf{mayan-haab-ordinal}\,(haab) \big) \bmod 365 \Big)$$

This is an instance of formula (1.42) with the ordinal position of R.D. 0 being $\Delta = (0 - \textbf{mayan-haab-epoch}) \bmod 365$.

The third Mayan calendar, the tzolkin (or sacred) calendar, was a religious calendar consisting of two cycles: a 13-day count and a cycle of 20 names:

(1) Imix	(5) Chicchan	(9) Muluc	(13) Ben	(17) Caban
(2) Ik	(6) Cimi	(10) Oc	(14) Ix	(18) Etznab
(3) Akbal	(7) Manik	(11) Chuen	(15) Men	(19) Cauac
(4) Kan	(8) Lamat	(12) Eb	(16) Cib	(20) Ahau

The pictographs for the tzolkin names are shown in Figure 10.2.

Figure 10.2 The tzolkin name signs. Adapted from Spinden [10, Fig. 1].

Unlike the haab months and days, the counts and names cycle *simultaneously*, and thus, for example, 13 Etznab precedes 1 Cauac, which precedes 2 Ahau, which precedes 3 Imix, and so on. Because 20 and 13 are relatively prime, this progression results in 260 unique dates, forming the "divine" year.

The long count date 0.0.0.0.0 is taken to be tzolkin date 4 Ahau. (The different correlations agree on this, too.) Representing tzolkin dates as pairs of positive integers

$$\boxed{\textit{number} \mid \textit{name}},$$

where *number* and *name* are integers in the ranges 1 to 13 and 1 to 20, respectively, we specify

$$\textbf{mayan-tzolkin-epoch} \overset{\text{def}}{=} \qquad (10.8)$$

$$\textbf{mayan-epoch} - \textbf{mayan-tzolkin-ordinal}\left(\boxed{4 \mid 20} \right)$$

where the function **mayan-tzolkin-ordinal** is explained below.

We can convert from an R.D. date to a tzolkin date with

$$\textbf{mayan-tzolkin-from-fixed}\,(\textit{date}) \overset{\text{def}}{=} \qquad (10.9)$$

$$\boxed{\textit{number} \mid \textit{name}}$$

where

$$\textit{count} \quad = \quad \textit{date} - \textbf{mayan-tzolkin-epoch} + 1$$

$$\textit{number} \quad = \quad \textit{count} \text{ amod } 13$$

$$\textit{name} \quad = \quad \textit{count} \text{ amod } 20$$

Just as with the haab calendar, it is impossible to convert a tzolkin date to an R.D. date. Unlike the haab calendar, however, because day numbers and day names cycle simultaneously, to calculate the number of days between two given tzolkin dates requires the solution to a pair of simultaneous linear congruences, as we did in Section 1.11. (See [7] for a general discussion of this topic and [5] for a specific discussion relating to the Mayan calendars.)

Suppose we want to know the number of days x from tzolkin date $\boxed{1 \mid 1}$ until the next occurrence of tzolkin date $\boxed{m \mid n}$. We apply formula (1.52) with $a = m - 1, b = n - 1, c = 13, d = 20, \Gamma = \Delta = 0$. Because $k = -3$ is the multiplicative inverse of 13 modulo 20, we get

$$x = (m - 1 + 13[-3(n - m)]) \bmod 260.$$

Accordingly, we define

$$\textbf{mayan-tzolkin-ordinal}\left(\boxed{\textit{number} \mid \textit{name}} \right) \overset{\text{def}}{=} \qquad (10.10)$$

$$(\textit{number} - 1 + 39 \times (\textit{number} - \textit{name})) \bmod 260$$

As with the haab calendar, this function can be used to compute the R.D. date of the Mayan tzolkin date on or before a given R.D. date:

$$\textbf{mayan-tzolkin-on-or-before}\,(\textit{tzolkin}, \textit{date}) \stackrel{\text{def}}{=} \qquad (10.11)$$

$$\textit{date} - \Big(\big(\textit{date} - \textbf{mayan-tzolkin-epoch} - $$

$$\textbf{mayan-tzolkin-ordinal}\,(\textit{tzolkin}) \big) \bmod 260 \Big)$$

This is another instance of formula (1.42).

A popular way for the Mayans to specify a date was to use the haab and tzolkin dates together, forming a cycle of the least common multiple of 365 and 260 days: 18,980 days or approximately 52 solar years. This cycle is called a *calendar round*, and we seek the latest date, on or before a given R.D. *date*, that falls on a specified date of the calendar round, with Haab date *haab* and Tzolkin date *tzolkin*. Again we apply formula (1.52), this time with $c = 365$ and $d = 260$, and no shifts. The greatest common divisor of c and d is 5. The inverse of $365/5 = 73$ modulo $260/5 = 52$ is (by coincidence) also 5. Plugging these values into (1.52), we get

$$(a + 365[b - a]) \bmod 18980,$$

for the position of the pair of dates, a and b, in the calendar round. Using formula (1.42) to go back to the last occurrence of *haab* and *tzolkin* before *date*, with k and Δ determined in this way—once with $a = \textbf{mayan-haab-ordinal}(\textit{haab})$ and $b = \textbf{mayan-tzolkin-ordinal}(\textit{tzolkin})$ and again with $a = \textbf{mayan-haab-epoch}$ and $b = \textbf{mayan-tzolkin-epoch}$—and simplifying, we have:

$$\textbf{mayan-calendar-round-on-or-before} \qquad (10.12)$$

$$(\textit{haab}, \textit{tzolkin}, \textit{date}) \stackrel{\text{def}}{=}$$

$$\begin{cases} \textit{date} - ((\textit{date} - \textit{haab-count} - 365 \times \textit{diff}) \bmod 18980) \\ \qquad\qquad\qquad\qquad\qquad\qquad \textbf{if } (\textit{diff} \bmod 5) = 0 \\ \textbf{bogus} \qquad\qquad\qquad\qquad\qquad\qquad\qquad \textbf{otherwise} \end{cases}$$

where

$$\begin{aligned} \textit{haab-count} \quad &= \quad \textbf{mayan-haab-ordinal}\,(\textit{haab}) + \\ &\qquad \textbf{mayan-haab-epoch} \\ \textit{tzolkin-count} \quad &= \quad \textbf{mayan-tzolkin-ordinal}\,(\textit{tzolkin}) + \\ &\qquad \textbf{mayan-tzolkin-epoch} \\ \textit{diff} \quad &= \quad \textit{tzolkin-count} - \textit{haab-count} \end{aligned}$$

For impossible combinations the constant **bogus** is returned.

This function can be used to compute the number of days between a pair of dates on the calendar round or to write a function **mayan-calendar-round-on-or-after**; we leave these to the reader.

References

[1] A. F. Aveni, *Empires of Time: Calendars, Clocks, and Cultures*, Basic Books, Inc., New York, 1989. Republished by Kondasha America, Inc., New York, 1995.

[2] C. P. Bowditch, *The Numeration, Calendar Systems and Astronomical Knowledge of the Mayas*, Cambridge University Press, Cambridge, 1910.

[3] J. T. Goodman, *The Archaic Maya Inscriptions*, Appendix to volume VIII of *Biologia Centrali-Americanna*, ed. by F. D. Godman and O. Salvin, R. H. Porter and Dulau & Co., London, 1897.

[4] J. S. Justeson, "Ancient Mayan Ethnoastronomy: An Overview of Epigraphic Sources," *World Archeoastronomy* (Selected Papers from the 2nd Oxford International Conference on Archaeoastronomy, Merida, Yucatan, Mexico, January 13–17 1986), A. F. Aveni, ed., chap. 8 (pp. 76–129), 1989.

[5] F. G. Lounsbury, "Maya Numeration, Computation, and Calendrical Astronomy," *Dictionary of Scientific Bibliography*, volume 15, supplement 1, pp. 759–818, Charles Scribner's Sons, New York, 1978.

[6] S. G. Morley, *The Ancient Maya*, revised by G. W. Brainerd, Stanford University Press, Stanford, CA, 1963.

[7] Ø. Ore, *Number Theory and Its History*, McGraw-Hill Book Co., Inc., New York, 1948. Reprinted by Dover Publications, Inc., Mineola, NY, 1987.

[8] L. Satterwaite, "Concepts and Structures of Maya Calendrical Arithmetics," Ph.D. Thesis, University of Pennsylvania, Philadelphia, 1947.

[9] H. J. Spinden, "Central American Calendars and the Gregorian Day," *Proceedings of the National Academy of Sciences* (*USA*), volume 6, pp. 56–59 (1920).

[10] H. J. Spinden, "The Reduction of Maya Dates," *Peabody Museum Papers*, volume VI, no. 4, 1924.

[11] H. J. Spinden, "Maya Dates and What They Reveal," *Science Bulletin* (The Museum of the Brooklyn Institute of Arts and Sciences), volume IV, no. 1, 1930.

[12] J. E. S. Thompson, *Maya Hieroglyphic Writing*, 3rd ed., University of Oklahoma Press, Norman, OK, 1971.

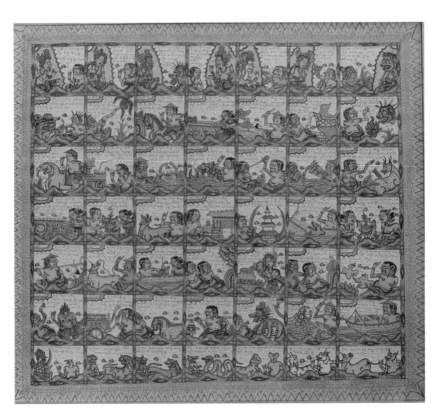

Balinese *plintangen* calendar, by Ni Made Widiarki of Kamasan, Klungkung, Bali, showing a combination of the 5-day market week (*pancawara* cycle) and the 7-day week (*saptawara* cycle). Reproduced, with permission, from *Myths & Symbols in Indonesian Art*, curated by M.-A. Milford-Lutzker, Antonio Prieto Memorial Gallery, Mills College, Oakland, CA, 1991.

11

The Balinese Pawukon Calendar

What is "really real" is the name... of the day, its place in the
transempirical taxonomy of days, not its epiphenomenal reflection
in the sky.
—Clifford Geertz: *The Interpretation of Cultures* (1973)

The Pawukon calendar of Bali is a complex example of a calendar based on
concurrent cycles (see Section 1.11). The whole calendar repeats every 210
days, but these 210-day "years" are unnumbered. The calendar comprises 10
subcycles of lengths 1 through 10, all running simultaneously. The subcycles
that determine the calendar are those of length 5, 6, 7; the others are altered to
fit, by repetitions or other complications.

Like many other cultures in the region, the Balinese also have a lunisolar
calendar of the old Hindu style (see Chapter 9), but leap months have been
added erratically; we do not describe its details. This lunisolar calendar is used
to determine only one holiday: Nyepi, a "New Year's Day" marking the start
of the tenth lunar month, near the onset of spring.

11.1 Structure and Implementation

The cycles and supercycles are endless, unanchored,
unaccountable, and, as their internal order has no significance,
without climax. They do not accumulate, they do not build, and
they are not consumed. They don't tell you what time it is; they
tell you what kind of time it is.
—Clifford Geertz: *The Interpretation of Cultures* (1973)

The main subcycles of the Pawukon calendar are those of length 5, 6, and 7,
and the whole calendar repeats every 210 days, the least common multiple of
5, 6, and 7. The names of the various cycles and of the days in each are given in

Table 11.1. There is no notion of a calendar month; rather any 35-day interval is called a *bulan*.

Each day is named according to the value assigned to the day in each of the 10 cycles:

$$\textbf{bali-pawukon-from-fixed}\,(date) \stackrel{\mathrm{def}}{=} \tag{11.1}$$

bali-luang-from-fixed (*date*)	bali-dwiwara-from-fixed (*date*)	bali-triwara-from-fixed (*date*)	bali-caturwara-from-fixed (*date*)	bali-pancawara-from-fixed (*date*)
bali-sadwara-from-fixed (*date*)	bali-saptawara-from-fixed (*date*)	bali-asatawara-from-fixed (*date*)	bali-sangawara-from-fixed (*date*)	bali-dasawara-from-fixed (*date*)

The day names for the periods of length 3, 6, and 7 cycle in their natural order. In particular, the 7-day cycle corresponds to the day of the week on other calendars. The 30 weeks of a full 210-day cycle are also named (see Table 11.2).

Cycles on the Pawukon calendar—like the Mayan haab and tzolkin calendars (see Chapter 10)—are unnumbered, and thus we can take any start of the 210-day period as its epoch; for example:

$$\textbf{bali-epoch} \stackrel{\mathrm{def}}{=} \textbf{fixed-from-jd}\,(146) \tag{11.2}$$

We can determine the position (beginning with 0) of any fixed date within the full 210-day cycle easily:

$$\textbf{bali-day-from-fixed}\,(date) \stackrel{\mathrm{def}}{=} \tag{11.3}$$

$$(date - \textbf{bali-epoch})\ \mathrm{mod}\ 210$$

The simple cycles of length 3 (*triwara*), 6 (*sadwara*), and 7 (*saptawara*) are then trivial to implement:

$$\textbf{bali-triwara-from-fixed}\,(date) \stackrel{\mathrm{def}}{=} \tag{11.4}$$

$$(\textbf{bali-day-from-fixed}\,(date)\ \mathrm{mod}\ 3) + 1$$

$$\textbf{bali-sadwara-from-fixed}\,(date) \stackrel{\mathrm{def}}{=} \tag{11.5}$$

$$(\textbf{bali-day-from-fixed}\,(date)\ \mathrm{mod}\ 6) + 1$$

$$\textbf{bali-saptawara-from-fixed}\,(date) \stackrel{\mathrm{def}}{=} \tag{11.6}$$

$$(\textbf{bali-day-from-fixed}\,(date)\ \mathrm{mod}\ 7) + 1$$

Table 11.1 *Names of days on each of the 10 simultaneous cycles of the Pawukon calendar.*

	Cycle Length									
	1	2	3	4	5	6	7	8	9	10	
	Ekawara	Dwiwara	Triwara	Caturwara	Pancawara	Sadwara	Saptawara	Asatawara	Sangawara	Dasawara	
Luang		Menga	Pasah	Sri	Umanis	Tungleh	Redite	Sri	Dangu	Pandita	1
		Pepet	Beteng	Laba	Paing	Aryang	Coma	Indra	Jangur	Pati	2
			Kajeng	Jaya	Pon	Urukung	Anggara	Guru	Gigis	Suka	3
				Menala	Wage	Paniron	Buda	Yama	Nohan	Duka	4
					Keliwon	Was	Wraspati	Ludra	Ogan	Sri	5
						Maulu	Sukra	Brahma	Erangan	Manuh	6
							Saniscara	Kala	Urungan	Manusa	7
								Uma	Tulus	Raja	8
									Dadi	Dewa	9
										Raksasa	0

Week	1	2	3	4	5	6	7	8	9	10	11	12	13	14	15	16	17	18	19	20	21	22	23	24	25	26	27	28	29	30
	Sinta	Landep	Ukir	Kulantir	Taulu	Gumbreg	Wariga	Warigadian	Jukungwangi	Sungsang	Dunggulan	Kuningan	Langkir	Medangsia	Pujut	Pahang	Krulut	Merakih	Tambir	Medangkungan	Matal	Uye	Menail	Prangbakat	Bala	Ugu	Wayang	Kelawu	Dukut	Watugunung
Redite (Sunday)																														
Coma (Monday)																														
Anggara (Tuesday)																														
Buda (Wednesday)																														
Wraspati (Thursday)																														
Sukra (Friday)																														
Saniscara (Saturday)																														

156

Table 11.2 (*Opposite*) *The 210-day Balinese Pawukon cycle can be divided into 30 weeks of 7 days. Reading clockwise from the upper left in each box of 8 numbers, the positions of each day on the cycles of length 3, 5, 4, 2, 9, 8, 10, and 6 are given. Italics and boldface are used to indicate important conjunctions: Kajeng-Keliwon is italic; Tumpek is bold. For example, consider the box Saniscarra (Saturday) for the twelfth week (Kuningan): The italic 3 in the upper left means that the day is in position 3 in the 3-day (triwara) cycle; it is italic because that day is the conjunction Kajeng-Keliwon. The boldface 5 in the upper right means that the day is in position 5 in the 5-day (pancawara) cycle; it is in bold because that day is the conjunction Tumpek. The 2 below the boldface 5 means that the day is the second day of the 4-day (caturwara) cycle, and so on. Traditional calendars, called tika, use symbols rather than numbers to punctuate each cycle; modern calendars would use the names instead of numbers and are typically arranged in a circular order as displayed here.*

157

The only complication of the 5-day (*pancawara*) cycle is that the Pawukon cycle begins with day 2 of the 5-day cycle, and thus we need to add 1 before taking the modulus:

$$\textbf{bali-pancawara-from-fixed}\,(date) \quad \overset{\text{def}}{=} \tag{11.7}$$

$$((\textbf{bali-day-from-fixed}\,(date) + 1) \mod 5) + 1$$

Calculating the week number is also trivial:

$$\textbf{bali-week-from-fixed}\,(date) \quad \overset{\text{def}}{=} \tag{11.8}$$

$$\left\lfloor \frac{\textbf{bali-day-from-fixed}\,(date)}{7} \right\rfloor + 1$$

The position of a day in the 10-day cycle depends on numbers, called *urips*, that are associated with the 5- and 7-day cycles by the sacred palm-leaf scriptures. Taking the sum of the two appropriate *urips*, modulo 10 gives the position in the 10-day (*dasawara*) cycle:[1]

$$\textbf{bali-dasawara-from-fixed}\,(date) \quad \overset{\text{def}}{=} \tag{11.9}$$

$$\left(\langle 5, 9, 7, 4, 8 \rangle_{[i]} + \langle 5, 4, 3, 7, 8, 6, 9 \rangle_{[j]} + 1 \right) \mod 10$$

where

$$i \quad = \quad \textbf{bali-pancawara-from-fixed}\,(date) - 1$$

$$j \quad = \quad \textbf{bali-saptawara-from-fixed}\,(date) - 1$$

The position of a day on the 2-day (*dwiwara*) cycle is simply the parity of its position on the 10-day cycle:

$$\textbf{bali-dwiwara-from-fixed}\,(date) \quad \overset{\text{def}}{=} \tag{11.10}$$

$$\textbf{bali-dasawara-from-fixed}\,(date) \quad \text{amod } 2$$

Similarly, the "1-day" (*ekawara*) cycle names only the even days of the 10-day cycle, which are called Luang. We use a boolean function to indicate whether

---

[1] The sequence 9, 7, 4, 8, 5 can be calculated as

$$a + \begin{cases} 4 & a \leq 1 \\ 5 & \text{otherwise} \end{cases}$$

where $a = (3d) \mod 5$, and $d = \textbf{bali-day-from-fixed}\,(date) - 2$.

a day is Luang:

$$\textbf{bali-luang-from-fixed}\,(date) \quad \stackrel{\mathrm{def}}{=} \tag{11.11}$$

$$(\,\textbf{bali-dasawara-from-fixed}$$

$$(date)\ \ \mathrm{mod}\ \ 2\,) = 0$$

Because 210 is not divisible by 8 or 9, to squeeze in subcycles of lengths 8 and 9, certain values must be repeated. The 9-day (*sangawara*) cycle begins with 4 occurrences of the value 1, which can be computed as follows:

$$\textbf{bali-sangawara-from-fixed}\,(date) \quad \stackrel{\mathrm{def}}{=} \tag{11.12}$$

$$(\max\,\{0,\ \textbf{bali-day-from-fixed}\,(date)\ -3\}\ \ \mathrm{mod}\ \ 9) + 1$$

The 8-day (*asatawara*) cycle runs normally except that days 70, 71, and 72 all get the value 7. This is a bit more complicated to compute:

$$\textbf{bali-asatawara-from-fixed}\,(date) \quad \stackrel{\mathrm{def}}{=} \tag{11.13}$$

$$(\max\,\{6, 4 + ((day - 70)\ \ \mathrm{mod}\ \ 210)\}\ \ \mathrm{mod}\ \ 8) + 1$$

where

$$day \quad = \quad \textbf{bali-day-from-fixed}\,(date)$$

Finally, the 4-day (*caturwara*) cycle depends directly on the 8-day cycle:

$$\textbf{bali-caturwara-from-fixed}\,(date) \quad \stackrel{\mathrm{def}}{=} \tag{11.14}$$

$$\textbf{bali-asatawara-from-fixed}\,(date)\ \ \mathrm{amod}\ \ 4$$

The full 210-day cycle is shown in Table 11.2. A traditional calendar, called a *tika*, uses symbols to mark one of the days of each of the 8 cycles shown in the chart.

Without numbering the cycles, there is no way to convert a Pawukon date into a fixed date. Instead, as for the Mayan calendars of Chapter 10, we use formulas (1.52) and (1.42) to determine the last occurrence of a Pawukon date before a given fixed date. The 10 components of the Pawukon date are fully determined by the values on the cycles of relatively prime lengths 5, 6, and 7; thus we apply (1.52) twice: once to compute the position b_{35} of a Pawukon date within a 35-day subcycle from its position a_5 in the 5-day week and b_7 in the 7-day week, and then again, to combine its position a_6 in the 6-day week with b_{35}. Recalling the offset of 1 in the 5-day cycle, we let $c = 5$ and $d = 7$ be the cycle lengths, $\Gamma = 1$ and $\Delta = 0$ be the offsets, and $k = 3$ be the inverse of 5 modulo 7 in (1.52), to obtain

$$b_{35} = (a_5 - 1 + 5 \times 3(b_7 - a_5 + 1)) \bmod 35$$
$$= (a_5 + 14 + 15(b_7 - a_5)) \bmod 35$$

For the full cycle of 210 days, we let $c = 6$, $d = 35$, $\Gamma = \Delta = 0$, and $k = 6$, to get

$$n = (a_6 + 36(b_{35} - a_6)) \bmod 210$$

Before applying (1.42), we also need to find the offset Δ of the Pawukon cycle vis-à-vis R.D. dates:

$$\textbf{bali-on-or-before}\,(b\text{-}date, date) \stackrel{\text{def}}{=} \qquad\qquad (11.15)$$

$$date - ((date + \Delta - days) \bmod 210)$$

where

$$a_5 = \textbf{bali-pancawara}\,(b\text{-}date) - 1$$

$$a_6 = \textbf{bali-sadwara}\,(b\text{-}date) - 1$$

$$b_7 = \textbf{bali-saptawara}\,(b\text{-}date) - 1$$

$$b_{35} = (a_5 + 14 + 15 \times (b_7 - a_5)) \bmod 35$$

$$days = a_6 + 36 \times (b_{35} - a_6)$$

$$\Delta = \textbf{bali-day-from-fixed}\,(0)$$

There is no need to take *days* modulo 210 before applying (1.42).

11.2 Conjunction Days

> The main...ceremony occurs on each temple's "birthday," every
> 210 days, at which time the gods descend from their homes atop
> the great volcano in the center of the island, enter iconic figurines
> placed on an altar in the temple, remain three days, and
> then return.
> —Clifford Geertz: *The Interpretation of Cultures* (1973)

The holidays on the Balinese Pawukon calendar are based on conjunctions of dates on individual cycles.

To collect all occurrences of holidays in a Gregorian year, we write a generic function to find the first occurrence on or after a given date of the *n*th day of a c-day cycle and then recursively find the remaining occurrences. To find the first occurrence, we use an analogue of formula (1.42):

$$\textbf{positions-in-interval}\,(n, c, \Delta, start, end) \;\overset{\text{def}}{=} \tag{11.16}$$

$$\begin{cases} \langle\,\rangle & \textbf{if } pos > end \\ \langle pos\rangle \;\|\; \textbf{positions-in-interval}\,(n, c, \Delta, pos+1, end) & \\ & \textbf{otherwise} \end{cases}$$

where

$$pos \quad = \quad start + ((n - start - \Delta - 1) \bmod c)$$

Here Δ is the position in the cycle of R.D. 0.

The ninth day of every 15-day subcycle is important: on this day, called Kajeng-Keliwon, the last day of the 3-day cycle (Kajeng) and last day of the 5-day cycle (Keliwon) coincide. (It is the ninth because the first day of the Pawukon cycle is day 2 of the 5-day cycle.) With **positions-in-interval**, it is easy to compute:

$$\textbf{kajeng-keliwon-in-gregorian}\,(g\text{-}year) \;\overset{\text{def}}{=} \tag{11.17}$$

$$\textbf{positions-in-interval}\,\big(9, 15, \Delta, jan_1, dec_{31}\big)$$

where

$$jan_1 \quad = \quad \textbf{fixed-from-gregorian}$$

$$\left(\boxed{\;g\text{-}year\;\mid\;\textbf{january}\;\mid\;1\;} \right)$$

$$dec_{31} \quad = \quad \textbf{fixed-from-gregorian}$$

$$\left(\boxed{\;g\text{-}year\;\mid\;\textbf{december}\;\mid\;31\;} \right)$$

$$\Delta \quad = \quad \textbf{bali-day-from-fixed}\,(0)$$

The 5-day and 7-day cycles together create a 35-day cycle. The second Saturday of the Pawukon cycle, and every subsequent fifth Saturday, are both the last day of the week and the last day of the 5-day cycle. Each such conjunction is also called Tumpek and is computed as follows:

$$\textbf{tumpek-in-gregorian}\,(g\text{-}year) \;\overset{\text{def}}{=} \tag{11.18}$$

$$\textbf{positions-in-interval}\,\big(14, 35, \Delta, jan_1, dec_{31}\big)$$

where

$$jan_1 \quad = \quad \textbf{fixed-from-gregorian}$$

$$\left(\boxed{\;g\text{-}year\;\mid\;\textbf{january}\;\mid\;1\;} \right)$$

$$dec_{31} = \textbf{fixed-from-gregorian}$$

$$\left(\begin{array}{|c|c|c|} \hline \textit{g-year} & \textbf{december} & 31 \\ \hline \end{array} \right)$$

$$\Delta = \textbf{bali-day-from-fixed}\,(0)$$

The 6 Tumpeks in each Pawukon cycle are named Tumpek Landep (day 14 of the 210-day cycle), Tumpek Uduh (day 49), Tumpek Kuningan (day 84), Tumpek Krulut (day 119), Tumpek Kandang (day 154), and Tumpek Ringgit (day 189).

Other significant conjunctions occur on days 4 (Buda-Keliwon), 18 (Buda-Cemeng), 24 (Anggara Kasih), and 29 (Pengembang) of each 35-day subcycle.

Day 74 of the Pawukon is Galungan; day 84 is Kuningan Day, which is both a Tumpek day and Kajeng-Keliwon; and the period from Galungan through Kuningan Day is called the Galungan Days, during which the most important celebrations are held.

References

[1] F. B. Eiseman, Jr., *Bali: Sekala and Niskala, volume I: Essays on Religion, Ritual, and Art, with two chapters by Margaret Eiseman*, chapter 17, Periplus Editions, Berkeley, CA, 1989.

[2] M. Kudlek, "Calendar Systems," *Mitteilungen der mathematischen Gesellschaft in Hamburg*, volume XII, number 2, pp. 395–428, 1991.

Part II

Astronomical Calendars

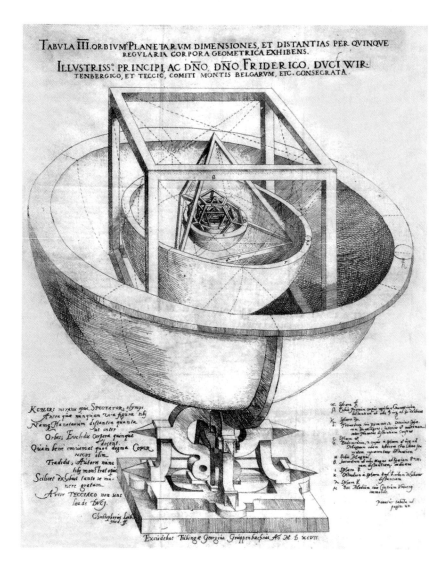

Geometrical explanation of the planetary distances—the mystical harmony of the spheres. From Johannes Kepler's *Prodromus Dissertationum Cosmographicarum Continens Mysterium Cosmographicum* (1596). (Courtesy of the University of Illinois, Urbana, IL.)

12

Time and Astronomy

Ask my friend l'Abbé Sallier to recommend to you some meagre
philomath, to teach you a little geometry and astronomy; not
enough to absorb your attention, and puzzle your intellects, but
only enough, not to be grossly ignorant of either. I have of late
been a sort of an *astronome malgré moy*, by bringing last Monday,
into the house of Lords, a bill for reforming our present Calendar,
and taking the New Style. Upon which occasion I was obliged to
talk some astronomical jargon, of which I did not understand one
word, but got it by heart, and spoke it by rote from a master.
I wished that I had known a little more of it myself; and so much
I would have you know.
—Letter from Philip Dormer Stanhope (Fourth Earl of
Chesterfield) to his son, February 28, 1751 C.E. (Julian)

The calendars in the second part of this book are based on accurate astronomical calculations. This chapter defines the essential astronomical terms and describes the necessary astronomical functions. Fuller treatment can be found in
the references—an especially readable discussion is given in [9].

We begin with an explanation of how positions of locations on Earth and
of heavenly bodies are specified followed by an examination of the notion
of time itself. After discussing the 24-hour day, we summarize the different
types of years and months used by various calendars along with algorithms that
closely approximate the times of astronomical events—notably equinoxes, solstices, and new moons. These astronomical functions are adapted from those
in [13] and [3] and require 64-bit arithmetic. Most of the algorithms are centered around the present date, for which they are accurate to within about 2
minutes. Their accuracy decreases for the far-distant past or future. More accurate algorithms exist [2] but are extremely complex and not needed for our
purposes.

165

We conclude this chapter with descriptions of several "speculative" astronomical calendars: the future version of the Bahá'í solar calendar, the observational Islamic lunar calendar, the classical Hebrew lunisolar calendar, and the proposed uniform date of Easter.

12.1 Position

> The cause of the error is very simple.... In journeying eastward he
> had gone towards the sun, and the days therefore diminished for
> him as many times four minutes as he crossed degrees in this
> direction. There are three hundred and sixty degrees in the
> circumference of the Earth; and these three hundred and sixty
> degrees, multiplied by four minutes, gives precisely twenty-four
> hours—that is, the day unconsciously gained.
> —Jules Verne: *Around the World in Eighty Days* (1873)

Locations on Earth are specified by giving their latitude and longitude. The *(terrestrial) latitude* of a geographic location is the angular distance on the Earth, measured in degrees from the equator, along the meridian of the location. Similarly, the *(terrestrial) longitude* of a geographic location is the angular distance on the Earth measured in degrees from the Greenwich meridian (which is $0°$), on the outskirts of London. Thus, for example, the location of Jerusalem is described as being $31.8°$ north, $35.2°$ east. In the algorithms, we take north as positive latitude and south as negative. For longitudes, we take east from Greenwich as positive and west as negative,[1] and thus positive longitude means a time later than Greenwich, and a negative longitude means a time earlier than in Greenwich.

As we will see in the next section, locations on Earth are also associated with a *time zone*, which is needed for determining local clock time. For some calculations (local sunrise and sunset, in particular), elevation above sea level is also a factor. Thus, the complete specification of a location that we use is

latitude	longitude	elevation	zone

We specify the time zone in hours difference from Universal Time (U.T.; see Section 12.2) and measure elevation above sea level in meters. For example, the specification of Urbana, Illinois, is

$$\textbf{urbana} \stackrel{\text{def}}{=} \boxed{\begin{array}{|c|c|c|c|} \hline 40.1° & -88.2° & 225m & -6 \\ \hline \end{array}} \qquad (12.1)$$

---

[1] This is in agreement with the standard of the International Astronomical Union but inconsistent with common sense and a century of common practice. See [13, p. 89].

because Urbana is at latitude 40.1° north, longitude 88.2° west, 225 meters above sea level, and 6 hours before U.T.

Moslems turn towards Mecca for prayer, and Jews face Jerusalem. Their locations are, respectively:

$$\textbf{mecca} \overset{\text{def}}{=} \tag{12.2}$$

| 21°25′24″ | 39°49′24″ | 1000m | 2 |

$$\textbf{jerusalem} \overset{\text{def}}{=} \boxed{\begin{array}{c|c|c|c} 31.8° & 35.2° & 800m & 2 \end{array}} \tag{12.3}$$

If a spherical Earth is assumed, the direction (measured in degrees, east of due north) of location *focus*, along a great circle, when one stands at location *locale*, can be determined by spherical trigonometry:

$$\textbf{direction}\,(locale, focus) \overset{\text{def}}{=} \tag{12.4}$$

$$\begin{cases} 0 & \textbf{if } denom = 0 \\[2ex] \textbf{arctan} \\ \left(\dfrac{\sin\left(\psi' - \psi\right)}{denom}, \begin{cases} 2 & \textbf{if } denom < 0 \\ 1 & \textbf{otherwise} \end{cases} \right) \text{ mod } 360 \\[2ex] \hspace{10em} \textbf{otherwise} \end{cases}$$

where

$$\begin{aligned} \phi &= locale_{\text{latitude}} \\ \phi' &= focus_{\text{latitude}} \\ \psi &= locale_{\text{longitude}} \\ \psi' &= focus_{\text{longitude}} \\ denom &= \cos\phi \times \tan\phi' - \sin\phi \times \cos\left(\psi - \psi'\right) \end{aligned}$$

This formula uses the two-argument function

$$\textbf{arctan}\,(x, quad) \overset{\text{def}}{=} \tag{12.5}$$

$$\begin{cases} \alpha & \textbf{if } quad = 1 \text{ or } quad = 4 \\ \alpha + 180° & \textbf{otherwise} \end{cases} \text{ mod } 360$$

where

$$\alpha = \arctan x$$

to find the arc tangent of x appropriate for *quadrant*, which changes when the two locations are on opposite sides of the globe. For example, in Urbana, Illinois, the *qibla* (direction of Mecca) is about 49° east of due north, whereas Jerusalem is at 45° east.[2]

The position of heavenly bodies can be measured in a manner corresponding to terrestrial longitude and latitude by reference to meridians (great circles passing through the two poles) of the celestial sphere. In this *equatorial* coordinate system, *right ascension* corresponds to longitude, and *declination* to latitude. For marking the position of the sun and moon, however, astronomers usually use an alternative coordinate system in which (*celestial* or *ecliptical*) *longitude* is measured along the ecliptic (the sun's apparent path among the stars) and (*celestial*) *latitude* is measured from the ecliptic. Zero longitude is at a position called the *First Point of Aries* (see page 179).

12.2 Time

> What, then, is time? I know well enough what it is, provided that
> nobody asks me; but if I am asked what it is and try to explain,
> I am baffled.
> —Saint Augustine: *Confessions* (circa 400)

Three distinct methods of measuring time are in use today:[3]

- *Solar time* is based on the solar day, which measures the time between successive transits of the sun across the meridian (the north-south line, through the zenith, overhead in the sky). As we will see, this period varies because of the nonuniform motion of the Earth.
- *Sidereal time* varies less than solar time. It is measured as the right ascension of a point in the sky crossing the meridian at any given moment. Thus, *local* sidereal time depends on terrestrial longitude and differs from observatory to observatory.
- *Dynamical time* is a uniform measure taking the frequency of oscillation of certain atoms as the basic building block. Various forms of dynamical time use different frames of reference, which make a difference in a universe governed by relativity.

The ordinary method of measuring time is called *Universal Time* (U.T.). It is local mean solar time, reckoned from midnight, at the observatory in

---

[2] Despite the antiquity of such great-circle calculations in Moslem and Jewish sources, many mosques and synagogues are designed according to other conventions.

[3] Ephemeris time, which takes the orbital motions in the solar system as the basic building block, is an outdated time scale as of 1984.

Greenwich, England, the 0° meridian.[4] The equivalent designation "Greenwich Mean Time," abbreviated G.M.T., has fallen into disfavor with astronomers because of confusion as to whether days begin at midnight or noon (before 1925, 0^h G.M.T. meant noon; from 1925 onwards it has meant midnight).

There are several closely related types of Universal Time. Civil time keeping uses Coordinated Universal Time (U.T.C.), which since 1972 has been atomic time adjusted periodically by leap seconds to keep it close to the prime meridian's mean solar time; see [11] and [18]. We use U.T.C. for calendrical purposes (except that we ignore the fact that leap seconds are also occasionally added mid-year) expressed as a fraction of a solar day.

From the spread of clocks and pocket watches in Europe until the early 1800s, each locale would set its clocks to local mean time. Each longitudinal degree of separation gives rise to a 4-minute difference in local time. For example, because the meridian of Paris is $2°20'15''$ east, its local mean time is 9 minutes, 21 seconds ahead of U.T. As another example, Beijing is $116°25'$ east; the time difference from U.T. is $7^h45^m40^s$.

"Standard time" was first used by British railway companies starting in 1840; time zones were first adopted by North American railway companies in the late 1800s [6]. Most of Western Europe is today in one zone; the 48 contiguous states of the United States are divided into 4 zones. An incredible list of locations and the times they use today and used historically appears in [21] (for outside the United States) and [20] (for the United States). We ignore the issue of daylight saving (summer) time because it is irrelevant to the calendars we discuss.

Converting between Universal and local mean time is easy, based on the longitude of the locale:

$$\textbf{universal-from-local}\,(t_\ell, locale) \overset{\text{def}}{=} \qquad (12.6)$$

$$t_\ell - \frac{locale_{\textbf{longitude}}}{360°}$$

$$\textbf{local-from-universal}\,(t_u, locale) \overset{\text{def}}{=} \qquad (12.7)$$

$$t_u + \frac{locale_{\textbf{longitude}}}{360°}$$

[4] The formal recognition of Greenwich as the "prime meridian" dates from the International Meridian Conference of 1884, but it had been informal practice from 1767. The French, however, continued to treat Paris as the prime meridian until 1911, when they switched to Greenwich, referring to it as "Paris Mean Time, minus nine minutes twenty-one seconds." France did not formally switch to Universal Time until 1978; see [22] and [6].

To convert between Universal Time and standard zone time, we need to use the time zone of the locale:

$$\textbf{standard-from-universal}\,(t_\mathrm{u}, \textit{locale}) \overset{\text{def}}{=} \tag{12.8}$$

$$t_\mathrm{u} + \tfrac{1}{24} \times \textit{locale}_{\textbf{zone}}$$

$$\textbf{universal-from-standard}\,(t_\mathrm{s}, \textit{locale}) \overset{\text{def}}{=} \tag{12.9}$$

$$t_\mathrm{s} - \tfrac{1}{24} \times \textit{locale}_{\textbf{zone}}$$

where time differences or zones are expressed in hours after Greenwich. To convert from local mean time to standard zone time, or vice versa, we combine the differences between Universal and standard time and between local mean and Universal time:

$$\textbf{standard-from-local}\,(t_\ell, \textit{locale}) \overset{\text{def}}{=} \tag{12.10}$$

$$\textbf{standard-from-universal}$$

$$(\textbf{universal-from-local}\,(t_\ell, \textit{locale})\,, \textit{locale})$$

$$\textbf{local-from-standard}\,(t_\mathrm{s}, \textit{locale}) \overset{\text{def}}{=} \tag{12.11}$$

$$\textbf{local-from-universal}$$

$$(\textbf{universal-from-standard}\,(t_\mathrm{s}, \textit{locale})\,, \textit{locale})$$

For example, Jerusalem is $35.2°$ east of Greenwich; its time zone is U.T.$+2^\mathrm{h}$. Therefore, to obtain standard time in Jerusalem from local mean time, a net offset of $20^\mathrm{m}48^\mathrm{s}$, is subtracted.

Astronomical calculations are typically done using Dynamical Time with its unchanging time units. (There are various forms of Dynamical Time, but the differences are too small to be of concern to us.) Solar time units, on the other hand, are not constant mainly because of the retarding effects of tides and the atmosphere, which cause a relatively steady lengthening of the day and contribute what is called a "secular" (that is, steadily changing) term to its length. This slowdown causes the mean solar day to increase in length by about 1.7 milliseconds per century. Because Universal Time is based on the Earth's speed of rotation, which is slowly decreasing, the discrepancy between Universal and Dynamical Time is growing. It now stands at about 65 seconds and is currently increasing at about an average of 1 second per year. To account for the vagaries in the length of an astronomical day, every now and then a *leap second* is inserted (usually between December 31 and January 1), thereby keeping our clocks—which show Universal Time—in tune with the gradually slowing rotation of Earth. Because the accumulated discrepancy is not entirely predictable, we use the following ad hoc function:

$$\textbf{ephemeris-correction}\,(t) \quad \overset{\text{def}}{=} \tag{12.12}$$

$$
\begin{cases}
\dfrac{year - 1933}{24 \times 60 \times 60} & \textbf{if } 1988 \le year \le 2019 \\[2ex]
\begin{aligned}
& -0.00002 + 0.000297 \times c + 0.025184 \times c^2 - \\
& 0.181133 \times c^3 + 0.553040 \times c^4 - 0.861938 \times c^5 + \\
& 0.677066 \times c^6 - 0.212591 \times c^7
\end{aligned} & \\
& \textbf{if } 1900 \le year \le 1987 \\[2ex]
\begin{aligned}
& -0.000009 + 0.003844 \times c + 0.083563 \times c^2 + \\
& 0.865736 \times c^3 + 4.867575 \times c^4 + 15.845535 \times c^5 + \\
& 31.332267 \times c^6 + 38.291999 \times c^7 + 28.316289 \times c^8 \\
& + 11.636204 \times c^9 + 2.043794 \times c^{10}
\end{aligned} & \\
& \textbf{if } 1800 \le year \le 1899 \\[2ex]
\dfrac{\begin{aligned}
& 8.118780842 - \\
& 0.005092142 \times (year - 1700) + \\
& 0.003336121 \times (year - 1700)^2 - \\
& .0000266484 \times (year - 1700)^3
\end{aligned}}{24 \times 60 \times 60} & \\
& \textbf{if } 1700 \le year \le 1799 \\[2ex]
\dfrac{\begin{aligned}
& 196.58333 - 4.0675 \times (year - 1600) + \\
& 0.0219167 \times (year - 1600)^2
\end{aligned}}{24 \times 60 \times 60} & \\
& \textbf{if } 1620 \le year \le 1699 \\[2ex]
\dfrac{\dfrac{x^2}{41048480} - 15}{24 \times 60 \times 60} & \textbf{otherwise}
\end{cases}
$$

where

$$year \quad = \quad \textbf{gregorian-year-from-fixed}\,(\lfloor t \rfloor)$$

To convert from U.T. to Dynamical Time, we add the correction:

$$\textbf{dynamical-from-universal}\,(t) \quad \overset{\text{def}}{=} \tag{12.13}$$

$$t + \textbf{ephemeris-correction}\,(t)$$

where t is an R.D. date and U.T. time. We approximate the inverse of (12.2) by

$$\textbf{universal-from-dynamical}\,(t) \quad \overset{\text{def}}{=} \tag{12.14}$$

$$t - \textbf{ephemeris-correction}\,(t)$$

The function **gregorian-date-difference** is given on page 54 and **gregorian-year-from-fixed** on page 53.

Figures 12.1 and 12.2 plot the difference between Universal and Dynamical time for ancient and modern eras, respectively.

To keep the numbers within reasonable bounds, our astronomical algorithms usually convert dates and times into "Julian centuries," that is, into the number (and fraction) of uniform-length centuries (36,525 days, measured in Dynamical Time) before or after noon on January 1, 2000 (Gregorian):

$$\textbf{julian-centuries}\,(t) \quad \overset{\text{def}}{=} \tag{12.15}$$

$$\tfrac{1}{36525} \times (\textbf{dynamical-from-universal}\,(t) - \textbf{j2000})$$

$$\textbf{j2000} \quad \overset{\text{def}}{=} \tag{12.16}$$

$$12^{\text{h}} + \textbf{fixed-from-gregorian}\left(\boxed{\;2000\;\vert\;\textbf{january}\;\vert\;1\;} \right)$$

To bring the time to noon from the R.D. moment of the start of the millennium,[5] we add a half day ($= 12^{\text{h}}$). The calendar conversion function **fixed-from-gregorian** was defined on page 51.

Sidereal time is discussed in the following section.

---

[5] Because Gregorian years in this book include a year 0, it is consistent to refer to January 2000 as the start of a Gregorian millennium.

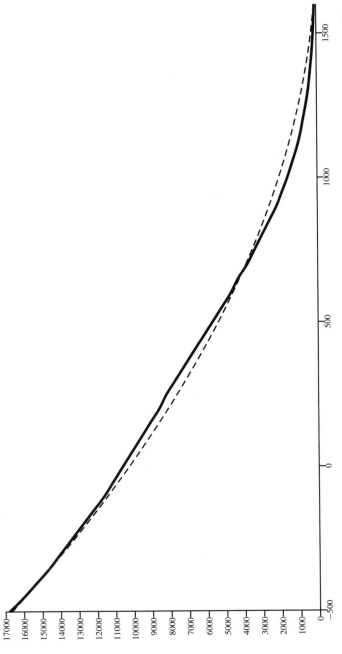

Figure 12.1 Difference between Dynamical (terrestrial) Time and Universal Time in atomic seconds plotted by Gregorian year. The dashed line shows the simple parabolic approximation $31 \left(\frac{y - 1820}{100} \right)^2 - 20$. Suggested by R. H. van Gent [personal communication] and based on [23, Chapter 14].

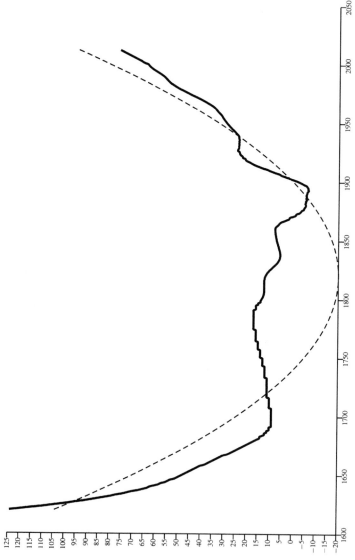

Figure 12.2 Difference between Dynamical (terrestrial) Time and Universal Time in atomic seconds plotted by Gregorian year. The dashed line shows the simple parabolic approximation $31 \left(\frac{y-1820}{100} \right)^2 - 20$. Data supplied by R. H. van Gent [personal communication] based on *Astronomical Almanac for the Year 2000*, Nautical Almanac Office, United States Naval Observatory, Washington, D.C., pp. K8–K9; the extrapolated values to 2012 were obtained from the National Earth Orientation Service.

12.3 The Day

> Some, like the Chaldees and the ancient Jews, define such a day as
> the time between two sunrises; others, like the Athenians, as that
> between two sunsets; or, like the Romans, from midnight to
> midnight; or like the Egyptians, from noon to noon.... It was
> necessary... to choose some mean and equal day, by which it
> would be possible to measure regularity of movement without
> trouble.
>
> —Nicolaus Copernicus: *De revolutionibus orbium coelestium*
> (1543)

The Earth rotates around its axis, causing the sun, moon, and stars to move
across the sky from east to west in the course of a day. The most obvious
way of measuring days is from sunrise to sunrise or from sunset to sunset
because sunrise and sunset are unmistakable. The Islamic, Hebrew, and Bahá'í
calendars begin their days at sunset, whereas the Hindu day starts and ends
with sunrise. The disadvantage of these methods of reckoning days is the wide
variation in the beginning and ending times. For example, in London, sunrise
occurs anywhere from 3:42 a.m. to 8:06 a.m., and sunset varies from 3:51 p.m.
to 8:21 p.m. By contrast, noon (the middle point of the day) and midnight
(the middle point of the night) vary only by about half an hour in London or
elsewhere. Thus, in many parts of the world, sunset or sunrise definitions of
the day have been superseded by a midnight-to-midnight day. For instance, the
Chinese in the twelfth century B.C.E. began their day with the crowing of the
rooster at 2 a.m., but more recently they have been using midnight. A noon-to-
noon day is also plausible and indeed is used in the julian day system described
in Section 1.5, but it has the disadvantage that the date changes in the middle
of the working day.

Even with solar days measured from midnight to midnight there are seasonal
variations. With the advent of mechanical clocks, introduced in the 1600s, the
use of *mean* solar time, in which a day is 24 equal-length hours,[6] was preferred
over the *apparent* time as measured by a sundial[7] (during the daytime, at least).
The elliptical orbit of the Earth and the obliquity (inclination) of the Earth's
equator with respect to its orbit cause a difference between the time the sun
crosses the (upper) meridian and 12 noon on a clock—the difference can be

---

[6] The 24-hour day is sometimes called a *nychthemeron* to distinguish it from the shorter period of
daylight.

[7] The hands on early mechanical clocks were imitating the movement of the shadow of the
gnomon (in the northern hemisphere where clocks were developed) as the sun crosses the sky.
This is the origin of our notion of "clockwise." See "The Last Word," *New Scientist*, March 27,
1999.

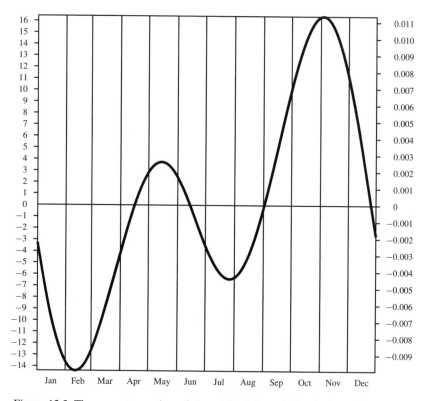

Figure 12.3 The current equation of time. The left vertical axis is marked in minutes and the right vertical axis is marked in fractions of a day (as computed by **equation-of-time**).

more than 16 minutes. This discrepancy is called the *equation of time*, where the term *equation* has its medieval meaning of "corrective factor."

The equation of time gives the difference between apparent midnight (when the sun crosses the lower meridian that passes through the nadir; this is virtually the same as the midpoint between sunset and sunrise) and mean midnight (0 hours on the 24-hour clock). Similarly, at other times of day the equation of time gives the difference between mean solar time and apparent solar time. In the past, when apparent time was the more readily available, the equation of time conventionally had the opposite sign.

The periodic pattern of the equation of time, shown in Figure 12.3, is sometimes inscribed as part of the analemma on sundials (usually in mirror image); the frontispiece for Appendix A (page 302) shows a three-dimensional image of the equation of time. During the twentieth century, the equation of time had zeroes around April 15, June 14, September 1, and December 25; it is at its maximum at the beginning of November and at its minimum in mid-February. The equation of time is needed for the French Revolutionary and Persian astronomical calendars, and a rough approximation is used in the modern Hindu calendars. We use the following function for the equation of time:

$$\textbf{equation-of-time}\,(t) \quad \overset{\text{def}}{=} \qquad\qquad (12.17)$$

$$\text{signum}\,(equation) \times \min\left\{|equation|\,, 12^{\text{h}}\right\}$$

where

c	$=$	$\textbf{julian-centuries}\,(t)$
longitude	$=$	$280.46645° + 36000.76983° \times c + 0.0003032° \times c^2$
anomaly	$=$	$357.52910° + 35999.05030° \times c - 0.0001559° \times c^2 - 0.00000048° \times c^3$
eccentricity	$=$	$0.016708617° - 0.000042037° \times c - 0.0000001236° \times c^2$
ε	$=$	$\textbf{obliquity}\,(t)$
y	$=$	$\tan^2\left(\dfrac{\varepsilon}{2}\right)$

$$
\begin{aligned}
equation \quad = \quad & \frac{1}{2 \times \pi} \times \Big(y \times \sin\,(2 \times longitude) + \\
& (-2 \times eccentricity \times \sin anomaly) + \\
& 4 \times eccentricity \times y \times \sin anomaly \\
& \times \cos\,(2 \times longitude) \\
& + \left(-0.5 \times y^2 \times \sin\,(4 \times longitude)\right) + \\
& \Big(-1.25 \times eccentricity^2 \\
& \qquad \times \sin\,(2 \times anomaly)\,\Big)\,\Big)
\end{aligned}
$$

The parameter t is an instant of time (R.D. day and fraction); it is converted to "Julian centuries," c. The function for obliquity is given below (page 180). The preceding approximation of the equation of time is not valid for dates that are many millennia in the past or future; hence, for robustness, we limit the calculated value to half a day.

The equation of time permits us to convert easily to and from apparent time:

$$\textbf{apparent-from-local}\,(t) \quad \overset{\text{def}}{=} \quad \text{(12.18)}$$

$$t + \textbf{equation-of-time}\,(t)$$

$$\textbf{local-from-apparent}\,(t) \quad \overset{\text{def}}{=} \quad \text{(12.19)}$$

$$t - \textbf{equation-of-time}\,(t)$$

The latter function is slightly inaccurate because the function **equation-of-time** takes local mean time, not apparent time, as its argument; the difference in the value of the equation of time in those few minutes is negligible, however.

Using the time conversion functions and those for the equation of time, we can find the true middle of the night (true, or apparent, midnight) or the true middle of the day (apparent noon) in standard time:

$$\textbf{midnight}\,(date, locale) \quad \overset{\text{def}}{=} \quad \text{(12.20)}$$

$$\textbf{standard-from-local}$$
$$(\textbf{local-from-apparent}\,(date)\,, locale)$$

$$\textbf{midday}\,(date, locale) \quad \overset{\text{def}}{=} \quad \text{(12.21)}$$

$$\textbf{standard-from-local}$$
$$\left(\textbf{local-from-apparent}\left(date + 12^{\text{h}}\right), locale\right)$$

A *sidereal day* is the time it takes for the Earth to rotate once around its axis, namely $23^{\text{h}}56^{\text{m}}4.0989^{\text{s}}$. In the course of one rotation on its axis, the Earth has also revolved somewhat in its orbit around the sun, and thus the sun is not quite in the same position as it was one rotation prior. This accounts for the difference of almost 4 minutes with respect to the solar day. The sidereal day is employed in the Hindu calendar.

Like the solar day, the sidereal day is not fixed; it is constantly growing longer. In practice, *sidereal time* is measured by the *hour angle* between the meridian (directly overhead) and the position of the First Point of Aries (see page 179). This definition of sidereal time is affected by precession of the equinoxes (see next page). Converting between mean solar and mean sidereal time amounts to evaluating a polynomial:

$$\textbf{sidereal-from-moment}\,(t) \stackrel{\text{def}}{=} \tag{12.22}$$

$$\Big(280.46061837° +$$

$$36525 \times 360.98564736629° \times c +$$

$$0.000387933° \times c^2 - \tfrac{1°}{38710000} \times c^3 \Big) \bmod 360$$

where

$$c = \frac{1}{36525} \times (t - \textbf{j2000})$$

The modern Hindu lunar calendar uses an approximation to this conversion.

12.4 The Year

> One who is capable of making astronomical calculations, but
> does not make them, is unworthy of being spoken to.
> —*Babylonian Talmud* (Sabbath, 75a)

The *vernal equinox* is the moment when the sun crosses the *true celestial equator* (the line in the sky above the Earth's equator) from south to north, on approximately March 20 each year. At that time the day and night are 12 hours each all over the world, and the Earth's axis of rotation is perpendicular to the line connecting the centers of the Earth and sun.[8] The point of intersection of the ecliptic, inclined from south to north, and the celestial equator is called the *true vernal equinox* or the "First Point of Aries," but it is currently in the constellation Pisces, not Aries, on account of a phenomenon called *precession of the equinoxes*. In its gyroscopic motion, the Earth's rotational axis migrates in a slow circle mainly as a consequence of the moon's pull on a nonspherical Earth. This nearly uniform motion causes the position of the equinoxes to move backwards along the ecliptic in a period of about 25,725 years. Precession has caused the vernal equinox to cease to coincide with the day when the sun enters Aries, as it did some 2300 years ago. Celestial longitude is measured from the First Point of Aries. As a consequence, the longitudes of the stars are constantly changing (in addition to the measurable motions of many of the "fixed" stars). Precession also causes the celestial pole to rotate slowly in a circular pattern. This is why the "pole star" has changed over the course of history; in 13,000 B.C.E., Vega was near the pole. In contrast, the Hindu calendar is

---

[8] Perhaps this perpendicularity explains the odd belief that fresh eggs balance more easily on the day of the vernal equinox. This turned into a minor craze in the United States; see Martin Gardner's "Notes of a Fringe Watcher," *The Skeptical Inquirer*, May/June 1996.

based on calculations in terms of *sidereal* longitude, which ignores precession and remains fixed against the backdrop of the stars.

The equator is currently inclined approximately $23.441884° = 23°26'21.448''$ with respect to the plane of revolution of the Earth around the sun. As a result, the sun, in the course of a year, traces a path through the stars that varies in distance from the celestial North Pole (which is near the star Polaris). This value, called *obliquity*, varies in a 100,000-year cycle, ranging from $24.2°$ 10,000 years ago to $22.6°$ in another 10,000 years. The ecliptic (the sun's apparent path through the constellations of the zodiac) is inclined the same $23.44°$ to the celestial equator (the plane passing through the center of the Earth, perpendicular to the axis of Earth's rotation). The following function gives an approximate value:

$$\textbf{obliquity}\,(t) \overset{\text{def}}{=} \tag{12.23}$$

$$23°26'21.448'' +$$
$$\Big(-46.8150'' \times c - 0.00059'' \times c^2 +$$
$$0.001813'' \times c^3 \,\Big)$$

where

$$c \quad = \quad \textbf{julian-centuries}\,(t)$$

In addition to precession, the pole of rotation of the Earth wobbles like a top in an 18.6-year period about its mean position. This effect is called *nutation* and is caused by the gravitational pull of the moon and sun on the unevenly shaped Earth. Nutation causes slight changes in the celestial latitudes and longitudes of stars and planets. It also causes a periodic variation in the lengths of the sidereal (and solar) day of up to about 0.01 second. *Mean sidereal time* smoothes out (subtracts) nutation, which can accumulate to a difference of about 1 second from actual sidereal time. The moon also causes small oscillations in the length of the day with periods ranging from 12 hours to 1 (sidereal) month, but these can safely be ignored.

The seasons are governed by the *tropical year*, which is the time it takes for the mean sun to return in its apparent path to the same position relative to the celestial equator. The precise value depends on which starting point is chosen. The mean length of a tropical year is today defined with respect to a "dynamical" equinox [16]; its current value is 365.242177 mean solar days, and it is decreasing by about 1.3×10^{-5} solar days per century. We use the following value in our calculations for estimation purposes:

$$\textbf{mean-tropical-year} \overset{\text{def}}{=} 365.242189 \tag{12.24}$$

Figure 12.4 compares the fluctuating equinox-to-equinox and solstice-to-solstice year lengths, measured in mean solar days, with the mean year length used in various arithmetical calendars.

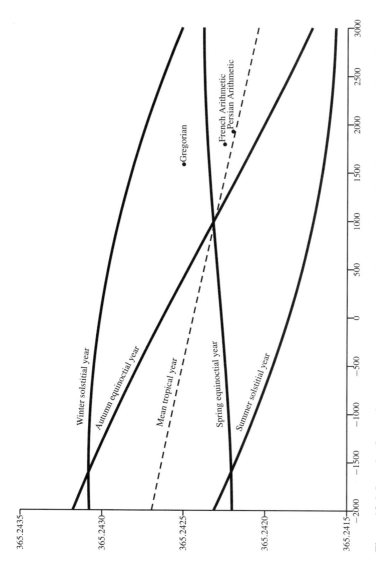

Figure 12.4 Length of year, in contemporaneous mean solar days, plotted by Gregorian year. (The value for the Julian/Coptic/Ethiopic calendars, 365.25, is omitted because it is far above the values plotted.) Suggested by R. H. van Gent [personal communication] and based on formulas from [13, Chapter 27] and the parabolic approximation from Figure 12.1.

181

A *sidereal year* is the time it takes for the Earth to revolve once around the sun, or for the (mean) sun to return to the same position relative to the background of the fixed stars. The sidereal year is 365.25636 days, or about 20 minutes more than the tropical. The modern Hindu calendar (Chapter 17) uses approximations of the sidereal and tropical year.

To determine the time of equinoxes or solstices, as required for the French Revolutionary (Chapter 15), Chinese (Chapter 16), Persian astronomical (Chapter 13), and proposed Bahá'í (Section 12.7) calendars, we need to be able to calculate the longitude of the sun at any given time. The following function takes an astronomical time, given as an R.D. moment t, converts it to Julian centuries, sums a long sequence of periodic terms, and adds terms to compensate for aberration (the effect of the sun's apparent motion while its light is traveling towards Earth) and nutation (caused by the wobble of the Earth):

$$\textbf{solar-longitude}\,(t) \quad \overset{\text{def}}{=} \qquad\qquad\qquad\qquad (12.25)$$

$$\big(\textit{longitude} + \textbf{aberration}\,(t)\; + \textbf{nutation}\,(t) \big)\; \bmod\; 360$$

where

$$
\begin{aligned}
c &= \textbf{julian-centuries}\,(t) \\[4pt]
\textit{longitude} &= 282.7771834° + 36000.76953744 \times c + \\
&\quad\; 0.000005729577951308232 \\
&\quad\; \times \sum (\tilde{x} \times \sin (\tilde{y} + \tilde{z} \times c)) \\[4pt]
\tilde{x} &= \text{(see Table 12.1)} \\[4pt]
\tilde{y} &= \text{(see Table 12.1)} \\[4pt]
\tilde{z} &= \text{(see Table 12.1)}
\end{aligned}
$$

To avoid cluttering the page with subscripts, we use vector notation, with the intention that the operations within the sum are performed on like-indexed elements of $\tilde{x}$, $\tilde{y}$, and $\tilde{z}$, displayed in Table 12.1. This function is accurate to within 10 minutes of arc for current times.

The effect of nutation on longitude is approximately

$$\textbf{nutation}\,(t) \quad \overset{\text{def}}{=} \qquad\qquad\qquad\qquad (12.26)$$

$$(-0.004778° \times \sin A) + \big(-0.0003667° \times \sin B \big)$$

where

$$
\begin{aligned}
c &= \textbf{julian-centuries}\,(t) \\[4pt]
A &= 124.90° - 1934.134° \times c + 0.002063° \times c^2 \\[4pt]
B &= 201.11° + 72001.5377° \times c + 0.00057° \times c^2
\end{aligned}
$$

Table 12.1 *Arguments for **solar-longitude** (page 182).*

$\tilde{x}$	$\tilde{y}$	$\tilde{z}$	$\tilde{x}$	$\tilde{y}$	$\tilde{z}$
403406	270.54861	0.9287892	195207	340.19128	35999.1376958
119433	63.91854	35999.4089666	112392	331.26220	35998.7287385
3891	317.843	71998.20261	2819	86.631	71998.4403
1721	240.052	36000.35726	660	310.26	71997.4812
350	247.23	32964.4678	334	260.87	−19.4410
314	297.82	445267.1117	268	343.14	45036.8840
242	166.79	3.1008	234	81.53	22518.4434
158	3.50	−19.9739	132	132.75	65928.9345
129	182.95	9038.0293	114	162.03	3034.7684
99	29.8	33718.148	93	266.4	3034.448
86	249.2	−2280.773	78	157.6	29929.992
72	257.8	31556.493	68	185.1	149.588
64	69.9	9037.750	46	8	107997.405
38	197.1	−4444.176	37	250.4	151.771
32	65.3	67555.316	29	162.7	31556.080
28	341.5	−4561.540	27	291.6	107996.706
27	98.5	1221.655	25	146.7	62894.167
24	110	31437.369	21	5.2	14578.298
21	342.6	−31931.757	20	230.9	34777.243
18	256.1	1221.999	17	45.3	62894.511
14	242.9	−4442.039	13	115.2	107997.909
13	151.8	119.066	13	285.3	16859.071
12	53.3	−4.578	10	126.6	26895.292
10	205.7	−39.127	10	85.9	12297.536
10	146.1	90073.778			

Aberration—the effect of the sun's moving about 20.47 seconds of arc during the 8 minutes its light is en route to Earth—is calculated as follows:

$$\textbf{aberration}\,(t) \overset{\text{def}}{=} \tag{12.27}$$

$$0.0000974° \times \cos\,(177.63° + 35999.01848° \times c) - 0.005575°$$

where

$$c = \textbf{julian-centuries}\,(t)$$

We determine the time of an equinox or solstice by giving a generic function that takes a moment t (in U.T.) and number of degrees ϕ, indicating the season, and searches for the moment when the longitude of the sun is next ϕ degrees.

Table 12.2 *The solar longitudes and approximate current dates of equinoxes and solstices along with approximate length of the following season.*

Name	Solar Longitude	Approximate Date	Season Length
Vernal (spring) Equinox	0°	March 20	92.76 days
Summer Solstice	90°	June 21	93.65 days
Autumnal (fall) Equinox	180°	September 22–23	89.84 days
Winter Solstice	270°	December 21–22	88.99 days

The search is bisection (see page 22) within an interval beginning 5 days before the estimate τ (or at the given moment, whichever comes later) and ending 5 days after. The process terminates when the time is ascertained within a hundred-thousandth of a day ($\varepsilon \approx 0.9$ seconds):

$$\textbf{solar-longitude-after}\,(t, \phi) \;\overset{\text{def}}{=} \tag{12.28}$$

$$\underset{x \in [l:u]}{\overset{u-l<\varepsilon}{\text{MIN}}} \left\{ \left(\left(\textbf{solar-longitude}\,(x) - \phi \right) \bmod 360 \right) < 180° \right\}$$

where

$$\varepsilon \;=\; 10^{-5}$$

$$rate \;=\; \frac{\textbf{mean-tropical-year}}{360°}$$

$$\tau \;=\; t + rate \times ((\phi - \textbf{solar-longitude}\,(t)) \bmod 360)$$

$$l \;=\; \max\{t, \tau - 5\}$$

$$u \;=\; \tau + 5$$

The equinoxes and solstices occur when the sun's longitude is a multiple of 90°. Specifically, Table 12.2 gives the names, solar longitudes, and approximate Gregorian dates, and the following constants define them:

$$\textbf{spring} \;\overset{\text{def}}{=}\; 0° \tag{12.29}$$

$$\textbf{summer} \;\overset{\text{def}}{=}\; 90° \tag{12.30}$$

$$\textbf{autumn} \;\overset{\text{def}}{=}\; 180° \tag{12.31}$$

$$\textbf{winter} \;\overset{\text{def}}{=}\; 270° \tag{12.32}$$

To use **solar-longitude-after** to determine, say, the standard time of the winter solstice in Urbana, Illinois, we write

urbana-winter (*g-year*) $\stackrel{\text{def}}{=}$ (12.33)

standard-from-universal

$\Big($ **solar-longitude-after**

$\Big($ **fixed-from-gregorian**

$\Big($ | *g-year* | **january** | 1 | $\Big)$,

winter $\Big)$,

urbana $\Big)$

For year 2000 this gives us the answer R.D. 730,475.31751, which is 7:37:13 a.m. on December 21.

12.5 The Month

> You have already seen... how much computation is involved, how many additions and subtractions are still necessary, despite our having exerted ourselves greatly to invent approximations that do not require complicated calculations. For the path of the moon is convoluted. Hence wise men have said: the sun knows its way, the moon does not....
>
> —Moses Maimonides: *Mishneh Torah,*
> *Book of Seasons* (1178)

The *new moon* occurs when the sun and moon have the same longitude; it is not necessarily the time of their closest encounter, as viewed from Earth, because the orbits of the Earth and moon are not coplanar. The time from new moon (*conjunction* of sun and moon) to new moon, a *lunation*, is called the *synodic month*. Its value today ranges from approximately 29.27 to 29.84 days [14], with a mean currently of about 29.530588 mean solar days, which translates into

mean-synodic-month $\stackrel{\text{def}}{=}$ 29.530588853   (12.34)

in days of 86,400 atomic seconds. Approximations of this value are used in lunar and lunisolar calendars, except observation-based calendars and the Chinese calendar, which uses actual values in its determinations. The mean and true times of the new moon can differ by up to about 14 hours. Figure 12.5 compares the changing length of the month with the value used on several arithmetic calendars.

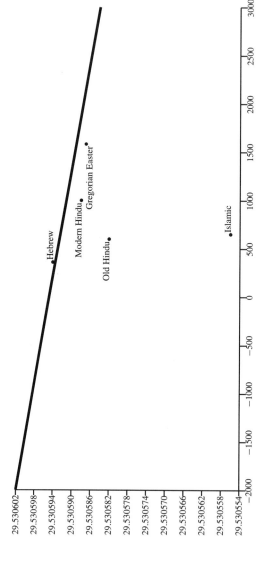

Figure 12.5 Length of synodic month, in contemporaneous mean solar days, plotted by Gregorian year. (The value for Orthodox Easter, 29.530851, is omitted because it is far above the values plotted.) Suggested by R. H. van Gent [personal communication] and based on data from [13, Chapter 49] and [23, Chapter 14].

The synodic month is not constant but is decreasing in mean length by about 3.6×10^{-7} solar days per century (though it is *increasing* in length by about 0.021 atomic seconds per century). The net effect of the decreases in synodic month and tropical year is to increase the number of months from its current value of about 12.3682670 per year by 0.3×10^{-6} months per century.

The *sidereal month* is the time it takes the moon to make one revolution around the Earth. Its mean value is 27.32166 days. In the interim, the Earth has moved in its orbit around the sun, and thus the difference in longitude between the sun and moon has increased, which is why the synodic month is longer. The mean values of these types of month should satisfy the equation

$$\frac{1}{\text{sidereal month}} - \frac{1}{\text{synodic month}} = \frac{1}{\text{sidereal year}}.$$

The *anomalistic month* is the time between consecutive perigees (points at which the moon is closest to Earth). The anomalistic month averages 27.55455 days. Approximations to these values are used in calculating the position of the moon for the modern Hindu lunisolar calendar.

We also use a notion of a *solar month*, the time for the sun's position in the sky to traverse one sign of the zodiac ($30°$ of longitude). Its mean value is one-twelfth of a solar year and ranges from 29.44 days in Northern Hemisphere winter (to traverse Capricorn) to 31.43 days in Northern Hemisphere summer. Solar months play an important rôle in the Chinese calendar (which uses tropical longitude) and the Hindu calendar (which uses sidereal longitude).

The time of new moon can be determined directly using sums of periodic terms. We use the following function for the moment (in U.T.) of the nth new moon after (before, if n is negative) the first new moon after R.D. 0, which was on January 11, 1 (Gregorian):

$$\textbf{nth-new-moon}\,(n) \quad \overset{\text{def}}{=} \quad \tag{12.35}$$

$$\textbf{universal-from-dynamical}$$

$$(approx + correction + extra + additional)$$

where

$$k \qquad = \qquad n - 24724$$

$$c \qquad = \qquad \frac{k}{1236.85}$$

approx $\quad = \quad$ 730125.59765 +

mean-synodic-month $\times$ 1236.85 $\times$ c

$+ 0.0001337 \times c^2 - 0.000000150 \times c^3 +$

$0.00000000073 \times c^4$

$E \quad = \quad 1 - 0.002516 \times c - 0.0000074 \times c^2$

solar-anomaly $\quad = \quad 2.5534° + 1236.85 \times 29.10535669° \times c$

$- 0.0000218° \times c^2 - 0.00000011° \times c^3$

lunar-anomaly $\quad = \quad 201.5643° +$

$385.81693528° \times 1236.85° \times c +$

$0.0107438° \times c^2 + 0.00001239° \times c^3 -$

$0.000000058° \times c^4$

moon-argument $\quad = \quad 160.7108° +$

$390.67050274 \times 1236.85° \times c -$

$0.0016341° \times c^2 - 0.00000227° \times c^3 +$

$0.000000011° \times c^4$

$\Omega \quad = \quad 124.7746 +$

$(-1.56375580 \times 1236.85) \times c$

$+ 0.0020691 \times c^2 + 0.00000215 \times c^3$

correction $\quad = \quad (-.00017 \times \sin \Omega) +$

$\sum \left(\tilde{v} \times E^{\tilde{w}} \times \sin \left(\tilde{x} \times \textit{solar-anomaly} + \right.\right.$

$\tilde{y} \times \textit{lunar-anomaly} +$

$\left.\left.\tilde{z} \times \textit{moon-argument} \right) \right)$

extra $\quad = \quad 0.000325°$

$\times \sin \left(299.77° + 132.8475848° \times c - \right.$

$\left. 0.009173° \times c^2 \right)$

additional $\quad = \quad \sum \left(\tilde{i} \times \sin \left(\tilde{i} + \tilde{j} \times k \right) \right)$

$\tilde{v} \quad = \quad$ (see Table 12.3)

$\tilde{w} \quad = \quad$ (see Table 12.3)

Table 12.3 *Arguments for **nth-new-moon** (page 189).*

$\tilde{v}$	$\tilde{w}$	$\tilde{x}$	$\tilde{y}$	$\tilde{z}$	$\tilde{v}$	$\tilde{w}$	$\tilde{x}$	$\tilde{y}$	$\tilde{z}$
−0.40720	0	0	1	0	0.17241	1	1	0	0
0.01608	0	0	2	0	0.01039	0	0	0	2
0.00739	1	−1	1	0	−0.00514	1	1	1	0
0.00208	2	2	0	0	−0.00111	0	0	1	−2
−0.00057	0	0	1	2	0.00056	1	1	2	0
−0.00042	0	0	3	0	0.00042	1	1	0	2
0.00038	1	1	0	−2	−0.00024	1	−1	2	0
−0.00007	0	2	1	0	0.00004	0	0	2	−2
0.00004	0	3	0	0	0.00003	0	1	1	−2
0.00003	0	0	2	2	−0.00003	0	1	1	2
0.00003	0	−1	1	2	−0.00002	0	−1	1	−2
−0.00002	0	1	3	0	0.00002	0	0	4	0

Table 12.4 *Arguments for **nth-new-moon** (page 189).*

$\tilde{i}$	$\tilde{j}$	$\tilde{l}$	$\tilde{i}$	$\tilde{j}$	$\tilde{l}$
251.88	0.016321	0.000165	251.83	26.641886	0.000164
349.42	36.412478	0.000126	84.66	18.206239	0.000110
141.74	53.303771	0.000062	207.14	2.453732	0.000060
154.84	7.306860	0.000056	34.52	27.261239	0.000047
207.19	0.121824	0.000042	291.34	1.844379	0.000040
161.72	24.198154	0.000037	239.56	25.513099	0.000035
331.55	3.592518	0.000023			

$$\tilde{x} \quad = \quad \text{(see Table 12.3)}$$

$$\tilde{y} \quad = \quad \text{(see Table 12.3)}$$

$$\tilde{z} \quad = \quad \text{(see Table 12.3)}$$

$$\tilde{i} \quad = \quad \text{(see Table 12.4)}$$

$$\tilde{j} \quad = \quad \text{(see Table 12.4)}$$

$$\tilde{l} \quad = \quad \text{(see Table 12.4)}$$

There were 24,724 months between January 1 C.E. and January 2000 C.E. upon which time this function is centered. The value of E depends on the eccentricity of Earth's elliptical orbit; Ω is the longitude of the moon's "ascending node."

To find a new moon preceding a given date or moment, we can use

$$\textbf{new-moon-before}\,(t) \quad \stackrel{\text{def}}{=} \tag{12.36}$$

$$\textbf{nth-new-moon}\left(\underset{k \geq n-1}{\text{MAX}}\ \left\{\textbf{nth-new-moon}\,(k) < t\right\}\right)$$

where

$$t_0 \quad = \quad \textbf{nth-new-moon}\,(0)$$

$$\phi \quad = \quad \textbf{lunar-phase}\,(t)$$

$$n \quad = \quad \text{round}\left(\frac{t - t_0}{\textbf{mean-synodic-month}} - \frac{\phi}{360°}\right)$$

For the following new moon, we have

$$\textbf{new-moon-after}\,(t) \quad \stackrel{\text{def}}{=} \tag{12.37}$$

$$\textbf{nth-new-moon}\left(\underset{k \geq n}{\text{MIN}}\ \left\{\textbf{nth-new-moon}\,(k) \geq t\right\}\right)$$

where

$$t_0 \quad = \quad \textbf{nth-new-moon}\,(0)$$

$$\phi \quad = \quad \textbf{lunar-phase}\,(t)$$

$$n \quad = \quad \text{round}\left(\frac{t - t_0}{\textbf{mean-synodic-month}} - \frac{\phi}{360°}\right)$$

Alternatively, one can determine the time of new moon indirectly from the longitude of the moon. The moon's longitude is significantly more difficult to compute than that of the Sun, because it is affected in a nonnegligible way by the pull of the Sun, Venus, and Jupiter. The function for longitude of the moon is given by

$$\textbf{lunar-longitude}\,(t) \quad \stackrel{\text{def}}{=} \tag{12.38}$$

$$\big(\ \textit{mean-moon} + \textit{correction} + \textit{venus} + \textit{jupiter} +$$

$$\textit{flat-earth} + \textbf{nutation}\,(t)\ \big) \ \bmod\ 360$$

where

$$c \quad = \quad \textbf{julian-centuries}\,(t)$$

$$\textit{mean-moon} \quad = \quad 218.3164591° +$$

$$481267.88134236° \times c - .0013268° \times c^2$$

$$+\ \frac{1°}{538841} \times c^3 - \frac{1°}{65194000} \times c^4$$

$$
\begin{aligned}
\textit{elongation} \quad =\quad & 297.8502042° + \\
& 445267.1115168° \times c - .00163° \times c^2 + \\
& \tfrac{1°}{545868} \times c^3 - \tfrac{1°}{113065000} \times c^4
\end{aligned}
$$

$$
\begin{aligned}
\textit{solar-anomaly} \quad =\quad & 357.5291092° + \\
& 35999.0502909° \times c - .0001536° \times c^2 + \\
& \tfrac{1°}{24490000} \times c^3
\end{aligned}
$$

$$
\begin{aligned}
\textit{lunar-anomaly} \quad =\quad & 134.9634114° + \\
& 477198.8676313° \times c + 0.008997° \times c^2 \\
& + \tfrac{1°}{69699} \times c^3 - \tfrac{1°}{14712000} \times c^4
\end{aligned}
$$

$$
\begin{aligned}
\textit{moon-node} \quad =\quad & 93.2720993° + \\
& 483202.0175273° \times c - .0034029° \times c^2 \\
& - \tfrac{1°}{3526000} \times c^3 + \tfrac{1°}{863310000} \times c^4
\end{aligned}
$$

$$
E \quad =\quad 1 - 0.002516 \times c - 0.0000074 \times c^2
$$

$$
\begin{aligned}
\textit{correction} \quad =\quad & \tfrac{1°}{1000000} \\
& \times \sum \Big(\tilde{v} \times E^{|\tilde{x}|} \\
& \qquad \times \sin \big(\tilde{w} \times \textit{elongation} + \\
& \qquad\qquad \tilde{x} \times \textit{solar-anomaly} + \\
& \qquad\qquad \tilde{y} \times \textit{lunar-anomaly} + \\
& \qquad\qquad \tilde{z} \times \textit{moon-node} \big) \Big)
\end{aligned}
$$

$$
\textit{venus} \quad =\quad \frac{3958°}{1000000} \times \sin(119.75 + c \times 131.849)
$$

$$
\textit{jupiter} \quad =\quad \frac{318°}{1000000} \times \sin(53.09 + c \times 479264.29)
$$

$$
\begin{aligned}
\textit{flat-earth} \quad =\quad & \tfrac{1962°}{1000000} \\
& \times \sin(\textit{mean-moon} - \textit{moon-node})
\end{aligned}
$$

$$
\begin{aligned}
\tilde{v} \quad &=\quad \text{(see Table 12.5)} \\
\tilde{w} \quad &=\quad \text{(see Table 12.5)} \\
\tilde{x} \quad &=\quad \text{(see Table 12.5)} \\
\tilde{y} \quad &=\quad \text{(see Table 12.5)} \\
\tilde{z} \quad &=\quad \text{(see Table 12.5)}
\end{aligned}
$$

Table 12.5 *Arguments for **lunar-longitude** (page 192).*

$\tilde{v}$	$\tilde{w}$	$\tilde{x}$	$\tilde{y}$	$\tilde{z}$	$\tilde{v}$	$\tilde{w}$	$\tilde{x}$	$\tilde{y}$	$\tilde{z}$
6288774	0	0	1	0	1274027	2	0	−1	0
658314	2	0	0	0	213618	0	0	2	0
−185116	0	1	0	0	−114332	0	0	0	2
58793	2	0	−2	0	57066	2	−1	−1	0
53322	2	0	1	0	45758	2	−1	0	0
−40923	0	1	−1	0	−34720	1	0	0	0
−30383	0	1	1	0	15327	2	0	0	−2
−12528	0	0	1	2	10980	0	0	1	−2
10675	4	0	−1	0	10034	0	0	3	0
8548	4	0	−2	0	−7888	2	1	−1	0
−6766	2	1	0	0	−5163	1	0	−1	0
4987	1	1	0	0	4036	2	−1	1	0
3994	2	0	2	0	3861	4	0	0	0
3665	2	0	−3	0	−2689	0	1	−2	0
−2602	2	0	−1	2	2390	2	−1	−2	0
−2348	1	0	1	0	2236	2	−2	0	0
−2120	0	1	2	0	−2069	0	2	0	0
2048	2	−2	−1	0	−1773	2	0	1	−2
−1595	2	0	0	2	1215	4	−1	−1	0
−1110	0	0	2	2	−892	3	0	−1	0
−810	2	1	1	0	759	4	−1	−2	0
−713	0	2	−1	0	−700	2	2	−1	0
691	2	1	−2	0	596	2	−1	0	−2
549	4	0	1	0	537	0	0	4	0
520	4	−1	0	0	−487	1	0	−2	0
−399	2	1	0	−2	−381	0	0	2	−2
351	1	1	1	0	−340	3	0	−2	0
330	4	0	−3	0	327	2	−1	2	0
−323	0	2	1	0	299	1	1	−1	0
294	2	0	3	0					

Using **solar-longitude** and **lunar-longitude**, one can determine the phase of the moon—defined as the difference in longitudes of the sun and moon—at any moment t:

$$\textbf{lunar-phase}\,(t) \;\overset{\text{def}}{=} \tag{12.39}$$

$$\big(\,\textbf{lunar-longitude}\,(t)\; -$$

$$\textbf{solar-longitude}\,(t)\,\big) \;\bmod\; 360$$

To determine the time of the new moon, or other phases of the moon, we search for a time before moment t when the solar and lunar longitudes differ by the desired amount, ϕ:

$$\textbf{lunar-phase-before}\,(t, \phi) \quad \stackrel{\text{def}}{=} \tag{12.40}$$

$$\operatorname*{MIN}_{x\in[l:u]}^{u-l<\varepsilon} \left\{ ((\textbf{lunar-phase}\,(x) - \phi) \bmod 360) < 180° \right\}$$

where

$$\varepsilon = 10^{-5}$$

$$\tau = t - \tfrac{1}{360} \times \textbf{mean-synodic-month}$$
$$\times ((\textbf{lunar-phase}\,(t) - \phi) \bmod 360°)$$

$$l = \tau - 2$$

$$u = \min\{t, \tau + 2\}$$

The bisection search is centered around the last time the *mean* moon had that phase and is performed until an accuracy of ε is obtained. That moment τ is calculated by a variant of equation (1.42) based on the average rate at which the phase changes 1 degree.

The search for the next time the moon has a given phase is analogous:

$$\textbf{lunar-phase-after}\,(t, \phi) \quad \stackrel{\text{def}}{=} \tag{12.41}$$

$$\operatorname*{MIN}_{x\in[l:u]}^{u-l<\varepsilon} \left\{ ((\textbf{lunar-phase}\,(x) - \phi) \bmod 360) < 180° \right\}$$

where

$$\varepsilon = 10^{-5}$$

$$\tau = t + \tfrac{1}{360} \times \textbf{mean-synodic-month}$$
$$\times ((\phi - \textbf{lunar-phase}\,(t)) \bmod 360°)$$

$$l = \max\{t, \tau - 2\}$$

$$u = \tau + 2$$

For the computation of specific phases of the moon, new moon, first quarter, full moon, and last quarter, we can use **lunar-phase-before** and **lunar-phase-after**, along with the following set of constants:

$$\textbf{new} \stackrel{\text{def}}{=} 0° \tag{12.42}$$

$$\textbf{full} \stackrel{\text{def}}{=} 180° \tag{12.43}$$

$$\text{\textbf{first-quarter}} \overset{\text{def}}{=} 90° \tag{12.44}$$

$$\text{\textbf{last-quarter}} \overset{\text{def}}{=} 270° \tag{12.45}$$

For obscure reasons, when four full moons occur within one solar season (from equinox to solstice or solstice to equinox), the third is termed a *blue moon*; see [17]. This event is similar to the conditions for a leap month on the Chinese calendar and Hindu lunisolar calendars, which mandate a leap month whenever two new moons occur within the same solar month.

Lunar latitude is computed in nearly the same way as longitude:

$$\text{\textbf{lunar-latitude}} (t) \overset{\text{def}}{=} \tag{12.46}$$

$$(latitude + venus + flat\text{-}earth + extra) \mod 360$$

where

$$c = \text{\textbf{julian-centuries}} (t)$$

$$
\begin{aligned}
longitude = \ & 218.3164591° + \\
& 481267.88134236° \times c - .0013268° \times c^2 \\
& + \tfrac{1°}{538841} \times c^3 - \tfrac{1°}{65194000} \times c^4
\end{aligned}
$$

$$
\begin{aligned}
elongation = \ & 297.8502042° + \\
& 445267.1115168° \times c - .00163° \times c^2 + \\
& \tfrac{1°}{545868} \times c^3 - \tfrac{1°}{113065000} \times c^4
\end{aligned}
$$

$$
\begin{aligned}
solar\text{-}anomaly = \ & 357.5291092° + \\
& 35999.0502909° \times c - .0001536° \times c^2 + \\
& \tfrac{1°}{24490000} \times c^3
\end{aligned}
$$

$$
\begin{aligned}
lunar\text{-}anomaly = \ & 134.9634114° + \\
& 477198.8676313° \times c + 0.008997° \times c^2 \\
& + \tfrac{1°}{69699} \times c^3 - \tfrac{1°}{14712000} \times c^4
\end{aligned}
$$

$$
\begin{aligned}
moon\text{-}node = \ & 93.2720993° + \\
& 483202.0175273° \times c - .0034029° \times c^2 \\
& - \tfrac{1°}{3526000} \times c^3 + \tfrac{1°}{863310000} \times c^4
\end{aligned}
$$

$$E = 1 - 0.002516 \times c - 0.0000074 \times c^2$$

$$latitude \quad = \quad \frac{1°}{1000000}$$
$$\times \sum \left(\tilde{v} \times E^{|\tilde{x}|} \right.$$
$$\times \sin \left(\tilde{w} \times elongation + \right.$$
$$\tilde{x} \times solar\text{-}anomaly +$$
$$\tilde{y} \times lunar\text{-}anomaly +$$
$$\left. \left. \tilde{z} \times moon\text{-}node \right) \right)$$

$$venus \quad = \quad \frac{175°}{1000000}$$
$$\times \left(\sin (119.75° + c \times 131.849° + moon\text{-}node) \right.$$
$$\left. + \sin \left(119.75° + c \times 131.849° - moon\text{-}node \right) \right)$$

$$flat\text{-}earth \quad = \quad \frac{-2235°}{1000000} \times \sin longitude +$$
$$\frac{127°}{1000000}$$
$$\times \sin (longitude - lunar\text{-}anomaly)$$
$$+ \frac{-115°}{1000000}$$
$$\times \sin (longitude + lunar\text{-}anomaly)$$

$$extra \quad = \quad \frac{382°}{1000000}$$
$$\times \sin (313.45° + c \times 481266.484°)$$

$\tilde{v} \quad = \quad$ (see Table 12.6)

$\tilde{w} \quad = \quad$ (see Table 12.6)

$\tilde{x} \quad = \quad$ (see Table 12.6)

$\tilde{y} \quad = \quad$ (see Table 12.6)

$\tilde{z} \quad = \quad$ (see Table 12.6)

Finally, the altitude of the moon above the horizon at any given time depends on the ecliptical position of the moon, on the time, and on the viewing location:

$$\textbf{lunar-altitude}\,(t, locale) \quad \overset{\text{def}}{=} \quad \text{(12.47)}$$

$$((altitude + 180°) \bmod 360) - 180°$$

where

$$\phi \quad = \quad locale_{\text{latitude}}$$
$$\psi \quad = \quad locale_{\text{longitude}}$$

Table 12.6 *Arguments for **lunar-latitude** (page 195).*

$\tilde{v}$	$\tilde{w}$	$\tilde{x}$	$\tilde{y}$	$\tilde{z}$	$\tilde{v}$	$\tilde{w}$	$\tilde{x}$	$\tilde{y}$	$\tilde{z}$
5128122	0	0	0	1	280602	0	0	1	1
277693	0	0	1	−1	173237	2	0	0	−1
55413	2	0	−1	1	46271	2	0	−1	−1
32573	2	0	0	1	17198	0	0	2	1
9266	2	0	1	−1	8822	0	0	2	−1
8216	2	−1	0	−1	4324	2	0	−2	−1
4200	2	0	1	1	−3359	2	1	0	−1
2463	2	−1	−1	1	2211	2	−1	0	1
2065	2	−1	−1	−1	−1870	0	1	−1	−1
1828	4	0	−1	−1	−1794	0	1	0	1
−1749	0	0	0	3	−1565	0	1	−1	1
−1491	1	0	0	1	−1475	0	1	1	1
−1410	0	1	1	−1	−1344	0	1	0	−1
−1335	1	0	0	−1	1107	0	0	3	1
1021	4	0	0	−1	833	4	0	−1	1
777	0	0	1	−3	671	4	0	−2	1
607	2	0	0	−3	596	2	0	2	−1
491	2	−1	1	−1	−451	2	0	−2	1
439	0	0	3	−1	422	2	0	2	1
421	2	0	−3	−1	−366	2	1	−1	1
−351	2	1	0	1	331	4	0	0	1
315	2	−1	1	1	302	2	−2	0	−1
−283	0	0	1	3	−229	2	1	1	−1
223	1	1	0	−1	223	1	1	0	1
−220	0	1	−2	−1	−220	2	1	−1	−1
−185	1	0	1	1	181	2	−1	−2	−1
−177	0	1	2	1	176	4	0	−2	−1
166	4	−1	−1	−1	−164	1	0	1	−1
132	4	0	1	−1	−119	1	0	−2	−1
115	4	−1	0	−1	107	2	−2	0	1

ε = **obliquity** (t)

λ = **lunar-longitude** (t)

β = **lunar-latitude** (t)

α = **arctan**

$$\left(\frac{\sin \lambda \times \cos \varepsilon - \tan \beta \times \sin \varepsilon}{\cos \lambda}, \left\lfloor \frac{\lambda}{90°} \right\rfloor + 1 \right)$$

$$\delta \quad = \quad \arcsin\,(\sin\beta \times \cos\varepsilon + \cos\beta \times \sin\varepsilon \times \sin\lambda)$$

$$\theta_0 \quad = \quad \textbf{sidereal-from-moment}\,(t)$$

$$H \quad = \quad (\theta_0 + \psi - \alpha)\ \bmod\ 360$$

$$\mathit{altitude} \quad = \quad \arcsin\,(\sin\phi \times \sin\delta + \cos\phi \times \cos\delta \times \cos H)$$

Here α is the moon's right ascension, δ, its declination, ε is the obliquity of the ecliptic, and H is the local sidereal hour angle. The result ranges from $-180°$ up to, but not including, $180°$.

12.6 Times of Day

> There is a time for the mountain top and a time for the market, a
> time for social withdrawal and a time for social participation.
> —Balinese proverb

Our civil day is divided into 24 hours, each hour is divided into 60 minutes, and each minute is divided into 60 seconds (if we assume no leap second is added to that day). Accordingly, we represent the time of day as a triple

hour : *minute* : *second*

where *hour* is an integer in the range 0 to 23, *minute* is an integer in the range 0 to 59, and *second* is a nonnegative real number less than 60. Other cultures subdivided the day differently. For instance, the ancient Egyptians—as well as the Greeks and Romans in classical times—divided the day and night *separately* into 12 equal "hours" each. Because, except at the equator, the length of daylight and nighttime varies with the seasons, the length of such daytime and nighttime hours also vary with the season. These seasonally varying *temporal* (or *seasonal*) hours (*horæ temporales*) are still used for ritual purposes among Jews. In London, for example, the length of such an hour varies from about 39 minutes in December to about 83 minutes in June.

From the first century B.C.E. until 1670, Chinese astronomers divided the day, which began at midnight, into 12 *shih* and also into 100 *ko*. The Hindus divide the civil day into 60 *ghaṭikás* of 24-minute duration, each of which is divided into 60 *palas*, each of which is 24 seconds. They also divide the sidereal day into 60 *nádís*, each *nádí* into 60 *vinadis*, and each of the latter into 6 *asus*. The Hebrew calendar divides hours into 1080 *ḥalaqim* (parts) of $3\frac{1}{3}$ seconds each; each part is divided into 76 *regaim* (moments). The French Revolutionary calendar divided each day into 10 "hours," each "hour" into 100 "minutes," and each "minute" into 100 "seconds."

We occasionally need the time of sunrise or sunset for a locale. Astronomical sunrise is nowadays defined as the time of first appearance of the upper limb of the sun; sunset is the moment of disappearance, again of the upper limb. This is also the definition used for calendars that begin their day at sunset (for example, the Islamic and Hebrew calendars) or sunrise (the Hindu calendar, for example). Because of the asymmetry involved, on the day of the equinox the intervals from sunrise to sunset and from sunset to sunrise differ by a few minutes. This discrepancy is further compounded by atmospheric refraction that makes the sun visible 2 to 3 minutes before a straight line to the sun is actually above the horizon and keeps the sun visible for a few minutes after it is geometrically below the horizon at sunset time.

We first write a general function to calculate the moment, in local mean time, when the "depression angle" of the geometric center of the sun is α degrees below the *geometric horizon* (at sea level) at *locale* around fixed moment *approx*, either in the morning (eastern horizon) or the evening (western horizon):

$$\textbf{moment-from-depression}\,(approx, locale, \alpha) \quad \overset{\text{def}}{=} \quad (12.48)$$

$$
\begin{cases}
\textbf{local-from-apparent} \\
\quad \left(\lfloor approx \rfloor + 0.5 + \right. \\
\qquad \begin{cases} -1 & \textbf{if } morning \\ 1 & \textbf{otherwise} \end{cases} \\
\qquad \times \left(\left(\left(0.5 + \dfrac{\arcsin\, sine\text{-}offset}{360°} \right) \bmod 1 \right) - 0.25 \right) \right) \\
\hspace{10cm} \textbf{if } |sine\text{-}offset| \leq 1 \\
\textbf{bogus} \hspace{6cm} \textbf{otherwise}
\end{cases}
$$

where

$$
\begin{aligned}
\phi &= locale_{\text{latitude}} \\
t &= \textbf{universal-from-local}\,(approx, locale) \\
\delta &= \arcsin\left(\sin\left(\textbf{obliquity}\,(t) \right) \right. \\
&\qquad \left. \times \sin\left(\textbf{solar-longitude}\,(t) \right) \right) \\
morning &= (approx \bmod 1) < 0.5 \\
sine\text{-}offset &= \tan\phi \times \tan\delta + \frac{\sin\alpha}{\cos\delta \times \cos\phi}
\end{aligned}
$$

The result cannot be perfectly accurate because the observed position of the sun depends on atmospheric conditions, such as atmospheric temperature, humidity, and pressure. In polar regions, when the sun does not reach the stated depression angle, this function returns the constant **bogus**.

The function **moment-from-depression** is then used in a two-stage computation for the determination of the local time in the morning or evening when the sun reaches a specified angle below (above, if the angle is negative) the true horizon. First, an approximation is determined, then that approximation is refined:

$$\textbf{dawn}\,(date,\,locale,\,\alpha) \quad \overset{\text{def}}{=} \tag{12.49}$$

$$\begin{cases} \textbf{bogus} & \textbf{if } result = \textbf{bogus} \\ \textbf{standard-from-local}\,(result,\,locale) & \textbf{otherwise} \end{cases}$$

where

$$approx \quad = \quad \textbf{moment-from-depression}$$
$$(date + 0.25,\,locale,\,\alpha)$$

$$result \quad = \quad \textbf{moment-from-depression}$$
$$\left(\begin{cases} date & \textbf{if } approx = \textbf{bogus} \\ approx & \textbf{otherwise} \end{cases} ,locale,\,\alpha \right)$$

Similarly for the evening we have:

$$\textbf{dusk}\,(date,\,locale,\,\alpha) \quad \overset{\text{def}}{=} \tag{12.50}$$

$$\begin{cases} \textbf{bogus} & \textbf{if } result = \textbf{bogus} \\ \textbf{standard-from-local}\,(result,\,locale) & \textbf{otherwise} \end{cases}$$

where

$$approx \quad = \quad \textbf{moment-from-depression}$$
$$(date + 0.75,\,locale,\,\alpha)$$

$$result \quad = \quad \textbf{moment-from-depression}$$
$$\left(\begin{cases} date + 0.99 & \textbf{if } approx = \textbf{bogus} \\ approx & \textbf{otherwise} \end{cases} ,locale,\,\alpha \right)$$

The *visible horizon* depends on the elevation of the observer. The half diameter of the sun ($16'$) plus the average effect of refraction ($34'$) amount to a depression angle of $50'$. If the observer is above sea level, then the sun is even lower (*dip* degrees) when its upper limb touches the observer's horizon. Hence, for sunrise we write

$$\textbf{sunrise}\,(date, locale) \stackrel{\text{def}}{=} \textbf{dawn}\,(date, locale, \alpha) \qquad (12.51)$$

where

$$h \quad = \quad \max\{0, locale_{\textbf{elevation}}\}$$

$$R \quad = \quad 6.372 \times 10^6 m$$

$$dip \quad = \quad \arccos\left(\frac{R}{R+h}\right)$$

$$\alpha \quad = \quad 50' + dip$$

The value for R is the radius of the Earth. This function ignores elevations below sea level or obstructions of the line of sight to the horizon. For sunset,

$$\textbf{sunset}\,(date, locale) \stackrel{\text{def}}{=} \textbf{dusk}\,(date, locale, \alpha) \qquad (12.52)$$

where

$$h \quad = \quad \max\{0, locale_{\textbf{elevation}}\}$$

$$R \quad = \quad 6.372 \times 10^6 m$$

$$dip \quad = \quad \arccos\left(\frac{R}{R+h}\right)$$

$$\alpha \quad = \quad 50' + dip$$

To convert these local times to standard time in (nonpolar regions) we would use **standard-from-local** (page 170). For example, to calculate the standard time of sunset in Urbana, Illinois, on a given Gregorian date we could write

$$\textbf{urbana-sunset}\,(g\text{-}date) \stackrel{\text{def}}{=} \qquad (12.53)$$

$$\textbf{time-from-moment}\,(\textbf{sunset}\,(d, \textbf{urbana}))$$

where

$$d \quad = \quad \textbf{fixed-from-gregorian}\,(g\text{-}date)$$

The times of occurrence of certain depression angles have religious significance for Jews and Moslems. Some Jews, for example, end Sabbath on

Table 12.7 *Significance of various solar depression angles. Islamic values are derived from [8]; Jewish values are from [10], primarily, and from [4].*

Angle	Time	Significance
20°	a.m.	Alternative Jewish dawn (Rabbenu Tam)
18°	a.m.	Astronomical and Islamic dawn
16°	a.m.	Jewish dawn (Maimonides)
15°	a.m.	Alternative Islamic dawn
12°	a.m.	Nautical twilight begins
6°	a.m.	Civil twilight begins
0°50′	a.m.	Sunrise
0°50′	p.m.	Sunset
4°40′	p.m.	Jewish dusk (Vilna Gaon)
6°	p.m.	Civil twilight ends
7° 5′	p.m.	Jewish sabbath ends (Cohn)
8°30′	p.m.	Alternative Jewish sabbath ends (Tykocinski)
12°	p.m.	Nautical twilight ends
15°	a.m.	Alternative Islamic dusk
18°	p.m.	Astronomical and Islamic dusk
20°	p.m.	Alternative Jewish dusk (Rabbenu Tam)

Saturday night when the sun reaches a depression angle of $7°5'$:

$$\textbf{jewish-sabbath-ends}\,(date, locale) \overset{\text{def}}{=} \tag{12.54}$$

$$\textbf{dusk}\,\big(date, locale, 7°5'\big)$$

but for other purposes consider dusk to end earlier:

$$\textbf{jewish-dusk}\,(date, locale) \overset{\text{def}}{=} \tag{12.55}$$

$$\textbf{dusk}\,\big(date, locale, 4°40'\big)$$

Table 12.7 gives some depression angles and their significance.

With the preceding functions for local sunrise and sunset times we can compute time based on temporal hours still used by Jews and Hindus. At *locale* on fixed *date*, the length of a daytime temporal hour is given by

$$\textbf{temporal-hour}\,(date, locale) \overset{\text{def}}{=} \tag{12.56}$$

$$\begin{cases} \textbf{bogus} & \textbf{if sunrise}\,(date, locale) = \textbf{bogus or} \\ & \textbf{sunset}\,(date, locale) = \textbf{bogus} \\[4pt] \dfrac{\textbf{sunset}\,(date, locale) \,-\, \textbf{sunrise}\,(date, locale)}{12} \\[6pt] \hspace{6cm} \textbf{otherwise} \end{cases}$$

This allows us to convert "sundial time" to standard time for daytime hours with

$$\textbf{standard-from-sundial}\,(date, hour, locale) \overset{\text{def}}{=} \qquad (12.57)$$

$$
\begin{cases}
\textbf{bogus} & \textbf{if } t = \textbf{bogus} \\[2mm]
\textbf{sunrise}\,(date, locale) + \\[1mm]
\quad \begin{cases} (hour - 6) \times t & \textbf{if } 6 \leq hour \leq 18 \\[1mm] (hour - 6) \times \left(\frac{1}{12} - t\right) & \textbf{otherwise} \end{cases} \\[4mm]
\qquad\qquad\qquad\qquad \textbf{otherwise}
\end{cases}
$$

where

$$t \quad = \quad \textbf{temporal-hour}\,(date, locale)$$

which in turn allows us to determine, say, the end of morning according to Jewish ritual:

$$\textbf{jewish-morning-end}\,(date, locale) \overset{\text{def}}{=} \qquad (12.58)$$

$$\textbf{standard-from-sundial}\,(date, 10, locale)$$

In the past, temporal hours were also used for the canonical hours of the Church breviary: Matins (midnight), Laud (dawn), Prime (sunrise), Terce (9 a.m.), Sext (noon), None (3 p.m.), Vesper (sunset), and Compline (dusk).

The times of apparent noon and midnight could be calculated using temporal hours, but the times can differ by a few seconds from **midday** and **midnight** because the times of sunrise and sunset sometimes change relatively quickly.

An important time of day for Moslem prayer is *asr*, which is defined as the moment in the afternoon when the shadow of a gnomon has increased by double its own length (just by its length for some Moslems) over the shadow length at noon. By trigonometry, we get the following determination:

$$\textbf{asr}\,(date, locale) \overset{\text{def}}{=} \textbf{dusk}\,(date, locale, -h) \qquad (12.59)$$

where

$$noon \quad = \quad \textbf{universal-from-standard}$$
$$\qquad\qquad\qquad (\textbf{midday}\,(date, locale)\,, locale)$$
$$\phi \quad = \quad locale_{\text{latitude}}$$
$$\delta \quad = \quad \arcsin\left(\,\sin\,(\textbf{obliquity}\,(noon))\right.$$
$$\qquad\qquad\qquad\qquad \left. \times \sin\,(\textbf{solar-longitude}\,(noon))\,\right)$$
$$altitude \quad = \quad \arcsin\,(\sin\phi \times \sin\delta + \cos\phi \times \cos\delta)$$

$$h \quad = \quad \arctan \left(\frac{\tan altitude}{2 \times \tan altitude + 1} \right)$$

where δ is the solar declination at noon.

12.7 Astronomical Solar Calendars

Astronomical solar calendars are based on the precise solar longitude at a specified time. For example, the astronomical Persian calendar begins its New Year on the day when the vernal equinox occurs before apparent noon (the middle point of the day, sundial time, not clock time) in Tehran; the start of the New Year is postponed to the next day if the equinox is after noon (see Chapter 13). Other calendars of this type include the original French Revolutionary calendar (Chapter 15) and the future form of the Bahá'í calendar (Chapter 14).

The key to implementing an astronomical solar calendar is to determine the day of the New Year on or before a given fixed date. In general, the New Year begins on the day when the solar longitude reaches a certain value at some critical moment, such as midnight. For this purpose, we first estimate the time using the current solar longitude:

$$\textbf{estimate-prior-solar-longitude}\,(t, \phi) \quad \overset{\text{def}}{=} \quad \text{(12.60)}$$

$$\min \{t, \tau - rate \times \Delta\}$$

where

$$rate \quad = \quad \frac{\textbf{mean-tropical-year}}{360°}$$

$$\tau \quad = \quad t - rate \times ((\textbf{solar-longitude}\,(t) - \phi) \bmod 360)$$

$$\Delta \quad = \quad \left(\left(\textbf{solar-longitude}\,(\tau) - \phi + 180° \right) \bmod 360\right) - 180°$$

This is done in a two-step process: First we go back to the time when the sun, traveling at mean speed, was last at longitude ϕ; then the error Δ in longitude is used to refine the estimate to within a day of the correct time. The only complication is handling the discontinuity from 360° to 0° by adding and then subtracting 180°.

For the future Bahá'í calendar (Section 14.3), the critical time is sunset in a yet-to-be-determined location, say (for the purposes of illustration) Haifa. The determination of the moment of sunset on any specified day is straightforward, given the parameters of Haifa:

$$\textbf{haifa} \quad \overset{\text{def}}{=} \quad \boxed{32.82° \mid 35° \mid 0m \mid 2} \quad \text{(12.61)}$$

$$\textbf{sunset-in-haifa}\,(\textit{date}) \;\stackrel{\text{def}}{=} \tag{12.62}$$

universal-from-standard

(sunset (*date*, **haifa**) , **haifa**)

The year on the future Bahá'í calendar begins with the vernal equinox (that is, solar longitude 0°). More precisely, the day on which the equinox falls before sunset is the first day of the year:

$$\textbf{future-bahai-new-year-on-or-before} \tag{12.63}$$
$$(\textit{date}) \;\stackrel{\text{def}}{=}$$

$$\operatorname*{MIN}_{day \geq \lfloor approx \rfloor - 1} \left\{ \begin{array}{l} \textbf{solar-longitude} \\ \quad (\textbf{sunset-in-haifa}\,(day)) \\ \leq \textbf{spring} + 2° \end{array} \right\}$$

where

$$\textit{approx} \quad = \quad \textbf{estimate-prior-solar-longitude}$$
$$(\textbf{sunset-in-haifa}\,(\textit{date})\,,\,\textbf{spring})$$

On account of the unequal distribution of leap years on the Gregorian calendar, the equinox in Haifa was as early as 4:23 a.m. on March 20 in 1896 and as late as 9:15 p.m. on March 21 in 1903; it will be even earlier in 2044 (at 1:19 a.m.).

12.8 Astronomical Lunar Calendars

So patent are the evils of a purely lunar year whose length varies,
owing to primitive methods of observation and determination of
the new moon, that efforts to correct them have never ceased from
the beginning to the present day.
—K. Vollers: *Encyclopædia of Religion and Ethics,* vol. III, p. 127
(1911)[9]

Astronomical methods, as well as rules of thumb, for predicting the time of first visibility of the crescent moon (the *phasis*) were developed over the

<hr>

[9] المؤلفون ليس بالّضرورة موافقون للآراء الموجودة في الأقتباس.

millennia by the ancient Babylonians, medieval Moslem and Hindu scientists, and by modern astronomers. One suggested criterion for likely visibility of the crescent moon (proposed by S. K. Shaukat [1]) requires a minimum difference in altitudes between the setting sun and moon (with parallax and refraction ignored) and a minimum-size crescent (which depends on the angular separation *arc-of-light* between the two bodies):

$$\textbf{visible-crescent}\,(date, locale) \overset{\text{def}}{=} \qquad\qquad (12.64)$$

$$\textbf{new} < phase < \textbf{first-quarter} \text{ and}$$
$$10.6° \leq arc\text{-}of\text{-}light \leq 90° \text{ and } altitude > 4.1°$$

where

$$t \quad = \quad \textbf{universal-from-standard}$$
$$(\textbf{dusk}\,(date - 1, locale, 4.5°)\,, locale)$$

$$phase \quad = \quad \textbf{lunar-phase}\,(t)$$

$$altitude \quad = \quad \textbf{lunar-altitude}\,(t, locale)$$

$$arc\text{-}of\text{-}light \quad = \quad \arccos\,(\cos\,(\textbf{lunar-latitude}\,(t)) \times \cos phase)$$

With this boolean function, we can calculate the day after the new moon is first observable by approximating the date and checking for visibility:

$$\textbf{phasis-on-or-before}\,(date, locale) \overset{\text{def}}{=} \qquad\qquad (12.65)$$

$$\underset{d \geq \tau}{\text{MIN}} \left\{ \textbf{visible-crescent}\,(d, locale) \right\}$$

where

$$mean \quad = \quad date - \left\lfloor \frac{\textbf{lunar-phase}\,(date + 1)}{360°} \right.$$
$$\left. \times \textbf{mean-synodic-month} \right\rfloor$$

$$\tau \quad = \quad \begin{cases} mean - 30 & \text{if } date - mean \leq 3 \text{ and} \\ & \text{not } \textbf{visible-crescent} \\ & (date, locale) \\ mean - 2 & \textbf{otherwise} \end{cases}$$

With these functions we can approximate the observation-based Islamic calendar that is used in practice. Suppose we take Cairo as the location of observation:

$$\textbf{islamic-locale} \;\overset{\text{def}}{=}\; \boxed{\begin{array}{c|c|c|c} 30.1^\circ & 31.3^\circ & 200m & 2 \end{array}} \tag{12.66}$$

Then we calculate the calendar as follows:

$$\textbf{fixed-from-observational-islamic} \tag{12.67}$$

$$\left(\boxed{\begin{array}{c|c|c} year & month & day \end{array}} \right) \;\overset{\text{def}}{=}\;$$

$$\textbf{phasis-on-or-before} \,(midmonth, \textbf{islamic-locale}) \;+$$

$$day - 1$$

where

$$midmonth \;=\; \textbf{islamic-epoch} +$$

$$\left\lfloor \left((year - 1) \times 12 + month - \tfrac{1}{2} \right) \right.$$

$$\left. \times \textbf{mean-synodic-month} \right\rfloor$$

$$\textbf{observational-islamic-from-fixed}\,(date) \;\overset{\text{def}}{=}\; \tag{12.68}$$

$$\boxed{\begin{array}{c|c|c} year & month & day \end{array}}$$

where

$$crescent \;=\; \textbf{phasis-on-or-before}$$

$$(date, \textbf{islamic-locale})$$

$$elapsed\text{-}months \;=\; \text{round}\left(\frac{crescent - \textbf{islamic-epoch}}{\textbf{mean-synodic-month}} \right)$$

$$year \;=\; \left\lfloor \frac{elapsed\text{-}months}{12} \right\rfloor + 1$$

$$month \;=\; (elapsed\text{-}months \bmod 12) + 1$$

$$day \;=\; date - crescent + 1$$

These functions for the Islamic calendar are approximate at best for many reasons: The phenomenon of visibility is still an area of astronomical research and is not yet fully understood; this criterion is just one of many suggestions.

It ignores the distance to the moon and also clarity of the atmosphere, which depends on location and season as well as on unpredictable factors. Moslem countries base the calendar on reported observations, not calculated observability. The best location for seeing the new moon varies from month to month (western locations are always better), and different religious authorities accept testimony from within different regions.

12.9 Astronomical Lunisolar Calendars

In 1997, the World Council of Churches [24] proposed a uniform date for Easter for both Eastern and Western churches (see Chapter 8). With the algorithms of this chapter, the proposed astronomical determination of Easter is straightforward. We need to find the first Sunday in Jerusalem after the first true full moon after the true vernal equinox:

$$\textbf{astronomical-easter}\,(g\text{-}year) \;\overset{\text{def}}{=} \tag{12.69}$$

$$\textbf{kday-after}\,(paschal\text{-}moon, \textbf{sunday})$$

where

$$jan_1 \quad = \quad \textbf{fixed-from-gregorian}$$
$$\left(\;\boxed{\;g\text{-}year\;\mid\;\textbf{january}\;\mid\;1\;}\;\right)$$

$$equinox \quad = \quad \textbf{solar-longitude-after}\,(jan_1, \textbf{spring})$$

$$paschal\text{-}moon \quad = \quad \lfloor\, \textbf{apparent-from-local}$$
$$(\,\textbf{local-from-universal}$$
$$(\,\textbf{lunar-phase-after}$$
$$(equinox, \textbf{full})\,,$$
$$\textbf{jerusalem}\,)\,)\,\rfloor$$

In classical times, the Hebrew month began with the reported observation of the crescent new moon like the Islamic religious calendar of the previous section. Unlike the Islamic calendar, leap months were intercalated so that the spring equinox always fell before the onset of Nisan 16 [12, 4:2]. Using our algorithm for visibility, we arrive at the following approximation for the date of Passover Eve (Nisan 14) in any given Gregorian year:

$$\textbf{classical-passover-eve}\,(g\text{-}year) \;\overset{\text{def}}{=}\; nisan_1 + 13 \tag{12.70}$$

where

$$jan_1 \quad = \quad \textbf{fixed-from-gregorian}$$

$$\left(\boxed{\begin{array}{|c|c|c|} \hline g\text{-}year & \textbf{january} & 1 \\ \hline \end{array}} \right)$$

$$equinox \quad = \quad \textbf{solar-longitude-after} \left(jan_1, \textbf{spring}\right)$$

$$new\text{-}moon \quad = \quad \textbf{phasis-on-or-before}$$

$$\left(\lfloor equinox \rfloor + 10, \textbf{jerusalem} \right)$$

$$set \quad = \quad \textbf{universal-from-standard}$$

$$\left(\textbf{sunset} \left(new\text{-}moon + 14, \textbf{jerusalem}\right), \right.$$

$$\left. \textbf{jerusalem} \right)$$

$$nisan_1 \quad = \quad \begin{cases} new\text{-}moon & \textbf{if } equinox < set \\ \textbf{phasis-on-or-before} & \\ \quad (new\text{-}moon + 45, \textbf{jerusalem}) & \\ & \textbf{otherwise} \end{cases}$$

Karaite Jews use this form of the Hebrew calendar.

Table 8.1 in Chapter 8 (page 123) compares the traditional dates of Passover and Easter with those obtained by the preceding astronomical calculations.

References

[1] K. Abdali, O. Afzal, I. A. Ahmad, M. Durrani, A. Salama, and S. K. Shaukat, "Crescent Moon Visibility: Consensus on Moon-Sighting and Determination of an Islamic Calendar," manuscript, 1996.

[2] P. Bretagnon and G. Francou, "Planetary Theories in Rectangular and Spherical Coordinates—VSOP87 Solutions," *Astronomy and Astrophysics*, volume 202, pp. 309–315, 1988.

[3] P. Bretagnon and J.-L. Simon, *Planetary Programs and Tables from* −4000 *to* +2800, Willmann-Bell, Inc., Richmond, VA, 1986.

[4] B. Cohn, *Tabellen enthaltend die Zeitangaben für den Beginn der Nacht und des Tages für die Breitengrade* +66° *bis* −38°. *Zum Gebrauch für den jüdischen Ritus*, Verlag von Josef Singer, Strasbourg, 1899.

[5] N. Dershowitz and E. M. Reingold, "Implementing Solar Astronomical Calendars," *Birashknāme*, ed. by M. Akrami, Shahid Beheshti University, Tehran (1998), 477–487.

[6] D. Howse, *Greenwich Time and the Discovery of the Longitude*, Oxford University Press, Oxford, 1980. Republished (with some variations in the appendices) as *Greenwich Time and the Longitude*, Philip Wilson Publishers, London, 1997.

[7] M. Ilyas, *A Modern Guide to Astronomical Calculations of Islamic Calendar, Times & Qibla*, Berita Publishing Sdn. Bhd., Kuala Lampur, 1984.

[8]   M. Ilyas, *Astronomy of Islamic Times for the Twenty-first Century*, Mansell Publishing Limited, London, 1988.

[9]   J. B. Kaler, *The Ever-Changing Sky*, Cambridge University Press, Cambridge, 1996.

[10] L. Levi, *Jewish Chrononomy: The Calendar and Times of Day in Jewish Law*, Gur Aryeh Institute for Advanced Jewish Scholarship, Brooklyn, NY, 1967. Revised edition published under the title *Halachic Times for Home and Travel*, Rubin Mass, Ltd., Jerusalem, 1992; expanded 3rd ed., 2000.

[11] D. D. McCarthy, "Astronomical Time," *Proc. IEEE*, volume 79, pp. 915–920, 1991.

[12] Maimonides (= Moshe ben Maimon), *Mishneh Torah: Sefer Zemanim—Hilhot Kiddush HaHodesh*, 1178. Translated by S. Gandz (with commentary by J. Obermann and O. Neugebauer), as *Code of Maimonides, Book Three, Treatise Eight, Sanctification of the New Moon*, Yale Judaica Series, volume XI, Yale University Press, New Haven, CT, 1956. Addenda and corrigenda by E. J. Wiesenberg appear at the end of *Code of Maimonides, Book Three, The Book of Seasons*, translated by S. Gandz and H. Klein, Yale Judaica Series, volume XIV, Yale University Press, New Haven, CT, 1961.

[13] J. Meeus, *Astronomical Algorithms*, 2nd ed., Willmann-Bell, Inc., Richmond, VA, 1998.

[14] J. Meeus, "Les durées extrêmes de la lunaison," *L'Astronomie* (Société Astronomique de France), volume 102, pp. 288–289, July–August 1988.

[15] J. Meeus, *Mathematical Astronomy Morsels*, Willmann-Bell, Inc., Richmond, VA, 1997.

[16] J. Meeus and D. Savoie, "The history of the tropical year," *Journal of the British Astronomical Association*, volume 102, no.1, pp. 40-42, 1992.

[17] D. W. Olson, R. T. Fienberg, and R. W. Sinnott, "What's a Blue Moon?" *Sky & Telescope*, volume 97, pp. 36–39, 1999.

[18] T. J. Quinn, "The BIPM and the Accurate Measure of Time," *Proc. IEEE*, volume 79, pp. 894–905, 1991.

[19] P. K. Seidelmann, B. Guinot, and L. E. Doggett, "Time," Chapter 2 in *Explanatory Supplement to the Astronomical Almanac*, P. K. Seidelmann, ed., U.S. Naval Observatory, University Science Books, Mill Valley, CA, 1992.

[20] T. G. Shanks, *The American Atlas: U.S. Longitudes & Latitudes Time Changes and Time Zones*, 5th ed., ACS Publications, San Diego, CA, 1996.

[21] T. G. Shanks, *The International Atlas: World Longitudes & Latitudes Time Changes and Time Zones*, 5th ed., ACS Publications, San Diego, CA, 1999.

[22] D. Sobel, *Longitude*, Walker, New York, 1995.

[23] F. R. Stephenson, *Historical Eclipses and Earth's Rotation*, Cambridge University Press, Cambridge, 1997.

[24] World Council of Churches, "The Date of Easter: Science Offers Solution to Ancient Religious Problem," Press release, March 24, 1997.

First 14 of 28 Arabian lunar stations from a late fourteenth-century manuscript of *Kitāb al-Bulhān* by the celebrated ninth-century Muslim astrologer Abu-Ma'shar al-Falaki (Albumazar) of Balkh, Khurasan, Persia. (Courtesy of the Bodleian Library, University of Oxford, Oxford.)

13

The Persian Calendar

It was the custom of the Persians not to begin a march before
sunrise. When the day was already bright, the signal was given
from the king's tent with the horn; above the tent, from which it
might be seen by all, there gleamed an image of the sun enclosed
in crystal. Now the order of march was as follows. In front on
silver altars was carried the fire which they called sacred and
eternal. Next came the Magi, chanting their traditional hymn.
These were followed by three hundred and sixty five young men
clad in purple robes, equal in number to the days of the whole
year; for the Persians also divided the year into that number
of days.

—Quintus Curtius Rufus:
History of Alexander, III, iii (circa 35 C.E.)

The modern Persian calendar, adopted in 1925, is a solar calendar based on
the Jalālī calendar designed in the eleventh century by a committee of astronomers, including a young Omar Khayyām, the noted Persian mathemati-
cian, astronomer, and poet. The Jalālī calendar had 12 months of 30 days each,
followed by a 5-day period (6 in leap years), just like the Coptic/Ethiopic calendar described in Chapter 4. In addition to the Jalālī calendar, the Zoroastrian
and Yazdegerd calendars, whose structure is described in Section 1.9, were
also used historically in Persia. The lengthy history of Persian calendars is
discussed in [4] and [6]; [1] gives a briefer history, together with tables and
computational rules for the arithmetic form of the calendar discussed in Section 13.3. A calendar identical to the modern Persian calendar, but with different month names, was adopted in Afghanistan in 1957.

13.1 Structure

The epoch of the modern Persian calendar is the date of the vernal equinox prior to the epoch of the Islamic calendar; that is, 1 A.P.[1] began on

$$\textbf{persian-epoch} \overset{\text{def}}{=} \tag{13.1}$$

$$\textbf{fixed-from-julian}\left(\boxed{\text{622 C.E.} \mid \textbf{march} \mid 19} \right)$$

According to Birashk [1], there is no Persian year 0 (as on the Julian calendar).

The year begins on the day when the vernal equinox (approximately March 21) occurs before true noon (midday) and is postponed to the next day if the equinox is after true noon. To implement the astronomical form of the calendar, we imitate the method used for the Future Bahá'í calendar in Section 12.7.

There are 12 Persian months, containing 29, 30, or 31 days, as follows:

(1) Farvardīn	فروردین	31 days
(2) Ordībehesht	اردیبهشت	31 days
(3) Xordād	خرداد	31 days
(4) Tīr	تیر	31 days
(5) Mordād	مرداد	31 days
(6) Shahrīvar	شهریور	31 days
(7) Mehr	مهر	30 days
(8) Abān	آبان	30 days
(9) Āzar	آزر	30 days
(10) Dey	دی	30 days
(11) Bahman	بهمن	30 days
(12) Esfand	اسفند	29 {30} days

The leap-year structure is given in curly brackets—the last month, Esfand, contains 30 days in leap years. Thus, an ordinary year has 365 days, and a leap year has 366 days.

The 1925 law establishing the modern Persian calendar is silent on the matter of leap-year determination, possibly intending a purely astronomical calendar in which the accurate determination of the vernal equinox defines the calendar—a leap year occurs when successive spring equinoxes are separated by 366 days. However, various commentators ([1] and [6], for example) have suggested arithmetic rules approximating such a calendar. In this chapter we give implementations of the pure astronomical form and Birashk's complex arithmetic form [1]. We briefly discuss how to implement the simpler

---

[1] *Anno Persico* or *Anno Persarum*; Persian year.

arithmetic form in [6]; implementing other arithmetic rules ([4, pp. 115–116]) would be similar.

Days begin at local zone midnight just like the Gregorian day. The week begins on Saturday; the days of the week are numbered, not named:

Saturday	Shanbēh	شنبه
Sunday	Yek-shanbēh	یکشنبه
Monday	Do-shanbēh	دوشنبه
Tuesday	Se-shanbēh	سه شنبه
Wednesday	Chār-shanbēh	چهارشنبه
Thursday	Panj-shanbēh	پنجشنبه
Friday	Jom'ēh	جمعه

13.2 The Astronomical Calendar

Because the occurrence of the New Year depends on true noon in Iran, we define

$$\textbf{tehran} \stackrel{\text{def}}{=} \boxed{35.68° \mid 51.42° \mid 1100m \mid 3.5} \tag{13.2}$$

and

$$\textbf{midday-in-tehran}\,(date) \stackrel{\text{def}}{=} \tag{13.3}$$

$$\textbf{universal-from-standard}$$

$$(\textbf{midday}\,(date, \textbf{tehran})\,, \textbf{tehran})$$

Historically, Isfahan might have been used, but because the 1925 law does not give a location, we opt for the capital, Tehran. The difference in longitudes is only a negligible $11'$ of arc.

We find the date of the New Year (vernal equinox) on or before a given fixed date in a manner identical to our determination of the New Year of the Future Bahá'í calendar (see Section 14.3)—all that changes is the location (Tehran instead of Haifa) and the critical moment (true noon instead of sunset):

$$\textbf{persian-new-year-on-or-before}\,(date) \stackrel{\text{def}}{=} \tag{13.4}$$

$$\underset{day \geq \lfloor approx \rfloor - 1}{\text{MIN}}$$

$$\left\{ \begin{array}{l} \textbf{solar-longitude} \\ \quad (\textbf{midday-in-tehran}\,(day)) \\ \leq \textbf{spring} + 2° \end{array} \right\}$$

where

$$approx \quad = \quad \textbf{estimate-prior-solar-longitude}$$
$$(\textbf{midday-in-tehran}\,(date)\,,\textbf{spring})$$

Once we know the date of the New Year it is straightforward to convert to an R.D. date from a Persian date by finding the R.D. date of the appropriate Persian year (correcting for the absence of a year 0) and adding the elapsed days so far that year:

$$\textbf{fixed-from-persian}\left(\begin{array}{|c|c|c|} \hline year & month & day \\ \hline \end{array}\right) \overset{\text{def}}{=} \tag{13.5}$$

$$new\text{-}year - 1 + \begin{cases} 31 \times (month - 1) & \textbf{if } month \leq 7 \\ 30 \times (month - 1) + 6 & \textbf{otherwise} \end{cases} + day$$

where

$$new\text{-}year \quad = \quad \textbf{persian-new-year-on-or-before}$$
$$\left(\textbf{persian-epoch} + 180 + \right.$$
$$\left\lfloor \textbf{mean-tropical-year} \right.$$
$$\left. \times \begin{cases} year - 1 & \textbf{if } 0 < year \\ year & \textbf{otherwise} \end{cases} \right\rfloor \right)$$

Similarly, to convert an R.D. date to a Persian date, we find the Persian New Year preceding the R.D. date and base our calculations on that (again, correcting for the absence of a year 0):

$$\textbf{persian-from-fixed}\,(date) \overset{\text{def}}{=} \begin{array}{|c|c|c|} \hline year & month & day \\ \hline \end{array} \tag{13.6}$$

where

$$new\text{-}year \quad = \quad \textbf{persian-new-year-on-or-before}\,(date)$$

$$y \quad = \quad \text{round}\left(\frac{new\text{-}year - \textbf{persian-epoch}}{\textbf{mean-tropical-year}}\right) + 1$$

$$year \quad = \quad \begin{cases} y & \textbf{if } 0 < y \\ y - 1 & \textbf{otherwise} \end{cases}$$

$$day\text{-}of\text{-}year \quad = \quad date - \textbf{fixed-from-persian} + 1$$
$$\left(\begin{array}{|c|c|c|} \hline year & 1 & 1 \\ \hline \end{array}\right)$$

$$
month = \begin{cases} \left\lceil \dfrac{day\text{-}of\text{-}year}{31} \right\rceil & \textbf{if } day\text{-}of\text{-}year \leq 186 \\[2em] \left\lceil \dfrac{day\text{-}of\text{-}year - 6}{30} \right\rceil & \textbf{otherwise} \end{cases}
$$

$$
day = date - \textbf{fixed-from-persian} \left(\boxed{year \mid month \mid 1} \right) + 1
$$

13.3 The Arithmetic Calendar

Birashk, [1, page 38], [2], explicitly rejects determination of leap years by the occurrence of the astronomical equinox. He favors the fixed arithmetic intercalation scheme we now describe.[2]

The intricate arithmetic leap year pattern chosen by Birashk follows a cycle of 2820 years, containing a total of 683 leap years, with the following structure. The 2820-year cycle consists of twenty-one 128-year subcycles followed by a 132-year subcycle:

$$2820 = 21 \times 128 + 132.$$

Each 128-year subcycle is divided into one 29-year sub-subcycle followed by three 33-year sub-subcycles:

$$128 = 29 + 3 \times 33.$$

Similarly, the 132-year subcycle is divided into one 29-year sub-subcycle followed by two 33-year sub-subcycles, followed by one 37-year sub-subcycle:

$$132 = 29 + 2 \times 33 + 37.$$

Finally, a year y in a sub-subcycle is a leap year if $y > 1$ and $y \bmod 4 = 1$. That is, years 5, 9, 13, ... of a sub-subcycle are leap years. Thus, a 29-year sub-subcycle has 7 leap years, a 33-year sub-subcycle has 8 leap years, and a 37-year sub-subcycle has 9 leap years for a total of

$$21 \times (7 + 3 \times 8) + (7 + 2 \times 8 + 9) = 683$$

---

[2] Birashk [1] contains some significant numerical errors in the treatment of negative Persian years. For example, his leap-year test in Section 2.5.2 works only for positive years. His Table 2.2 shows the subcycle $-41 \ldots 86$, which contains only 127 years because there is no year 0; this leads to errors in his examples in his Section 2.6.2. His Table I shows -1260 as a leap year, which it is not. There are various other minor errors in his Table I as well.

leap years and a total of

$$2820 \times 365 + 683 = 1{,}029{,}983$$

days in the 2820-year cycle. The true number of days in 2820 tropical years is

$$2820 \times 365.242199 = 1{,}029{,}983.00118,$$

and thus Birashk claims that the arithmetic Persian calendar is in error by only a few minutes in 2820 years.[3]

Years 475 A.P., 3295 A.P., ... are the first years of the cycle. To facilitate the use of modular arithmetic, however, it is more convenient for us to view the cycles as beginning in the years 474 A.P., 3294 A.P., ..., which we consider the zeroth years of the cycle rather than the 2820th years.

Unfortunately, the distribution of the 683 leap years in the cycle of 2820 years does not obey the cycle-of-years formulas from Section 1.12, and thus our implementation must be more complex than in, say, the Islamic calendar described in Chapter 6. Fortunately, the distribution of the leap years in the range of 443–3293 A.P. *does* satisfy the cycle-of-years formulas with $c = 2816$, $l = 682$, and $\Delta = 38$. This range of years contains a full cycle of 2820 Persian years, 474–3293 A.P.; consequently, by shifting into that range we *can* use the cycle-of-years formulas from Section 1.12. First we find the number of years since the zeroth year of Persian cycle that started in 474 A.P.; then we find the equivalent position to that year in the range 474–3293 A.P.; and then we apply formula (1.57). Our test for a Persian leap year is thus

$$\textbf{arithmetic-persian-leap-year?}\ (\textit{p-year}) \ \overset{\text{def}}{=} \tag{13.7}$$

$$((\textit{year} + 38) \times 682 \ \ \text{mod} \ \ 2816) < 682$$

where

$$y \quad = \quad \begin{cases} \textit{p-year} - 474 & \textbf{if } 0 < \textit{p-year} \\ \textit{p-year} - 473 & \textbf{otherwise} \end{cases}$$

$$\textit{year} \quad = \quad (y \ \text{mod} \ 2820) + 474$$

However, we do not need this function to convert Persian dates to and from R.D. dates. We include it because it is much simpler than the rule given in [1].

---

[3] Birashk's calculation is overly simplistic: the length of the spring equinoctial year is not the same as the tropical year, and in either case the year length is slowly changing, as is the length of a day. See Section 12.4.

Abdollahy [6, page 672] gives a simpler leap-year rule for the modern Persian calendar in which the 128-year cycle has 31 leap years following formula (1.57) with $c = 128, l = 31$, and $\Delta = 38$. This rule repeats the pattern of the first 128-year cycle of Birashk's rule. Implementing the arithmetic Persian calendar with Abdollahy's leap year rule is a simple combination of the ideas used in implementing the arithmetic Islamic calendar in Chapter 6 together with the method used below.

To convert a Persian date to an R.D. date we first find the equivalent year in the 2820-year cycle 474–3293 A.P.; then we use *that* year and imitate our function for converting from an Islamic date to an R.D. date (page 89): We add together the number of days before the epoch of the calendar, the number of days in 2820-year cycles before 474 A.P., the number of nonleap days in prior years, the number of leap days in prior years—computed using formula (1.59) with $\Delta = 474 + 38 = 512$, the number of days in prior months of the given date, and the number of days in the given month up to and including the given date:

fixed-from-arithmetic-persian $\hspace{4cm}$ (13.8)

$$\left(\begin{array}{|c|c|c|} \hline \textit{p-year} & \textit{month} & \textit{day} \\ \hline \end{array} \right) \overset{\text{def}}{=}$$

$$\textbf{persian-epoch} - 1 + 1029983 \times \left\lfloor \frac{y}{2820} \right\rfloor + 365 \times (\textit{year} - 1)$$

$$+ \left\lfloor \frac{682 \times \textit{year} - 110}{2816} \right\rfloor + \begin{cases} 31 \times (\textit{month} - 1) & \textbf{if } \textit{month} \leq 7 \\ 30 \times (\textit{month} - 1) + 6 & \textbf{otherwise} \end{cases} +$$

day

where

$$y \quad = \quad \begin{cases} \textit{p-year} - 474 & \textbf{if } 0 < \textit{p-year} \\ \textit{p-year} - 473 & \textbf{otherwise} \end{cases}$$

$$\textit{year} \quad = \quad (y \bmod 2820) + 474$$

The inverse problem, determining the Persian date corresponding to a given R.D. date, must be handled as on the Gregorian calendar (page 54). First we must determine the Persian year in which a given R.D. date occurs. This calculation is done as in the Gregorian calendar (page 53), but by taking the number of days elapsed since Farvardīn 1, 475 A.P., dividing by 1,029,983 to get the number of completed 2820-year cycles, and using the remainder of that division to get the number of prior days since the start of the last 2820-year cycle.

Then we add together 474 (the number of years before the 2820-year cycles), $2820 \times n_{2820}$ (the number of years in prior 2820-year cycles), and the number of years since the start of the last 2820-year cycle. The last of these is computed from formula (1.64). However, that formula is based on a cycle of years numbered $1, 2, \ldots, c = 2820$, whereas the range of applicability of our approximate cycle structure is 474–3293 A.P., which corresponds to years in the cycle numbered $0, 1, \ldots, 2819$; hence, formula (1.64) does not apply to the last year. The last year differs from the cycle-of-years formula only because it is a leap year, and thus it is only to the last day of that year that the formula does not apply—that is, day 1,029,982, the last day of a 2820-year cycle—and we must handle that as an exception. Therefore we have

$$\textbf{arithmetic-persian-year-from-fixed} \qquad\qquad (13.9)$$
$$(\textit{date}) \quad \overset{\text{def}}{=}$$

$$\begin{cases} \textit{year} & \textbf{if } 0 < \textit{year} \\ \textit{year} - 1 & \textbf{otherwise} \end{cases}$$

where

$$d_0 \;=\; \textit{date} - \textbf{fixed-from-arithmetic-persian}$$
$$\left(\boxed{475 \;|\; 1 \;|\; 1} \right)$$

$$n_{2820} \;=\; \left\lfloor \frac{d_0}{1029983} \right\rfloor$$

$$d_1 \;=\; d_0 \bmod 1029983$$

$$y_{2820} \;=\; \begin{cases} 2820 & \textbf{if } d_1 = 1029982 \\[2mm] \left\lfloor \dfrac{2816 \times d_1 + 1031337}{1028522} \right\rfloor & \textbf{otherwise} \end{cases}$$

$$\textit{year} \;=\; 474 + 2820 \times n_{2820} + y_{2820}$$

The computation of y_{2820} in **arithmetic-persian-year-from-fixed** requires a numerator as large as $2816 \times 1{,}029{,}981 = 2{,}900{,}426{,}496$, which approaches our limit of 32-bit arithmetic. One can avoid such large numbers by expressing

$d_1 = 366a + b, 0 \le b < 366$, and rewriting that computation as

$$a = \left\lfloor \frac{d_1}{366} \right\rfloor,$$

$$b = d_1 \bmod 366,$$

$$y_{2820} = 1 + a + \left\lfloor \frac{2134a + 2816b + 2815}{1028522} \right\rfloor.$$

We chose 366 as the divisor because $(2816 \times 366) \bmod 1{,}028{,}522 = 2134$ is small.

Now that we can determine the Persian year of an R.D. date, we can easily find the day number in the Persian year of an R.D. date; from that we can compute the Persian month number by division. Knowing the year and month, we determine the day of the month by subtraction. Putting these pieces together, we have

arithmetic-persian-from-fixed (*date*) $\overset{\text{def}}{=}$ (13.10)

$$\boxed{\; year \;|\; month \;|\; day \;}$$

where

$$year = \textbf{arithmetic-persian-year-from-fixed}$$
$$(date)$$

$$day\text{-}of\text{-}year = date - \textbf{fixed-from-arithmetic-persian} + 1$$
$$\left(\boxed{\; year \;|\; 1 \;|\; 1 \;} \right)$$

$$month = \begin{cases} \left\lceil \dfrac{day\text{-}of\text{-}year}{31} \right\rceil & \textbf{if } day\text{-}of\text{-}year \le 186 \\[2ex] \left\lceil \dfrac{day\text{-}of\text{-}year - 6}{30} \right\rceil & \textbf{otherwise} \end{cases}$$

$$day = date - \textbf{fixed-from-arithmetic-persian} + 1$$
$$\left(\boxed{\; year \;|\; month \;|\; 1 \;} \right)$$

Comparing the dates of the Persian New Year on the astronomical calendar to those of the arithmetic calendar, for 1000–1800 A.P. (= 1637–2417 Gregorian), we find they disagree on the 28 years shown in Table 13.1. Outside of this range disagreement is far more common, occurring almost every fourth year. Notice that there is complete agreement for the range of Gregorian years 1865–2024 (1244–1403 A.P.).

Table 13.1 *Years in the range 1000–1800* A.P. *on which the astronomical Persian calendar differs from the arithmetic Persian calendar.*

Persian Year	Astronomical New Year R.D.	Gregorian	Arithmetic New Year R.D.	Gregorian
1016	597,616 = March 20, 1637		597,617 = March 21, 1637	
1049	609,669 = March 20, 1670		609,670 = March 21, 1670	
1078	620,261 = March 20, 1699		620,262 = March 21, 1699	
1082	621,722 = March 21, 1703		621,723 = March 22, 1703	
1111	632,314 = March 20, 1732		632,315 = March 21, 1732	
1115	633,775 = March 20, 1736		633,776 = March 21, 1736	
1144	644,367 = March 20, 1765		644,368 = March 21, 1765	
1177	656,420 = March 20, 1798		656,421 = March 21, 1798	
1210	668,473 = March 21, 1831		668,474 = March 22, 1831	
1243	680,526 = March 20, 1864		680,527 = March 21, 1864	
1404	739,331 = March 21, 2025		739,330 = March 20, 2025	
1437	751,384 = March 21, 2058		751,383 = March 20, 2058	
1532	786,082 = March 21, 2153		786,081 = March 20, 2153	
1565	798,135 = March 21, 2186		798,134 = March 20, 2186	
1569	799,596 = March 21, 2190		799,595 = March 20, 2190	
1598	810,188 = March 22, 2219		810,187 = March 21, 2219	
1631	822,241 = March 21, 2252		822,240 = March 20, 2252	
1660	832,833 = March 21, 2281		832,832 = March 20, 2281	
1664	834,294 = March 21, 2285		834,293 = March 20, 2285	
1693	844,886 = March 22, 2314		844,885 = March 21, 2314	
1697	846,347 = March 22, 2318		846,346 = March 21, 2318	
1726	856,939 = March 22, 2347		856,938 = March 21, 2347	
1730	858,400 = March 22, 2351		858,399 = March 21, 2351	
1759	868,992 = March 21, 2380		868,991 = March 20, 2380	
1763	870,453 = March 21, 2384		870,452 = March 20, 2384	
1788	879,584 = March 21, 2409		879,583 = March 20, 2409	
1792	881,045 = March 21, 2413		881,044 = March 20, 2413	
1796	882,506 = March 21, 2417		882,505 = March 20, 2417	

13.4 Holidays

> A philosopher of the Ḥashwiyya-school relates that when
> Solomon the son of David had lost his seal and his empire, but was
> reinstated after forty days, he at once regained his former majesty,
> the princes came before him, and the birds were busy in his
> service. Then the Persians said, *"Naurôz âmadh,"* i.e. the new day
> has come. Therefore that day was called Naurôz.
> —Abū-Raiḥān Muḥammad ibn 'Aḥmad al-Bīrūnī:
> *Al-Āthār al-Bāqiyah 'an al-Qurūn al-Khāliyah* (1000)

As throughout this book, we consider our problem to be the determination of holidays that occur in a specified Gregorian year. Because the Persian year is almost consistently aligned with the Gregorian year, each Persian holiday (as long as it is not very near January 1) occurs just once in a given Gregorian year. Holidays that occur on fixed days on the Persian calendar are almost fixed on the Gregorian calendar—such holidays are easy to determine on the Gregorian calendar by observing that the Persian year beginning in Gregorian year y is given by

Persian New Year occurring in March of Gregorian year y

$= y + 1 - \textbf{gregorian-year-from-fixed}(\textbf{persian-epoch}),$

but we must compensate for the lack of year 0 by subtracting 1 if the above value is not positive. Thus, to find the R.D. date of *Naw Ruz* (Persian New Year, Farvardīn 1) according to the astronomical Persian calendar, which falls in a specified Gregorian year, we would use

$$\textbf{naw-ruz}\,(\textit{g-year}) \;\overset{\text{def}}{=} \tag{13.11}$$

$\textbf{fixed-from-persian}$

$$\left(\left\lfloor \begin{cases} \textit{persian-year} - 1 & \textbf{if } \textit{persian-year} \le 0 \\ \textit{persian-year} & \textbf{otherwise} \end{cases} \right\rfloor \; 1 \; 1 \right)$$

where

$$\textit{persian-year} \;=\; \textit{g-year} - \textbf{gregorian-year-from-fixed} \;+\; 1$$

$$(\textbf{persian-epoch})$$

If we want the date of Naw Ruz according to the arithmetic Persian calendar, we would substitute the function **fixed-from-arithmetic-persian** for **fixed-from-persian** in (13.4).

References

[1] A. Birashk, *A Comparative Calendar of the Iranian, Muslim Lunar, and Christian Eras for Three Thousand Years*, Mazda Publishers (in association with Bibliotheca Persica), Costa Mesa, CA, 1993.

[2] Letter to Edward Reingold from A. Birashk, editor of *Dāneshnāme-ye Bozorg-e Farsi* (*The Larger Persian Encyclopædia*), Tehran, June 21, 1996.

[3] F. C. de Blois and B. van Dalen, "Ta'rikh" (Part I), *The Encyclopaedia of Islam*, 2nd ed. volume 10, pp. 257–271, E. J. Brill, Leiden, 1998.

[4] S. H. Taqizadeh, "Various Eras and Calendars Used in the Countries of Islam," *Bulletin of the School of Oriental Studies (University of London)*, volume 9, pp. 903–922, 1937–39, and volume 10, pp. 107–132, 1939.

[5] S. H. Taqizadeh, "Djalali," *The Encyclopaedia of Islam*, 2nd ed. volume 2, pp. 397–400, E. J. Brill, Leiden, 1962.

[6] E. Yarshater, ed., *Encyclopædia Iranica*, Routledge & Kegan Paul, Ltd., London, 1990.

Shrine of the Bāb, located on Mount Carmel, Israel and built in stages from 1899 to 1953. The Bāb (Mirzā Ali Muhammad of Shiraz), who died 1850, was the originator of the 19-year cycle of the Bahá'í calendar. (Courtesy of the Bahá'í National Center, Wilmette, IL.)

14

The Bahá'í Calendar

In the not far distant future it will be necessary that all peoples in
the world agree on a common calendar. It seems, therefore, fitting
that the new age of unity should have a new calendar free from the
objections and associations which make each of the older
calendars unacceptable to large sections of the world's population,
and it is difficult to see how any other arrangement could exceed
in simplicity and convenience that proposed by the Báb.
—John Ebenezer Esslemont: *Bahá'u'lláh and the New Era:*
An Introduction to the Bahá'í Faith (1923)

14.1 Structure

The Bahá'í (or Badí') calendar begins its years on the day of the vernal
equinox. Theoretically, if the actual time of the equinox occurs after sunset,
then the year should begin a day later [2]. Current practice in the West, however, is to begin on March 21 of the Gregorian calendar, regardless. The calendar is based on the 19-year cycle 1844–1863 of the Báb, the martyred forerun-
ner of Bahá'u'lláh and co-founder of the Bahá'í faith.

As in the Islamic calendar, days are from sunset to sunset. Unlike those of
the Islamic calendar, years are solar; they are composed of 19 months of 19
days each with an additional period of 4 or 5 days after the eighteenth month.
Leap years in the West follow the same pattern as in the Gregorian calendar.

As on the Persian calendar, the week begins on Saturday; weekdays have
the following names (in Arabic):

Saturday	Jalāl	جلال	(Glory)
Sunday	Jamāl	جمال	(Beauty)
Monday	Kamāl	كمال	(Perfection)
Tuesday	Fiḍāl	فضال	(Grace)

Wednesday	'Idāl	عدال	(Justice)
Thursday	Istijlāl	استجلال	(Majesty)
Friday	Istiqlāl	استقلال	(Independence)

The months are called

(1) Bahā'	بهاء	(Splendor)	19 days
(2) Jalāl	جلال	(Glory)	19 days
(3) Jamāl	جمال	(Beauty)	19 days
(4) 'Aẓamat	عظمة	(Grandeur)	19 days
(5) Nūr	نور	(Light)	19 days
(6) Raḥmat	رحمة	(Mercy)	19 days
(7) Kalimāt	كلمات	(Words)	19 days
(8) Kamāl	كمال	(Perfection)	19 days
(9) Asmā'	اسماء	(Names)	19 days
(10) 'Izzat	عزّة	(Might)	19 days
(11) Mashīyyat	مشيّة	(Will)	19 days
(12) 'Ilm	علم	(Knowledge)	19 days
(13) Qudrat	قدرة	(Power)	19 days
(14) Qawl	قول	(Speech)	19 days
(15) Masā'il	مسائل	(Questions)	19 days
(16) Sharaf	شرف	(Honor)	19 days
(17) Sulṭān	سلطان	(Sovereignty)	19 days
(18) Mulk	مُلك	(Dominion)	19 days
Ayyām-i-Hā	ايّام ها	(Days of God)	4 {5} days
(19) 'Alā'	علاء	(Loftiness)	19 days

The leap-year variation is given in curly brackets. The 19 days of each month have the same names as the months, except that there is no intercalary Ayyām-i-Hā.

Years are also named in a 19-year cycle, called *Vāḥid*, meaning "unity" and having a numerological value of 19 in Arabic letters:

(1) Alif	الف	(A)
(2) Bā'	باء	(B)
(3) Āb	أب	(Father)
(4) Dāl	دال	(D)
(5) Bāb	باب	(Gate)
(6) Vāv	واو	(V)

(7) Abad	ابد	(Eternity)
(8) Jād	جاد	(Generosity)
(9) Bahā'	بهاء	(Splendor)
(10) Ḥubb	حبّ	(Love)
(11) Bahhāj	بهّاج	(Delightful)
(12) Javāb	جواب	(Answer)
(13) Aḥad	احد	(Single)
(14) Vahhāb	وهّاب	(Bountiful)
(15) Vidād	وداد	(Affection)
(16) Badī'	بدیء	(Beginning)
(17) Bahī	بهی	(Luminous)
(18) Abhā	ابهی	(Most Luminous)
(19) Vāḥid	واحد	(Unity)

There is also a 361-year major cycle, called *Kull-i-Shay* (the name has numerological value $361 = 19^2$ in Arabic). Thus, for example, Monday, April 21, 1930 would be called "Kamāl (Monday), the day of Qudrat (the thirteenth), of the month of Jalāl, of the year Bahhāj (the eleventh), of the fifth Vāḥid, of the first Kull-i-Shay, of the Bahá'í Era."

Accordingly, we represent a Bahá'í date by a list

major	cycle	year	month	day

The first component, *major*, is an integer (positive for real Bahá'í dates); the components *cycle*, *year*, and *day*, take on integer values in the range 1...19; because the intercalary period interrupts the sequence of month numbers, *month* is either an integer between 1 and 19 or else the special constant value

$$\textbf{ayyam-i-ha} \overset{\text{def}}{=} 0 \tag{14.1}$$

The epoch of the calendar, day 1 of year 1 B.E.,[1] is March 21, 1844 (Gregorian):

$$\textbf{bahai-epoch} \overset{\text{def}}{=} \tag{14.2}$$

$$\textbf{fixed-from-gregorian}\left(\begin{array}{|c|c|c|} \hline 1844 & \textbf{march} & 21 \\ \hline \end{array} \right)$$

which is R.D. 673,222.

---

[1] Bahá'í Era.

14.2 Western Version

The Bahá'í calendar in use in the West is based on the Gregorian calendar, and thus our functions are relatively straightforward:

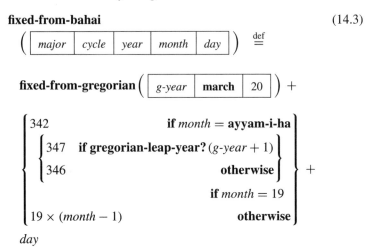

fixed-from-bahai $\qquad$ (14.3)

$$
\left(\begin{array}{|c|c|c|c|c|} \hline major & cycle & year & month & day \\ \hline \end{array} \right) \overset{\text{def}}{=}
$$

$$
\textbf{fixed-from-gregorian} \left(\begin{array}{|c|c|c|} \hline g\text{-}year & \textbf{march} & 20 \\ \hline \end{array} \right) +
$$

$$
\begin{cases} 342 & \text{if } month = \textbf{ayyam-i-ha} \\ \begin{cases} 347 & \textbf{if gregorian-leap-year? } (g\text{-}year + 1) \\ 346 & \textbf{otherwise} \end{cases} & \\ & \textbf{if } month = 19 \\ 19 \times (month - 1) & \textbf{otherwise} \end{cases} +
$$

$$ day $$

where

$$
g\text{-}year = 361 \times (major - 1) + 19 \times (cycle - 1) + year - 1 +
$$
$$
\textbf{gregorian-year-from-fixed}
$$
$$
(\textbf{bahai-epoch})
$$

We first find the corresponding Gregorian year by counting how many years (361 for each major cycle and 19 for each minor cycle) have elapsed since the epoch in 1844. Starting with the R.D. date of the last day (March 20) of the prior Bahá'í year, we add the number of days in the given month plus 19 days for each month, except that the intercalary period has only 4 or 5 days (for a total of 346 or 347 days), depending on whether February of the Gregorian calendar had a leap-day or not.

The inverse function is

$$
\textbf{bahai-from-fixed} \, (date) \overset{\text{def}}{=} \qquad (14.4)
$$

$$
\begin{array}{|c|c|c|c|c|} \hline major & cycle & year & month & day \\ \hline \end{array}
$$

where

$$
g\text{-}year = \textbf{gregorian-year-from-fixed} \, (date)
$$

$$
start = \textbf{gregorian-year-from-fixed}
$$
$$
(\textbf{bahai-epoch})
$$

$$years = \textit{g-year} - start -
\begin{cases}
1 & \text{if } date \leq \textbf{fixed-from-gregorian} \\
& \left(\boxed{\begin{array}{|c|c|c|} \textit{g-year} & \textbf{march} & 20 \end{array}} \right) \\
0 & \textbf{otherwise}
\end{cases}$$

$$major = \left\lfloor \frac{years}{361} \right\rfloor + 1$$

$$cycle = \left\lfloor \frac{years \bmod 361}{19} \right\rfloor + 1$$

$$year = (years \bmod 19) + 1$$

$$days = date - \textbf{fixed-from-bahai}
\left(\boxed{\begin{array}{|c|c|c|c|c|} \textit{major} & \textit{cycle} & \textit{year} & 1 & 1 \end{array}} \right)$$

$$month =
\begin{cases}
19 & \text{if } date \geq \textbf{fixed-from-bahai} \\
& \left(\boxed{\begin{array}{|c|c|c|c|c|} \textit{major} & \textit{cycle} & \textit{year} & 19 & 1 \end{array}} \right) \\
\textbf{ayyam-i-ha} & \\
& \text{if } date \geq \textbf{fixed-from-bahai} \\
& \left(\boxed{\begin{array}{|c|c|c|c|c|} \textit{major} & \textit{cycle} & \textit{year} & \textbf{ayyam-i-ha} & 1 \end{array}} \right) \\
\left\lfloor \dfrac{days}{19} \right\rfloor + 1 & \textbf{otherwise}
\end{cases}$$

$$day = date + 1 - \textbf{fixed-from-bahai}
\left(\boxed{\begin{array}{|c|c|c|c|c|} \textit{major} & \textit{cycle} & \textit{year} & \textit{month} & 1 \end{array}} \right)$$

Here we compute the number of years that have elapsed since the start of the Bahá'í calendar by looking at the Gregorian year number and considering whether the date is before or after Bahá'í New Year and then using the result to get the number of elapsed major and minor cycles and years within the cycle. The remaining days divided by 19, the length of a month, gives the month number, but again special consideration must be given for the intercalary period and for the last month of the Bahá'í year.

14.3 Future Calendar

The Bahá'í year was intended by the official rules [2] to begin at sunset preceding the vernal equinox, which is frequently a day before or after March 21. The New Year calculation for this intended version of the calendar involves astronomical computations and was given in Section 12.7.

To convert a future Bahá'í date into a fixed date, we take the R.D. date of the Bahá'í New Year and add 19 days for each full month plus the number of elapsed days in the current month. The intercalary days and last month of the year must be treated exceptionally: days in Ayyám-i-Há are preceded by 18 full months (that is, 342 days); because the length of that period differs in ordinary and leap years, for dates in the last month, we count backwards from the following New Year. In the following function, we multiply the number of years since the epoch by the mean tropical year length, plus or minus half a year, and then use **future-bahai-new-year-on-or-before** (page 204) to get the R.D. date of the subsequent or prior Bahá'í New Year:

fixed-from-future-bahai   (14.5)

$$\left(\boxed{\begin{array}{|c|c|c|c|c|} major & cycle & year & month & day \end{array}} \right) \quad \overset{\text{def}}{=}$$

$$\begin{cases}
\begin{aligned}
&\textbf{future-bahai-new-year-on-or-before} \\
&\quad \Big(\textbf{bahai-epoch} + \\
&\qquad \left\lfloor \textbf{mean-tropical-year} \times \left(years + \tfrac{1}{2} \right) \right\rfloor \Big) \\
&\quad - 19 + day - 1 \\
&\hspace{5cm} \textbf{if } month = 19 \\[2mm]
&\textbf{future-bahai-new-year-on-or-before} \\
&\quad \Big(\textbf{bahai-epoch} + \\
&\qquad \left\lfloor \textbf{mean-tropical-year} \times \left(years - \tfrac{1}{2} \right) \right\rfloor \Big) \\
&\quad + 342 + day - 1 \\
&\hspace{4cm} \textbf{if } month = \textbf{ayyam-i-ha} \\[2mm]
&\textbf{future-bahai-new-year-on-or-before} \\
&\quad \Big(\textbf{bahai-epoch} + \\
&\qquad \left\lfloor \textbf{mean-tropical-year} \times \left(years - \tfrac{1}{2} \right) \right\rfloor \Big) \\
&\quad + (month - 1) \times 19 + day - 1 \\
&\hspace{6cm} \textbf{otherwise}
\end{aligned}
\end{cases}$$

where

$$years \quad = \quad 361 \times (major - 1) + 19 \times (cycle - 1) + year$$

The inverse function is

future-bahai-from-fixed (*date*) $\overset{\text{def}}{=}$ (14.6)

major	*cycle*	*year*	*month*	*day*

where

new-year = **future-bahai-new-year-on-or-before**

(*date*)

$$years \quad = \quad \text{round} \left(\frac{new\text{-}year - \textbf{bahai-epoch}}{\textbf{mean-tropical-year}} \right)$$

$$major \quad = \quad \left\lfloor \frac{years}{361} \right\rfloor + 1$$

$$cycle \quad = \quad \left\lfloor \frac{years \bmod 361}{19} \right\rfloor + 1$$

$$year \quad = \quad (years \bmod 19) + 1$$

$$days \quad = \quad date - new\text{-}year$$

$$month \quad = \quad \begin{cases} 19 \qquad \textbf{if } date \geq \textbf{fixed-from-future-bahai} \\ \qquad \left(\begin{array}{|c|c|c|c|c|} \hline major & cycle & year & 19 & 1 \\ \hline \end{array} \right) \\[1em] \textbf{ayyam-i-ha} \\ \qquad \textbf{if } date \geq \textbf{fixed-from-future-bahai} \\ \qquad \left(\begin{array}{|c|c|c|c|c|} \hline major & cycle & year & \textbf{ayyam-i-ha} & 1 \\ \hline \end{array} \right) \\[1em] \left\lfloor \dfrac{days}{19} \right\rfloor + 1 \qquad\qquad \textbf{otherwise} \end{cases}$$

$$day \quad = \quad date + 1 - \textbf{fixed-from-future-bahai}$$

$$\left(\begin{array}{|c|c|c|c|c|} \hline major & cycle & year & month & 1 \\ \hline \end{array} \right)$$

Here we compute the number of years that have elapsed since the start of the Bahá'í calendar by dividing the numbers of days since the epoch by the mean tropical year length and then using the result to get the number of elapsed major and minor cycles and years within the cycle. The remaining days divided by 19 (the length of a Bahá'í month) give the month number, but again, consideration must be given to the intercalary days and for the last month of the Bahá'í year.

This astronomical version of the calendar is not yet in use, as explained in the following letter [1]:

> Until the Universal House of Justice decides upon the spot on which the calculations for establishing the date of Naw-Rūz each year are to be based it is not possible to state exactly the correspondence between Bahá'í dates and Gregorian dates for any year. Therefore for the present the believers in the West commemorate Bahá'í events on their traditional Gregorian anniversaries. Once the necessary legislation to determine Naw-Rūz has been made, the correspondence between Bahá'í and Gregorian dates will vary from year to year depending upon whether the Spring Equinox falls on the 20th, 21st or 22nd of March. In fact in Persia the friends have been, over the years, following the Spring Equinox as observed in Tehran, to determine Naw-Rūz, and the National Spiritual Assembly has to issue every year a Bahá'í calendar for the guidance of the friends. The Universal House of Justice feels that this is not a matter of urgency and, in the meantime, is having research conducted into such questions.

In fact, the version of the Bahá'í calendar currently employed in the Near East (Iran, Israel, Persian Gulf countries, and the Arabian Peninsula) uses Tehran (rather than Haifa as we did in Section 12.7) in the computation of sunset for **future-bahai-new-year-on-or-before**.

14.4 Holidays

Because the Bahá'í calendar used in the West is synchronized with the Gregorian (except that Ayyām-i-Hā 4 is March 1 in ordinary years, but February 29 in leap years), holidays are a trivial matter. Bahá'í New Year is always celebrated on March 21, the assumed date of the spring equinox. It is called the Feast of Naw-Rūz, as is the Persian New Year, which also celebrates the vernal equinox (see Chapter 13). Its computation is trivial:

$$\textbf{bahai-new-year}\,(g\text{-}year) \;\overset{\text{def}}{=} \tag{14.7}$$

$$\textbf{fixed-from-gregorian}\left(\boxed{\begin{array}{c|c|c} g\text{-}year & \textbf{march} & 21 \end{array}} \right)$$

The other major holidays on which work is proscribed are the Feast of Ridván (Jalāl 13 = April 21), Ridván 9 (Jamāl 2 = April 29), Ridván 12 (Jāmal 5 = May 2), Declaration of the Bāb ('Azamat 7 = May 23), Ascension of Bahā'u'llāh ('Azamat 13 = May 29), Martyrdom of the Bāb (Rahmat 16 = July 9), Birth of the Bāb ('Ilm 5 = October 20), and the Birth of Bahā'u'llāh (Qudrat 9 = November 12). Two other obligatory celebrations are the Birth of

'Abdu'l-Bahā (also 'Aẓamat 7 = May 23) and the Ascension of 'Abdu'l-Bahā (Qawl 6 = November 28). There are additional days of significance, including the first day of each month (a feast day) and the whole last month (fast days).

Determining holidays on the future Bahá'í calendar is more involved because they do not coincide with dates on another calendar. For example, we would have

$$\textbf{feast-of-ridvan}\,(g\text{-}year) \overset{\text{def}}{=} \tag{14.8}$$

$$\textbf{fixed-from-future-bahai}$$

$$\left(\boxed{\begin{array}{c|c|c|c|c} major & cycle & year & 2 & 13 \end{array}} \right)$$

where

$$
\begin{aligned}
years &= g\text{-}year - \textbf{gregorian-year-from-fixed} \\
&\qquad (\textbf{bahai-epoch}) \\[1em]
major &= \left\lfloor \frac{years}{361} \right\rfloor + 1 \\[1em]
cycle &= \left\lfloor \frac{years \bmod 361}{19} \right\rfloor + 1 \\[1em]
year &= (years \bmod 19) + 1
\end{aligned}
$$

In Near Eastern countries, as explained above, the date of the New Year is the one on which the equinox occurs before sunset in Tehran. Thus, Bahá'í Naw-Rūz coincides with Persian Naw Rūz unless the equinox occurs between noon and sunset. The other major holidays on the Near Eastern Bahá'í calendar are celebrated on their Bahá'í dates, except for four that follow the Islamic calendar instead: Declaration of the Bāb (Jamādā I 5), Martyrdom of the Bāb (Sh'abān 28), Birth of the Bāb (Muḥarram 1), and the Birth of Bahā'u'llāh (Muḥarram 2). In Israel, however, these four are observed on their Islamic dates, whereas the other five are observed on their Gregorian dates.

References

[1] Letter written on behalf of the Universal House of Justice to the National Spiritual Assembly of the Bahá'í of the United States, October 30, 1974.

[2] Universal House of Justice, *The Bahá'í World: An International Record*, volume xviii, Bahá'í World Center, Haifa, pp. 598–601, 1986.

Print of the French Revolutionary calendar month of Vendémiaire by Laurent Guyot, after Jean-Jacques Lagrenée, the younger, Paris. (Courtesy of Bibliothèque Nationale de France, Paris.)

15

The French Revolutionary Calendar

Of the Republican calendar, the late John Quincy Adams said:
"This system has passed away and is forgotten. This incongruous
composition of profound learning and superficial frivolity, of
irreligion and morality, of delicate imagination and coarse
vulgarity, is dissolved." Unfortunately the effects of this calendar,
though it was used for only about twelve years, have not passed
away. It has entailed a permanent injury on history and on
science.
—Joseph Lovering: *Proceedings of the American
Academy of Arts and Sciences,* p. 350 (1872)[1]

The French Revolutionary calendar (*Le Calendrier Républicain*) was instituted by the National Convention of the French Republic in October 1793. Its epoch is R.D. 654,415, that is, Saturday, September 22, 1792 (Gregorian), the day of the autumnal equinox of that year and also the first day following the establishment of the Republic. The calendar went into effect on Sunday, November 24, 1793 (Gregorian) and was used by the French until Tuesday, December 31, 1805 (Gregorian); on Wednesday, January 1, 1806 (Gregorian), the Revolutionary calendar was abandoned by Napoleonic edict and France reverted to the Gregorian calendar, but the Revolutionary calendar was used again during May 6–23, 1871.

Following the example of several ancient calendars, including the Coptic and Ethiopic (see Chapter 4), the French Revolutionary calendar divided the year into 12 months containing exactly 30 days each, followed by a period of 5 monthless days (6 in leap years). The poetic names of the months, coined by Fabre d'Églantine, were taken from the seasons in which they

---

[1] *Les auteurs ne souscrivent pas nécessairement aux opinions des auteurs des citations.*

occurred:[2]

(1) Vendémiaire (vintage)	(7) Germinal (seed)
(2) Brumaire (fog)	(8) Floréal (blossom)
(3) Frimaire (sleet)	(9) Prairial (pasture)
(4) Nivôse (snow)	(10) Messidor (harvest)
(5) Pluviôse (rain)	(11) Thermidor (heat)
(6) Ventôse (wind)	(12) Fructidor (fruit)

An English wit who was "disgusted with the 'namby pamby' style of the French calendar" dubbed them Slippy, Drippy, Nippy, Showery, Flowery, Bowery, Hoppy, Croppy, Poppy, Wheezy, Sneezy, Freezy [2, volume I, pp. 38–39].

As usual, we use

year	month	day

to represent the date, treating the monthless days as a thirteenth month, as in the Mayan haab calendar (Chapter 10).

Although not relevant to our calculations, each month was divided into 3 *décades* (decades) of 10 days each; the tenth day was considered a day of rest. This made the new calendar unpopular because, under the Gregorian calendar, the workers had had every seventh day off. The 10 days were named by their ordinal position in the decade:

(1) Primidi	(6) Sextidi
(2) Duodi	(7) Septidi
(3) Tridi	(8) Octidi
(4) Quartidi	(9) Nonidi
(5) Quintidi	(10) Decadi

The 5 or 6 monthless days that were added at the end of each year were holidays called *sansculottides* celebrating various attributes of the Revolution:

---

[2] Native American, old Vedic, and Gezer names of months have similar phenological flavor, as do the names of the 24 "solar terms" on the Chinese calendar (see Table 16.1 on page 243). Also, in the mid-eighteenth century Linnæus published *The Calendar of Flora* consisting of the 12 months Reviving Winter (December 22–March 19), Thawing (March 19–April 12), Budding (April 12–May 9), Leafing (May 9–May 25), Flowering (May 25–June 20), Fruiting (June 20–July 12), Ripening (July 12–August 4), Reaping (August 4–August 28), Sowing (August 28–September 22), Shedding (September 22–October 28), Freezing (October 28–November 5), and Dead Winter (November 5–December 22). See *Miscellaneous Tracts Relating to Natural History, Husbandry, and Physick* to which is added the *Calendar of Flora*, by B. Stillingfleet, R. and J. Dodsley, London, 1762. Stillingfleet is today best remembered as the original "bluestocking"; see the *Oxford English Dictionary*, 2nd ed., Oxford University Press, Oxford, 1989. We are indebted to Evan Melhado for pointing out the Linnæus and Stillingfleet references.

(1) Jour de la Vertu (virtue day)

(2) Jour du Génie (genius day)

(3) Jour du Labour (labor day)

(4) Jour de la Raison (reason day)

(5) Jour de la Récompense (reward day)

{(6) Jour de la Révolution (revolution day)}

The leap-year intercalary day is given in curly brackets.

15.1 The Original Form

> ... je ne regrette presque plus le calendrier républicain
> [... I almost no longer regret the French Revolutionary calendar]
> —Stendhal: *Journal* (January 20, 1806)

Originally, the calendar was kept in synchronization with the solar year by setting the first day of Vendémiaire to occur at the autumnal equinox, just as the Persian astronomical calendar fixes the start of the year according to the spring equinox. (See Chapter 13.) That is, there was no leap-year rule per se; a leap year occurred when successive autumnal equinoxes were 366 days apart, which happens roughly every 4 years. However, the pattern is not regular, and the precise calculation of the equinox is not easy, and thus the original rule was changed to the simple Gregorian-like rule that we discuss in the following section. In this section we give the original form of the calendar.

To implement the original form of the calendar we need to determine the moment of the autumnal equinox in Paris. The Paris Observatory is $48°50'11''$ ($= 175811°/3600$) north, $2°20'15''$ ($= 187°/80$) east, 27 meters above sea level, and 1 hour after Universal Time, so we define

$$\textbf{paris} \stackrel{\text{def}}{=} \tag{15.1}$$

$48°50'11''$	$2°20'15''$	$27m$	1

Because eighteenth-century France used local mean time, days began at true (apparent) midnight. The New Year began on the first day that the autumnal equinox is after true midnight. That is, the "critical moment" (in the sense of Section 12.7) for the French Revolutionary calendar is

$$\textbf{midnight-in-paris}\,(date) \stackrel{\text{def}}{=} \tag{15.2}$$

$$\textbf{universal-from-standard}$$

$$(\textbf{midnight}\,(date+1,\,\textbf{paris})\,,\,\textbf{paris})$$

We find the date of the New Year (autumnal equinox) on or before a given fixed date in a manner parallel to our determination of the New Year of the Future Bahá'í calendar (see Section 12.7):

$$\textbf{french-new-year-on-or-before}\,(date) \quad \overset{\text{def}}{=} \quad (15.3)$$

$$\underset{day \geq \lfloor approx \rfloor - 1}{\textbf{MIN}}$$

$$\left\{ \begin{array}{c} \textbf{autumn} \leq \textbf{solar-longitude} \\ (\ \textbf{midnight-in-paris}\,(day)\ ) \end{array} \right\}$$

where

$$approx \quad = \quad \textbf{estimate-prior-solar-longitude}$$
$$(\textbf{midnight-in-paris}\,(date)\,,\,\textbf{autumn})$$

We define

$$\textbf{french-epoch} \quad \overset{\text{def}}{=} \quad (15.4)$$

$$\textbf{fixed-from-gregorian}\,\left(\ \boxed{\ \begin{array}{c|c|c} 1792 & \text{september} & 22 \end{array}\ }\ \right)$$

Now we can convert from a French Revolutionary date to an R.D. date by finding the preceding New Year and doing some simple arithmetic:

$$\textbf{fixed-from-french}\,\left(\ \boxed{\begin{array}{c|c|c} year & month & day \end{array}}\ \right) \quad \overset{\text{def}}{=} \quad (15.5)$$

$$new\text{-}year - 1 + 30 \times (month - 1) + day$$

where

$$new\text{-}year \quad = \quad \textbf{french-new-year-on-or-before}$$
$$(\ \lfloor \textbf{french-epoch} + 180 +$$
$$\textbf{mean-tropical-year} \times (year - 1) \rfloor\ )$$

and in the other direction by

$$\textbf{french-from-fixed}\,(date) \quad \overset{\text{def}}{=} \quad \boxed{\begin{array}{c|c|c} year & month & day \end{array}} \quad (15.6)$$

where

$$new\text{-}year \quad = \quad \textbf{french-new-year-on-or-before}\,(date)$$

$$year \quad = \quad \text{round}\left(\frac{new\text{-}year - \textbf{french-epoch}}{\textbf{mean-tropical-year}}\right) + 1$$

$$month \quad = \quad \left\lfloor \frac{date - new\text{-}year}{30} \right\rfloor + 1$$

$$day \quad = \quad ((date - new\text{-}year) \bmod 30) + 1$$

15.2 The Modified Form

> We are informed, that the present French Calendar will soon be
> abolished, it being found productive of endless inconvenience in
> mercantile transactions, in comparing dates of letters and bills of
> exchange, and possessing not one advantage in return, as it was
> not even astronomically just, and actually separated us from all the
> rest of Europe.
>
> —*The Times* (London), August 8, 1805

A simpler, arithmetical leap-year rule for the French Revolutionary calendar
was proposed by Gilbert Romme in 1795:

> Every 4th year is a leap year, except
> every 100th year is not a leap year, except
> every 400th year is a leap year, except
> every 4000th year is not a leap year,

giving an average of $1,460,969/4000 = 365.24225$ days per year, which is
an error of about 1 day in 14,000 years compared to the present mean tropical year length. Although the calendar was abandoned before this rule could
be adopted, we show how to implement this strictly arithmetical form of the
calendar.

We do not need to use it, but we define

modified-french-leap-year? (*f-year*) $\overset{\text{def}}{=}$ (15.7)

$(f\text{-}year \bmod 4) = 0$ and

$(f\text{-}year \bmod 400) \notin \{100, 200, 300\}$ and

$(f\text{-}year \bmod 4000) \neq 0$

Conversion of a French Revolutionary date to an R.D. date is thus done by
summing all days before that date, including the number of days before the
calendar began, 365 days for each prior year, all prior leap days (using the

inclusion/exclusion method described for the Gregorian calendar—see page 52), and the number of prior days in the present year:

fixed-from-modified-french (15.8)

$$\left(\begin{array}{|c|c|c|}\hline year & month & day \\\hline\end{array}\right) \stackrel{\text{def}}{=}$$

$$\textbf{french-epoch} - 1 + 365 \times (year - 1) + \left\lfloor \frac{year - 1}{4} \right\rfloor -$$

$$\left\lfloor \frac{year - 1}{100} \right\rfloor + \left\lfloor \frac{year - 1}{400} \right\rfloor - \left\lfloor \frac{year - 1}{4000} \right\rfloor +$$

$$30 \times (month - 1) + day$$

Calculating the French Revolutionary date from the R.D. *date* involves sequentially determining the year, month, and day of the month. The year is first approximated within one of its true value and then found precisely by checking the two possible years. The month is then found exactly by division, and the day of the month is determined by subtraction:

modified-french-from-fixed (*date*) $\stackrel{\text{def}}{=}$ (15.9)

$$\begin{array}{|c|c|c|}\hline year & month & day \\\hline\end{array}$$

where

$$approx = \left\lfloor \frac{date - \textbf{french-epoch} + 2}{\frac{1460969}{4000}} \right\rfloor + 1$$

$$year = \begin{cases} approx - 1 & \text{if } date < \textbf{fixed-from-modified-french} \left(\begin{array}{|c|c|c|}\hline approx & 1 & 1 \\\hline\end{array}\right) \\ approx & \textbf{otherwise} \end{cases}$$

$$month = \left\lfloor \frac{date - \textbf{fixed-from-modified-french} \left(\begin{array}{|c|c|c|}\hline year & 1 & 1 \\\hline\end{array}\right)}{30} \right\rfloor + 1$$

$$day = date - \textbf{fixed-from-modified-french} \left(\begin{array}{|c|c|c|}\hline year & month & 1 \\\hline\end{array}\right) + 1$$

References

[1] *Le Calendrier Républicain*, Bureau des Longitudes et Observatoire de Paris, Paris, 1994.

[2] J. Brady, *Clavis Calendaria; or, a Compendious Analysis of the Calendar: Illustrated with Ecclesiastical, Historical, and Classical Anecdotes*, 2nd ed., printed privately for the author, London, 1812.

[3] M. Hamer, "A Calendar for All Seasons," *New Scientist*, volume 124, no. 1696/1697, pp. 9–12, December 23/30, 1989.

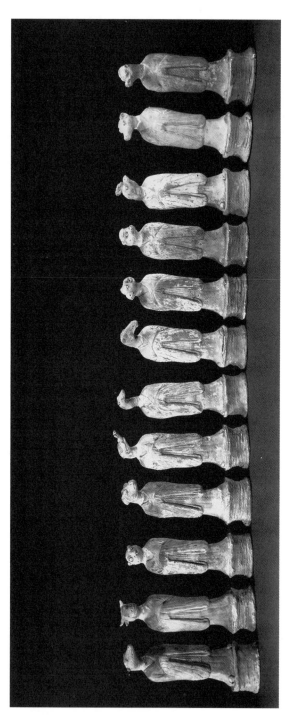

Pottery figurines of the 12 traditional Chinese calendrical animals (terrestrial branches) excavated in 1955 from a Táng Dynasty (618–907 C.E.), tomb in the suburbs of Xīān, Shǎnxī, China. These animals, shown left to right in the order given on page 257, are 38.5–41.5cm tall and have animal faces on human bodies with long robes; such funerary use of the 12 animals is still in practice. Reproduced with permission of the Department of Foreign Affairs, Art Exhibitions China.

16

The Chinese Calendar

> The complexity of calendars is due simply to the
> incommensurability of the fundamental periods on which they are
> based.... Calendars based on [the synodic month], depending only
> on lunations, make the seasons unpredictable, while calendars
> based on [the tropical year] cannot predict the full moons, the
> importance of which in ages before the introduction of artificial
> illuminants was considerable. The whole history of
> calendar-making, therefore, is that of successive attempts to
> reconcile the irreconcilable, and the numberless systems of
> intercalated months, and the like, are thus of minor scientific
> interest. The treatment here will therefore be deliberately brief.
> —Joseph Needham: *Science and Civilisation in China* (1959)[1]

The Chinese calendar is a lunisolar calendar based on astronomical events, not arithmetical rules. Days begin at civil midnight. Months are lunar, beginning on the day of the new moon and ending on the day before the next new moon. Years contain 12 or 13 such months, with the number of months determined by the number of new moons between successive winter solstices. The details of the Chinese calendar have varied greatly—there have been more than 50 calendar reforms—since its inception in the fourteenth century B.C.E.; some of its history, in particular its effect on the development of mathematics in China, is described in [8]; other historical details can be found in [3] and [11].[2] The version we implement here is the 1645 version, established in the second

---

[1] 作者可以不认同引文的见解

[2] The three most significant of calendar reforms were the following: In 104 B.C.E., the rule that the lunar month without a major solar term is intercalary was established (page 248), and *mean* values were used for both solar and lunar months, much like the old Hindu lunisolar calendar described in Chapter 9. In 619 C.E., the use of *true* new moons was introduced. In 1645 C.E., the use of *true* solar months was introduced.

year of the Qīng dynasty.[3] We discuss some common misconceptions about the Chinese calendar later in Section 16.5. The Japanese lunisolar calendar is nearly identical to the Chinese; we describe it in Section 16.8.

16.1 Solar Terms

> It is better to have no decent calendar than have Westerners in
> China.
> —Yáng Guāngxiān (1664)[4]

The Chinese year, called a nián (年), consists of true lunar months, but the arrangement of those months depends on the sun's course through the 12 zodiacal signs. Specifically, the Chinese divide the solar year into 24 solar terms or *jiéqì*: 12 major solar terms called *zhōngqì* and 12 minor solar terms known by the general term jiéqì. These terms correspond to 15° segments of solar longitude, with the major terms starting at $k \times 30°$ of solar longitude and the minor terms starting at $k \times 30° + 15°$ of solar longitude, $k = 0, 1, \ldots, 11$; the names of the 24 terms are shown in Table 16.1.

The dates of the terms in Table 16.1 are only approximate; the true motion of the sun varies, and thus to implement the Chinese calendar we need to calculate the precise date of a given solar longitude. We use the solar longitude function, equation (12.4), to determine the index of the last major solar term on or before a given date:

$$\textbf{current-major-solar-term}\,(date) \quad \overset{\text{def}}{=} \qquad (16.1)$$

$$\left(2 + \left\lfloor \frac{s}{30°} \right\rfloor \right) \text{ amod } 12$$

---

[3] Specifically, we follow the principles of Baolin Liú, the former calendrist of the Purple Mountain Observatory, Nanjing, China, as given in [9]; for a summary of this manuscript, see [4]. Our functions accurately reproduce the third printing of [16], of which Liú is the primary author, for 1907 onward; they reproduce Xú's table [22] for 1907 onward, except for 2033; Xú used the first printing of [16], which was later corrected (Xú takes the month beginning on August 25 as a leap month, forcing the solstice into the tenth month, thus violating Liú's basic principle given on page 247).

For years 1645–1906, our functions very occasionally err because of disagreements by a few minutes in the astronomical calculations (the Chinese used seventeenth-century models of the solar system until 1913, and thus their calculated times of solar and lunar events were not as accurate as ours); nevertheless, our calculated dates for Chinese New Year agree with Xú's table for 1644–2050.

[4] Yáng had attempted to amend the calendar, but his inadequate knowledge resulted in frequent errors [8]. He had had the Jesuits, who had—through superior astronomical calculations—achieved positions of importance in determining the calendar, framed and sentenced to death before the errors caused by his ignorance caused him to be sent into exile and the Jesuits to be released [1].

Table 16.1 *The solar terms of the Chinese year—major solar terms, zhōngqì (中气), are given in boldface; minor solar terms, jiéqì (节气), are given in lightface. Adapted from [4].*

Index	Chinese Name	Japanese Pronunciation	English Meaning	Solar Longitude	Approximate Starting Date
1.	Lìchūn (立春)	Risshun	Beginning of Spring	315°	February 4
1.	**Yǔshuǐ (雨水)**	Usui	**Rain Water**	**330°**	**February 19**
2.	Jīngzhé (惊蛰)	Kēchitsu	Waking of Insects	345°	March 6
2.	**Chūnfēn (春分)**	Shunbun	**Spring Equinox**	**0°**	**March 21**
3.	Qīngmíng (清明)	Sēmē	Pure Brightness	15°	April 5
3.	**Gǔyǔ (谷雨)**	Kokuu	**Grain Rain**	**30°**	**April 20**
4.	Lìxià (立夏)	Rikka	Beginning of Summer	45°	May 6
4.	**Xiǎomǎn (小满)**	Shōman	**Grain Full**	**60°**	**May 21**
5.	Mángzhòng (芒种)	Bōshu	Grain in Ear	75°	June 6
5.	**Xiàzhì (夏至)**	Geshi	**Summer Solstice**	**90°**	**June 21**
6.	Xiǎoshǔ (小暑)	Shōsho	Slight Heat	105°	July 7
6.	**Dàshǔ (大暑)**	Taisho	**Great Heat**	**120°**	**July 23**
7.	Lìqiū (立秋)	Risshū	Beginning of Autumn	135°	August 8
7.	**Chǔshǔ (处暑)**	Shosho	**Limit of Heat**	**150°**	**August 23**
8.	Báilù (白露)	Hakuro	White Dew	165°	September 8
8.	**Qiūfēn (秋分)**	Shūbun	**Autumnal Equinox**	**180°**	**September 23**
9.	Hánlù (寒露)	Kanro	Cold Dew	195°	October 8
9.	**Shuāngjiàng (霜降)**	Sōkō	**Descent of Frost**	**210°**	**October 24**
10.	Lìdōng (立冬)	Rittō	Beginning of Winter	225°	November 8
10.	**Xiǎoxuě (小雪)**	Shōsetsu	**Slight Snow**	**240°**	**November 22**
11.	Dàxuě (大雪)	Taisetsu	Great Snow	255°	December 7
11.	**Dōngzhì (冬至)**	Tōji	**Winter Solstice**	**270°**	**December 22**
12.	Xiǎohán (小寒)	Shōkan	Slight Cold	285°	January 6
12.	**Dàhán (大寒)**	Taikan	**Great Cold**	**300°**	**January 20**

where

$$s \quad = \quad \textbf{solar-longitude}$$
$$(\textbf{ universal-from-standard}$$
$$(date, \textbf{chinese-location}\,(date)) \,)$$

We define

$$\textbf{chinese-location}\,(t) \quad \overset{\text{def}}{=} \tag{16.2}$$

$$\begin{cases} \boxed{39.55° \quad 116°25' \quad 43.5m \quad \tfrac{1397}{180}} \\ \qquad\qquad\qquad \textbf{if } year < 1929 \\ \boxed{39.55° \quad 116°25' \quad 43.5m \quad 8} \\ \qquad\qquad\qquad\qquad \textbf{otherwise} \end{cases}$$

where

$$year \quad = \quad \textbf{gregorian-year-from-fixed}\,(\lfloor t \rfloor)$$

because before 1929 local mean time of Beijing was used—since Beijing is at longitude 116°25′ east, the time difference from U.T. was $7^{\text{h}}45^{\text{m}}40^{\text{s}} = 1397/180$ hours. After 1928, however, China adopted the standard time zone, and calendar makers used the 120° meridian, or 8 hours after U.T.[5]

Although not needed for date conversion, a printed Chinese calendar usually indicates the major and minor solar terms. The solar longitude functions in Section 12.4 also allow us to calculate the moment after the start of a given R.D. date when the solar longitude will be θ degrees:

$$\textbf{chinese-solar-longitude-on-or-after} \tag{16.3}$$
$$(date, \theta) \quad \overset{\text{def}}{=}$$

$$\textbf{standard-from-universal}\,(t, \textbf{chinese-location}\,(t))$$

where

$$t \quad = \quad \textbf{solar-longitude-after}$$
$$(\textbf{ universal-from-standard}$$
$$(date, \textbf{chinese-location}\,(date))\,, \theta \,)$$

from which we can determine the start of the major solar term on or after a

---

[5] Actual practice for 1928 is uncertain.

given date:

$$\textbf{major-solar-term-on-or-after}\,(date) \overset{\text{def}}{=} \tag{16.4}$$

$$\textbf{chinese-solar-longitude-on-or-after}\,(date, l)$$

where

$$l = 30 \times \left\lceil \dfrac{\begin{array}{c}\textbf{solar-longitude}\\ (\textbf{midnight-in-china}\,(date))\end{array}}{30} \right\rceil \bmod 360$$

We can also compute the index of the last minor solar term prior to a given date:

$$\textbf{current-minor-solar-term}\,(date) \overset{\text{def}}{=} \tag{16.5}$$

$$\left(3 + \left\lfloor \dfrac{s - 15°}{30°} \right\rfloor \right) \text{ amod } 12$$

where

$$s = \textbf{solar-longitude}\,(\textbf{midnight-in-china}\,(date))$$

and the date of the minor solar term on or after a given date:

$$\textbf{minor-solar-term-on-or-after}\,(date) \overset{\text{def}}{=} \tag{16.6}$$

$$\textbf{chinese-solar-longitude-on-or-after}\,(date, l)$$

where

$$l = \left(30 \times \left\lceil \dfrac{\begin{array}{c}\textbf{solar-longitude}\\ (\,\textbf{midnight-in-china}\,(date)\,)\end{array} - 15°}{30} \right\rceil + 15° \right) \bmod 360$$

One of the solar terms, the winter solstice (dōngzhì), plays a dominant role in the calendar, and we need to determine the date it occurs; because days end at civil midnight, the U.T. moment of midnight is given by

$$\textbf{midnight-in-china}\,(date) \overset{\text{def}}{=} \tag{16.7}$$

$$\textbf{universal-from-standard}$$

$$(date, \textbf{chinese-location}\,(date))$$

Now, using the same method used for the future Bahá'í calendar in Section 12.7, we have

chinese-winter-solstice-on-or-before (16.8)

$$(date) \stackrel{\text{def}}{=}$$

$$\underset{day \geq \lfloor approx \rfloor - 1}{\text{MIN}}$$

$$\left\{ \begin{array}{c} \textbf{winter} \leq \textbf{solar-longitude} \\ (\textbf{ midnight-in-china} \\ (day + 1) \,) \end{array} \right\}$$

where

$$approx = \textbf{estimate-prior-solar-longitude}$$
$$(\textbf{midnight-in-china} \, (date + 1) \,, \textbf{winter})$$

16.2 Months

Chinese months begin on the day of the new moon in Beijing, and thus we must be able to calculate that. We use the function **new-moon-after** (see page 190) to tell us the moment in universal time of the first new moon on or after *date* and the function **standard-from-universal** to convert to standard Beijing time (Section 12.2). With these functions we can write

chinese-new-moon-on-or-after $(date) \stackrel{\text{def}}{=}$ (16.9)

$$\left\lfloor \textbf{standard-from-universal} \right.$$
$$\left. (t, \textbf{chinese-location} \, (t)) \right\rfloor$$

where

$$t = \textbf{new-moon-after} \, (\textbf{midnight-in-china} \, (date))$$

Similarly, we use **new-moon-before** (page 190) in

chinese-new-moon-before $(date) \stackrel{\text{def}}{=}$ (16.10)

$$\left\lfloor \textbf{standard-from-universal} \right.$$
$$\left. (t, \textbf{chinese-location} \, (t)) \right\rfloor$$

where

$$t \quad = \quad \textbf{new-moon-before}$$

$$(\textbf{midnight-in-china} \, (date))$$

Once we can calculate the solar terms and new moons, we are ready to compute the arrangement of months in a Chinese year. The basic rule that determines the calendar is

The winter solstice (dōngzhì) always occurs during the eleventh month of the year.

To enforce this rule for a given Chinese year, we must examine the winter-solstice-to-winter-solstice period, called a *suì* (岁). Hence, we must compute the dates of two successive winter solstices. For example, in 1989 the winter solstice occurred at 9:23 p.m. U.T. on December 21, which was December 22 (R.D. 726,458) in Beijing. The next winter solstice was at 3:08 a.m. U.T. on December 22, 1990 (R.D. 726,823), which was the same date in Beijing. The list of the new moons in Beijing with R.D. dates d such that $726{,}458 < d \leq 726{,}823$ is

(i)	R.D. 726,464	(December 28, 1989)
(ii)	R.D. 726,494	(January 27, 1990)
(iii)	R.D. 726,523	(February 25, 1990)
(iv)	R.D. 726,553	(March 27, 1990)
(v)	R.D. 726,582	(April 25, 1990)
(vi)	R.D. 726,611	(May 24, 1990)
(vii)	R.D. 726,641	(June 23, 1990)
(viii)	R.D. 726,670	(July 22, 1990)
(ix)	R.D. 726,699	(August 20, 1990)
(x)	R.D. 726,729	(September 19, 1990)
(xi)	R.D. 726,758	(October 18, 1990)
(xii)	R.D. 726,788	(November 17, 1990)
(xiii)	R.D. 726,818	(December 17, 1990)

These 13 dates are the beginnings of months on the Chinese calendar during the suì from December 23, 1989 to December 22, 1990.

The average length of a lunar month is about 29.53 days and varies from approximately 29.27 to 29.84. Because there can be 365 or 366 days between successive solstices, there will be either 12 or 13 new moons: Fewer than 12 new moons is impossible because the longest period containing at most 11 new moons is just short of 12 consecutive lunar months and considerably less than 365 days; more than 13 new moons is also impossible because the shortest period containing at least 14 new moons contains 13 full lunar months, which is much more than 366 days. The 12 or 13 months thus found form the months following the eleventh month of the preceding Chinese year to the eleventh month of the Chinese year in question.

Months on the Chinese calendar are numbered 1 to 12; a leap month duplicates the number of the preceding month. The possible numberings of the 12 or 13 months from a winter solstice to the following winter solstice are thus as shown in Figure 16.1. It is clear from this figure that if there are only 12 new moons, they must be numbered 12, 1, 2, ..., 11; but if there are 13 new moons, which one is the leap month? The answer follows from the rule

The leap month of a 13-month winter-solstice-to-winter-solstice period is the first month that does not contain a major solar term—that is, the first lunar month that is wholly within a solar month.

There *must* be such a lunar month because the period from one winter solstice to the next contains only 12 major solar terms, yet there are 13 lunar months. (This is an application of the famous "Dirichlet box principle" or "pigeonhole principle"—see, for example, [10, Section 4.8].) A solar month can also fall entirely within a lunar month—that is, a lunar month can contain *two* major solar terms. Such an occurrence in a 13-month Chinese year can cause two or more lunar months without major solar terms; in a 12-month Chinese year it can cause one or more months without major solar terms.

We can test for a leap year by computing its first new moon, computing its last new moon, and rounding

$$\frac{last\text{-}new\text{-}moon - first\text{-}new\text{-}moon}{29.53}$$

to the nearest integer—if the value obtained is 12, the year is a leap year with 13 months.

There cannot be more than one leap month in a suì, but how do we know that a Chinese year cannot require two leap months? That is impossible because the two-solar-year period between the winter solstice of year $y - 2$ and the winter solstice of year y can contain either 24 or 25 lunar months; because the period from the winter solstice of year $y - 1$ to the winter solstice of year y has 13 months, the period from the winter solstice of year $y - 2$ to the winter solstice of year $y - 1$ can have only 12 lunar months and hence no leap month. Thus, the first month in a winter-solstice-to-winter-solstice period without a major solar term will be the leap month, and no second leap month is possible.

To determine whether a given month lacks a major solar term, we write a function that compares the major solar term at a given date with that at the

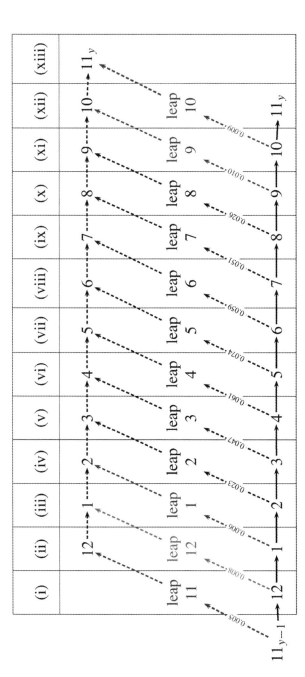

Figure 16.1 The theoretical possible numberings of the lunar months (i)–(xiii) for the Chinese calendar in the solstice to solstice period of year y. Each column corresponds to the new moon beginning a lunar month and each column contains the number of that lunar month. The winter solstice of Gregorian year $y - 1$ occurs in the lunar month numbered 11_{y-1}, that is, in the month before the new moon (i), and the winter solstice for Gregorian year y occurs in the lunar month numbered 11_y, that is, in the month of the new moon (xii) or (xiii). The solid arrows show the only possible numbering when there are 12 new moons between the successive solstices. Dashed lines show possible numberings when there are 13 new moons between successive solstices. Before 1645, when *mean* solar terms were used, any month could be followed by a leap month. The relatively swift movement of the sun in the winter means that in current practice, because *true* solar terms are used, leap months 9, 10, 11, or 1 are rare (these numberings are shown in gray); leap month 12 is exceptionally rare (this rare numbering is shown in light gray). The dashed lines from a month to a following leap month are labeled with the approximate probability of that transition based on data from [1] for the Chinese calendar for the thousand years 1645–2644.

249

beginning of the next month:

$$\textbf{no-major-solar-term?} \, (date) \quad \overset{\text{def}}{=} \tag{16.11}$$

$$\textbf{current-major-solar-term} \, (date)$$

$$= \textbf{current-major-solar-term}$$

$$(\textbf{chinese-new-moon-on-or-after} \, (date + 1))$$

Applying this function to the first day of a month tells us if the month lacks a solar term. Because we want only the first month missing a major term to be a leap month, we also need the following function:

$$\textbf{prior-leap-month?} \, \left(m', m\right) \quad \overset{\text{def}}{=} \tag{16.12}$$

$$m \geq m' \text{ and } \Big\{ \, \textbf{no-major-solar-term?} \, (m) \ \text{ or}$$

$$\textbf{prior-leap-month?}$$

$$\left(m', \textbf{chinese-new-moon-before} \, (m)\right) \, \Big\}$$

which determines (recursively) whether there is a Chinese leap month on or after the lunar month starting on fixed day m' and at or before the lunar month starting at fixed date m.

Figure 16.2 shows the structure of the Chinese calendar for a hypothetical year. Notice that the winter solstice is in the eleventh month, as required, and the month following the tenth month is a leap month containing no major solar term. Major terms and new moons are considered *without regard to their time of day*. Thus, for example, even if the major term, dōngzhì, occurred in Beijing *before* the new moon on that date, dōngzhì (the winter solstice) is considered to be in that month, not the previous month. In contrast, in the modern Hindu calendars (Chapter 17) the predicted time of day of an event is critical.

Continuing our example of 1989–90, we have the following dates for the major solar terms:

12.	Dàhán	R.D. 726,487	(January 20, 1990)
1.	Yǔshuǐ	R.D. 726,517	(February 19, 1990)
2.	Chūnfēn	R.D. 726,547	(March 21, 1990)
3.	Gǔyǔ	R.D. 726,577	(April 20, 1990)
4.	Xiǎomǎn	R.D. 726,608	(May 21, 1990)
5.	Xiàzhì	R.D. 726,639	(June 21, 1990)
6.	Dàshǔ	R.D. 726,671	(July 23, 1990)

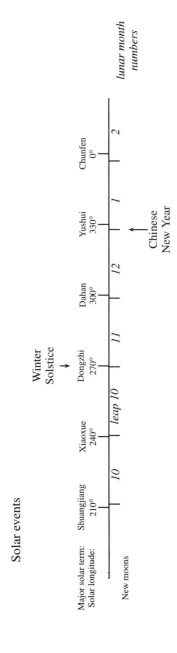

Figure 16.2 The Chinese calendar for a hypothetical year. Division into major solar terms is shown above the time line and new moons are shown below. Solar and lunar events are specified by the day of occurrence irrespective of the exact time of day. Chinese month numbers are in italic.

251

7.	Chǔshǔ	R.D. 726,702	(August 23, 1990)
8.	Qiūfēn	R.D. 726,733	(September 23, 1990)
9. Shuāngjiàng		R.D. 726,764	(October 24, 1990)
10.	Xiǎoxuě	R.D. 726,793	(November 22, 1990)
11.	Dōngzhì	R.D. 726,823	(December 22, 1990)

Collating this list with the list of new moons, we find

(i)		R.D. 726,464	(December 28, 1989)
12.	Dàhán	R.D. 726,487	(January 20, 1990)
(ii)		R.D. 726,494	(January 27, 1990)
1.	Yǔshuǐ	R.D. 726,517	(February 19, 1990)
(iii)		R.D. 726,523	(February 25, 1990)
2.	Chūnfēn	R.D. 726,547	(March 21, 1990)
(iv)		R.D. 726,553	(March 27, 1990)
3.	Gǔyǔ	R.D. 726,577	(April 20, 1990)
(v)		R.D. 726,582	(April 25, 1990)
4.	Xiǎomǎn	R.D. 726,608	(May 21, 1990)
(vi)		R.D. 726,611	(May 24, 1990)
5.	Xiàzhì	R.D. 726,639	(June 21, 1990)
(vii)		R.D. 726,641	(June 23, 1990)
(viii)		R.D. 726,670	(July 22, 1990)
6.	Dàshǔ	R.D. 726,671	(July 23, 1990)
(ix)		R.D. 726,699	(August 20, 1990)
7.	Chǔshǔ	R.D. 726,702	(August 23, 1990)
(x)		R.D. 726,729	(September 19, 1990)
8.	Qiūfēn	R.D. 726,733	(September 23, 1990)
(xi)		R.D. 726,758	(October 18, 1990)
9. Shuāngjiàng		R.D. 726,764	(October 24, 1990)
(xii)		R.D. 726,788	(November 17, 1990)
10.	Xiǎoxuě	R.D. 726,793	(November 22, 1990)
(xiii)		R.D. 726,818	(December 17, 1990)
11.	Dōngzhì	R.D. 726,823	(December 22, 1990)

Hence month (vii), from June 23 to July 21, 1990, is a leap month; that is, the numbering of the 13 months (i)–(xiii) must be (see Figure 16.1)

Month 12	R.D. 726,464	(December 28, 1989)
Month 1	R.D. 726,494	(January 27, 1990)
Month 2	R.D. 726,523	(February 25, 1990)
Month 3	R.D. 726,553	(March 27, 1990)
Month 4	R.D. 726,582	(April 25, 1990)

Month 5	R.D. 726,611	(May 24, 1990)
Leap month 5	R.D. 726,641	(June 23, 1990)
Month 6	R.D. 726,670	(July 22, 1990)
Month 7	R.D. 726,699	(August 20, 1990)
Month 8	R.D. 726,729	(September 19, 1990)
Month 9	R.D. 726,758	(October 18, 1990)
Month 10	R.D. 726,788	(November 17, 1990)
Month 11	R.D. 726,818	(December 17, 1990)

Thus the date of the Chinese New Year in this suì is found to be R.D. 726,494.

Describing the process outlined above algorithmically, we find the Chinese New Year in the suì containing *date*:

$$\textbf{chinese-new-year-in-sui}\,(date) \quad \overset{\text{def}}{=} \qquad\qquad (16.13)$$

$$\begin{cases} \textbf{chinese-new-moon-on-or-after}\,(m_{13}+1) \\ \qquad \textbf{if } \text{round}\left(\dfrac{next\text{-}m_{11} - m_{12}}{\textbf{mean-synodic-month}}\right) = 12 \text{ and} \\ \qquad \big\{\ \textbf{no-major-solar-term?}\,(m_{12}) \ \text{ or} \\ \qquad\quad \textbf{no-major-solar-term?}\,(m_{13})\ \big\} \\ m_{13} \hfill \textbf{otherwise} \end{cases}$$

where

$$s_1 \quad = \quad \textbf{chinese-winter-solstice-on-or-before}$$
$$(date)$$

$$s_2 \quad = \quad \textbf{chinese-winter-solstice-on-or-before}$$
$$(s_1 + 370)$$

$$m_{12} \quad = \quad \textbf{chinese-new-moon-on-or-after}\,(s_1 + 1)$$

$$m_{13} \quad = \quad \textbf{chinese-new-moon-on-or-after}\,(m_{12} + 1)$$

$$next\text{-}m_{11} \quad = \quad \textbf{chinese-new-moon-before}\,(s_2 + 1)$$

This latter function allows us to find the Chinese New Year on or before a given *date*:

$$\textbf{chinese-new-year-on-or-before}\,(date) \quad \overset{\text{def}}{=} \qquad\qquad (16.14)$$

$$\begin{cases} new\text{-}year & \textbf{if } date \geq new\text{-}year \\ \textbf{chinese-new-year-in-sui}\,(date - 180) & \textbf{otherwise} \end{cases}$$

where

$$new\text{-}year \quad = \quad \textbf{chinese-new-year-in-sui} \, (date)$$

We first find the Chinese New Year in the suì containing the given *date*; if that New Year is after *date* (which can happen if *date* is late in the Chinese year), we go back to the previous suì.

16.3 Conversions to and from Fixed Dates

> Ancient Chinese texts say that "the calendar and the pitch pipes have such a close fit, that you could not slip a hair between them."
> —Giorgio de Santillana and Hertha von Dechend: *Hamlet's Mill*
> (1969)

By tradition, Chinese years go in cycles of 60, each year having a special sexagenary name (discussed in the next section), with the first year of the first cycle commencing in year −2636 (Gregorian). Thus we define

$$\textbf{chinese-epoch} \quad \overset{\text{def}}{=} \tag{16.15}$$

$$\textbf{fixed-from-gregorian} \left(\quad \boxed{\begin{array}{c|c|c} -2636 & \textbf{february} & 15 \end{array}} \quad \right)$$

This is the traditional date of the first use of the sexagesimal cycle, February 15, −2636 (Gregorian) = March 8, 2637 B.C.E. (Julian).

Although it is not traditional to count these cycles, we do so for convenience to identify a year uniquely. The conversion between Chinese dates and R.D. dates can now be done by a method nearly identical to our function **chinese-new-year-in-sui**. Notice that most of the work lies in determining the month number and whether it is a leap month:

$$\textbf{chinese-from-fixed} \, (date) \quad \overset{\text{def}}{=} \tag{16.16}$$

cycle	year	month	leap-month	day

where

s_1	=	**chinese-winter-solstice-on-or-before**
		(*date*)
s_2	=	**chinese-winter-solstice-on-or-before**
		$(s_1 + 370)$
m_{12}	=	**chinese-new-moon-on-or-after** $(s_1 + 1)$
$next\text{-}m_{11}$	=	**chinese-new-moon-before** $(s_2 + 1)$
m	=	**chinese-new-moon-before** $(date + 1)$

$$leap\text{-}year \quad = \quad \text{round}\left(\frac{next\text{-}m_{11} - m_{12}}{\textbf{mean-synodic-month}}\right) = 12$$

$$month \quad = \quad \left(\text{round}\left(\frac{m - m_{12}}{\textbf{mean-synodic-month}}\right) \right.$$

$$\left. - \begin{cases} 1 & \textbf{if } leap\text{-}year \textbf{ and} \\ & \textbf{prior-leap-month?} \\ & (m_{12}, m) \\ 0 & \textbf{otherwise} \end{cases}\right) \ \text{amod } 12$$

$$leap\text{-}month \quad = \quad leap\text{-}year \textbf{ and}$$
$$\textbf{no-major-solar-term? } (m) \textbf{ and}$$
$$\text{not } \textbf{prior-leap-month?}$$
$$\left(m_{12}, \textbf{chinese-new-moon-before}\right.$$
$$(m)\left.\right)$$

$$elapsed\text{-}years \quad = \quad \left\lfloor 1.5 - \frac{1}{12} \times month + \frac{date - \textbf{chinese-epoch}}{\textbf{mean-tropical-year}} \right\rfloor$$

$$cycle \quad = \quad \left\lfloor \frac{elapsed\text{-}years - 1}{60} \right\rfloor + 1$$

$$year \quad = \quad elapsed\text{-}years \text{ amod } 60$$

$$day \quad = \quad date - m + 1$$

The calculation of *elapsed-years* is done by finding the elapsed years to the mid-summer of the desired Chinese year so that the irregular character of leap years cannot affect the truncation.

Finally, to convert a Chinese date to an R.D. date, we find a mid-year date of the given cycle and year, find the prior Chinese New Year, go forward to the appropriate months, and add the day of the month:

fixed-from-chinese (16.17)

$$\left(\begin{array}{|c|c|c|c|c|} \hline cycle & year & month & leap & day \\ \hline \end{array}\right) \stackrel{\text{def}}{=}$$

$$prior\text{-}new\text{-}moon + day - 1$$

where

$$mid\text{-}year = \left\lfloor \textbf{chinese-epoch} + \right.$$
$$((cycle - 1) \times 60 + year - 1 + 0.5)$$
$$\left. \times \textbf{mean-tropical-year} \right\rfloor$$

$$new\text{-}year = \textbf{chinese-new-year-on-or-before}$$
$$(mid\text{-}year)$$

$$p = \textbf{chinese-new-moon-on-or-after}$$
$$(new\text{-}year + (month - 1) \times 29)$$

$$d = \textbf{chinese-from-fixed}\,(p)$$

$$prior\text{-}new\text{-}moon = \begin{cases} p & \textbf{if } month = d_{\textbf{month}} \text{ and} \\ & leap = d_{\textbf{leap}} \\ \textbf{chinese-new-moon-on-or-after} \\ (p+1) \\ & \textbf{otherwise} \end{cases}$$

16.4 The Sexagesimal Cycle of Names

The Chinese calendar uses a cycle of 60 names for years. The name is formed by combining a *celestial stem*, tiān gān (天干), with a *terrestrial branch*, dì zhī (地支). The celestial stems,

(1) Jiǎ (甲)	(6) Jǐ (己)
(2) Yǐ (乙)	(7) Gēng (庚)
(3) Bǐng (丙)	(8) Xīn (辛)
(4) Dīng (丁)	(9) Rén (壬)
(5) Wù (戊)	(10) Guǐ (癸)

are untranslatable, though they are sometimes associated with the 5 elements (tree, fire, earth, metal, and water), each in its male and female form. These stems have another use as well—they correspond to "A, B, C, D, ..." For example, because written Chinese uses word symbols, rather than an alphabet, jiǎ, yǐ, bǐng, and dīng are used as letter grades on Chinese exam papers.

The terrestrial branches

(1) Zǐ (子)	(Rat)	(7) Wǔ (午)	(Horse)
(2) Chǒu (丑)	(Ox)	(8) Wèi (未)	(Sheep)
(3) Yín (寅)	(Tiger)	(9) Shēn (申)	(Monkey)
(4) Mǎo (卯)	(Hare)	(10) Yǒu (酉)	(Fowl)
(5) Chén (辰)	(Dragon)	(11) Xū (戌)	(Dog)
(6) Sì (巳)	(Snake)	(12) Hài (亥)	(Pig)

are also untranslatable; the English names—traditional animal totems—given for the 12 branches corresponding to the years of the Chinese "Zodiac" are not translations from the Chinese.

Names are assigned sequentially, running through the decimal and duo-denary lists simultaneously: The first name is jiǎzǐ, the second is yǐchǒu, the third is bǐngyín, and so on. Because the least common multiple of 10 and 12 is 60, the cycle of names repeats after the sixtieth name, guǐhài. Representing the name as a pair of numbers giving the celestial stem and the terrestrial branch (which must have the same parity), respectively, and using equation (1.50), we can thus obtain the nth name of the sexagenary cycle of names by the function

$$\textbf{chinese-sexagesimal-name}\ (n) \stackrel{\text{def}}{=} \tag{16.18}$$

$$\boxed{\ n \text{ amod } 10\ \big|\ n \text{ amod } 12\ }$$

Determining the number of names between given sexagesimal names is an instance of formula (1.53):

$$\textbf{chinese-name-difference} \tag{16.19}$$

$$\left(\boxed{\ stem_1\ \big|\ branch_1\ }, \boxed{\ stem_2\ \big|\ branch_2\ } \right) \stackrel{\text{def}}{=}$$

$$\Big(\big(stem\text{-}difference - 1 + $$
$$25 \times (branch\text{-}difference - stem\text{-}difference) \big) \bmod 60 \Big) + 1$$

where

$$stem\text{-}difference \quad = \quad stem_2 - stem_1$$

$$branch\text{-}difference \quad = \quad branch_2 - branch_1$$

Because the name of the first year of any cycle is jiǎzǐ, the name of Chinese *year* in any cycle is given by

$$\textbf{chinese-name-of-year}\ (year) \stackrel{\text{def}}{=} \tag{16.20}$$

$$\textbf{chinese-sexagesimal-name}\ (year)$$

This representation can be inverted to give the year within a cycle corresponding to a given sexagesimal name by using formula (1.53), as described on page 31.

At one time the Chinese used the same sequence of 60 names to name months and days as well. Extrapolating backward from known dates, we find

$$\textbf{chinese-month-name-epoch} \;\stackrel{\text{def}}{=}\; 3 \tag{16.21}$$

Because leap months were unnamed, we can write

$$\textbf{chinese-name-of-month}\,(\textit{year}, \textit{month}) \;\stackrel{\text{def}}{=} \tag{16.22}$$

$$\textbf{chinese-sexagesimal-name}$$

$$(\textit{elapsed-months} + \textbf{chinese-month-name-epoch})$$

where

$$\textit{elapsed-months} \;=\; 12 \times (\textit{year} - 1) + \textit{month} - 1$$

For days, the repeating sequence of 60 names acts like a "week." We have

$$\textbf{chinese-day-name-epoch} \;\stackrel{\text{def}}{=}\; 15 \tag{16.23}$$

$$\textbf{chinese-name-of-day}\,(\textit{date}) \;\stackrel{\text{def}}{=} \tag{16.24}$$

$$\textbf{chinese-sexagesimal-name}$$

$$(\textit{date} + \textbf{chinese-day-name-epoch})$$

Just as we did for the 7-day week in **kday-on-or-before**, we can apply formula (1.42) to compute the R.D. date of the last date with a given sexagesimal name on or before a given R.D. date:

$$\textbf{chinese-day-name-on-or-before}\,(\textit{name}, \textit{date}) \;\stackrel{\text{def}}{=} \tag{16.25}$$

$$\textit{date} - \Big(\Big(\,\textit{date} + \textbf{chinese-name-difference}$$

$$\big(\,\textit{name}, \textbf{chinese-sexagesimal-name}$$

$$(\textbf{chinese-day-name-epoch}\,)\big)\Big)\bmod 60\,\Big)$$

The 60-element cycle of stem-branch combinations is applied to Chinese hours as well as to years, months, and days. Because the Chinese hours are intervals that are 2 ordinary hours in length (from odd hour to odd hour), the 60-element cycle repeats in 5 days, and the 12-element cycle of branches repeats daily from 11 p.m. to 11 p.m. The 12 branches are therefore used on Chinese medicine labels—the herbalist tells the patient to take the medicine everyday in time slots yín and shēn, for example.

16.5 Common Misconceptions

> Please note... Islamic and Chinese new year dates are
> approximate.
> —American Express Publishing Company: *1995 Pocket Diary*

Not much has been written in Western languages about the Chinese calendar, but much of what has been written is ill-informed, out of date, or oversimplified.

For instance, the 19-year Metonic cycle is not used to determine leap years. Since 1645, true, not mean, behavior of the moon and sun is used in calculations, and as a consequence, months 11 and 12 can be followed by a leap month (rarely—but it can happen: in 2033 on the Chinese calendar there will be a leap month 11 and in 1890 on the Japanese lunisolar calendar, identical to the Chinese except for the location at which the calculations are done, there was a leap month 12). Thus, Chinese New Year is *not* always the second new moon after the winter solstice, as is sometimes claimed ([21], for example). Far enough in the future, as perihelion moves, winter leap months will become more and more common, including leap twelfth months.

There is a popular "rule" that says that Chinese New Year is the new moon closest to lìchūn (beginning of spring), which occurs approximately on February 4 (see, for example, [15]). Most of the time this is true, but if there is a new moon around January 21 (and hence again around February 20), the rule is difficult to apply. In such close situations, the rule can fail, as it did for 1985.

It is not traditional to count cycles or years; years are generally given as regnal years and by sexagesimal name. Our code describes the Chinese New Year that began on January 28, 1998 as year 15 in cycle 78, making it year $60 \times (78 - 1) + 15 = 4635$ in Chinese chronology. This era agrees with that used in Fritsche [5]. However, the popular press at the time described that new Chinese year as year 4696. The difference in year numbers stems from different choices of epoch and a likely error in calculation: We chose the traditional date of the first use of the sexagesimal cycle, February 15, -2636 (Gregorian) = March 8, 2637 B.C.E. (Julian); hence $1998 - (-2636) = 4634$ Chinese years elapsed prior to January 28, 1998. Others, including Sun Yat-sen, choose to number years from 2697 B.C.E., the first year of Emperor Huángdì, the traditional ancestor of the Chinese nation; this starting point would correctly give 4694 elapsed years as of January 28, 1998. Then, erroneously adding 1 to compensate for a year 0 on the Gregorian calendar gives 4695 elapsed years and hence year number 4696, as reported in the press. In any case, because the epoch in 2637 B.C.E. corresponds to year 61 of Huángdì, the sexagesimal name of a Chinese year is independent of the epoch.

The calculations are done for the 120° east meridian (after 1928). Calendars for other Asian countries may use other points of reference—see Section 16.8, for example.

16.6 Holidays

The last day of the Chinese lunisolar year, followed by the first day of the next year, is a major celebration on the Chinese calendar. We have already seen how to determine the Chinese New Year on or before a given fixed date. It is easy to use this to determine Chinese New Year in a given Gregorian year:

$$\textbf{chinese-new-year}\,(g\text{-}year) \;\overset{\text{def}}{=} \tag{16.26}$$

chinese-new-year-on-or-before

$$\Big(\, \textbf{fixed-from-gregorian}\,\Big(\; \boxed{\;g\text{-}year\;\vert\;\textbf{july}\;\vert\;1\;}\;\Big)\,\Big)$$

We ask for the New Year on or before a summer date because that New Year is the one found in the first suì examined in **chinese-new-year-on-or-before**. The more obvious choice of asking for the New Year on or before December 31 results in two suìs being examined because December 31 always falls at the end of the Chinese year.

Because the Chinese calendar is consistently aligned with the sufficiently accurate Gregorian calendar, the determination of holidays is handled, as on the Hebrew calendar, by observing that fixed dates on the Chinese calendar occur in fixed seasons of the year. Specifically,

Chinese New Year occurring in the winter of Gregorian year y

$$= y + 1 - \textbf{gregorian-year-from-fixed}(\textbf{chinese-epoch}).$$

For example, the Chinese year that began in the winter of year 0 (Gregorian) was 2637 (cycle 44, year 57). This means that holidays occurring in the spring, summer, and fall of Gregorian year y occur in the Chinese year $y + 2637$, whereas holidays in the winter occur in either Chinese year $y + 2637$ or $y + 2636$, depending on whether they are before or after January 1; such holidays need to be handled like Islamic holidays (Section 6.2).

Aside from Chinese New Year, the main fixed-Chinese-date holidays on the Chinese calendar are the Lantern Festival (fifteenth day of first month); the Dragon Festival (fifth day of the fifth month); Qǐqiǎo or Qīxī, called "Chinese Valentine's Day" (seventh day of the seventh month); Hungry Ghosts (fifteenth day of the seventh month); the Mid-Autumn Festival (fifteenth day of the eighth month); and the Double-Ninth Festival (ninth day of the ninth month). Holidays are never observed in leap months. For example, to find the R.D. date of the Dragon Festival in a Gregorian year, we would use

$$\textbf{dragon-festival}\,(g\text{-}year) \overset{\text{def}}{=} \tag{16.27}$$

$$\textbf{fixed-from-chinese}\left(\;\boxed{\begin{array}{c|c|c|c|c} cycle & year & 5 & false & 5 \end{array}}\;\right)$$

where

$$elapsed\text{-}years \quad = \quad g\text{-}year - \textbf{gregorian-year-from-fixed}\ +1$$
$$(\textbf{chinese-epoch})$$

$$cycle \quad = \quad \left\lfloor \frac{elapsed\text{-}years - 1}{60} \right\rfloor + 1$$

$$year \quad = \quad elapsed\text{-}years\ \text{amod}\ 60$$

In addition to the fixed-date holidays, two holidays are determined by solar terms, Qīngmíng and Dōngzhì (the winter solstice). To determine the exact dates for Gregorian year *g-year* we look for the next (major or minor) solar term after a date shortly before the approximate date of the term of interest. For example,

$$\textbf{qing-ming}\,(g\text{-}year) \overset{\text{def}}{=} \tag{16.28}$$

$$\left\lfloor\;\textbf{minor-solar-term-on-or-after}\right.$$
$$\left(\;\textbf{fixed-from-gregorian}\left(\;\boxed{\begin{array}{c|c|c} g\text{-}year & \textbf{march} & 30 \end{array}}\;\right)\right)\left.\right\rfloor$$

16.7 Chinese Age

According to the Chinese custom, a person's age is considered to be 1 immediately at birth; a person becomes a year older with each subsequent Chinese New Year, and thus a child born a week before the New Year is considered age 2 a week after birth! This difference in the meaning of "age" has caused difficulties in gathering and interpreting sociological data [17]. To compute the age of a person according to this custom, given the Chinese date of birth and the present fixed *date*, we would use

$$\textbf{chinese-age}\,(birthdate, date) \overset{\text{def}}{=} \tag{16.29}$$

$$\begin{cases} 60 \times \left(today_{\textbf{cycle}} - birthdate_{\textbf{cycle}}\right) + today_{\textbf{year}} - \\ birthdate_{\textbf{year}} + 1 \\ \qquad \textbf{if } date \geq \textbf{fixed-from-chinese}\,(birthdate) \\ \textbf{bogus} \qquad\qquad\qquad\qquad\qquad \textbf{otherwise} \end{cases}$$

where

$$today \quad = \quad \textbf{chinese-from-fixed}\,(date)$$

16.8 The Japanese Calendar

> It has often been remarked that the Japanese do many things in a way that runs directly counter to European ideas of what is natural and proper. To the Japanese themselves our ways appear equally unaccountable.
> —B. H. Chamberlain: *Things Japanese* (1911)[6]

The development of calendars in Japan closely paralleled that in China with similar improvements to the traditional Japanese calendar in years following those improvements to the Chinese calendar. For example, the use of true new moons began in China in 619 C.E., but in Japan in 697 C.E.; true solar months have been used in the Chinese calendar since 1645 and in the Japanese calendar since 1798. Since 1844, the traditional Japanese calendar has followed the principles described in this chapter except that the calculations are done based on locations in Japan. Although Japan officially changed over to the Gregorian calendar in 1873, the traditional calendar continues to be published and used, if only for astrological purposes. During 1873–1887 calculations were done using Tokyo longitude, 139°46′ east, which is $9^h19^m4^s$ ($= 9\frac{143}{450}$) after U.T. Since 1888, longitude 135° east (9 hours after U.T.) has been used. Thus, we define

$$\textbf{japanese-location}\,(t) \quad \overset{\mathrm{def}}{=} \qquad\qquad\qquad (16.30)$$

$$\begin{cases} \boxed{\begin{array}{c|c|c|c} 35.7° & 139°46′ & 24m & 9\frac{143}{450} \end{array}} \\ \qquad\qquad\qquad \textbf{if } year < 1888 \\ \boxed{\begin{array}{c|c|c|c} 35° & 135° & 0m & 9 \end{array}} \quad \textbf{otherwise} \end{cases}$$

where

$$year \quad = \quad \textbf{gregorian-year-from-fixed}\,(\lfloor t \rfloor)$$

As with the Chinese calendar, the sexagesimal cycles are not numbered. Rather, years are given according to the *nengō system*; this is a system of eras, the most recent of which are

Hēsē (平成)	1989–
Shōwa (昭和)	1926–1988
Taishō (大正)	1912–1925

---

[6] 筆者らは，必ずしも引用に同意というわけではない．

Mēji (明治)   1868–1911
Kēō (慶應)   1865–1867

Some tables (like [11]) give not only nengō years but also the *kigen*, a count of years since the mythological founding of the Japanese empire in 660 B.C.E. by Emperor Jimmu Tennō. Months are numbered as in Chinese; solar terms are given by the Chinese ideograms in Table 16.1, but they are pronounced using Japanese pronunciation of the Chinese characters.

To calculate the Japanese calendar, we just replace **chinese-location** with **japanese-location** throughout our functions for the Chinese calendar and change the epoch. The results match those in [12], which covers the period 1873–2050.[7] For earlier years, our results approximate those in [20] for 1844–1872 fairly well.[8] The Japanese dates given in [22] are untrustworthy.

The function **chinese-age** also conforms to Japanese system of determining age in the "kazoe doshi" (literally, "counted-year") system.

References

[1] H. Aslaksen, "The Mathematics of the Chinese Calendar," preprint, Department of Mathematics, National University of Singapore, manuscript, 1999.

[2] W. Bramsen, *Japanese Chronological Tables*, Seishi Bunsha, Tokyo, 1880.

[3] J. Chen, "Chinese Calendars," *Ancient China's Technology and Science*, compiled by the Institute of the History of Natural Sciences, Chinese Academy of Sciences, Foreign Language Press, Beijing, pp. 33–49, 1983.

[4] L. E. Doggett, "Calendars," *Explanatory Supplement to the Astronomical Almanac*, P. K. Seidelmann, ed., University Science Books, Mill Valley, CA, pp. 575–608, 1992.

[5] H. Fritsche, *On Chronology and the Construction of the Calendar with Special Regard to the Chinese Computation of Time Compared with the European*, R. Laverentz, St. Petersburg, 1886.

[6] P. Hoang, *A Notice of the Chinese Calendar and a Concordance with the European Calendar*, 2nd ed., Catholic Mission Press, Shanghai, 1904.

[7] P. Hoang, *Concordance des Chronologies Néoméniques Chinoise et Européene*, 12th ed., Kuangchi Press, Taiwan, 1968.

---

[7] Except for 1947; Nishizawa [12] follows the published calendar for 1947, which erroneously had a leap month 3 instead of a leap month 2 as the rules would dictate (in fact, the correct time is given for Gǔyǔ in [12] but is inconsistent with the calendar there!). Nishizawa [13] suggests that the erroneous calendar occurred because of post-war confusion. Our algorithms give the "correct" calendar.

[8] Perfectly from 1860 onward with occasional minor errors in 1844–1859, except for a major disagreement from the end of 1851 to the spring of 1852. Such disagreement is not surprising because, during 1844–1872, the Japanese calendar was based on *apparent time*, whereas our functions use *local mean time*. Furthermore, as with the Chinese calendar before the twentieth century, the astronomical models used for the Japanese calendar in the nineteenth century are less accurate than our astronomical functions.

[8] Y. Lǐ and S. Dù, *Chinese Mathematics: A Concise History*, translated by J. N. Crossley and A. W.-C. Lun, Oxford University Press, Oxford, 1987.

[9] B. Liú and F. R. Stephenson, "The Chinese Calendar and Its Operational Rules," manuscript, 1990.

[10] C. L. Liu, *Elements of Discrete Mathematics*, 2nd. ed., McGraw-Hill Book Co., Inc., New York, 1985.

[11] S. Nakayama, *A History of Japanese Astronomy: Chinese Background and Western Impact*, Harvard University Press, Cambridge, MA, 1969.

[12] Y. Nishizawa, *Rekijitsu Taikan (Treatise on the Japanese Calendar)*, Shinjinbutsu-Ōraisha, Tokyo, 1994.

[13] Y. Nishizawa, personal communication, September 3, 1999.

[14] J. Needham, *Science and Civilisation in China, Vol. 3: Mathematics and the Sciences of the Heavens and the Earth*, Cambridge University Press, Cambridge, 1959.

[15] F. Parise, ed., *The Book of Calendars*, Facts on File, New York, 1982.

[16] Purple Mountain Observatory, *Xīn biān wàn nián lì (The Newly Compiled Perpetual Chinese Calendar) 1840–2050*, Kē xué pǔ jí chū bǎn shè (Popular Science Press), Beijing, 1984. Third and subsequent printings correct the structure of the year 2033.

[17] S.-H. Saw, "Errors in Chinese Age Statistics," *Demography*, volume 4, pp. 859–875, 1967.

[18] F. R. Stephenson and B. Liú, "A Brief Contemporary History of the Chinese Calendar," manuscript, 1990.

[19] P. Y. Tsuchihashi, *Japanese Chronological Tables from 601 to 1872*, Monumenta Nipponica Monograph 11, Sophia University, Tokyo, 1988.

[20] M. Uchida, *Nihon Rekijitsu Genten (Sourcebook for the Japanese Calendar System)*, Yūzankaku-Shuppan, Inc., Tokyo, 1994.

[21] W. C. Welch, *Chinese-American Calendar for the 102 Chinese Years Commencing January 24, 1849 and Ending February 5, 1951*, U.S. Department of Labor, Bureau of Immigration, United States Government Printing Office, Washington, 1928.

[22] H. C. Xú, *Xīn biān Zhōng-guó sān qiān nián lì rì jiǎn suǒ biǎo (The Newly Compiled Chinese 3000-Year Calendar Indexing Table)*, Rén mín jiào yù chū bǎn shè (People's Education Press), Beijing, 1992.

Twelfth-century black stone slab from Andhra Pradesh, India, depicting the 12 signs of the zodiac surrounding a lotus in full bloom representing the sun. (Courtesy of the Prince of Wales Museum of Western India, Bombay.)

17

The Modern Hindu Calendars

Adhika months are the cream of the Indian Calendar, while *kshaya* are its *crème de la crème*. Figures of speech apart, it is certainly true that the success or failure of any computer in deducing *adhika* and *kshaya* months is the measure of the success or failure, as a whole, with the Indian Calendar. How far the present method satisfies this ordeal, will be for competent judges to decide.
—Dewan Bahadur L. D. Swamikannu Pillai:
Indian Chronology (1911)

Today, numerous calendars are used in India for different purposes. The Gregorian calendar is used by the government for civil matters; the Islamic calendar is used by Moslems; the Hindus employ both solar and lunisolar calendars. Indeed, there are over 30 variations of the Hindu calendar in active use. In March 1957, an attempt was made to revise the traditional calendar to follow the pattern of the Gregorian leap year structure [1]. The proposed reform has not, however, been widely accepted, though the new, National Calendar dates appear in published calendars.

The best known of several related systems used on the Indian subcontinent is the classical Hindu calendar of the (Present) *Sūrya-Siddhānta* (circa 1000), said to have been revealed to Maya the Assyrian at the end of the last "Golden Age," in the year 2,163,154 B.C.E.[1] This work introduced a calendar based on approximations to the true times of astronomical events rather than the mean values used in the earlier, simpler calendar described in Chapter 9. This calendar is somewhat similar to the Chinese, beginning its months according to the actual time of new moon; however, the Chinese calendar today uses modern astronomical methods to determine these times, whereas the Hindu calendar

---

[1] Not 2,163,102 B.C.E., as stated in [9, p. ix], on account of the discrepancy between the Julian and Hindu average year lengths.

applies fixed, ancient methods to approximate the true positions of the sun and moon.

In the mean Hindu calendar (Chapter 9), the calculations are simple. The necessary computational mechanisms for the true system are, by contrast, very complex; experts have attempted over the centuries to reduce hand calculations to table lookup and the very simplest arithmetical operations, avoiding nuisances like large numbers or even signed numbers but requiring logarithms and a multiplicity of tables covering various periods of time. However, shortcuts for humans are unnecessary complications for computers, and we avoid all of them. Unlike table-based methods, the use of rational numbers gives perfect fidelity to the sources. We believe that an algorithmic description is the simplest and most concise way of describing the rules; it has allowed us to condense many pages of words and tables into a few hundred lines of computer code.

The modern Hindu calendar depends on the computed positions of the sun and moon, taking into account that solar and lunar motions vary in speed across the celestial sphere. We refer to these positions as "true," though they are not true in the astronomical sense but rather approximate the irregular apparent motions of the sun and moon. The Hindu sidereal year is the time it takes for the position of the sun to return to the constellation Aries; its length averages $365.25875648\cdots$ days. The length of a solar month varies from 29.318 days to 31.644; that of a Hindu lunar month varies from 29.305 to 29.812 days. The sidereal month is the mean time it takes for the moon to return to the same (longitudinal) point vis-à-vis the stars and is given as $27.321674\cdots$ days. The synodic month takes the motion of the sun into account; it is the mean time between new moons (lunar conjunctions) and is taken to be $29.5305879\cdots$ days. (See Section 12.5.) The mean values for years and months are given in the *Sūrya-Siddhānta* as rational numbers:

$$\textbf{hindu-sidereal-year} \ \overset{\text{def}}{=}\ 365\frac{279457}{1080000} \tag{17.1}$$

$$\textbf{hindu-sidereal-month} \ \overset{\text{def}}{=}\ 27\frac{4644439}{14438334} \tag{17.2}$$

$$\textbf{hindu-synodic-month} \ \overset{\text{def}}{=}\ 29\frac{7087771}{13358334} \tag{17.3}$$

The modern and old Hindu solar calendars have the same basic structure and are based on the sidereal year. Each solar month begins when the sun enters a new sign of the zodiac. Hindu longitudes are sidereal (relative to the fixed stars, not to the precessing equinoctial point) and have as their origin a point near ζ Piscium (Revatī, the sixth brightest star—actually a binary star—in constellation Pisces, near the ecliptic), or (according to other opinions) 180° from the star Spica (= α Virginis), rather than from the equinoctial point—but this has no impact on the calculations. (See Section 12.1.) If the sign is entered before some critical time (see page 279 for details), then the day is day 1 of a new month; otherwise, it is the last day of the previous month. However, because the solar months vary in length, we cannot know when successive months begin without calculating the position of the sun. The result is that a solar month can have 29, 30, 31, or 32 days. The lunar month is either 29 or 30 days long. The (solar) day begins at sunrise. Because (in the variant we implement) it is the zodiacal position of the sun at sunrise that determines the month name, we will have to compute sunrise as well.

As with the old Hindu calendar (Chapter 9), lunar month names are determined by the (first) zodiacal sign entered by the sun during the month. When no sign is entered, the month is considered leap; leap months take the same name as the following month. This method of reckoning also leads occasionally to lost months. When, very rarely, a solar month elapses with no new moon, a lunar month is skipped (called *kshaya*). There is a 19- to 141-year gap between occurrences of skipped months; they occur in the winter, near perihelion, when the apparent motion of the sun is fastest. As in the Chinese calendar with its similar leap-month scheme (see page 247), a lunisolar year must have either 12 or 13 months. Thus, a year with a skipped month perforce contains either 1 leap month (as in 1963[2]) or (extremely rarely) 2 leap months (as in 4576 K.Y. = 1475–1476 C.E. and in 5083 K.Y. = 1982–1983[3]).

As in Chapter 9, we follow here the *amânta* scheme in which months begin and end with new moons; in the alternative *pûrṇimânta* scheme (used primarily in the states of Bihar, Uttar Pradesh, Madhya Pradesh, Rajasthan, Haryana, and Kashmir), months go from full moon to full moon. A peculiarity of the latter method [2] is that the New Year begins with the new moon in the middle of the first month.

The month names (page 134) are derived from asterisms (star groups) along the ecliptic. They are a subset of the original names for the (unequal) division of the ecliptic into 27 or 28 lunar stations or "mansions," one for each day of the sidereal month. The lunar month name is that of the asterism in which the full moon occurs. The exact star groups were already uncertain in the time of al-Bīrūnī; one suggestion is given in Table 17.1.

---

[2] In 1897, Sewell and Dîkshit [8] wrote, "We are led by these peculiarities to suppose that there will be no suppressed month till at earliest A.D. 1944, and possibly not till A.D. 1963." Pillai's [5] reaction was that "there is no reason why this matter should be treated as one for conjecture, since anybody familiar with the present method can calculate that the next *Kshaya* month will be in A.D. 1963."

[3] From 1300 C.E. until 1980 C.E., only Mārgaśīrsha (in the years beginning in 1315, 1380, 1521), Pausha (1334, 1399, 1540, 1681, 1822, 1963), and Māgha (1418, 1475) have been skipped. The omission of Māgha (and concomitant intercalation of Phālguna) in 1418 is not listed in [9] (only 4 minutes separate the start of the solar and lunar months). Also according to our calculations Māgha should have been omitted in 5083 K.Y. This is a close call, for the sun entered Māgha on February 13, 1983 (Gregorian) at 4:10:18 a.m., and the new moon occurred half an hour later at 4:43:56. The prior new moon was on January 14 at 9:03:53 a.m., which was before the sun entered Makara at 5:26:14 p.m.; Āśvina and Phālguna were leap.

Table 17.1 *Suggested correspondence of lunar stations and asterisms. Boldface indicates stations after which lunar months are named. The Greek letters indicate the relative brightness of the star in its constellation. (Popular names are given in parentheses.) Thus, α Tauri is the brightest star in Taurus, called Aldebaran ("the follower" in Arabic, a red star of first magnitude in the eye of the bull and part of the Hyades). A twenty-eighth station, omitted from some lists, is unnumbered.*

	Lunar station	Prominent star	Associated deity
1.	**Aśvinī**	α Arietis (Hamal)	Aśvinau
2.	Bharaṇī	35 Arietis	Yama
3.	**Kṛittikâ**	η Tauri (Alcyone)	Agni
4.	Rohiṇī	α Tauri (Aldebaran)	Prajāpati
5.	**Mṛigaśiras**	λ Orionis (Meissa)	Soma
6.	Ārdrā	α Orionis (Betelgeuse)	Rudra
7.	Punarvasu	β Geminorum (Pollux)	Aditi
8.	**Pushya**	δ Cancri (Asellus Australis)	Bṛhaspati
9.	Āśleshā	α Cancri (Acubens)	Sarpāḥ
10.	**Maghā**	α Leonis (Regulus)	Pitaraḥ
11.	Pūrva Phalgunī	δ Leonis (Zosma)	Aryaman
12.	**Uttara Phalgunī**	β Leonis (Denebola)	Bhaga
13.	Hasta	γ Corvi (Gienah)	Savitṛ
14.	**Chitrā**	α Virginis (Spica)	Indra
15.	Svāti	α Bootis (Arcturus)	Vāyu
16.	**Viśākhā**	α Libræ (Zubenelgenubi)	Indrāgni
17.	Anurādhā	δ Scorpii (Dschubba)	Mitra
18.	**Jyeshṭhā**	α Scorpii (Antares)	Indra
19.	Mūla	γ Scorpii	Pitaraḥ
20.	Pūrva Āshāḍhā	δ Sagittarii (Kaus Media)	Āpaḥ
21.	**Uttara Āshāḍhā**	σ Sagittarii (Nunki)	Viśve devāḥ
	Abhijit	α Lyræ (Vega)	Brahmā
22.	**Śravaṇā**	α Aquilæ (Altair)	Viṣṇu
23.	Dhanishthā	α Delphini (Sualocin)	Vasavaḥ
24.	Śatatārakā	λ Aquarii	Indra
25.	Pūrva Bhādrapadā	α Pegasi (Markab)	Aja Ekapād
26.	**Uttara Bhādrapada**	α Andromedæ (Alpheratz)	Ahirbudhnya
27.	Revatī	ζ Piscium	

Day numbers are determined by the lunar phase, or *tithi*, current at sunrise (see Chapter 9). The varying motion of the moon—a "lunar day" ranges in length from 21.5 to 26.2 hours—can cause two sunrises to fall within 1 lunar day, or (every 2 months, or so) for a lunar day to begin and end between one sunrise and the next. This situation leads to a unique aspect of the Hindu scheme: Consecutive days can bear the *same* ordinal number (an "intercalated" day), and any number can be skipped (an "extracalated" day). In the case of days, the second of 2 days with the same number is considered extra (*adhika*). A day may therefore be named "Second 7 in the dark half of the first Mārgaśira."

Suppose we can determine the sidereal longitudes of the Sun and Moon at any given time. To determine the Hindu lunar date of any given day, we perform the following sequence of operations:

1. Determine the phase of the moon at sunrise of the given day by taking the difference of longitudes between the positions of the sun and moon. Dividing the difference in degrees by 12 gives an integer in the range 0 ... 29, corresponding to (one less than) the ordinal number of the lunar day current at sunrise.
2. Compare the current day number with that of the previous. If they are the same, then it is a leap day (and "*adhika*" is appended to the number).
3. Determine when the last new moon at or before sunrise of the current day occurred.
4. Determine the position of the sun (which is the same as that of the moon) at that new moon. The zodiacal sign in which it occurs establishes the name (that of the next sign) of the current month.
5. Compare the current month name with that of the next new moon. If they are the same, then it is a leap month (and "*adhika*" is appended to the month's name).

In contrast, the calculations of the old (mean) Hindu lunisolar calendar can result in added months and lost days but not lost months nor added days. Because the mean lunar month is shorter than the mean solar month, there is never a situation on the mean calendar in which an expunged lunar month is called for. Similarly, because a civil day is longer than a thirtieth of a mean synodic month, leap days were never needed.

17.1 Hindu Astronomy

From a chronological point of view the substitution for the mean calendric system of one based on the true movements of the sun and moon, was anything but an improvement, as it destabilized the foundations of the time reckoning. Indeed, the system may have had the charm of adapting daily life as nearly as the astronomical knowledge permitted to the movement of the heavenly bodies, but on the other hand it broke ties with history, as there was no unity of elements or systems. The very complexity of the system is proof of its primitiveness.

—W. E. van Wijk: *Decimal Tables for the Reduction of Hindu Dates from the Data of the Sūrya-Siddhānta* (1938)

From the time of Ptolemy's *Almagest* in the second century until the Keplerian Revolution of the seventeenth century, it was well known that the motions of the seven heavenly bodies visible to the naked eye (the sun, the moon, Mercury, Venus, Mars, Jupiter, and Saturn) can best be described by combinations of circular motions, that is, cycles and epicycles.[4] The Hindu calendar approximations are based on such epicycles.

To find the true positions of the sun and moon we need to adjust their mean longitudes by the contribution of the epicycle. The heavenly body is assumed to remain on the *deferent* (the main circle) but to be "pulled" in one direction or the other by "winds" and "cords of air" originating on the epicycle. If we assume the center of the epicycle is at longitude β and the *anomaly* (angle of the heavenly body around the epicycle, measured from the farthest point from Earth along the epicycle) is α, the angular position is approximately

$$\beta + \arcsin(r \sin \alpha),$$

where r is the ratio of radii of epicycle and deferent. Figure 17.1 illustrates this arrangement.

The *Sūrya-Siddhānta* and earlier Hindu astronomical tracts give a table of sines for angles of $0°$ to $90°$, in increments of 225 minutes of arc, and interpolation is used for intermediate values. The sines, shown in Table 17.2, are given as integers in the range $0 \ldots 3438$ (that is, in terms of a radius of 3438 units) and serve as close approximations to the true sine.[5] We implement the table by means of the following ad hoc function, which returns an amplitude in the range $[0 : 1]$ for angles given in degrees:

$$\textbf{hindu-sine-table} \, (entry) \;\overset{\text{def}}{=}\; \frac{1}{3438} \times \text{round} \, (exact + error) \quad (17.4)$$

where

$$exact \;=\; 3438 \times \sin \left(entry \times \frac{225}{60} \right)$$

$$error \;=\; 0.215 \times \text{signum} \, (exact) \times \text{signum} \, (|exact| - 1716)$$

---

[4] Elliptical motion is indeed exactly characterized by one retrograde epicycle, on which motion is in the opposite direction of that along the deferent and the period is double (see Figure 17.1); the distinction between elliptical motion and epicyclical motion is conceptual. Kepler's second law of 1609 explains that the motion is not uniform.

[5] A radius of 3438 and a quadrant comprising 5400 minutes imply a value of $\frac{5400 \times 4}{3438 \times 2} \approx 3.141361$ for π. A recurrence is given in the *Sūrya-Siddhānta* for producing this table of sines, namely

$$\sin(n+1)\alpha = n\alpha - \frac{1}{225} \sum_{i<n} (n - i) \sin(n\alpha),$$

where $\alpha = 225'$. The table given in *Sūrya-Siddhānta*, however, is more accurate than this formula and, as seen in Table 17.2, is correct, except for erratic rounding. The recurrence would be precise with $(225/3438)^2 \approx 1/233.5$ instead of $1/225$. See Burgess's comments in [9, p. 335].

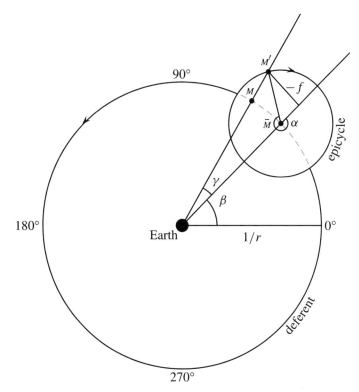

Figure 17.1 The motion of the moon viewed from above the North Pole. The mean position of the moon, $\overline{M}$, revolves in a circle, called the *deferent*, of radius $1/r$ at a steady rate (once every mean sidereal month). At the same time, a "being" M' rotates around an epicycle of unit radius centered at $\overline{M}$ in the opposite direction of the motion of $\overline{M}$ so that it returns to the apogee (the point at which it is farthest from Earth) in a period called the *anomalistic month*. Let β be the longitude of $\overline{M}$, α be the angle of M' from the apogee, called the *anomaly*, and f be $\sin \alpha$, which we call the *offset*. The true longitude of the moon, M, on the deferent along a radius from Earth to M', is $\beta + \gamma$, where $\sin \gamma \approx -fr = -(\sin \alpha)r$. Thus we have for the *equation of center* $\gamma = 360° - \arcsin(r \sin \alpha) = \arcsin(r \sin \alpha)$. In addition, the ratio r changes as $\overline{M}$ revolves around Earth (see the text). The figure is not drawn to scale.

Linear interpolation is used for in-between values:

$$\textbf{hindu-sine}\,(\theta) \quad \overset{\text{def}}{=} \tag{17.5}$$

$$\textit{fraction} \times \textbf{hindu-sine-table}\,(\lceil \textit{entry} \rceil) \,+$$

$$(1 - \textit{fraction}) \times \textbf{hindu-sine-table}\,(\lfloor \textit{entry} \rfloor)$$

Table 17.2 *Hindu sine table, 0–90° (with radius 3438)*

Table Entry	Angle (Minutes)	Hindu Sine	Precise Value	Table Entry	Angle (Minutes)	Hindu Sine	Precise Value
0	0	0	0.00				
1	225	225	224.86	13	2925	2585	2584.83
2	450	449	448.75	14	3150	2728	2727.55
3	675	671	670.72	15	3375	2859	2858.59
4	900	890	889.82	16	3600	2978	2977.40
5	1125	1105	1105.11	17	3825	3084	3083.45
6	1350	1315	1315.67	18	4050	3177	3176.30
7	1575	1520	1520.59	19	4275	3256	3255.55
8	1800	1719	1719.00	20	4500	3321	3320.85
9	2025	1910	1910.05	21	4725	3372	3371.94
10	2250	2093	2092.92	22	4950	3409	3408.59
11	2475	2267	2266.83	23	5175	3431	3430.64
12	2700	2431	2431.03	24	5400	3438	3438.00

where

$$entry = \theta \times \frac{60}{225}$$

$$fraction = entry \bmod 1$$

To invert **hindu-sine** we use,

$$\textbf{hindu-arcsin}\,(amp) \stackrel{\text{def}}{=} \tag{17.6}$$

$$\begin{cases} -\,\textbf{hindu-arcsin}\,(-amp) & \textbf{if } amp < 0 \\[2ex] \frac{225}{60} \times \left(pos - 1 + \dfrac{amp - below}{\textbf{hindu-sine-table}\,(pos) \,-\, below} \right) & \\[2ex] & \textbf{otherwise} \end{cases}$$

where

$$pos = \underset{k \geq 0}{\text{MIN}} \left\{ amp \leq \textbf{hindu-sine-table}\,(k) \right\}$$

$$below = \textbf{hindu-sine-table}\,(pos - 1)$$

Again, interpolation is used for intermediate values not appearing in the table.

To determine the position of the mean sun or moon, we have the generic function

$$\textbf{mean-position}\,(t, period) \stackrel{\text{def}}{=} \tag{17.7}$$

$$360° \times \left(\frac{t - \textbf{hindu-creation}}{period} \bmod 1 \right)$$

which calculates the longitude (in degrees) at a given moment t when the period of rotation is *period* days. The visible planets, according to the *Sūrya-Siddhānta*, were in mean conjunction at the epoch but in *true* conjunction at the end of creation, 1,955,880,000 years (sidereal, not tropical—the difference is slight; see Section 12.4) prior to the onset of the Kali Yuga:

$$\textbf{hindu-creation} \;\overset{\text{def}}{=} \tag{17.8}$$

$$\textbf{hindu-epoch} - 1955880000 \times \textbf{hindu-sidereal-year}$$

Thus, the anomaly is taken to be 0 at (the end of) creation. The size of the sun's epicycle is $14/360$ of its deferent; for the moon the ratio is larger: $32/360$. The period of revolution of the (cords of air around the) epicycles are

$$\textbf{hindu-anomalistic-year} \;\overset{\text{def}}{=}\; \frac{1577917828000}{4320000000 - 387} \tag{17.9}$$

$$\textbf{hindu-anomalistic-month} \;\overset{\text{def}}{=} \tag{17.10}$$

$$\frac{1577917828}{57753336 - 488199}$$

for the sun and moon, respectively. These values are derived from the stated speed of rotation of the apsides, $387/1000$ times in 4,320,000 years ($= 1,577,917,828$ days) for the sun and 488,199 times in the same period for the moon.[6] The anomalistic month is the corrected (*bija*) value introduced in the mid-sixteenth century by Gaṇeśa Daivajña and still in use today, not that originally given in the *Sūrya-Siddhānta*.

To complicate matters, in the scheme of *Sūrya-Siddhānta*, the epicycle actually shrinks as it revolves (almost as if there were an epicycle on the epicycle). For both the sun and moon, the change amounts to $20'$ and reaches its minimum value when entering the even quadrants. Changes in the size of the epicycle are reflected in the following function:

$$\textbf{true-position}\,(t,\,period,\,size,\,anomalistic,\,change) \;\overset{\text{def}}{=} \tag{17.11}$$

$$(long - equation) \;\bmod\; 360$$

---

[6] Whereas we compute the anomaly from creation, traditionally one precomputes the position of perihelion at some base date, and the time between true and mean New Year for that base, called *sodhya*, because the solar anomaly changes very slowly. "The difference in the sun's equation of the centre and true longitude, caused by the shift of the apsin, is exceedingly small and may well be ignored" [7, p. 55].

where

$$long \qquad = \quad \textbf{mean-position}\,(t, period)$$

$$offset \qquad = \quad \textbf{hindu-sine}$$

$$(\textbf{mean-position}\,(t, anomalistic))$$

$$contraction \quad = \quad |offset| \times change \times size$$

$$equation \qquad = \quad \textbf{hindu-arcsin}\,(offset \times (size - contraction))$$

which adjusts the mean longitudinal position (center of the epicycle) by the equation of motion (the longitudinal displacement caused by epicyclic motion), calculated from creation, and normalizes the resultant angle by using the modulus function.

Plugging in the relevant constants, we have

$$\textbf{hindu-solar-longitude}\,(t) \quad \stackrel{\text{def}}{=} \qquad\qquad\qquad (17.12)$$

true-position
$$\left(t, \textbf{hindu-sidereal-year}, \tfrac{14}{360}, \textbf{hindu-anomalistic-year}, \tfrac{1}{42} \right)$$

from which the zodiacal position follows:

$$\textbf{hindu-zodiac}\,(t) \quad \stackrel{\text{def}}{=} \qquad\qquad\qquad (17.13)$$

$$\left\lfloor \frac{\textbf{hindu-solar-longitude}\,(t)}{30°} \right\rfloor + 1$$

The position of the moon is calculated in a similar fashion:

$$\textbf{hindu-lunar-longitude}\,(t) \quad \stackrel{\text{def}}{=} \qquad\qquad\qquad (17.14)$$

true-position
$$\left(t, \textbf{hindu-sidereal-month}, \tfrac{32}{360}, \textbf{hindu-anomalistic-month}, \tfrac{1}{96} \right)$$

Now we have all the information needed to determine the phase of the moon at any given time. It is simply the difference in longitudes:

$$\textbf{hindu-lunar-phase}\,(t) \quad \stackrel{\text{def}}{=} \qquad\qquad\qquad (17.15)$$

$$\left(\textbf{hindu-lunar-longitude}\,(t) - \right.$$
$$\left. \textbf{hindu-solar-longitude}\,(t) \right) \bmod 360$$

This translates into the number of the lunar day by dividing the difference by one-thirtieth of a full circle (that is, 12°):

$$\textbf{lunar-day}\,(t) \quad \overset{\text{def}}{=} \quad \left\lfloor \frac{\textbf{hindu-lunar-phase}\,(t)}{12°} \right\rfloor + 1 \qquad (17.16)$$

To find the time of the new moon, we need to search for the day when the difference in longitudes of the sun and moon is nil. The exact time can be found by bisection (see page 22):

$$\textbf{hindu-new-moon-before}\,(t) \quad \overset{\text{def}}{=} \qquad\qquad\qquad (17.17)$$

$$\underset{x\in[\tau-1:\min\{t,\tau+1\}]}{\overset{p(l,u)}{\text{MIN}}} \left\{ \textbf{hindu-lunar-phase}\,(x) < 180° \right\}$$

where

$$\varepsilon \quad = \quad 2^{-1000}$$

$$\tau \quad = \quad t - \frac{1}{360°} \times \textbf{hindu-lunar-phase}\,(t)$$

$$\times \textbf{hindu-synodic-month}$$

$$p\,(l,u) \quad = \quad \textbf{hindu-zodiac}\,(l) = \textbf{hindu-zodiac}\,(u) \ \text{or}$$

$$u - l < \varepsilon$$

The search can terminate as soon as it has narrowed the position of the new moon down to one zodiacal sign. (To prevent any possibility of an infinite loop, the search is limited here to 1000 bisections.)

17.2 Calendars

> I dare not hope that I have made myself quite clear, simply because [my explanation] involves too many fractions and details. To tell the truth it took me several days to get familiar with the [calendar] system.... . Several of my Brahmin friends themselves were unable to explain the intricacies of the Hindu calendar.... But let me not leave the impression that these attempts on the part of the Brahmins of old to reconcile the seemingly irreconcilable have been futile... There can be no doubt that, from the point of view of correctness and exactitude, the Hindu calendars are by far the nearest approaches to the actual machinery of astronomical phenomena governing life on our planet. The only fault of the Hindu calendars is that they are unintelligible to the common man.
> —Hashim Amir Ali: *Facts and Fancies* (1946)

To determine the Hindu year for a given R.D. date (or time), it is not enough to take the quotient of the number of days elapsed with the mean length of a year. A correction must be applied based on where the sun actually is vis-à-vis the start of the zodiac:

$$\textbf{hindu-calendar-year}\,(t) \quad \stackrel{\text{def}}{=} \tag{17.18}$$

$$\text{round}$$

$$\left(\frac{t - \textbf{hindu-epoch}}{\textbf{hindu-sidereal-year}} - \frac{\textbf{hindu-solar-longitude}\,(t)}{360°} \right)$$

If the true solar longitude at the given time is a bit less than $360°$, then the mean value is decreased by 1.

The Kali Yuga Era is used today only for calculations. Instead, one commonly used starting point is the Śaka Era in which (elapsed) year 0 began in the spring of 78 C.E., or 3179 K.Y.:

$$\textbf{hindu-solar-era} \quad \stackrel{\text{def}}{=} \quad 3179 \tag{17.19}$$

In West Bengal an era that began in 593 C.E. is used instead.

The solar date is determined by approximation followed by search:

$$\textbf{hindu-solar-from-fixed}\,(date) \quad \stackrel{\text{def}}{=} \tag{17.20}$$

year	month	day

where

$$critical \quad = \quad \textbf{hindu-sunrise}\,(date + 1)$$

$$month \quad = \quad \textbf{hindu-zodiac}\,(critical)$$

$$year \quad = \quad \textbf{hindu-calendar-year}\,(critical) \, - $$
$$\qquad\qquad \textbf{hindu-solar-era}$$

$$approx \quad = \quad date - 3 - \big(\lfloor \, \textbf{hindu-solar-longitude}$$
$$\qquad\qquad\qquad (critical) \, \rfloor \bmod 30° \,\big)$$

$$begin \quad = \quad \underset{i \geq approx}{\text{MIN}} \left\{ \begin{array}{l} \textbf{hindu-zodiac} \\ \quad (\textbf{hindu-sunrise}\,(i + 1)) \\ = month \end{array} \right\}$$

$$day \quad = \quad date - begin + 1$$

To determine the day of the month, we underestimate the day when the sun entered the current zodiacal sign (*approx*) and search forward for the start of the month *begin*. The calculation of **hindu-sunrise** is given in the next section.

For example, R.D. 0 is Makara 20 of year -78 S.E.,[7] the same month but a day later than the mean solar calendar (page 131).

The preceding function follows the Orissa rule according to which the solar month of a given day is determined by the zodiacal position of the sun at sunrise the following morning. This is just one of various critical times that have been used (see [8, pp. 12–13] and [2, p. 282]):

- According to the Orissa rule, sunrise of the following day is used.
- According to the Tamil rule, sunset of the current day is used.
- According to the Malayali rule, 1:12 p.m. (seasonal time) on the current day is used.
- According to the Bengal rule, midnight at the start of the day is usually used unless the zodiac sign changes between 11:36 p.m. and 12:24 a.m., in which case various special rules apply.
- According to some calendars from Madras, midnight at the start of the previous day is used.

Unlike the mean calendar, determining the R.D. date now requires a search, for which we also need to compare solar dates:

hindu-solar-on-or-before? (17.21)

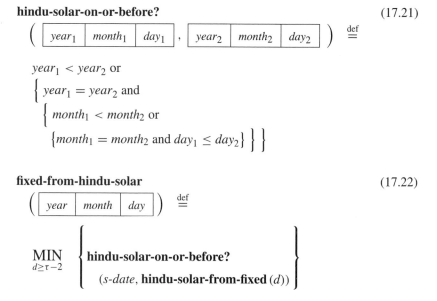

$$\left(\boxed{\ year_1\ |\ month_1\ |\ day_1\ } , \boxed{\ year_2\ |\ month_2\ |\ day_2\ } \right) \overset{\text{def}}{=}$$

$$year_1 < year_2 \text{ or}$$
$$\left\{ year_1 = year_2 \text{ and} \right.$$
$$\left\{ month_1 < month_2 \text{ or} \right.$$
$$\left\{ month_1 = month_2 \text{ and } day_1 \le day_2 \right\} \left. \right\} \left. \right\}$$

fixed-from-hindu-solar (17.22)

$$\left(\boxed{\ year\ |\ month\ |\ day\ } \right) \overset{\text{def}}{=}$$

$$\underset{d \ge \tau - 2}{\text{MIN}} \left\{ \begin{array}{l} \textbf{hindu-solar-on-or-before?} \\ (s\text{-}date, \textbf{hindu-solar-from-fixed}\,(d)) \end{array} \right\}$$

---

[7] Śaka (Scythian) Era (expired).

where

$$s\text{-}date = \boxed{\begin{array}{|c|c|c|} year & month & day \end{array}}$$

$$approx = \left\lfloor \left(year + \mathbf{hindu\text{-}solar\text{-}era} + \tfrac{1}{12} \times (month - 1) \right) \times \mathbf{hindu\text{-}sidereal\text{-}year} \right\rfloor + \mathbf{hindu\text{-}epoch} + day - 1$$

$$rate = \frac{360°}{\mathbf{hindu\text{-}sidereal\text{-}year}}$$

$$\phi = (month - 1) \times 30° + (day - 1) \times rate$$

$$\Delta = \left(\left(\mathbf{hindu\text{-}solar\text{-}longitude}\left(approx + \tfrac{1}{4}\right) - \phi + 180° \right) \bmod 360 \right) - 180°$$

$$\tau = approx - \left\lceil \frac{\Delta}{rate} \right\rceil$$

This function begins its linear search for the fixed date corresponding to the Hindu solar date *s-date* from R.D. date $\tau - 1$, which is obtained by refining the initial estimate *approx*.

As explained earlier, there are both leap months and leap days on the true Hindu lunisolar calendar; hence, we use quintuples

$$\boxed{\begin{array}{|c|c|c|c|c|} year & month & leapmonth & day & leapday \end{array}}$$

for lunisolar dates. For the lunisolar year, we use another common era, the Vikrama, which begins in 58 B.C.E., and differs from the Kali Yuga by 3044 years:

$$\mathbf{hindu\text{-}lunar\text{-}era} \stackrel{\text{def}}{=} 3044 \tag{17.23}$$

$$\mathbf{hindu\text{-}lunar\text{-}from\text{-}fixed}\,(date) \stackrel{\text{def}}{=} \tag{17.24}$$

$$\boxed{\begin{array}{|c|c|c|c|c|} year & month & leapmonth & day & leapday \end{array}}$$

where

$$critical = \mathbf{hindu\text{-}sunrise}\,(date)$$

$$day = \mathbf{lunar\text{-}day}\,(critical)$$

$$\textit{leapday} \quad = \quad \textit{day} = \textbf{lunar-day}$$
$$(\textbf{hindu-sunrise} \; (\textit{date} - 1))$$

$$\textit{last-new-moon} \quad = \quad \textbf{hindu-new-moon-before} \; (\textit{critical})$$

$$\textit{next-new-moon} \quad = \quad \textbf{hindu-new-moon-before}$$
$$(\lfloor \textit{last-new-moon} \rfloor + 35)$$

$$\textit{solar-month} \quad = \quad \textbf{hindu-zodiac} \; (\textit{last-new-moon})$$

$$\textit{leapmonth} \quad = \quad \textit{solar-month}$$
$$= \textbf{hindu-zodiac} \; (\textit{next-new-moon})$$

$$\textit{month} \quad = \quad (\textit{solar-month} + 1) \quad \text{amod} \; 12$$

$$\textit{year} \quad = \quad \textbf{hindu-calendar-year} \; (\textit{next-new-moon})$$
$$- \textbf{hindu-lunar-era} -$$
$$\begin{cases} -1 & \textbf{if } \textit{leapmonth} \text{ and } \textit{month} = 1 \\ 0 & \textbf{otherwise} \end{cases}$$

This function uses the Hindu approximations to true times of new moons, true position of the sun at new moon, and true phase of the moon at sunrise (*critical*) to determine the *month* and *day*. The lunisolar month name and K.Y. year are those of the solar month and year in effect 1 solar month after the beginning (*last-new-moon*) of the current lunar month. The function checks whether it is a leap month (*leapmonth*) with the same name as the following month (*next-new-moon*), or a leap day (*leapday*) with the same ordinal number as the previous day. Our fixed date R.D. 0 is the fourth day of the dark half (that is, lunar day 19) of Māgha (the eleventh month) in year 57 V.E.;[8] neither the day nor month is leap. This date is 1 month later than on the mean calendar (see page 135).

To invert the process and derive the R.D. date from a lunar date, we first find a lower bound on the possible R.D. date and then search for the exact correspondence. As Jacobi [3, p. 409] explains: "The problem must be solved indirectly, *i.e.,* we must ascertain approximately the day on which the given *tithi* was likely to end, and then calculate...the *tithi* that really ends on that day."

---

[8] Vikrama Era (expired).

We need to compare the five components of lunar dates lexicographically:

hindu-lunar-on-or-before? (17.25)

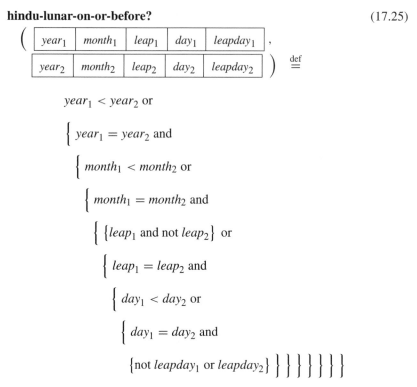

$year_1 < year_2$ or

$\Big\{\ year_1 = year_2$ and

$\Big\{\ month_1 < month_2$ or

$\Big\{\ month_1 = month_2$ and

$\Big\{\ \{leap_1$ and not $leap_2\}$ or

$\Big\{\ leap_1 = leap_2$ and

$\Big\{\ day_1 < day_2$ or

$\Big\{\ day_1 = day_2$ and

$\{$not $leapday_1$ or $leapday_2\}\ \Big\}\Big\}\Big\}\Big\}\Big\}\Big\}$

With this we can convert to a fixed date:

fixed-from-hindu-lunar (17.26)

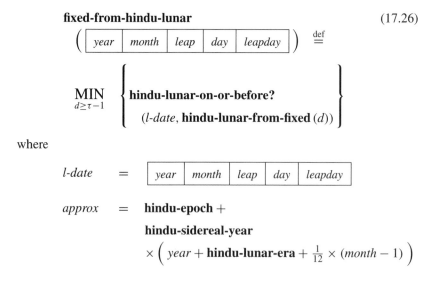

$$\underset{d \geq \tau - 1}{\text{MIN}} \left\{ \begin{array}{l} \textbf{hindu-lunar-on-or-before?} \\ (\textit{l-date},\ \textbf{hindu-lunar-from-fixed}\,(d)) \end{array} \right\}$$

where

$l\text{-}date$ =

$year$	$month$	$leap$	day	$leapday$

$approx$ = **hindu-epoch** +

hindu-sidereal-year

$\times \left(year + \textbf{hindu-lunar-era} + \tfrac{1}{12} \times (month - 1) \right)$

$$s \quad = \quad \left\lfloor approx - \frac{1}{360°} \times \textbf{hindu-sidereal-year} \right.$$
$$\times \Big(\big(\big(\textbf{ hindu-solar-longitude } (approx)$$
$$- \big(month - 1 \big) \times 30° +$$
$$180° \big) \bmod 360° \big) - 180 \big) \Big\rfloor$$

$$k \quad = \quad \textbf{lunar-day} \left(s + \frac{1}{4} \right)$$

$$est \quad = \quad s + day - \begin{cases} k & \textbf{if } 3 < k < 27 \\ ((k+15) \bmod 30) - 15 & \\ \qquad \textbf{if } mid_{\textbf{month}} < month \text{ or} \\ \qquad \{ mid_{\textbf{leap-month}} \text{ and not } leap \} \\ ((k-15) \bmod 30) + 15 & \textbf{otherwise} \end{cases}$$

$$\tau \quad = \quad est - \left(\left(\textbf{lunar-day} \left(est + \frac{1}{4} \right) - day + 15 \right) \bmod 30 \right) + 15$$

$$mid \quad = \quad \textbf{hindu-lunar-from-fixed} \, (s - 15)$$

We use mean solar months to estimate the fixed date. That estimate may be a month off in either direction because a true new moon might occur near the start of a true solar month. After the correct month is determined, a search is still necessary because of the variability in month length.

17.3 Sunrise

> It should, however, be remarked that if the interval between true sunrise and the end of a *tithi*, &c. is *very* small … the case must be regarded as doubtful; though our calculations materially agree with those of the Hindus, still an almanac-maker avails himself of abbreviations which in the end may slightly influence the result.
> —Hermann Jacobi: "The Computation of Hindu Dates in Inscriptions & c.," *Epigraphia Indica* (1892)

It remains to compute the actual time of sunrise for any particular day. We use the standard location, Ujjain, a city holy to the Hindus situated at $23°9'$ north, $75°46'6''$ east:

$$\textbf{ujjain} \quad \overset{\text{def}}{=} \qquad\qquad\qquad\qquad\qquad (17.27)$$

23°9'	75°46'6''	0m	$5\frac{461}{9000}$

$$\textbf{hindu-locale} \ \overset{\text{def}}{=} \ \textbf{ujjain} \tag{17.28}$$

Other locales employ local variants of the calendar that depend on the zodiacal constellation and lunar phase in effect at true local sunrise. Despite the comment of van Wijk [11, p. 24], that "the rules the Sūrya-Siddhānta gives for calculating the time of true sunrise are exceedingly complicated, and inapplicable in practice," so that no one seems to bother with all the corrections mandated for the calculation of local sunrise, and the inaccuracy of the methods, we include them here exactly as ordained by the *Sūrya-Siddhānta* (see [13]).

Four corrections to mean sunrise (6 a.m.) are necessary:

1. The latitude of the location affects the time of sunrise by an amount that also depends on the season. This is called the "ascensional difference":

$$\textbf{ascensional-difference} \, (date, locale) \ \overset{\text{def}}{=} \tag{17.29}$$

$$\textbf{hindu-arcsin} \left(- \frac{earth\text{-}sine}{diurnal\text{-}radius} \right)$$

where

$$sin\text{-}decl \quad = \quad \tfrac{1397}{3438} \times \textbf{hindu-sine}$$
$$(\textbf{hindu-tropical-longitude}$$
$$(date) \,)$$

$$lat \quad = \quad locale_{\text{latitude}}$$

$$diurnal\text{-}radius \quad = \quad \textbf{hindu-sine}$$
$$(90° + \textbf{hindu-arcsin} \, (sin\text{-}decl))$$

$$tan\text{-}lat \quad = \quad \frac{\textbf{hindu-sine} \, (lat)}{\textbf{hindu-sine} \, (90° + lat)}$$

$$earth\text{-}sine \quad = \quad sin\text{-}decl \times tan\text{-}lat$$

This computation requires *tropical longitude*, which is affected by precession of the equinoxes. The value given in the *Sūrya-Siddhānta* for the maximum precession is 27°, and it is said to cycle once every 7200 years:[9]

$$\textbf{hindu-tropical-longitude} \, (date) \ \overset{\text{def}}{=} \tag{17.30}$$

$$(\textbf{hindu-solar-longitude} \, (date) - precession) \ \bmod \ 360$$

---

[9] The correct value is about 26,000 years with no maximum; see page 179. It was a common pre-Newtonian misconception, called "trepidation," that precession cycles in this way.

where

$$days \quad = \quad \lfloor date - \textbf{hindu-epoch} \rfloor$$

$$precession \quad = \quad 27° - \left| 54° - \left(\left(27° + 108° \times \frac{600}{1577917828} \right. \right. \right.$$
$$\left. \left. \left. \times days \right) \bmod 108 \right) \right|$$

2. There is a small difference between the length of the sidereal day (one rotation of the Earth) and the solar day (from midnight to midnight) which amounts to almost a minute in a quarter of a day (see page 178). The function

$$\textbf{solar-sidereal-difference} \, (date) \quad \overset{\text{def}}{=} \qquad\qquad (17.31)$$

$$\textbf{daily-motion} \, (date) \times \textbf{rising-sign} \, (date)$$

comprises a factor for the speed of the sun along the ecliptic:

$$\textbf{daily-motion} \, (date) \quad \overset{\text{def}}{=} \quad mean\text{-}motion \times (factor + 1) \quad (17.32)$$

where

$$mean\text{-}motion \quad = \quad \frac{360°}{\textbf{hindu-sidereal-year}}$$

$$anomaly \quad = \quad \textbf{mean-position}$$
$$(date, \textbf{hindu-anomalistic-year})$$

$$epicycle \quad = \quad \frac{14}{360} - \frac{1}{1080} \times |\textbf{hindu-sine} \, (anomaly)|$$

$$entry \quad = \quad \left\lfloor \frac{anomaly}{\frac{225°}{60}} \right\rfloor$$

$$sine\text{-}table\text{-}step \quad = \quad \textbf{hindu-sine-table} \, (entry + 1) \, -$$
$$\textbf{hindu-sine-table} \, (entry)$$

$$factor \quad = \quad sine\text{-}table\text{-}step \times \left(-\frac{3438}{225} \right) \times epicycle$$

that depends on the solar anomaly, and a tabulated factor that depends on the distance of the sun from the celestial equator:

$$\textbf{rising-sign} \, (date) \quad \overset{\text{def}}{=} \qquad\qquad (17.33)$$

$$\left\langle \frac{1670}{1800}, \frac{1795}{1800}, \frac{1935}{1800}, \frac{1935}{1800}, \frac{1795}{1800}, \frac{1670}{1800} \right\rangle [i \bmod 6]$$

where

$$i = \left\lfloor \frac{\textbf{hindu-tropical-longitude}\,(\textit{date})}{30°} \right\rfloor$$

3. The *equation of time* gives the difference between local and civil midnight caused by the uneven (apparent) motion of the sun through the seasons (see page 178). The *Sūrya-Siddhānta* uses the following very rough approximation:

$$\textbf{hindu-equation-of-time}\,(\textit{date}) \overset{\text{def}}{=} \tag{17.34}$$

$$\textbf{daily-motion}\,(\textit{date}) \times \frac{1}{360°} \times \textit{equation-sun} \times \frac{1}{360°}$$

$$\times \textbf{hindu-sidereal-year}$$

where

$$\textit{offset} = \textbf{hindu-sine}$$
$$(\textbf{mean-position}$$
$$(\textit{date}, \textbf{hindu-anomalistic-year}))$$

$$\textit{equation-sun} = \textit{offset} \times \frac{3438°}{60} \times \left(\frac{1}{1080} \times |\textit{offset}| - \frac{14}{360} \right)$$

4. For locations other than Ujjain, the difference in longitude affect the local time of astronomical events by 4 minutes for every degree of longitude.

Putting the preceding corrections together, we have

$$\textbf{hindu-sunrise}\,(\textit{date}) \overset{\text{def}}{=} \tag{17.35}$$

$$\textit{date} + \tfrac{1}{4} + \frac{\textbf{ujjain}_{\text{longitude}} - \textbf{hindu-locale}_{\text{longitude}}}{360°}$$

$$+ \textbf{hindu-equation-of-time}\,(\textit{date}) +$$

$$\frac{1577917828/1582237828}{360°}$$

$$\times \left(\textbf{ascensional-difference}\,(\textit{date}, \textbf{hindu-locale}) + \right.$$
$$\left. \tfrac{1}{4} \times \textbf{solar-sidereal-difference}\,(\textit{date}) \right)$$

The factor $\frac{1,577,917,828}{1,582,237,828} \approx 0.9972697$ converts a sidereal hour angle to solar time. The definition of **hindu-locale** must be changed to get the time of sunrise at other locations.

17.4 Alternatives

> Every year a great number of pañcāṅgs [almanacs] is still printed all over India, and some are calculated entirely after the prescriptions of the *Sūrya-Siddhānta* (or of another Siddhānta or Karaṇa), and some take their astronomical data from the Greenwich Nautical Almanac. Now there is something in favour of both ways, and one who wishes to know the exact moment of conjunctions, &c., must certainly use the second type. But that which is won on the one side is lost on the other: the Indians are possessors of an old tradition, and they ought to preserve that and glorify it....
>
> —Walther E. van Wijk: "On Hindu Chronology IV: Decimal Tables for Calculating the Exact Moments of Beginning of Mean and True Tithis, Karaṇas, Nakṣatras and Yogas, According to the Sūrya-Siddhānta; Together with Some Miscellaneous Notes on the Subject of Hindu Chronology," *Acta Orientalia,* volume IV (1926)

An alternative to the calculations we have presented would be to utilize the same accurate astronomical functions used for the Chinese calendar. Indeed, some Indian calendar makers have substituted such ephemeris data for the traditional methods, but they are the exception. Though it is generally agreed that one should follow the rules dictated by the *Sūrya-Siddhānta* for calculating lunar days, for sunrise it seems that most calendars use tabulated times, not the approximate values obtained by following the strictures of the *Sūrya-Siddhānta*, which can be off by more than 16 minutes. Thus, one would get better agreement with published Hindu calendars by incorporating modern computations of local sunrise in place of those we gave in the previous section. To use astronomical sunrise at the Hindu "prime meridian," or elsewhere, we would need to substitute the following calculation for **hindu-sunrise**:

$$\textbf{alt-hindu-sunrise}\ (date) \;\stackrel{\text{def}}{=} \tag{17.36}$$

$$\frac{1/60}{24} \times \text{round}\,(rise \times 24 \times 60)$$

where

$$rise \quad = \quad \textbf{sunrise}\ (date,\ \textbf{hindu-locale})$$

The calculated moment of sunrise is rounded to the nearest minute and left as a rational number.

We should also point out that the "infinite" precision of our algorithms is, from a mathematical point of view, specious, because the "true" motions are only approximations, and the sine table used to calculate the epicyclic adjustments is accurate to only three decimal places. There is therefore nothing gained by our keeping the fractions obtained by interpolation and calculation to greater accuracy than the table lookup methods other than fidelity to the traditional sources. Our formulas, as stated, can involve numbers with hundreds of digits! For example, sunrise on July 31, 2000 (Gregorian) is calculated to be at R.D. moment

$$\frac{16156338896158375802621798219261001624039028849594030929652148187157637097641105866059236333664880575338386352129}{221219033733836060119643335886889570536130275573660722821902376023876524764679192295008453132500000000000000}$$

which is 5:22:58.45 a.m. (about 7 minutes before the actual sunrise). At that time, the phase of the moon is

$$\frac{913324356901304171084477500391296417948145381648270971896801383089033773617058009593206479465642170886346433096201309411553875228505696882978684649285603688577652256590634265169898501128562506425453912817819022826188247513633012672275423592737}{254545357983774225624971570338796632702918326208834491685033569007734979259603479141694851067944441211859430267279331509850515775980101037031794700022766198809573599812527678656718585693056233786341051252656250000000000000000000000000000000000000}$$

which is just shy of 359° (whereas it is actually a bit past new moon). Double-precision arithmetic suffices for all practical purposes.

17.5 Holidays

> In what manner the *Hindus* contrive so far to reconcile the lunar
> and solar years, as to make them proceed concurrently in their
> ephemerides, might easily have been shown by exhibiting a
> version of their *Nadíyu* or *Varánes* almanack; but their modes of
> intercalation form no part of my present subject, and would injure
> the simplicity of my work, without throwing any light on the
> religion of the *Hindus*.
> —Sir William Jones: "Asiatick Researches," *Transactions of the*
> *Bengal Society* (1801)

As with the Hindu calendars, so too with the holidays; there are a plethora of regional holidays and local variants of widespread holidays. The most complete reference in English is [10], but sufficient details to handle exceptional circumstances (leap months, skipped months, leap days, omitted days, and borderline cases) are lacking.

Certain hours, days, and months are more auspicious than others. For example, Wednesday and Saturday are "unlucky" days, as is the dark half of each month. Leap months and civil days containing lost lunar days are considered inauspicious. Astronomical events, such as actual or computed solar and lunar eclipses and planetary conjunctions, are usually auspicious.

The chief solar festivals are solar New Year (Sowramana Ugadi) on Mesha 1, the day following the Hindu vernal equinox, and Ayyappa Jyothi Darshanam (Pongal) on Makara 1 and on the preceding day, celebrating the winter solstice. Solar New Year in Gregorian year y is always (for many millennia, at least) in year $y - 78$ s.e., and the winter solstice of Gregorian year y occurs in year $y - 79$ s.e.; thus, the computation of the corresponding R.D. dates is straightforward.

The precise times of solar and lunar events are usually included in published Indian calendars. The fixed moment of entry of the sun into a Hindu zodiacal sign, called the *saṃkrānti*, can be computed in the following manner:

$$\textbf{hindu-solar-longitude-after}\,(t, \phi) \overset{\text{def}}{=} \tag{17.37}$$

$$\underset{x \in [l:u]}{\overset{u-l<\varepsilon}{\text{MIN}}} \left\{ \begin{array}{l} \left(\left(\textbf{hindu-solar-longitude} \; - \phi \right) \bmod 360 \right) < 180° \\ (x) \end{array} \right\}$$

where

$$\varepsilon \quad = \quad \frac{1}{1000000}$$

$$\tau \quad = \quad t + \tfrac{1}{360} \times \textbf{hindu-sidereal-year}$$
$$\times \left(\left(\phi - \textbf{hindu-solar-longitude}\,(t) \right) \bmod 360° \right)$$

$$l \quad = \quad \max\{t, \tau - 5\}$$

$$u \quad = \quad \tau + 5$$

This is simply a bisection search for the moment when the true (sidereal) solar longitude is ϕ. Mesha saṃkrānti, in Gregorian year *g-year*, when the longitude of the sun is 0 by Hindu reckoning, is, then,

$$\textbf{mesha-samkranti}\,(g\text{-}year) \overset{\text{def}}{=} \tag{17.38}$$

$$\textbf{hindu-solar-longitude-after}\,\left(jan_1, 0°\right)$$

where

$$jan_1 \quad = \quad \textbf{fixed-from-gregorian}$$

$$\left(\boxed{\; g\text{-}year \;}\; \boxed{\; \text{january} \;}\; \boxed{\; 1 \;} \right)$$

This function gives R.D. moment

$$\frac{4867740413951421371524212135643}{6666094378185523200000000000}$$

as the time of Mesha saṃkrānti in the Gregorian year 2000, which is 5:55:31 p.m. on April 13.

Most Indian holidays, however, depend on the lunar date. Festivals are usually celebrated on the day a specified lunar day is current at sunrise; other events may depend on the phase of the moon at noon, sunset, or midnight. Some lunar holidays require that the specified lunar day be current at noon rather than at sunrise. Sometimes, if the lunar day in question begins at least 1/15 of a day before sunset of one day and ends before sunset of the next, the corresponding holiday is celebrated on the first day [5, Section 113]. For example, Nāga Panchamī (a day of snake worship) is normally celebrated on Śrāvaṇa 5 but is advanced 1 day if lunar day 5 begins in the first 1.2 temporal hours of day 4 and ends within the first tenth of day 5. Technically, such determinations require computation of the time of sunset in a manner analogous to that of sunrise.

The search for the new moon, given as **hindu-new-moon** on (page 277), is halted once the position of the moon (and sun) at the time of conjunction has been narrowed down to a particular constellation on the zodiac. When greater accuracy is needed, and for the arbitrary phases needed for holiday calculations, we use the following function—the inverse of equation (17.1)—which gives the moment at which the kth lunar day occurred after moment t:

$$\textbf{lunar-day-after}\,(t, k) \quad \overset{\text{def}}{=} \tag{17.39}$$

$$\underset{x\in[\max\{t,\tau-2\}:\tau+2]}{\overset{u-l<\varepsilon}{\text{MIN}}}$$

$$\left\{ \begin{array}{l} (\,(\,\textbf{hindu-lunar-phase}\ -phase\,)\ \text{mod}\ 360\,) < 180° \\ (x) \end{array} \right\}$$

where

$$\varepsilon \quad = \quad 2^{-17}$$

$$phase \quad = \quad (k-1)\times 12$$

$$\tau \quad = \quad t + \tfrac{1}{360}\times(\,(\,phase - \textbf{hindu-lunar-phase}$$

$$(t)\,)\ \text{mod}\ 360°\,)$$

$$\times\,\textbf{hindu-synodic-month}$$

The value of τ is the most recent mean moment when $k - 1$ thirtieths of a lunar month has elapsed. For the time of new moon, k should be 1; $k = 16$ for the time of full moon.

The beginning of the lunisolar New Year (Chandramana Ugadi), usually Chaitra 1, is the day of the first sunrise after the new moon preceding Mesha saṃkrānti, or the prior new moon in the case when the first month of the lunar year is leap:

$$\textbf{hindu-lunar-new-year}\,(g\text{-}year) \quad \overset{\text{def}}{=} \qquad\qquad (17.40)$$

$$h\text{-}day + \begin{cases} 0 & \textbf{if } new\text{-}moon < critical \textbf{ or} \\ & \textbf{lunar-day} \\ & (\ \textbf{hindu-sunrise} \\ & \quad (h\text{-}day + 1)\ )\ ) = 2 \\ 1 & \textbf{otherwise} \end{cases}$$

where

$$jan_1 \quad = \quad \textbf{fixed-from-gregorian}$$

$$\left(\boxed{\;g\text{-}year\;\mid\;\textbf{january}\;\mid\;1\;} \right)$$

$$mina \quad = \quad \textbf{hindu-solar-longitude-after}\,\left(jan_1, 330°\right)$$

$$new\text{-}moon \quad = \quad \textbf{lunar-day-after}\,(mina, 1)$$

$$h\text{-}day \quad = \quad \lfloor new\text{-}moon \rfloor$$

$$critical \quad = \quad \textbf{hindu-sunrise}\,(h\text{-}day)$$

If the first lunar day of the New Year is wholly contained in the interval between one sunrise and the next, then this function returns the fixed date on which the new moon occurs, which is also the last day of the previous lunisolar year, Phālguna 30.[10]

The major Hindu lunar holidays include the Birthday of Rāma (Rāma Navamī), celebrated on Chaitra 9; Varalakshmi Vratam on the Friday prior

---

[10] The results obtained with our functions are in complete agreement with Sewell and Dîkshit's tables [8] for added and expunged months from 1500 to 1900. Furthermore, our functions are in agreement with the calculations in [5, pp. 97–101] for the earlier disputed years considered there. They also agree on the date of the lunisolar New Years in the period 1500–1900, except for spring 1600, when the first new moon of 1657 V.E. occurred on March 5, 1600 C.E. (Julian) after sunrise, but the second lunar day began at 6:07 a.m. on March 6. Reckoning with mean sunrise, as in [8, p. lxxxii], March 6 is the first day of the New Year, because at 6 a.m. that day the new moon was still in its first tithi. However, at the true time of sunrise, 6:13 according to the *Sūrya-Siddhānta*, or 6:08 using our astronomical code, lunar day 1 had already ended and, therefore, the New Year is considered to have started on the previous day.

to Śrāvaṇa 15; the Birthday of Krishna (Janmāshṭamī) on Śrāvaṇa 23; Gaṇēśa Chaturthī, held on Bhādrapada 4;[11] Durgā Ashtami on Āśvina 8; Saraswati Puja on Āśvina 9, when books are worshipped in honor of the goddess of eloquence and arts, Sarasvatī; Dasra on Āśvina 10; Diwali, a major autumn festival celebrated Āśvina 29–Kārtika 1 (Kārtika 1 is the main day of festivity and marks the beginning of the year in some regions); the festival Karthikai Deepam on Kārtika 15; the main festival of the year, Vaikunta Ekadashi on Mārgaśīra 11, honoring Vishnu; Maha Shivaratri, the Great Night of Shiva, celebrated on the day that lunar day Māgha 29 is current at midnight, and preceded by a day of fasting by devotees of Shiva; and the spring festival, Holi, which takes place in the evening of lunar day Phālguna 15.

In general, holidays are not held in leap months. When a month is skipped, its holidays are usually celebrated in the following month. Festivals are generally celebrated on the second of two days with the same lunar day number; if a day is expunged, the festival takes place on the civil day containing that lunar day.

For some holidays, the location of the moon may be more important in some regions than the lunar date. A lunar station, called *nakṣatra* is associated with each civil day and is determined by the (sidereal) longitude of the moon at sunrise:

$$
\textbf{lunar-station}\ (date)\ \overset{\text{def}}{=} \tag{17.41}
$$

$$
\left\lfloor \frac{\textbf{hindu-lunar-longitude}\ (critical)}{\frac{800°}{60}} \right\rfloor + 1
$$

where

$$
critical\quad =\quad \textbf{hindu-sunrise}\ (date)
$$

The names of the 27 stations are given in Table 17.1.

The function **lunar-day-after** can also be used to determine the time of onset of *karanas*, which are each half of a lunar day in duration, by using fractions for k. The most recent occurrence of the nth karana ($1 \le n \le 60$), prior to day d, begins within ε of **lunar-day-after**$(d, (n + 1)/2, \varepsilon)$. The names of the karanas follow the repeating pattern shown in Table 17.3. The following

---

[11] According to [4], the precise rule is that Gaṇēśa Chaturthī is celebrated on the day in which lunar day 4 is current in whole or in part during the midday period that extends from 1.2 temporal hours before noon until 1.2 temporal hours after noon. If, however, that lunar day is current during midday on 2 consecutive days, or if it extends from after midday on one day until before midday of the next, then it is celebrated on the former day.

Table 17.3 *The repeating pattern of names of karanas (half-days).*

Karanas	0	1	2	3	4	5	6	7	8	9	10
1–8	Kiṃstughna	Bava	Vālava	Kaulava	Taitila	Gara	Vaṇija	Viṣṭi			
9–15		Bava	Vālava	Kaulava	Taitila	Gara	Vaṇija	Viṣṭi			
16–22		Bava	Vālava	Kaulava	Taitila	Gara	Vaṇija	Viṣṭi			
23–29		Bava	Vālava	Kaulava	Taitila	Gara	Vaṇija	Viṣṭi			
30–36		Bava	Vālava	Kaulava	Taitila	Gara	Vaṇija	Viṣṭi			
37–43		Bava	Vālava	Kaulava	Taitila	Gara	Vaṇija	Viṣṭi			
44–50		Bava	Vālava	Kaulava	Taitila	Gara	Vaṇija	Viṣṭi			
51–60		Bava	Vālava	Kaulava	Taitila	Gara	Vaṇija	Viṣṭi	Śakuni	Nāga	Catuṣpada

function gives the column number of the nth karana:

$$\textbf{karana} (n) \overset{\text{def}}{=} \begin{cases} 0 & \textbf{if } n = 1 \\ n - 50 & \textbf{if } n > 57 \\ (n-1) \text{ amod } 7 & \textbf{otherwise} \end{cases} \qquad (17.42)$$

A *yoga* (meaning "addition") is the varying period of time during which the solar and lunar longitudes increase a *total* of 800 arcminutes ($13°20'$).[12] A full circle contains 27 segments of $800'$, corresponding to the 27 yogas:

(1) Viṣkamba	(15) Vajra
(2) Prīti	(16) Siddhi
(3) Ayuṣmān	(17) Vyatipāta
(4) Saubhāgya	(18) Varīyas
(5) Śobhana	(19) Parigha
(6) Atigaṇḍa	(20) Śiva
(7) Sukarmān	(21) Siddha
(8) Dhṛti	(22) Sādhya
(9) Śūla	(23) Śubha
(10) Gaṇḍa	(24) Śukla
(11) Vṛddhi	(25) Brahman
(12) Dhruva	(26) Indra
(13) Vyāghāta	(27) Vaidhṛti
(14) Harṣaṇa	

Because a full revolution of the sun or moon has no net effect on the yogas, we need only consider their longitudes, counted in increments of $800'$ modulo 27:

$$\textbf{yoga} (date) \overset{\text{def}}{=} \qquad (17.43)$$

$$\left\lfloor \left(\textbf{hindu-solar-longitude} (date) + 1 \right. \right.$$
$$\left. + \textbf{hindu-lunar-longitude} \right.$$
$$\left. (date) \right) \times \tfrac{60}{800} \text{ mod } 27° \right\rfloor$$

Inverting this function to determine the time of the last occurrence of a given yoga is similar to **lunar-day-after**.

There are also numerous days of lesser importance that depend on the lunisolar calendar. Certain combinations of events are also significant. As a

---

[12] Certain conjunctions of calendrical and astronomical events are also termed yogas.

relatively insignificant example, whenever lunar day 8 falls on Wednesday, the day is sacred:

$$\textbf{sacred-wednesdays-in-gregorian}\,(g\text{-}year) \quad \overset{\text{def}}{=} \qquad (17.44)$$

$$\textbf{sacred-wednesdays}$$

$$\left(\ \textbf{fixed-from-gregorian}\left(\ \boxed{g\text{-}year \mid \textbf{january} \mid 1}\ \right),\right.$$

$$\textbf{fixed-from-gregorian}$$

$$\left.\left(\ \boxed{g\text{-}year \mid \textbf{december} \mid 31}\ \right)\ \right)$$

This uses the following function to collect all such Wednesdays between fixed dates *start* and *end*:

$$\textbf{sacred-wednesdays}\,(start, end) \quad \overset{\text{def}}{=} \qquad (17.45)$$

$$\begin{cases} \langle\,\rangle & \textbf{if } start > end \\[4pt] \begin{cases} \langle wed \rangle & \textbf{if } h\text{-}date_{\textbf{day}} = 8 \\ \langle\,\rangle & \textbf{otherwise} \end{cases} \\ \|\ \textbf{sacred-wednesdays}\,(wed + 1, end) \\ \hspace{4cm} \textbf{otherwise} \end{cases}$$

where

$$wed = \textbf{kday-on-or-after}\,(start, \textbf{wednesday})$$

$$h\text{-}date = \textbf{hindu-lunar-from-fixed}\,(wed)$$

There are also auspicious and inauspicious days that depend on the position of the planets. These can be calculated in much the same way as that of the moon but with an additional epicyclic motion to contend with (see [6]).

The *panchang* is the traditional five-part Hindu calendar comprising for each civil day its lunar day (*tithi*), day of the week, *nakṣatra* (stellar position of the moon), *yoga*, and *karana* (based on the lunar phase). We have provided functions for each component.

References

[1] Calendar Reform Committee, *Report of the Calendar Reform Committee*, New Delhi, 1955.
[2] S. K. Chatterjee and A. K. Chakravarty, "Indian Calendar from Post-Vedic Period to A.D. 1900," *Indian Journal of History of Science*, volume 20, pp. 252–308, 1985.

[3] H. G. Jacobi, "The Computation of Hindu Dates in Inscriptions, & c.,"
J. Burgess, ed., *Epigraphia Indica: A Collection of Inscriptions Supplementary to
the Corpus Inscriptionum Indicarum of the Archæological Survey of India*,
Calcutta, pp. 403–460, p. 481, 1892.

[4] F. Kielhorn, "Festal Days of the Hindu Lunar Calendar," *The Indian Antiquary*,
volume XXVI, pp. 177–187, 1897.

[5] D. B. L. D. S. Pillai, *Indian Chronology, Solar, Lunar, and Planetary. A Practical
Guide*, Madras, 1911.

[6] D. Pingree, "History of Mathematical Astronomy in India," C. C. Gillispie, ed.,
Dictionary of Scientific Biography, volume XV, supplement I, 1978,
pp. 533–633.

[7] R. Sewell, *The Siddhantas and the Indian Calendar*, Government of India
Central Publication Branch, Calcutta, 1924.

[8] R. Sewell and S. B. Dîkshit, *The Indian Calendar, with Tables for the Conversion
of Hindu and Muhammadan into* A.D. *Dates, and Vice Versa, with Tables of
Eclipses Visible in India by R. Schram*, Motilal Banarsidass Publishers, Delhi,
1995. Originally published in 1896.

[9] *Sūrya-Siddhānta*, circa 1000. Translated by E. Burgess with notes by W. D.
Whitney, *Journal of the American Oriental Society*, volume 6, 1860. A new
edition, edited by P. Gangooly with an introduction by P. Sengupta, was
published by Calcutta University, 1935. Reprinted by Indological Book House,
Varanasi, India, 1977; also reprinted by Wizards Book Shelf, Minneapolis, 1978.

[10] M. M. Underhill, *The Hindu Religious Year*, Association Press, Calcutta and
Oxford University Press, London, 1921.

[11] W. E. van Wijk, *Decimal Tables for the Reduction of Hindu Dates from the Data
of the Sūrya-Siddhānta*, Martinus Nijhoff, The Hague, 1938.

[12] W. E. van Wijk, "On Hindu Chronology IV: Decimal Tables for Calculating the
Exact Moments of Beginning of Mean and True Tithis, Karaṇas, Nakṣatras and
Yogas, According to the Sūrya-Siddhānta; Together with Some Miscellaneous
Notes on the Subject of Hindu Chronology," *Acta Orientalia*, volume IV,
pp. 55–80, 1926.

[13] W. E. van Wijk, "On Hindu Chronology V: Decimal Tables for Calculating True
Local Time, According to the Sūrya-Siddhānta," *Acta Orientalia*, volume V,
pp. 1–27, 1927.

Blue and white glazed jar from the reign of Kāng Xī (1662–1722), showing plum blossoms against a background of melting ice and used to hold a gift of fragrant tea for New Year's Day. (Courtesy of the Victoria & Albert Museum, London.)

Coda

The following description of the presentation of the annual calendar in China is taken from Peter (Pierre) Hoang (*A Notice of the Chinese Calendar and a Concordance with the European Calendar*, 2nd ed., Catholic Mission Press, Shanghai, 1904):

Every year, on the 1st of the 2nd month, the Board of Mathematics presents to the Emperor three copies of the *Annual Calendar* for the following year, namely in Chinese, in Manchou and in Mongolian. Approbation being given, it is engraved and printed. Then on the 1st of the 4th month, two printed copies in Chinese are sent to the *Fan-t'ai* (Treasurer) of each province, that of Chih li excepted; one of which, stamped with the seal of the Board of Mathematics, is to be preserved in the archives of the Treasury, while the other is used for engraving and printing for public use in the province.

On the 1st day of the 10th month, early in the morning, the Board of Mathematics goes to offer Calendars to the Imperial court. The copies destined to the Emperor and Empresses are borne upon a sedan-like stand painted with figures of dragons (*Lung t'ing*), those for the Princes, the Ministers and officers of the court being carried on eight similar stands decorated with silk ornaments (*Ts'ai-t'ing*). They are accompanied by the officers of the Board with numerous attendants and the Imperial band of music. On arriving at the first entrance of the palace, the Calendars for the Emperor are placed upon an ornamented stand, those for other persons being put upon two other stands on each side. The copies for the Emperor and his family are not stamped with the seal of the Board of Mathematics, while the others are. The middle stand is taken into the palace, where the officers of the Board make three genuflections, each followed by three prostrations, after which the Calendars are handed to the eunuchs who present them to the Emperor, the Empress-mother, the Empress and other persons of the seraglio, two copies being given to each, viz. one in Chinese and one in Manchou. The master of ceremonies then proceeds to the entrance of the palace where the two other stands were left, and where the Princes, the Ministers with the civil and military mandarins, both Manchous and Mongols all in robes of state are in attendance. The master of ceremonies reads the Imperial decree of publication of the Calendars, namely: "The Emperor presents you all with the Annual Calendar of the year, and promulgates it throughout the Empire," which proclamation is heard kneeling. Then follow three genuflections and nine prostrations, after which all receive the Calendar on their knees, the Princes two copies, one in Chinese and one in Manchou, the ministers and other officers only one, each in his own language. Lastly the Corean envoy, who must attend every year on that day, is presented kneeling with one hundred Chinese copies, to take home with him.

In the provinces, the *Fan-t'ai* (Treasurer), after getting some printed copies of the Calendar stamped with a special seal, also on the 1st of the 10th month, sends them on a sedan-like stand to the Viceroy or Governor, accompanied by the mandarin called *Li-wen-t'ing*, who is instructed with the printing of the Calendar. The Viceroy or Governor receives them to the sound of music and of three cannon shots. The Calendars being set upon a stand between two tapers in the tribunal, the Viceroy or Governor, in robes of state, approaches the stand, and turning towards that quarter where Peking is situated, makes three genuflections and nine prostrations, after which ceremony he reverently receives the Calendars. The Treasurer sends the Calendar to all the civil and military Mandarins, all of whom, except those of inferior degree, receive it with the same forms. Any copies left are sold to the people. The reprinting of the Calendar is forbidden under a penalty (except in *Fu-chien* and *Kuang-tong* where it is tolerated). If therefore any copy is found without seal or with a false one, its author is sought after and punished. Falsification of the Calendar is punished with death; whoever reprints the *Annual Calendar* is liable to 100 blows and two months cangue.

Now that's a society that takes calendars (and copyrights) seriously!

Part III

Appendices

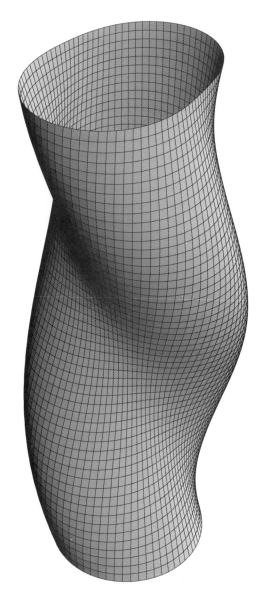

The equation of time wrapped onto a cylinder. The rotational range is 1 year; the axial range is Gregorian years 1500–12500. This rendering, by Stewart P. Dickson, was converted into a three-dimensional cam to be used as a mechanical cam in the "Clock of the Long Now" by W. Daniel Hillis and the Long Now Foundation. The clock is designed to keep local, absolute, and astronomical time over a span of 10,000 years. The cam resynchronizes the clock at local solar noon via a thermal trigger. See *The Clock of the Long Now: Time and Responsibility* by Stewart Brand, Basic Books, New York, 1999 for more information. (Reproduced by permission.)

Appendix A

Function, Parameter, and Constant Types

> You must never forget that programs will be read by people as
> well as machines. Write them carefully.
> —George E. Forsythe: Remark to Alan George (1967)

In this appendix we list all of the types of objects used in our calendar functions. After giving a list of the types themselves, we list, for each function, the types of its parameters and of its result. Then, we give a similar list for all constants.

A.1 Types

Name	Type or Range	Supertype
amplitude	$[-1:1]$	*real*
angle	$[0:360)$	*real*
	$[-180:180)$	*real*
armenian-date	⟨*armenian-year, armenian-month, armenian-day*⟩	*standard-date*
armenian-day	$1 \ldots 31$	*positive-integer*
armenian-month	$1 \ldots 13$	*positive-integer*
armenian-year	*integer*	
bahai-cycle	$1 \ldots 19$	*positive-integer*
bahai-date	⟨*bahai-major, bahai-cycle, bahai-year,* *bahai-month, bahai-day*⟩	*list-of-integers*
bahai-day	$1 \ldots 19$	*positive-integer*
bahai-major	*integer*	
bahai-month	$0 \ldots 19$	*nonnegative-integer*
bahai-year	$1 \ldots 19$	*positive-integer*
boolean	*true, false*	
chinese-branch	$1 \ldots 12$	*positive-integer*
chinese-cycle	*integer*	
chinese-date	⟨*chinese-cycle, chinese-year, chinese-month,* *chinese-leap-month, chinese-day*⟩	*list*
chinese-day	$1 \ldots 31$	*positive-integer*
chinese-leap	*boolean*	
chinese-month	$1 \ldots 12$	*positive-integer*
chinese-name	⟨*chinese-stem, chinese-branch*⟩	*list-of-nonnegative-integers*
chinese-stem	$1 \ldots 10$	*positive-integer*

Name	Type or Range	Supertype
chinese-year	1...60	*positive-integer*
coptic-date	⟨*coptic-year, coptic-month, coptic-day*⟩	*standard-date*
coptic-day	1...31	*positive-integer*
coptic-month	1...13	*positive-integer*
coptic-year	*integer*	
day-of-week	0...6	*nonnegative-integer*
distance		*real*
egyptian-date	⟨*egyptian-year, egyptian-month, egyptian-day*⟩	*standard-date*
egyptian-day	1...30	*positive-integer*
egyptian-month	1...13	*positive-integer*
egyptian-year	*integer*	
ethiopic-date	⟨*ethiopic-year, ethiopic-month, ethiopic-day*⟩	*standard-date*
ethiopic-day	1...31	*positive-integer*
ethiopic-month	1...13	*positive-integer*
ethiopic-year	*integer*	
fixed-date	*integer*	
fraction-of-day	[-0.5,0.5]	*real*
french-date	⟨*french-year, french-month, french-day*⟩	*standard-date*
french-day	1...30	*positive-integer*
french-month	1...13	*positive-integer*
french-year	*integer*	
gregorian-date	⟨*gregorian-year, gregorian-month, gregorian-day*⟩	*standard-date*
gregorian-day	1...31	*positive-integer*
gregorian-month	1...12	*positive-integer*
gregorian-year	*integer*	
hebrew-date	⟨*hebrew-year, hebrew-month, hebrew-day*⟩	*standard-date*
hebrew-day	1...30	*positive-integer*
hebrew-month	1...13	*positive-integer*
hebrew-year	*integer*	
hindu-lunar-date	⟨*hindu-lunar-year, hindu-lunar-month, hindu-lunar-leap-month, hindu-lunar-day, hindu-lunar-leap-day*⟩	*list*
hindu-lunar-day	1...30	*positive-integer*
hindu-lunar-leap-day	*boolean*	
hindu-lunar-leap-month	*boolean*	
hindu-lunar-month	1...12	*positive-integer*
hindu-lunar-year	*integer*	
hindu-solar-date	⟨*hindu-solar-year, hindu-solar-month, hindu-solar-day*⟩	*standard-date*
hindu-solar-day	1...32	*positive-integer*
hindu-solar-month	1...12	*positive-integer*
hindu-solar-year	*integer*	
hindu-year	*integer*	
hour	0...23	*nonnegative-integer*
ides	13,15	*roman-count*
integer		*rational*
interval		*real*
islamic-date	⟨*islamic-year, islamic-month, islamic-day*⟩	*standard-date*
islamic-day	1...30	*positive-integer*
islamic-month	1...12	*positive-integer*
islamic-year	*integer*	
iso-date	⟨*iso-year, iso-week, iso-day*⟩	*list-of-integers*
iso-day	1...7	*positive-integer*
iso-week	1...53	*positive-integer*
iso-year	*integer*	
julian-centuries	*real*	
julian-date	⟨*julian-year, julian-month, julian-day*⟩	*standard-date*
julian-day	1...31	*positive-integer*
julian-day-number	*real*	
julian-month	1...12	*positive-integer*
julian-year	*nonzero-integer*	

Name	Type or Range	Supertype
list		
list-of-angles		*list-of-reals*
list-of-fixed-dates		*list-of-integers*
list-of-integers		*list*
list-of-nonnegative-integers		*list-of-integers*
list-of-pairs		*list*
list-of-reals		*list*
location	⟨angle, angle, distance, real⟩	*list*
mayan-baktun	*integer*	
mayan-haab-date	⟨mayan-haab-month, mayan-haab-day⟩	*list-of-nonnegative-integers*
mayan-haab-day	0 . . . 19	*nonnegative-integer*
mayan-haab-month	1 . . . 19	*positive-integer*
mayan-katun	0 . . . 19	*nonnegative-integer*
mayan-kin	0 . . . 19	*nonnegative-integer*
mayan-long-count-date	⟨mayan-baktun, mayan-katun, mayan-tun, mayan-uinal, mayan-kin⟩	*list-of-integers*
mayan-tun	0 . . . 17	*nonnegative-integer*
mayan-tzolkin-date	⟨mayan-tzolkin-number, mayan-tzolkin-name⟩	*list-of-nonnegative-integers*
mayan-tzolkin-name	1 . . . 20	*nonnegative-integer*
mayan-tzolkin-number	1 . . . 13	*nonnegative-integer*
mayan-uinal	0 . . . 19	*nonnegative-integer*
minute	0 . . . 59	*nonnegative-integer*
moment	*real*	
nakshatra	1 . . . 27	*positive-integer*
nones	5, 7	*roman-count*
nonnegative-integer	0, 1, . . .	*integer*
nonzero-integer	. . . , −2, −1, 1, 2, . . .	*integer*
nonzero-real	(−∞ : 0) ∪ (0 : ∞)	*real*
old-hindu-lunar-date	⟨old-hindu-lunar-year, old-hindu-lunar-month, old-hindu-lunar-leap, old-hindu-lunar-day⟩	*list*
old-hindu-lunar-day	1 . . . 30	*positive-integer*
old-hindu-lunar-leap	*boolean*	
old-hindu-lunar-month	1 . . . 12	*positive-integer*
old-hindu-lunar-year	*integer*	
old-hindu-month	1 . . . 12	*positive-integer*
old-hindu-year	*integer*	
omer-count	⟨0 . . . 7, 0 . . . 6⟩	*list-of-nonnegative-integers*
persian-date	⟨persian-year, persian-month, persian-day⟩	*standard-date*
persian-day	1 . . . 31	*positive-integer*
persian-month	1 . . . 12	*positive-integer*
persian-year	*nonzero-integer*	
phase	[0 : 360)	*angle*
positive-integer	1, 2, . . .	*integer*
quadrant	1 . . . 4	*positive-integer*
radian	[0 : 2π)	*real*
rational		*real*
rational-amplitude	[−1 : 1]	*rational*
rational-angle	[0 : 360)	*rational*
rational-interval		*rational*
rational-moment	*rational*	*moment*
real	(−∞ : ∞)	
roman-count	1 . . . 19	*positive-integer*
roman-date	⟨roman-year, roman-month, roman-event, roman-count, roman-leap⟩	*list*
roman-event	1 . . . 3	*integer*
roman-leap	*boolean*	

Name	Type or Range	Supertype
roman-month	1 . . . 12	*positive-integer*
roman-year	*integer*	
season	[0 : 360)	*angle*
second	[0 : 60)	*real*
standard-date	⟨*standard-year, standard-month, standard-day*⟩	*list-of-integers*
standard-day	1 . . . 31	*positive-integer*
standard-month	1 . . . 13	*positive-integer*
standard-year	*integer*	
string		
time	⟨*hour, minute, second*⟩	*list-of-reals*
weekday	0 . . . 6	*nonnegative-integer*

A.2 Function Types

Function	Parameter Type(s)	Result Type
aberration	*moment*	*angle*
adjusted-mod	⟨*real, real*⟩	*real*
advent	*gregorian-year*	*fixed-date*
alt-orthodox-easter	*gregorian-year*	*fixed-date*
alt-fixed-from-gregorian	*gregorian-date*	*fixed-date*
alt-gregorian-from-fixed	*fixed-date*	*gregorian-date*
alt-gregorian-year-from-fixed	*fixed-date*	*gregorian-year*
alt-hindu-sunrise	*fixed-date*	*rational-moment*
apparent-from-local	*moment*	*moment*
arccos-degrees	*amplitude*	*angle*
arcsin-degrees	*amplitude*	*angle*
arctan-degrees	⟨*real, quadrant*⟩	*angle*
arithmetic-persian-from-fixed	*fixed-date*	*persian-date*
arithmetic-persian-leap-year?	*persian-year*	*boolean*
arithmetic-persian-year-from-fixed	*fixed-date*	*persian-year*
armenian-date	⟨*armenian-year, armenian-month, armenian-day*⟩	*armenian-date*
armenian-from-fixed	*fixed-date*	*armenian-date*
ascensional-difference	⟨*fixed-date, location*⟩	*rational-angle*
asr	⟨*fixed-date, location*⟩	*moment*
astronomical-easter	*gregorian-year*	*fixed-date*
bahai-cycle	*bahai-date*	*bahai-cycle*
bahai-date	⟨*bahai-major, bahai-cycle, bahai-year, bahai-month, bahai-day*⟩	*bahai-date*
bahai-day	*bahai-date*	*bahai-day*
bahai-from-fixed	*fixed-date*	*bahai-date*
bahai-major	*bahai-date*	*bahai-major*
bahai-month	*bahai-date*	*bahai-month*
bahai-new-year	*gregorian-year*	*fixed-date*
bahai-year	*bahai-date*	*bahai-year*
balinese-date	⟨*boolean,*1. . . 2, 1. . . 3, 1. . . 4, 1. . . 5, 1. . . 6, 1. . . 7, 1. . . 8, 1. . . 9, 0. . . 9⟩	*balinese-date*
bali-asatawara	*balinese-date*	1. . . 8
bali-asatawara-from-fixed	*fixed-date*	1. . . 8
bali-caturwara	*balinese-date*	1. . . 4
bali-caturwara-from-fixed	*fixed-date*	1. . . 4
bali-dasawara	*balinese-date*	0. . . 9
bali-dasawara-from-fixed	*fixed-date*	0. . . 9
bali-day-from-fixed	*fixed-date*	0. . . 209
bali-dwiwara	*balinese-date*	1. . . 2
bali-dwiwara-from-fixed	*fixed-date*	1. . . 2
bali-luang	*balinese-date*	*boolean*

Function	Parameter Type(s)	Result Type
bali-luang-from-fixed	*fixed-date*	*boolean*
bali-on-or-before	⟨*balinese-date, fixed-date*⟩	*fixed-date*
bali-pancawara	*balinese-date*	1...5
bali-pancawara-from-fixed	*fixed-date*	1...5
bali-pawukon-from-fixed	*fixed-date*	*balinese-date*
bali-sadwara	*balinese-date*	1...6
bali-sadwara-from-fixed	*fixed-date*	1...6
bali-sangawara	*balinese-date*	1...9
bali-sangawara-from-fixed	*fixed-date*	1...9
bali-saptawara	*balinese-date*	1...7
bali-saptawara-from-fixed	*fixed-date*	1...7
bali-triwara	*balinese-date*	1...3
bali-triwara-from-fixed	*fixed-date*	1...3
bali-week-from-fixed	*fixed-date*	1...30
bce	*standard-year*	*julian-year*
binary-search	⟨—, *real*, —, *real*, —, *real*→*boolean*, ⟨*real, real*⟩→*boolean*⟩	*real*
birkath-ha-hama	*gregorian-year*	*list-of-fixed-dates*
ce	*standard-year*	*julian-year*
chinese-age	⟨*chinese-date, fixed-date*⟩	*nonnegative-integer* (or **bogus**)
chinese-branch	*chinese-name*	*chinese-branch*
chinese-cycle	*chinese-date*	*chinese-cycle*
chinese-date	⟨*chinese-cycle, chinese-year, chinese-month,chinese-leap, chinese-day*⟩	*chinese-date*
chinese-day	*chinese-date*	*chinese-day*
chinese-day-name-on-or-before	⟨*chinese-name, fixed-date*⟩	*chinese-day*
chinese-from-fixed	*fixed-date*	*chinese-date*
chinese-leap	*chinese-date*	*chinese-leap*
chinese-location	*moment*	*location*
chinese-month	*chinese-date*	*chinese-month*
chinese-name-difference	⟨*chinese-name, chinese-name*⟩	*nonnegative-integer*
chinese-name	⟨*chinese-stem, chinese-branch*⟩	*chinese-name* (or **bogus**)
chinese-name-of-day	*chinese-date*	*chinese-name*
chinese-name-of-month	⟨*chinese-year, chinese-month*⟩	*chinese-name*
chinese-name-of-year	*chinese-year*	*chinese-name*
chinese-new-moon-before	*fixed-date*	*fixed-date*
chinese-new-moon-on-or-after	*fixed-date*	*fixed-date*
chinese-new-year	*gregorian-year*	*fixed-date*
chinese-new-year-in-sui	*fixed-date*	*fixed-date*
chinese-new-year-on-or-before	*fixed-date*	*fixed-date*
chinese-sexagesimal-name	*integer*	*chinese-name*
chinese-solar-longitude-on-or-after	⟨*fixed-date, season*⟩	*moment*
chinese-stem	*chinese-name*	*chinese-stem*
chinese-winter-solstice-on-or-before	*fixed-date*	*fixed-date*
chinese-year	*chinese-date*	*chinese-year*
christmas	*gregorian-year*	*fixed-date*
classical-passover-eve	*gregorian-year*	*fixed-date*
coptic-christmas	*gregorian-year*	*list-of-fixed-dates*
coptic-date	⟨*coptic-year, coptic-month, coptic-day*⟩	*coptic-date*
coptic-from-fixed	*fixed-date*	*coptic-date*
coptic-in-gregorian	⟨*coptic-month, coptic-day, gregorian-year*⟩	*list-of-fixed-dates*
coptic-leap-year?	*coptic-year*	*boolean*
cosine-degrees	*angle*	*amplitude*
current-major-solar-term	*fixed-date*	*integer*
current-minor-solar-term	*fixed-date*	*integer*
daily-motion	*fixed-date*	*rational-angle*
dawn	⟨*moment, location, angle*⟩	*moment*
day-number	*gregorian-date*	*positive-integer*

Function	Parameter Type(s)	Result Type
day-of-week-from-fixed	*fixed-date*	*day-of-week*
daylight-saving-end	*gregorian-year*	*fixed-date*
daylight-saving-start	*gregorian-year*	*fixed-date*
days-in-hebrew-year	*hebrew-year*	353,354,355,383, 384,385
days-remaining	*gregorian-date*	*nonnegative-integer*
deg	*real*	*angle*
	list-of-reals	*list-of-angles*
degrees	*real*	*angle*
degrees-to-radians	*real*	*radian*
direction	⟨*location, location*⟩	*angle*
dragon-festival	*gregorian-year*	*fixed-date*
dusk	⟨*moment, location, angle*⟩	*moment*
dynamical-from-universal	*moment*	*moment*
easter	*gregorian-year*	*fixed-date*
eastern-orthodox-christmas	*gregorian-year*	*list-of-fixed-dates*
egyptian-date	⟨*egyptian-year, egyptian-month, egyptian-day*⟩	*egyptian-date*
egyptian-from-fixed	*fixed-date*	*egyptian-date*
election-day	*gregorian-year*	*fixed-date*
elevation	*location*	*distance*
ephemeris-correction	*moment*	*fraction-of-day*
epiphany	*gregorian-year*	*fixed-date*
equation-of-time	*moment*	*fraction-of-day*
estimate-prior-solar-longitude	⟨*moment, season*⟩	*moment*
ethiopic-date	⟨*ethiopic-year, ethiopic-month, ethiopic-day*⟩	*ethiopic-date*
ethiopic-from-fixed	*fixed-date*	*ethiopic-date*
feast-of-ridvan	*gregorian-year*	*fixed-date*
final	⟨—, *integer, integer→boolean*⟩	*integer*
first-kday	⟨*weekday, gregorian-month, gregorian-day, gregorian-year*⟩	*fixed-date*
fixed-from-arithmetic-persian	*persian-date*	*fixed-date*
fixed-from-armenian	*armenian-date*	*fixed-date*
fixed-from-bahai	*bahai-date*	*fixed-date*
fixed-from-chinese	*chinese-date*	*fixed-date*
fixed-from-coptic	*coptic-date*	*fixed-date*
fixed-from-egyptian	*egyptian-date*	*fixed-date*
fixed-from-ethiopic	*ethiopic-date*	*fixed-date*
fixed-from-french	*french-date*	*fixed-date*
fixed-from-future-bahai	*bahai-date*	*fixed-date*
fixed-from-gregorian	*gregorian-date*	*fixed-date*
fixed-from-hebrew	*hebrew-date*	*fixed-date*
fixed-from-hindu-lunar	*old-hindu-lunar-date*	*fixed-date*
fixed-from-hindu-solar	*hindu-solar-date*	*fixed-date*
fixed-from-islamic	*islamic-date*	*fixed-date*
fixed-from-iso	*iso-date*	*fixed-date*
fixed-from-jd	*julian-day-number*	*fixed-date*
fixed-from-julian	*julian-date*	*fixed-date*
fixed-from-mjd	*julian-day-number*	*fixed-date*
fixed-from-mayan-long-count	*mayan-long-count-date*	*fixed-date*
fixed-from-modified-french	*french-date*	*fixed-date*
fixed-from-observational-islamic	*islamic-date*	*fixed-date*
fixed-from-old-hindu-lunar	*old-hindu-lunar-date*	*fixed-date*
fixed-from-old-hindu-solar	*hindu-solar-date*	*fixed-date*
fixed-from-persian	*persian-date*	*fixed-date*
fixed-from-roman	*roman-date*	*fixed-date*
french-date	⟨*french-year, french-month french-day*⟩	*french-date*
french-from-fixed	*fixed-date*	*french-date*
french-new-year-on-or-before	*fixed-date*	*fixed-date*
future-bahai-from-fixed	*fixed-date*	*bahai-date*
future-bahai-new-year-on-or-before	*fixed-date*	*fixed-date*

Function	Parameter Type(s)	Result Type
gregorian-date	⟨*gregorian-year, gregorian-month, gregorian-day*⟩	*gregorian-date*
gregorian-date-difference	⟨*gregorian-date, gregorian-date*⟩	*integer*
gregorian-from-fixed	*fixed-date*	*gregorian-date*
gregorian-leap-year?	*gregorian-year*	*boolean*
gregorian-year-from-fixed	*fixed-date*	*gregorian-year*
hebrew-birthday	⟨*hebrew-date, hebrew-year*⟩	*fixed-date*
hebrew-birthday-in-gregorian	⟨*hebrew-date, gregorian-year*⟩	*list-of-fixed-dates*
hebrew-calendar-elapsed-days	*hebrew-year*	*integer*
hebrew-date	⟨*hebrew-year, hebrew-month, hebrew-day*⟩	*hebrew-date*
hebrew-from-fixed	*fixed-date*	*hebrew-date*
hebrew-leap-year?	*hebrew-year*	*boolean*
hebrew-new-year	*hebrew-year*	*fixed-date*
hebrew-new-year-delay	*hebrew-year*	*0,1,2*
hindu-arcsin	*amplitude*	*rational-angle*
hindu-calendar-year	*rational-moment*	*hindu-solar-year*
hindu-day-count	*fixed-date*	*integer*
hindu-equation-of-time	*fixed-date*	*rational-moment*
hindu-lunar-date	⟨*hindu-lunar-year, hindu-lunar-month, hindu-lunar-leap-month, hindu-lunar-day, hindu-lunar-leap-day*⟩	*hindu-lunar-date*
hindu-lunar-day	*hindu-lunar-date*	*hindu-lunar-day*
hindu-lunar-from-fixed	*fixed-date*	*hindu-lunar-date*
hindu-lunar-leap-day	*hindu-lunar-date*	*hindu-lunar-leap-day*
hindu-lunar-leap-month	*hindu-lunar-date*	*hindu-lunar-leap-month*
hindu-lunar-longitude	*rational-moment*	*rational-angle*
hindu-lunar-month	*hindu-lunar-date*	*hindu-lunar-month*
hindu-lunar-new-year	*gregorian-year*	*fixed-date*
hindu-lunar-on-or-before?	⟨*hindu-lunar-date, hindu-lunar-date*⟩	*boolean*
hindu-lunar-phase	*rational-moment*	*rational-angle*
hindu-lunar-year	*hindu-lunar-date*	*hindu-lunar-year*
hindu-new-moon-before	*rational-moment*	*rational-moment*
hindu-sine	*angle*	*rational-amplitude*
hindu-sine-table	*integer*	*rational-angle*
hindu-solar-date	⟨*hindu-solar-year, hindu-solar-month, hindu-solar-day*⟩	*hindu-solar-date*
hindu-solar-from-fixed	*fixed-date*	*hindu-solar-date*
hindu-solar-longitude	*rational-moment*	*rational-angle*
hindu-solar-longitude-after	⟨*gregorian-year, hindu-solar-month*⟩	*moment*
hindu-solar-on-or-before?	⟨*hindu-solar-date, hindu-solar-date*⟩	*boolean*
hindu-sunrise	*fixed-date*	*rational-moment*
hindu-tropical-longitude	*fixed-date*	*rational-angle*
hindu-zodiac	*rational-moment*	*hindu-solar-month*
hr	*real*	*interval*
ides-of-month	*roman-month*	*ides*
independence-day	*gregorian-year*	*fixed-date*
islamic-date	⟨*islamic-year, islamic-month, islamic-day*⟩	*islamic-date*
islamic-from-fixed	*fixed-date*	*islamic-date*
islamic-in-gregorian	⟨*islamic-month, islamic-day, gregorian-year*⟩	*list-of-fixed-dates*
islamic-leap-year?	*islamic-year*	*boolean*
iso-date	⟨*iso-year, iso-week, iso-day*⟩	*iso-date*
iso-day	*iso-date*	*day-of-week*
iso-from-fixed	*fixed-date*	*iso-date*
iso-week	*iso-date*	*iso-week*
iso-year	*iso-date*	*iso-year*

Function	Parameter Type(s)	Result Type
japanese-location	*moment*	*location*
jd-from-fixed	*fixed-date*	*julian-day-number*
jd-from-moment	*moment*	*julian-day-number*
jewish-dusk	⟨*fixed-date, location*⟩	*moment*
jewish-morning-end	⟨*fixed-date, location*⟩	*moment*
jewish-sabbath-ends	⟨*fixed-date, location*⟩	*moment*
jovian-year	*fixed-date*	*1 . . . 60*
julian-centuries	*moment*	*real*
julian-date	⟨*julian-year, julian-month, julian-day*⟩	*julian-date*
julian-from-fixed	*fixed-date*	*julian-date*
julian-in-gregorian	⟨*julian-month, julian-day, gregorian-year*⟩	*list-of-fixed-dates*
julian-leap-year?	*julian-year*	*boolean*
kajeng-keliwon-in-gregorian	*gregorian-year*	*list-of-fixed-dates*
karana	*1 . . . 60*	*0 . . . 10*
kday-after	⟨*fixed-date, weekday*⟩	*fixed-date*
kday-before	⟨*fixed-date, weekday*⟩	*fixed-date*
kday-nearest	⟨*fixed-date, weekday*⟩	*fixed-date*
kday-on-or-after	⟨*fixed-date, weekday*⟩	*fixed-date*
kday-on-or-before	⟨*fixed-date, weekday*⟩	*fixed-date*
labor-day	*gregorian-year*	*fixed-date*
last-day-of-hebrew-month	⟨*hebrew-month, hebrew-year*⟩	*hebrew-day*
last-kday	⟨*weekday, gregorian-month,* *gregorian-day, gregorian-year*⟩	*fixed-date*
last-month-of-hebrew-year	*hebrew-year*	*hebrew-month*
latitude	*location*	*±angle*
local-from-apparent	*moment*	*moment*
local-from-standard	⟨*moment, location*⟩	*moment*
local-from-universal	⟨*moment, location*⟩	*moment*
location	⟨*angle, angle, distance, real*⟩	*location*
long-marheshvan?	*hebrew-year*	*boolean*
longitude	*location*	*±angle*
lunar-altitude	⟨*moment, location*⟩	*angle*
lunar-day	*rational-moment*	*hindu-lunar-day*
lunar-day-after	⟨*rational-moment, rational, real*⟩	*rational-moment*
lunar-latitude	*moment*	*angle*
lunar-longitude	*moment*	*angle*
lunar-station	*fixed-date*	*nakshatra*
lunar-phase	*moment*	*phase*
lunar-phase-after	⟨*phase, moment*⟩	*moment*
lunar-phase-before	⟨*phase, moment*⟩	*moment*
major-solar-term-on-or-after	*fixed-date*	*moment*
mawlid-an-nabi	*gregorian-year*	*list-of-fixed-dates*
mayan-baktun	*mayan-long-count-date*	*mayan-baktun*
mayan-calendar-round-on-or-before	⟨*mayan-haab-date, mayan-tzolkin-date,* *fixed-date*⟩	*fixed-date* (or **bogus**)
mayan-haab-date	⟨*mayan-haab-day, mayan-haab-month*⟩	*mayan-haab-date*
mayan-haab-day	*mayan-haab-date*	*mayan-haab-day*
mayan-haab-from-fixed	*fixed-date*	*mayan-haab-date*
mayan-haab-month	*mayan-haab-date*	*mayan-haab-month*
mayan-haab-on-or-before	⟨*mayan-haab-date, fixed-date*⟩	*fixed-date*
mayan-haab-ordinal	*mayan-haab-date*	*nonnegative-integer*
mayan-katun	*mayan-long-count-date*	*mayan-katun*
mayan-kin	*mayan-long-count-date*	*mayan-kin*
mayan-long-count-date	⟨*mayan-baktun, mayan-katun, mayan-tun,* *mayan-uinal, mayan-kin*⟩	*mayan-long-count-date*
mayan-long-count-from-fixed	*fixed-date*	*mayan-long-count-date*
mayan-tun	*mayan-long-count-date*	*mayan-tun*
mayan-tzolkin-date	⟨*mayan-tzolkin-number,* *mayan-tzolkin-name*⟩	*mayan-tzolkin-date*
mayan-tzolkin-from-fixed	*fixed-date*	*mayan-tzolkin-date*
mayan-tzolkin-name	*mayan-tzolkin-date*	*mayan-tzolkin-name*
mayan-tzolkin-number	*mayan-tzolkin-date*	*mayan-tzolkin-number*
mayan-tzolkin-on-or-before	⟨*mayan-tzolkin-date, fixed-date*⟩	*fixed-date*

Function	Parameter Type(s)	Result Type
mayan-tzolkin-ordinal	*mayan-tzolkin-date*	*nonnegative-integer*
mayan-uinal	*mayan-long-count-date*	*mayan-uinal*
mean-position	⟨*rational-moment, rational*⟩	*rational-angle*
memorial-day	*gregorian-year*	*fixed-date*
mesha-samkranti	*gregorian-year*	*moment*
midday	⟨*fixed-date, location*⟩	*moment*
midday-in-tehran	*fixed-date*	*moment*
midnight	⟨*fixed-date, location*⟩	*moment*
midnight-in-china	*fixed-date*	*moment*
midnight-in-paris	*fixed-date*	*moment*
minor-solar-term-on-or-after	*fixed-date*	*moment*
mjd-from-fixed	*fixed-date*	*julian-day-number*
modified-french-from-fixed	*fixed-date*	*french-year*
modified-french-leap-year?	*french-year*	*boolean*
molad	⟨*hebrew-month, hebrew-year*⟩	*moment*
moment-from-depression	⟨*moment, location, angle*⟩	*moment*
moment-from-jd	*julian-day-number*	*moment*
mt	*real*	*distance*
naw-ruz	*gregorian-year*	*fixed-date*
next	⟨—, *integer, integer→boolean*⟩	*integer*
new-moon-before	*moment*	*moment*
new-moon-after	*moment*	*moment*
no-major-solar-term?	*fixed-date*	*boolean*
nones-of-month	*roman-month*	*nones*
nth-kday	⟨*integer, weekday, gregorian-date*⟩	*fixed-date*
nth-new-moon	*integer*	*moment*
nutation	*moment*	*angle*
obliquity	*moment*	*angle*
observational-islamic-from-fixed	*fixed-date*	*islamic-date*
old-hindu-lunar-date	⟨*old-hindu-lunar-year,* *old-hindu-lunar-month,* *old-hindu-lunar-leap-month,* *old-hindu-lunar-day*⟩	*old-hindu-lunar-date*
old-hindu-lunar-day	*old-hindu-lunar-date*	*old-hindu-lunar-day*
old-hindu-lunar-from-fixed	*fixed-date*	*old-hindu-lunar-date*
old-hindu-lunar-leap	*old-hindu-lunar-date*	*old-hindu-lunar-leap*
old-hindu-lunar-leap-year?	*old-hindu-lunar-year*	*boolean*
old-hindu-lunar-month	*old-hindu-lunar-date*	*old-hindu-lunar-month*
old-hindu-lunar-year	*old-hindu-lunar-date*	*old-hindu-lunar-year*
old-hindu-solar-from-fixed	*fixed-date*	*hindu-solar-date*
omer	*fixed-date*	*omer-count* (or **bogus**)
orthodox-easter	*gregorian-year*	*fixed-date*
passover	*gregorian-year*	*fixed-date*
pentecost	*gregorian-year*	*fixed-date*
persian-date	⟨*persian-year, persian-month,* *persian-day*⟩	*persian-date*
persian-from-fixed	*fixed-date*	*persian-date*
persian-new-year-on-or-before	*fixed-date*	*fixed-date*
phasis-on-or-before	⟨*moment, location*⟩	*moment*
poly	⟨*real, list-of-reals*⟩	*real*
positions-in-interval	⟨*nonnegative-integer,* *positive-integer, nonnegative-integer,* *fixed-date, fixed-date*⟩	*list-of-fixed-dates*
prior-leap-month?	⟨*fixed-date, fixed-date*⟩	*boolean*
purim	*gregorian-year*	*fixed-date*
qing-ming	*gregorian-year*	*fixed-date*
quotient	⟨*real, nonzero-real*⟩	*integer*
radians-to-degrees	*radian*	*angle*
rising-sign	*fixed-date*	*integer*
roman-count	*roman-date*	*roman-count*
roman-date	⟨*roman-year, roman-month,* *roman-event, roman-count,* *roman-leap*⟩	*roman-date*

Function	Parameter Type(s)	Result Type
roman-event	*roman-date*	*roman-event*
roman-leap	*roman-date*	*roman-leap*
roman-month	*roman-date*	*roman-month*
roman-year	*roman-date*	*roman-year*
roman-from-fixed	*fixed-date*	*roman-date*
sacred-wednesdays	*gregorian-year*	*list-of-fixed-dates*
sacred-wednesdays-in-gregorian	*gregorian-year*	*list-of-fixed-dates*
yom-ha-zikkaron	*gregorian-year*	*fixed-date*
sh-ela	*gregorian-year*	*list-of-fixed-dates*
short-kislev?	*hebrew-year*	*boolean*
sidereal-from-moment	*moment*	*angle*
sigma	⟨*list-of-pairs, list-of-reals*→*real*⟩	*real*
sin-degrees	*angle*	*amplitude*
solar-longitude	*moment*	*season*
solar-longitude-after	⟨*moment, season*⟩	*moment*
solar-sidereal-difference	*fixed-date*	*rational-angle*
standard-day	*standard-date*	*standard-day*
standard-from-local	⟨*moment, location*⟩	*moment*
standard-from-sundial	⟨*fixed-date, real, location*⟩	*real*
standard-from-universal	⟨*moment, location*⟩	*moment*
standard-month	*standard-date*	*standard-month*
standard-year	*standard-date*	*standard-year*
sum	⟨*integer*→*real, —, integer,* *integer*→*boolean*⟩	*real*
sunrise	⟨*fixed-date, location*⟩	*moment*
sunset	⟨*fixed-date, location*⟩	*moment*
sunset-in-haifa	*fixed-date*	*moment*
ta-anit-esther	*gregorian-year*	*fixed-date*
tangent-degrees	*angle*	*real*
temporal-hour	⟨*fixed-date, location*⟩	*real*
time-from-moment	*moment*	⟨*hour, minute, second*⟩
time-of-day	⟨*hour, minute, second*⟩	*time*
tishah-be-av	*gregorian-year*	*fixed-date*

true-position	⟨*rational-moment, rational,*
	    positive-integer, rational,
	    nonnegative-integer⟩
		rational-angle

tumpek-in-gregorian	*gregorian-year*	*list-of-fixed-dates*
universal-from-dynamical	*moment*	*moment*
universal-from-local	⟨*moment, location*⟩	*moment*
universal-from-standard	⟨*moment, location*⟩	*moment*
visible-crescent	⟨*fixed-date, location*⟩	*boolean*
yahrzeit	⟨*hebrew-date, hebrew-year*⟩	*fixed-date*
yahrzeit-in-gregorian	⟨*hebrew-date, gregorian-year*⟩	*list-of-fixed-dates*
yoga	*fixed-date*	*1 . . . 27*
yom-kippur	*gregorian-year*	*fixed-date*
zone	*location*	*real*

A.3 Constant Types and Values

Constant	Type	Value
april	*standard-month*	4
armenian-epoch	*fixed-date*	201443
arya-jovian-period	*rational*	131493125/30352
arya-lunar-day	*rational*	26298625/26716668
arya-lunar-month	*rational*	131493125/4452778
arya-solar-month	*rational*	210389/6912
arya-solar-year	*rational*	210389/576
ayyam-i-ha	*bahai-month*	0

Constant	Type	Value
august	*standard-month*	8
autumn	*season*	180
bahai-epoch	*fixed-date*	673222
bali-epoch	*fixed-date*	−1721279
bogus	*string*	"bogus"
chinese-epoch	*fixed-date*	−963099
chinese-day-name-epoch	*integer*	15
chinese-month-name-epoch	*integer*	3
coptic-epoch	*fixed-date*	103605
december	*standard-month*	12
egyptian-epoch	*fixed-date*	−272787
ethiopic-epoch	*fixed-date*	2430
false	*boolean*	false
february	*standard-month*	2
first-quarter	*phase*	90
french-epoch	*fixed-date*	654415
friday	*weekday*	5
full	*phase*	180
gregorian-epoch	*fixed-date*	1
haifa	*location*	⟨32.82, 35.0, 0, 2⟩
hebrew-epoch	*fixed-date*	−1373427
hindu-anomalistic-month	*rational*	1577917828/57265137
hindu-anomalistic-year	*rational*	1577917828000/4319999613
hindu-creation	*fixed-date*	−714403429586
hindu-epoch	*fixed-date*	−1132959
hindu-locale	*location*	⟨463/20, 2273/30, 0, 383/75⟩
hindu-lunar-era	*standard-year*	3044
hindu-sidereal-month	*rational*	394479457/14438334
hindu-sidereal-year	*rational*	394479457/1080000
hindu-solar-era	*standard-year*	3179
hindu-synodic-month	*rational*	394479457/13358334
ides	*integer*	3
islamic-epoch	*fixed-date*	227015
islamic-locale	*location*	⟨30.1, 31.3, 200, 2⟩
j2000	*moment*	730120.5
january	*standard-month*	1
jd-epoch	*moment*	−1721424.5
jerusalem	*location*	⟨31.8, 35.2, 800, 2⟩
julian-epoch	*fixed-date*	−1
july	*standard-month*	7
june	*standard-month*	6
kalends	*integer*	1
last-quarter	*phase*	270
march	*standard-month*	3
may	*standard-month*	5
mayan-epoch	*fixed-date*	−1137142
mayan-haab-epoch	*fixed-date*	−1137490
mayan-tzolkin-epoch	*fixed-date*	−1137302
mean-synodic-month	*real*	29.530588853
mean-tropical-year	*real*	365.242189
mecca	*location*	⟨6427/300, 11947/300, 1000, 2⟩
mjd-epoch	*fixed-date*	678576
monday	*weekday*	1
new	*phase*	0
nisan	*hebrew-month*	1
nones	*integer*	2
november	*standard-month*	11
october	*standard-month*	10
paris	*location*	⟨175811/3600, 187/80, 27, 1⟩
persian-epoch	*fixed-date*	226896
pi	*real*	3.141592653589793

Constant	Type	Value
saturday	*weekday*	6
september	*standard-month*	9
spring	*season*	0
summer	*season*	90
sunday	*weekday*	0
tehran	*location*	⟨35.68, 51.42, 1100, 3.5⟩
thursday	*weekday*	4
tishri	*hebrew-month*	7
true	*boolean*	true
tuesday	*weekday*	2
ujjain	*location*	⟨1389/60, 4546/60, 0, 2273/450⟩
wednesday	*weekday*	3
winter	*season*	270

Astronomical clock designed and made in Norway by Rasmus Sornes between 1958 and 1964. It computes sidereal time, apparent solar time, mean solar time, Gregorian date (taking the leap rule fully into account), solar and lunar eclipses, precession, and the positions of all planets. (Courtesy of The Time Museum, Rockford, IL.)

Appendix B

Lisp Implementation

> It has been often said that a person does not really understand
> something until he teaches it to someone else. Actually a person
> does not *really* understand something until he can teach it to a
> *computer*, i.e., express it as an algorithm.
> —Donald E. Knuth: "Computer Science and its Relation to
> Mathematics,"
> *American Mathematical Monthly* (1974)

This appendix contains the complete Common Lisp implementation of the calendar functions described in the text. The functions in the text were automatically typeset from the definitions in this appendix. These functions are on the compact disc accompanying this book; errata are available over the World Wide Web at

    http://www.calendarists.com

Please bear in mind the limits of the License and that the copyright on this book includes the code. *Also please keep in mind that if the result of any calculation is critical, it should be verified by independent means.*

For licensing information about nonpersonal and other uses, contact the authors. The code is distributed in the hope that it may be useful but without any warranty as to the accuracy of its output and with liability limited to return of the price of this book, which restrictions are set forth on page xxxii.

B.1 Lisp Preliminaries

For readers unfamiliar with Lisp, this section provides the bare necessities. A complete description can be found in [1].

317

All functions in Lisp are written in prefix notation. If f is a defined function, then

```
(f e0 e1 e2 ... en)
```

applies f to the $n + 1$ arguments e0, e1, e2, ..., en. Thus, for example, + adds a list of numbers:

```
(+ 1 -2 3)
```

adds the three numbers and returns the value 2. The Lisp functions -, *, and / work similarly, to subtract, multiply, and divide, respectively, a list of numbers. In a similar fashion, <= ($\leq$) checks that the numbers are in nondecreasing order and yields true (t in Lisp) if the relations hold. For instance,

```
(<= 1 2 3)
```

evaluates to t. The Lisp functions =, /= (not equal), <, >, and >= (greater than or equal) are similar.

Lists are Lisp's main data structure. To construct a list (e0 e1 e2 ... en) the expression

```
(list e0 e1 e2 ... en)
```

is used. The function nth, used as (nth i l), extracts the ith element of the list l, indexing from 0; the predicate member, used as (member x l), tests if x is an element of l. To get the first (indexed 0), second, and so on, through tenth elements of a list, we use the functions first, second, third, fourth, fifth, sixth, seventh, eighth, ninth, and tenth. The empty list is represented by nil.

Constants are defined with the defconstant command, which has the syntax

```
(defconstant constant-name
    expression)
```

For example,

```
1   (defconstant sunday
2       ;; TYPE day-of-week
3       ;; Residue class for Sunday.
4       0)
```

```
1   (defconstant monday
2       ;; TYPE day-of-week
3       ;; Residue class for Monday.
4       (+ sunday 1))
```

```
1   (defconstant tuesday
2       ;; TYPE day-of-week
3       ;; Residue class for Tuesday.
4       (+ sunday 2))
```

```
1   (defconstant wednesday
2     ;; TYPE day-of-week
3     ;; Residue class for Wednesday.
4     (+ sunday 3))
```

```
1   (defconstant thursday
2     ;; TYPE day-of-week
3     ;; Residue class for Thursday.
4     (+ sunday 4))
```

```
1   (defconstant friday
2     ;; TYPE day-of-week
3     ;; Residue class for Friday.
4     (+ sunday 5))
```

```
1   (defconstant saturday
2     ;; TYPE day-of-week
3     ;; Residue class for Saturday.
4     (+ sunday 6))
```

The function 1+ increments a number by one (the similar function 1- decrements by one).

Notice that semicolons mark the start of comments. "Type" information is given in comments for each of these functions. Although Common Lisp has its own system of type declarations, we prefer the simpler, untyped Lisp but annotate each function and constant to aid the reader in translating our code into a typed language. The base types are defined in Table A.1 beginning on page 303.

To distinguish in the code between empty lists (nil) and the truth value "false," we define

```
1   (defconstant false
2     ;; TYPE boolean
3     ;; Constant representing false.
4     nil)
```

For "true," we define

```
1   (defconstant true
2     ;; TYPE boolean
3     ;; Constant representing true.
4     t)
```

We also use a string constant to signify an error value:

```
1   (defconstant bogus
2     ;; TYPE string
3     ;; Used to denote nonexistent dates.
4     "bogus")
```

The function equal can be used to check lists and strings for equality.

Functions are defined using the defun command, which has the following syntax:

```
(defun function-name (param1 ... paramn)
   expression)
```

For example, we compute the day of the week of an R.D. date (page 27) with

```
1    (defun day-of-week-from-fixed (date)
2      ;; TYPE fixed-date -> day-of-week
3      ;; The residue class of the day of the week of date.
4      (mod date 7))
```

and we implement julian day calculations by writing

```
1    (defconstant jd-epoch
2      ;; TYPE moment
3      ;; Fixed time of start of the julian day number.
4      -1721424.510)
```

Common Lisp uses 10 to specify unscaled maximum-precision (at least 50-bit) constants.

```
1    (defun moment-from-jd (jd)
2      ;; TYPE julian-day-number -> moment
3      ;; Moment of julian day number jd.
4      (+ jd jd-epoch))
```

```
1    (defun jd-from-moment (tee)
2      ;; TYPE moment -> julian-day-number
3      ;; Julian day number of moment tee.
4      (- tee jd-epoch))
```

```
1    (defun fixed-from-jd (jd)
2      ;; TYPE julian-day-number -> fixed-date
3      ;; Fixed date of julian day number jd.
4      (floor (moment-from-jd jd)))
```

```
1    (defun jd-from-fixed (date)
2      ;; TYPE fixed-date -> julian-day-number
3      ;; Julian day number of fixed date.
4      (jd-from-moment date))
```

```
1    (defconstant mjd-epoch
2      ;; TYPE fixed-date
3      ;; Fixed time of start of the modified julian day number.
4      678576)
```

```
1    (defun fixed-from-mjd (mjd)
2      ;; TYPE julian-day-number -> fixed-date
3      ;; Fixed date of modified julian day number mjd.
4      (+ mjd mjd-epoch))
```

```
1    (defun mjd-from-fixed (date)
2      ;; TYPE fixed-date -> julian-day-number
3      ;; Modified julian day number of fixed date.
4      (- date mjd-epoch))
```

As another example of a function definition, we can define a function (inconveniently named in Common Lisp) to return the (truncated) integer quotient of two integers, $\lfloor m/n \rfloor$:

```
1    (defun quotient (m n)
2      ;; TYPE (real nonzero-real) -> integer
3      ;; Whole part of m/n.
4      (floor m n))
```

The floor function can also be called with one argument:

```
(floor x)
```

is $\lfloor x \rfloor$, the greatest integer less than or equal to x.

As a final example of a function definition, note that the Common Lisp function mod *always returns a nonnegative value for a positive divisor*; we use this property occasionally, but we also need a function like mod with its values adjusted so that the modulus of a multiple of the divisor is the divisor itself rather than 0. To define this function, denoted "amod" in the text, we write

```
1   (defun adjusted-mod (x y)
2     ;; TYPE (real real) -> real
3     ;; The value of (x mod y) with y instead of 0.
4     (+ y (mod x (- y))))
```

For convenience in expressing our calendar functions in Lisp, we introduce a macro to compute sums (the few instances in which we use macros and not functions avoid the issue of passing functions to functions). The expression

```
(sum f i k p)
```

computes

$$\sum_{k \leq i < \min_{j \geq k}\{\neg p(j)\}} f(i);$$

that is, the expression $f(i)$ is summed for all $i = k, k+1, \ldots$, continuing only as long as the condition $p(i)$ holds. The sum is 0 if $p(k)$ is false. The (mysterious-looking) Common Lisp definition of sum is as follows:

```
1   (defmacro sum (expression index initial condition)
2     ;; TYPE ((integer->real) * integer (integer->boolean))
3     ;; TYPE -> real
4     ;; Sum expression for index = initial and successive
5     ;; integers, as long as condition holds.
6     (let* ((temp (gensym)))
7       `(do ((,temp 0 (+ ,temp ,expression))
8             (,index ,initial (1+ ,index)))
9            ((not ,condition) ,temp))))
```

The Common Lisp construct let* defines a sequence of constants (possibly in terms of previously defined constants) and ends with an expression whose value is returned by the construct.

A summation macro sigma and a summation function poly for polynomials are used in the astronomical code:

```
1   (defmacro sigma (list body)
2     ;; TYPE (list-of-pairs (list-of-reals->real))
3     ;; TYPE -> real
4     ;; list is of the form ((i1 l1)..(in ln)).
5     ;; Sum of body for indices i1..in
6     ;; running simultaneously thru lists l1..ln.
7     `(apply '+ (mapcar (function (lambda
```

```
 8                                 ,(mapcar 'car list)
 9                                 ,body))
10                            ,@(mapcar 'cadr list))))
```

```
 1   (defun poly (x a)
 2     ;; TYPE (real list-of-reals) -> real
 3     ;; Sum powers of x with coefficients (from order 0 up)
 4     ;; in list a.
 5     (if (equal a nil)
 6         0
 7         (+ (first a) (* x (poly x (cdr a)))))))
```

The function if has three arguments: a boolean condition, a then-expression, and an else-expression. The cond statement lists a sequence of tests and values such as a generalized case statement.

Two additional sum-like macros are used for searching:

```
 1   (defmacro next (index initial condition)
 2     ;; TYPE (* integer (integer->boolean)) -> integer
 3     ;; First integer greater or equal to initial such that
 4     ;; condition holds.
 5     '(do ((,index ,initial (1+ ,index)))
 6          ((,condition ,index)))
```

```
 1   (defmacro final (index initial condition)
 2     ;; TYPE (* integer (integer->boolean)) -> integer
 3     ;; Last integer greater or equal to initial such that
 4     ;; condition holds.
 5     '(do ((,index ,initial (1+ ,index)))
 6          ((not ,condition) (1- ,index))))
```

We use binary search—see equation (1.21)—expressed as the macro binary-search:

```
 1   (defmacro binary-search (l lo h hi x test end)
 2     ;; TYPE (* real * real * (real->boolean)
 3     ;; TYPE ((real real)->boolean)) -> real
 4     ;; Bisection search for x in lo..hi such that
 5     ;; end holds.  test determines when to go left.
 6     (let* ((left (gensym)))
 7       '(do* ((,x false (/ (+ ,h ,l) 2))
 8              (,left false ,test)
 9              (,l ,lo (if ,left ,l ,x))
10              (,h ,hi (if ,left ,x ,h)))
11          (,end (/ (+ ,h ,l) 2)))))
```

B.2 Basic Code

To extract a particular component from a date, we use, when necessary, the functions **standard-month**, **standard-day**, and **standard-year**. For example:

```
 1   (defun standard-month (date)
 2     ;; TYPE standard-date -> standard-month
 3     ;; Month field of date = (year month day).
 4     (second date))
```

```
 1   (defun standard-day (date)
 2     ;; TYPE standard-date -> standard-day
 3     ;; Day field of date = (year month day).
 4     (third date))
```

```
1   (defun standard-year (date)
2     ;; TYPE standard-date -> standard-year
3     ;; Year field of date = (year month day).
4     (first date))
```

Such constructors and selectors could be defined as macros.
We also have

```
1   (defun time-of-day (hour minute second)
2     ;; TYPE (hour minute second) -> time
3     (list hour minute second))
```

```
1   (defun time-from-moment (tee)
2     ;; TYPE moment -> time
3     ;; Time of day (hour minute second) from moment tee.
4     (let* ((hour (floor (mod (* tee 24) 24)))
5            (minute (floor (mod (* tee 24 60) 60)))
6            (second (mod (* tee 24 60 6010) 60)))
7       (time-of-day hour minute second)))
```

B.3 The Egyptian/Armenian Calendars

```
1   (defun egyptian-date (year month day)
2     ;; TYPE (egyptian-year egyptian-month egyptian-day)
3     ;; TYPE -> egyptian-date
4     (list year month day))
```

```
1   (defconstant egyptian-epoch
2     ;; TYPE fixed-date
3     ;; Fixed date of start of the Egyptian (Nabonasser)
4     ;; calendar.
5     ;; JD 1448638 = February 26, 747 BCE (Julian).
6     (fixed-from-jd 1448638))
```

```
1   (defun fixed-from-egyptian (e-date)
2     ;; TYPE egyptian-date -> fixed-date
3     ;; Fixed date of Egyptian date.
4     (let* ((month (standard-month e-date))
5            (day (standard-day e-date))
6            (year (standard-year e-date)))
7       (+ egyptian-epoch   ; Days before start of calendar
8          (* 365 (1- year)); Days in prior years
9          (* 30 (1- month)); Days in prior months this year
10         day -1)))         ; Days so far this month
```

```
1   (defun egyptian-from-fixed (date)
2     ;; TYPE fixed-date -> egyptian-date
3     ;; Egyptian equivalent of fixed date.
4     (let* ((days ; Elapsed days since epoch.
5            (- date egyptian-epoch))
6            (year ; Year since epoch.
7            (1+ (quotient days 365)))
8            (month; Calculate the month by division.
9            (1+ (quotient (mod days 365)
10                          30)))
11           (day   ; Calculate the day by subtraction.
12           (- days
13              (* 365 (1- year))
14              (* 30 (1- month))
15              -1)))
16       (egyptian-date year month day)))
```

```
1  (defun armenian-date (year month day)
2    ;; TYPE (armenian-year armenian-month armenian-day)
3    ;; TYPE -> armenian-date
4    (list year month day))
```

```
1  (defconstant armenian-epoch
2    ;; TYPE fixed-date
3    ;; Fixed date of start of the Armenian calendar.
4    ;; = July 11, 552 CE (Julian).
5    201443)
```

```
1   (defun fixed-from-armenian (a-date)
2     ;; TYPE armenian-date -> fixed-date
3     ;; Fixed date of Armenian date.
4     (let* ((month (standard-month a-date))
5            (day (standard-day a-date))
6            (year (standard-year a-date)))
7       (+ armenian-epoch
8          (- (fixed-from-egyptian
9               (egyptian-date year month day))
10             egyptian-epoch)))))
```

```
1  (defun armenian-from-fixed (date)
2    ;; TYPE fixed-date -> armenian-date
3    ;; Armenian equivalent of fixed date.
4    (egyptian-from-fixed
5      (+ date (- egyptian-epoch armenian-epoch))))
```

B.4 Cycles of Days

```
1  (defun kday-on-or-before (date k)
2    ;; TYPE (fixed-date weekday) -> fixed-date
3    ;; Fixed date of the k-day on or before fixed date.
4    ;; k=0 means Sunday, k=1 means Monday, and so on.
5    (- date (day-of-week-from-fixed (- date k))))
```

```
1  (defun kday-on-or-after (date k)
2    ;; TYPE (fixed-date weekday) -> fixed-date
3    ;; Fixed date of the k-day on or after fixed date.
4    ;; k=0 means Sunday, k=1 means Monday, and so on.
5    (kday-on-or-before (+ date 6) k))
```

```
1  (defun kday-nearest (date k)
2    ;; TYPE (fixed-date weekday) -> fixed-date
3    ;; Fixed date of the k-day nearest fixed date.
4    ;; k=0 means Sunday, k=1 means Monday, and so on.
5    (kday-on-or-before (+ date 3) k))
```

```
1  (defun kday-after (date k)
2    ;; TYPE (fixed-date weekday) -> fixed-date
3    ;; Fixed date of the k-day after fixed date.
4    ;; k=0 means Sunday, k=1 means Monday, and so on.
5    (kday-on-or-before (+ date 7) k))
```

```
1  (defun kday-before (date k)
2    ;; TYPE (fixed-date weekday) -> fixed-date
3    ;; Fixed date of the k-day before fixed date.
4    ;; k=0 means Sunday, k=1 means Monday, and so on.
5    (kday-on-or-before (- date 1) k))
```

B.5 The Gregorian Calendar

```
1   (defun gregorian-date (year month day)
2     ;; TYPE (gregorian-year gregorian-month gregorian-day)
3     ;; TYPE -> gregorian-date
4     (list year month day))
```

```
1   (defconstant gregorian-epoch
2     ;; TYPE fixed-date
3     ;; Fixed date of start of the (proleptic) Gregorian
4     ;; calendar.
5     1)
```

```
1   (defconstant january
2     ;; TYPE standard-month
3     ;; January on Julian/Gregorian calendar.
4     1)
```

```
1   (defconstant february
2     ;; TYPE standard-month
3     ;; February on Julian/Gregorian calendar.
4     (1+ january))
```

```
1   (defconstant march
2     ;; TYPE standard-month
3     ;; March on Julian/Gregorian calendar.
4     (+ january 2))
```

```
1   (defconstant april
2     ;; TYPE standard-month
3     ;; April on Julian/Gregorian calendar.
4     (+ january 3))
```

```
1   (defconstant may
2     ;; TYPE standard-month
3     ;; May on Julian/Gregorian calendar.
4     (+ january 4))
```

```
1   (defconstant june
2     ;; TYPE standard-month
3     ;; June on Julian/Gregorian calendar.
4     (+ january 5))
```

```
1   (defconstant july
2     ;; TYPE standard-month
3     ;; July on Julian/Gregorian calendar.
4     (+ january 6))
```

```
1   (defconstant august
2     ;; TYPE standard-month
3     ;; August on Julian/Gregorian calendar.
4     (+ january 7))
```

```
1   (defconstant september
2     ;; TYPE standard-month
3     ;; September on Julian/Gregorian calendar.
4     (+ january 8))
```

```
1   (defconstant october
2     ;; TYPE standard-month
3     ;; October on Julian/Gregorian calendar.
4     (+ january 9))
```

```
1   (defconstant november
2     ;; TYPE standard-month
3     ;; November on Julian/Gregorian calendar.
4     (+ january 10))
```

```
1   (defconstant december
2     ;; TYPE standard-month
3     ;; December on Julian/Gregorian calendar.
4     (+ january 11))
```

```
1   (defun gregorian-leap-year? (g-year)
2     ;; TYPE gregorian-year -> boolean
3     ;; True if g-year is a leap year on the Gregorian
4     ;; calendar.
5     (and (= (mod g-year 4) 0)
6          (not (member (mod g-year 400)
7                       (list 100 200 300)))))
```

```
1   (defun fixed-from-gregorian (g-date)
2     ;; TYPE gregorian-date -> fixed-date
3     ;; Fixed date equivalent to the Gregorian date.
4     (let* ((month (standard-month g-date))
5           (day (standard-day g-date))
6           (year (standard-year g-date)))
7       (+ (1- gregorian-epoch); Days before start of calendar
8          (* 365 (1- year)); Ordinary days since epoch
9          (quotient (1- year)
10                    4); Julian leap days since epoch...
11         (-        ; ...minus century years since epoch...
12          (quotient (1- year) 100))
13         (quotient   ; ...plus years since epoch divisible...
14          (1- year) 400)  ; ...by 400.
15         (quotient    ; Days in prior months this year...
16          (- (* 367 month) 362); ...assuming 30-day Feb
17          12)
18         (if (<= month 2) ; Correct for 28- or 29-day Feb
19             0
20             (if (gregorian-leap-year? year)
21                 -1
22                 -2))
23         day)))        ; Days so far this month.
```

```
1   (defun gregorian-year-from-fixed (date)
2     ;; TYPE fixed-date -> gregorian-year
3     ;; Gregorian year corresponding to the fixed date.
4     (let* ((d0          ; Prior days.
5           (- date gregorian-epoch))
6          (n400         ; Completed 400-year cycles.
7           (quotient d0 146097))
8          (d1           ; Prior days not in n400.
9           (mod d0 146097))
10         (n100         ; 100-year cycles not in n400.
11          (quotient d1 36524))
12         (d2           ; Prior days not in n400 or n100.
13          (mod d1 36524))
14         (n4           ; 4-year cycles not in n400 or n100.
15          (quotient d2 1461))
16         (d3           ; Prior days not in n400, n100, or n4.
17          (mod d2 1461))
18         (n1           ; Years not in n400, n100, or n4.
19          (quotient d3 365))
20         (year (+ (* 400 n400)
21                  (* 100 n100)
22                  (* 4 n4)
23                  n1)))
```

```
24          (if (or (= n100 4) (= n1 4))
25              year        ; Date is day 366 in a leap year.
26          (1+ year)))); Date is ordinal day (1+ (mod d3 365))
27                          ; in (1+ year).
```

```
1   (defun gregorian-from-fixed (date)
2     ;; TYPE fixed-date -> gregorian-date
3     ;; Gregorian (year month day) corresponding to fixed date.
4     (let* ((year (gregorian-year-from-fixed date))
5            (prior-days; This year
6             (- date (fixed-from-gregorian
7                      (gregorian-date year january 1))))
8            (correction; To simulate a 30-day Feb
9             (if (< date (fixed-from-gregorian
10                         (gregorian-date year march 1)))
11                0
12                (if (gregorian-leap-year? year)
13                    1
14                    2)))
15           (month      ; Assuming a 30-day Feb
16            (quotient
17             (+ (* 12 (+ prior-days correction)) 373)
18             367))
19           (day        ; Calculate the day by subtraction.
20            (1+ (- date
21                   (fixed-from-gregorian
22                    (gregorian-date year month 1))))))
23       (gregorian-date year month day)))
```

```
1   (defun gregorian-date-difference (g-date1 g-date2)
2     ;; TYPE (gregorian-date gregorian-date) -> integer
3     ;; Number of days from Gregorian date g-date1 until
4     ;; g-date2.
5     (- (fixed-from-gregorian g-date2)
6        (fixed-from-gregorian g-date1)))
```

```
1   (defun day-number (g-date)
2     ;; TYPE gregorian-date -> positive-integer
3     ;; Day number in year of Gregorian date g-date.
4     (gregorian-date-difference
5      (gregorian-date (1- (standard-year g-date)) december 31)
6      g-date))
```

```
1   (defun days-remaining (g-date)
2     ;; TYPE gregorian-date -> nonnegative-integer
3     ;; Days remaining in year after Gregorian date g-date.
4     (gregorian-date-difference
5      g-date
6      (gregorian-date (standard-year g-date) december 31)))
```

```
1   (defun alt-fixed-from-gregorian (g-date)
2     ;; TYPE gregorian-date -> fixed-date
3     ;; Alternative calculation of fixed date equivalent to the
4     ;; Gregorian date.
5     (let* ((month (standard-month g-date))
6            (day (standard-day g-date))
7            (year (standard-year g-date))
8            (m (adjusted-mod (- month 2) 12))
9            (y (+ year (quotient (+ month 9) 12))))
10       (+ (1- gregorian-epoch)
11          -306        ; Days in March...December.
12          (* 365 (1- y)); Ordinary days since epoch.
13          (quotient (1- y)
14                    4); Julian leap days since epoch...
```

```
15        (-              ; ...minus century years since epoch...
16          (quotient (1- y) 100))
17          (quotient     ; ...plus years since epoch divisible...
18          (1- y) 400); ...by 400.
19          (quotient     ; Days in prior months this year.
20          (1- (* 3 m))
21          5)
22        (* 30 (1- m))
23        day)))          ; Days so far this month.
```

```
1   (defun alt-gregorian-from-fixed (date)
2     ;; TYPE fixed-date -> gregorian-date
3     ;; Alternative calculation of Gregorian (year month day)
4     ;; corresponding to fixed date.
5     (let* ((y (gregorian-year-from-fixed
6                (+ (1- gregorian-epoch)
7                   date
8                   306)))
9            (prior-days
10             (- date (fixed-from-gregorian
11                      (gregorian-date (1- y) 3 1))))
12            (month
13             (adjusted-mod (+ (quotient
14                               (+ (* 5 prior-days) 155)
15                               153)
16                              2)
17                           12))
18            (year (- y (quotient (+ month 9) 12)))
19            (day
20             (1+ (- date
21                    (fixed-from-gregorian
22                     (gregorian-date year month 1))))))
23       (gregorian-date year month day)))
```

```
1   (defun alt-gregorian-year-from-fixed (date)
2     ;; TYPE fixed-date -> gregorian-year
3     ;; Gregorian year corresponding to the fixed date.
4     (let* ((approx ; approximate year
5                (quotient (- date gregorian-epoch -2)
6                          146097/400))
7            (start  ; start of next year
8                (+ gregorian-epoch
9                   (* 365 approx)
10                  (quotient approx 4)
11                  (- (quotient approx 100))
12                  (quotient approx 400))))
13       (if (< date start)
14           approx
15         (1+ approx)))))
```

```
1   (defun independence-day (g-year)
2     ;; TYPE gregorian-year -> fixed-date
3     ;; Fixed date of United States Independence Day in
4     ;; Gregorian year.
5     (fixed-from-gregorian (gregorian-date g-year july 4)))
```

```
1   (defun nth-kday (n k g-date)
2     ;; TYPE (integer weekday gregorian-date) -> fixed-date
3     ;; Fixed date of n-th k-day after Gregorian date.  If
4     ;; n>0, return the n-th k-day on or after date.
5     ;; If n<0, return the n-th k-day on or before date.
6     ;; A k-day of 0 means Sunday, 1 means Monday, and so on.
7     (if (> n 0)
8         (+ (* 7 n)
9            (kday-before (fixed-from-gregorian g-date) k))
```

```
10        (+ (* 7 n)
11           (kday-after (fixed-from-gregorian g-date) k)))))
```

```
1   (defun first-kday (k g-date)
2     ;; TYPE (weekday gregorian-date -> fixed-date
3     ;; Fixed date of first k-day on or after Gregorian date.
4     ;; A k-day of 0 means Sunday, 1 means Monday, and so on.
5     (nth-kday 1 k g-date))
```

```
1   (defun last-kday (k g-date)
2     ;; TYPE (weekday gregorian-date -> fixed-date
3     ;; Fixed date of last k-day on or before Gregorian date.
4     ;; A k-day of 0 means Sunday, 1 means Monday, and so on.
5     (nth-kday -1 k g-date))
```

```
1   (defun labor-day (g-year)
2     ;; TYPE gregorian-year -> fixed-date
3     ;; Fixed date of United States Labor Day in Gregorian
4     ;; year--the first Monday in September.
5     (first-kday monday (gregorian-date g-year september 1)))
```

```
1   (defun memorial-day (g-year)
2     ;; TYPE gregorian-year -> fixed-date
3     ;; Fixed date of United States Memorial Day in Gregorian
4     ;; year--the last Monday in May.
5     (last-kday monday (gregorian-date g-year may 31)))
```

```
1   (defun election-day (g-year)
2     ;; TYPE gregorian-year -> fixed-date
3     ;; Fixed date of United States Election Day in Gregorian
4     ;; year--the Tuesday after the first Monday in November.
5     (first-kday tuesday (gregorian-date g-year november 2)))
```

```
1   (defun daylight-saving-start (g-year)
2     ;; TYPE gregorian-year -> fixed-date
3     ;; Fixed date of the start of United States daylight saving
4     ;; time in Gregorian year--the first Sunday in April.
5     (first-kday sunday (gregorian-date g-year april 1)))
```

```
1   (defun daylight-saving-end (g-year)
2     ;; TYPE gregorian-year -> fixed-date
3     ;; Fixed date of the end of United States daylight saving
4     ;; time in Gregorian year--the last Sunday in October.
5     (last-kday sunday (gregorian-date g-year october 31)))
```

```
1   (defun christmas (g-year)
2     ;; TYPE gregorian-year -> fixed-date
3     ;; Fixed date of Christmas in Gregorian year.
4     (fixed-from-gregorian (gregorian-date g-year december 25)))
```

```
1   (defun advent (g-year)
2     ;; TYPE gregorian-year -> fixed-date
3     ;; Fixed date of Advent in Gregorian year
4     ;; --the Sunday closest to November 30.
5     (kday-nearest (fixed-from-gregorian
6                     (gregorian-date g-year november 30))
7                   sunday))
```

```
1   (defun epiphany (g-year)
2     ;; TYPE gregorian-year -> fixed-date
3     ;; Fixed date of Epiphany in U.S. in Gregorian year
4     ;; --the first Sunday after January 1.
5     (first-kday sunday (gregorian-date g-year january 2)))
```

B.6 The Julian Calendar

In the Lisp code we use −*n* for year *n* B.C.E. (Julian):

```
1   (defun bce (n)
2     ;; TYPE standard-year -> julian-year
3     ;; Negative value to indicate a BCE Julian year.
4     (- n))
```

and positive numbers for C.E. (Julian) years:

```
1   (defun ce (n)
2     ;; TYPE standard-year -> julian-year
3     ;; Positive value to indicate a CE Julian year.
4     n)
```

```
1   (defun julian-date (year month day)
2     ;; TYPE (julian-year julian-month julian-day)
3     ;; TYPE -> julian-date
4     (list year month day))
```

```
1   (defun julian-leap-year? (j-year)
2     ;; TYPE julian-year -> boolean
3     ;; True if j-year is a leap year on the Julian calendar.
4     (= (mod j-year 4) (if (> j-year 0) 0 3)))
```

```
1   (defconstant julian-epoch
2     ;; TYPE fixed-date
3     ;; Fixed date of start of the Julian calendar.
4     (fixed-from-gregorian (gregorian-date 0 december 30)))
```

```
1   (defun fixed-from-julian (j-date)
2     ;; TYPE julian-date -> fixed-date
3     ;; Fixed date equivalent to the Julian date.
4     (let* ((month (standard-month j-date))
5            (day (standard-day j-date))
6            (year (standard-year j-date))
7            (y (if (< year 0)
8                   (1+ year) ; No year zero
9                   year)))
10      (+ (1- julian-epoch)   ; Days before start of calendar
11         (* 365 (1- y))      ; Ordinary days since epoch.
12         (quotient (1- y) 4); Leap days since epoch...
13         (quotient           ; Days in prior months this year...
14          (- (* 367 month) 362); ...assuming 30-day Feb
15          12)
16         (if (<= month 2)    ; Correct for 28- or 29-day Feb
17             0
18             (if (julian-leap-year? year)
19                 -1
20                 -2))
21         day)))              ; Days so far this month.
```

```
1   (defun julian-from-fixed (date)
2     ;; TYPE fixed-date -> julian-date
3     ;; Julian (year month day) corresponding to fixed date.
4     (let* ((approx       ; Nominal year.
5            (quotient (+ (* 4 (- date julian-epoch)) 1464)
6                      1461))
7           (year (if (<= approx 0)
8                     (1- approx) ; No year 0.
9                     approx))
10          (prior-days; This year
11           (- date (fixed-from-julian
```

```
12                              (julian-date year january 1))))
13               (correction; To simulate a 30-day Feb
14                (if (< date (fixed-from-julian
15                              (julian-date year march 1)))
16                    0
17                  (if (julian-leap-year? year)
18                      1
19                    2)))
20               (month      ; Assuming a 30-day Feb
21                (quotient
22                 (+ (* 12 (+ prior-days correction)) 373)
23                 367))
24               (day        ; Calculate the day by subtraction.
25                (1+ (- date
26                      (fixed-from-julian
27                       (julian-date year month 1))))))
28      (julian-date year month day)))
```

```
1   (defun julian-in-gregorian (j-month j-day g-year)
2     ;; TYPE (julian-month julian-day gregorian-year)
3     ;; TYPE -> list-of-fixed-dates
4     ;; List of the fixed dates of Julian month, day
5     ;; that occur in Gregorian year.
6     (let* ((jan1 (fixed-from-gregorian
7                   (gregorian-date g-year january 1)))
8            (dec31 (fixed-from-gregorian
9                    (gregorian-date g-year december 31)))
10           (y (standard-year (julian-from-fixed jan1)))
11           (y-prime (if (= y -1)
12                        1
13                      (1+ y)))
14           ;; The possible occurrences in one year are
15           (date1 (fixed-from-julian
16                   (julian-date y j-month j-day)))
17           (date2 (fixed-from-julian
18                   (julian-date y-prime j-month j-day))))
19       (append
20        (if ; date1 occurs in current year
21            (<= jan1 date1 dec31)
22            ;; Then that date; otherwise, none
23            (list date1) nil)
24        (if ; date2 occurs in current year
25            (<= jan1 date2 dec31)
26            ;; Then that date; otherwise, none
27            (list date2) nil))))
```

In languages like Lisp that allow functions as parameters, one could write a generic version of this function to collect holidays of any given calendar and pass fixed-from-julian to it as an additional parameter. We have deliberately avoided this and similar advanced language features in the interests of portability.

```
1   (defconstant kalends
2     ;; TYPE roman-event
3     ;; Class of Kalends.
4     1)
```

```
1   (defconstant nones
2     ;; TYPE roman-event
3     ;; Class of Nones.
4     2)
```

```
1    (defconstant ides
2      ;; TYPE roman-event
3      ;; Class of Ides.
4      3)


1    (defun roman-date (year month event count leap)
2      ;; TYPE (roman-year roman-month roman-event roman-count
3      ;; TYPE  roman-leap) -> roman-date
4      (list year month event count leap))


1    (defun roman-year (date)
2      ;; TYPE roman-date -> roman-year
3      (first date))


1    (defun roman-month (date)
2      ;; TYPE roman-date -> roman-month
3      (second date))


1    (defun roman-event (date)
2      ;; TYPE roman-date -> roman-event
3      (third date))


1    (defun roman-count (date)
2      ;; TYPE roman-date -> roman-count
3      (fourth date))


1    (defun roman-leap (date)
2      ;; TYPE roman-date -> roman-leap
3      (fifth date))


1    (defun ides-of-month (month)
2      ;; TYPE roman-month -> ides
3      ;; Date of Ides in Roman month.
4      (if (member month (list march may july october))
5          15
6          13))


1    (defun nones-of-month (month)
2      ;; TYPE roman-month -> nones
3      ;; Date of Nones in Roman month.
4      (- (ides-of-month month) 8))


1    (defun roman-from-fixed (date)
2      ;; TYPE fixed-date -> roman-date
3      ;; Roman name for fixed date.
4      (let* ((j (julian-from-fixed date))
5             (month (standard-month j))
6             (day (standard-day j))
7             (year (standard-year j))
8             (month-prime (adjusted-mod (1+ month) 12))
9             (year-prime (if (= month-prime 1) (1+ year) year))
10            (kalends1 (fixed-from-roman
11                        (roman-date year-prime month-prime
12                                    kalends 1 false)))))
13       (cond
14        ((= day 1) (roman-date year month kalends 1 false))
15        ((<= day (nones-of-month month))
16         (roman-date year month nones
17                     (1+ (- (nones-of-month month) day)) false))
18        ((<= day (ides-of-month month))
19         (roman-date year month ides
```

```
20                         (1+ (- (ides-of-month month) day)) false))
21           ((or (/= month february)
22                (not (julian-leap-year? year)))
23            ; After the Ides, in a month that is not February of a
24            ; leap year
25            (roman-date year-prime month-prime kalends
26                        (1+ (- kalends1 date)) false))
27           ((< day 25)
28            ; February of a leap year, before leap day
29            (roman-date year march kalends (- 30 day) false))
30           (true
31            ; February of a leap year, on or after leap day
32            (roman-date year march kalends
33                        (- 31 day) (= day 25))))))))
```

```
1    (defun fixed-from-roman (r-date)
2      ;; TYPE roman-date -> fixed-date
3      ;; Fixed date for Roman name.
4      (let* ((leap (roman-leap r-date))
5             (count (roman-count r-date))
6             (event (roman-event r-date))
7             (month (roman-month r-date))
8             (year (roman-year r-date)))
9        (+ (cond
10            ((= event kalends)
11             (fixed-from-julian (julian-date year month 1)))
12            ((= event nones)
13             (fixed-from-julian
14              (julian-date year month (nones-of-month month))))
15            ((= event ides)
16             (fixed-from-julian
17              (julian-date year month (ides-of-month month)))))
18           (- count)
19           (if (and (julian-leap-year? year)
20                    (= month march)
21                    (= event kalends)
22                    (>= 16 count 6))
23               0 ; After Ides until leap day
24               1) ; Otherwise
25           (if leap
26               1 ; Leap day
27               0)))) ; Non-leap day
```

B.7 The Coptic and Ethiopic Calendars

```
1    (defun coptic-date (year month day)
2      ;; TYPE (coptic-year coptic-month coptic-day) -> coptic-date
3      (list year month day))
```

```
1    (defconstant coptic-epoch
2      ;; TYPE fixed-date
3      ;; Fixed date of start of the Coptic calendar.
4      (fixed-from-julian (julian-date (ce 284) august 29)))
```

```
1    (defun coptic-leap-year? (c-year)
2      ;; TYPE coptic-year -> boolean
3      ;; True if c-year is a leap year on the Coptic calendar.
4      (= (mod c-year 4) 3))
```

```
1    (defun fixed-from-coptic (c-date)
2      ;; TYPE coptic-date -> fixed-date
3      ;; Fixed date of Coptic date.
4      (let* ((month (standard-month c-date))
```

```
 5            (day (standard-day c-date))
 6            (year (standard-year c-date)))
 7      (+ coptic-epoch -1   ; Days before start of calendar
 8         (* 365 (1- year)); Ordinary days in prior years
 9         (quotient year 4); Leap days in prior years
10         (* 30 (1- month)); Days in prior months this year
11         day)))           ; Days so far this month
```

```
 1   (defun coptic-from-fixed (date)
 2     ;; TYPE fixed-date -> coptic-date
 3     ;; Coptic equivalent of fixed date.
 4     (let* ((year ; Calculate the year by cycle-of-years formula
 5             (quotient (+ (* 4 (- date coptic-epoch)) 1463)
 6                       1461))
 7            (month; Calculate the month by division.
 8             (1+ (quotient
 9                  (- date (fixed-from-coptic
10                           (coptic-date year 1 1)))
11                  30)))
12            (day  ; Calculate the day by subtraction.
13             (- date -1
14                (fixed-from-coptic
15                 (coptic-date year month 1)))))
16       (coptic-date year month day)))
```

```
 1   (defun ethiopic-date (year month day)
 2     ;; TYPE (ethiopic-year ethiopic-month ethiopic-day)
 3     ;; TYPE -> ethiopic-date
 4     (list year month day))
```

```
 1   (defconstant ethiopic-epoch
 2     ;; TYPE fixed-date
 3     ;; Fixed date of start of the Ethiopic calendar.
 4     (fixed-from-julian (julian-date (ce 8) august 29)))
```

```
 1   (defun fixed-from-ethiopic (e-date)
 2     ;; TYPE ethiopic-date -> fixed-date
 3     ;; Fixed date of Ethiopic date.
 4     (let* ((month (standard-month e-date))
 5            (day (standard-day e-date))
 6            (year (standard-year e-date)))
 7       (+ ethiopic-epoch
 8          (- (fixed-from-coptic
 9              (coptic-date year month day))
10             coptic-epoch))))
```

```
 1   (defun ethiopic-from-fixed (date)
 2     ;; TYPE fixed-date -> ethiopic-date
 3     ;; Ethiopic equivalent of fixed date.
 4     (coptic-from-fixed
 5      (+ date (- coptic-epoch ethiopic-epoch))))
```

```
 1   (defun coptic-in-gregorian (c-month c-day g-year)
 2     ;; TYPE (coptic-month coptic-day gregorian-year)
 3     ;; TYPE -> list-of-fixed-dates
 4     ;; List of the fixed dates of Coptic month, day
 5     ;; that occur in Gregorian year.
 6     (let* ((jan1 (fixed-from-gregorian
 7                   (gregorian-date g-year january 1)))
 8            (dec31 (fixed-from-gregorian
 9                    (gregorian-date g-year december 31)))
10            (y (standard-year (coptic-from-fixed jan1)))
11            ;; The possible occurrences in one year are
12            (date1 (fixed-from-coptic
```

```
13                      (coptic-date y c-month c-day)))
14          (date2 (fixed-from-coptic
15                      (coptic-date (1+ y) c-month c-day)))))
16      (append
17       (if ; date1 occurs in current year
18           (<= jan1 date1 dec31)
19           ;; Then that date; otherwise, none
20           (list date1) nil)
21       (if ; date2 occurs in current year
22           (<= jan1 date2 dec31)
23           ;; Then that date; otherwise, none
24           (list date2) nil)))))
```

```
1   (defun coptic-christmas (g-year)
2     ;; TYPE gregorian-year -> list-of-fixed-dates
3     ;; List of zero or one fixed dates of Coptic Christmas
4     ;; in Gregorian year.
5     (coptic-in-gregorian 4 29 g-year))
```

B.8 The ISO Calendar

```
1   (defun iso-date (year week day)
2     ;; TYPE (iso-year iso-week iso-day) -> iso-date
3     (list year week day))
```

```
1   (defun iso-week (date)
2     ;; TYPE iso-date -> iso-week
3     (second date))
```

```
1   (defun iso-day (date)
2     ;; TYPE iso-date -> day-of-week
3     (third date))
```

```
1   (defun iso-year (date)
2     ;; TYPE iso-date -> iso-year
3     (first date))
```

```
1   (defun fixed-from-iso (i-date)
2     ;; TYPE iso-date -> fixed-date
3     ;; Fixed date equivalent to ISO (year week day).
4     (let* ((week (iso-week i-date))
5            (day (iso-day i-date))
6            (year (iso-year i-date)))
7       ;; Add fixed date of Sunday preceding date plus day
8       ;; in week.
9       (+ (nth-kday
10          week sunday
11          (gregorian-date (1- year) december 28)) day)))
```

```
1   (defun iso-from-fixed (date)
2     ;; TYPE fixed-date -> iso-date
3     ;; ISO (year week day) corresponding to the fixed date.
4     (let* ((approx ; Year may be one too small.
5            (gregorian-year-from-fixed (- date 3)))
6           (year (if (>= date
7                          (fixed-from-iso
8                          (iso-date (1+ approx) 1 1)))
9                     (1+ approx)
10                    approx))
11          (week (1+ (quotient
12                     (- date
```

```
13                              (fixed-from-iso (iso-date year 1 1)))
14                        7)))
15              (day (adjusted-mod date 7)))
16        (iso-date year week day)))
```

B.9 The Islamic Calendar

```
1   (defun islamic-date (year month day)
2     ;; TYPE (islamic-year islamic-month islamic-day)
3     ;; TYPE -> islamic-date
4     (list year month day))
```

```
1   (defconstant islamic-epoch
2     ;; TYPE fixed-date
3     ;; Fixed date of start of the Islamic calendar.
4     (fixed-from-julian (julian-date (ce 622) july 16)))
```

```
1   (defun islamic-leap-year? (i-year)
2     ;; TYPE islamic-year -> boolean
3     ;; True if i-year is an Islamic leap year.
4     (< (mod (+ 14 (* 11 i-year)) 30) 11))
```

```
1   (defun fixed-from-islamic (i-date)
2     ;; TYPE islamic-date -> fixed-date
3     ;; Fixed date equivalent to Islamic date.
4     (let* ((month (standard-month i-date))
5            (day (standard-day i-date))
6            (year (standard-year i-date)))
7       (+ day                      ; Days so far this month.
8          (* 29 (1- month))        ; Days in prior months.
9          (quotient (1- (* 6 month)) 11)
10         (* (1- year) 354)        ; Nonleap days in prior years.
11         (quotient                ; Leap days in prior years.
12          (+ 3 (* 11 year)) 30)
13         islamic-epoch            ; Days before start of calendar.
14         -1)))
```

```
1   (defun islamic-from-fixed (date)
2     ;; TYPE fixed-date -> islamic-date
3     ;; Islamic date (year month day) corresponding to fixed
4     ;; date.
5     (let* ((year
6             (quotient
7              (+ (* 30 (- date islamic-epoch)) 10646)
8              10631))
9            (prior-days
10            (- date (fixed-from-islamic
11                     (islamic-date year 1 1))))
12           (month
13            (quotient
14             (+ (* 11 prior-days) 330)
15             325))
16           (day
17            (1+ (- date (fixed-from-islamic
18                         (islamic-date year month 1))))))
19       (islamic-date year month day)))
```

```
1   (defun islamic-in-gregorian (i-month i-day g-year)
2     ;; TYPE (islamic-month islamic-day gregorian-year)
3     ;; TYPE -> list-of-fixed-dates
4     ;; List of the fixed dates of Islamic month, day
5     ;; that occur in Gregorian year.
```

```
6     (let* ((jan1 (fixed-from-gregorian
7                     (gregorian-date g-year january 1)))
8            (dec31 (fixed-from-gregorian
9                     (gregorian-date g-year december 31)))
10           (y (standard-year (islamic-from-fixed jan1)))
11           ;; The possible occurrences in one year are
12           (date1 (fixed-from-islamic
13                    (islamic-date y i-month i-day)))
14           (date2 (fixed-from-islamic
15                    (islamic-date (1+ y) i-month i-day)))
16           (date3 (fixed-from-islamic
17                    (islamic-date (+ y 2) i-month i-day))))
18       ;; Combine in one list those that occur in current year
19       (append
20        (if (<= jan1 date1 dec31)
21            (list date1) nil)
22        (if (<= jan1 date2 dec31)
23            (list date2) nil)
24        (if (<= jan1 date3 dec31)
25            (list date3) nil))))
```

```
1     (defun mawlid-an-nabi (g-year)
2       ;; TYPE gregorian-year -> list-of-fixed-dates
3       ;; List of fixed dates of Mawlid-an-Nabi occurring in
4       ;; Gregorian year.
5       (islamic-in-gregorian 3 12 g-year))
```

B.10 The Hebrew Calendar

```
1     (defun hebrew-date (year month day)
2       ;; TYPE (hebrew-year hebrew-month hebrew-day) -> hebrew-date
3       (list year month day))
```

```
1     (defconstant nisan
2       ;; TYPE hebrew-month
3       ;; Nisan is month number 1.
4       1)
```

```
1     (defconstant tishri
2       ;; TYPE hebrew-month
3       ;; Tishri is month number 7.
4       7)
```

```
1     (defun hebrew-leap-year? (h-year)
2       ;; TYPE hebrew-year -> boolean
3       ;; True if h-year is a leap year on Hebrew calendar.
4       (< (mod (1+ (* 7 h-year)) 19) 7))
```

```
1     (defun last-month-of-hebrew-year (h-year)
2       ;; TYPE hebrew-year -> hebrew-month
3       ;; Last month of Hebrew year.
4       (if (hebrew-leap-year? h-year)
5           13
6         12))
```

```
1     (defconstant hebrew-epoch
2       ;; TYPE fixed-date
3       ;; Fixed date of start of the Hebrew calendar, that is,
4       ;; Tishri 1, 1 AM.
5       (fixed-from-julian (julian-date (bce 3761) october 7)))
```

```
1   (defun molad (h-month h-year)
2     ;; TYPE (hebrew-month hebrew-year) -> moment
3     ;; Moment of mean conjunction of h-month in Hebrew
4     ;; h-year.
5     (let* ((y ;; Treat Nisan as start of year.
6            (if (< h-month tishri)
7                (1+ h-year)
8              h-year))
9           (months-elapsed
10           (+ (- h-month tishri)  ;; Months this year.
11            (quotient ;; Months until New Year.
12             (- (* 235 y) 234)
13             19))))
14     (+ hebrew-epoch
15       -876/25920
16       (* months-elapsed (+ 29 (hr 12) 793/25920)))))
```

```
1   (defun hebrew-calendar-elapsed-days (h-year)
2     ;; TYPE hebrew-year -> integer
3     ;; Number of days elapsed from the (Sunday) noon prior
4     ;; to the epoch of the Hebrew calendar to the mean
5     ;; conjunction (molad) of Tishri of Hebrew year h-year,
6     ;; or one day later.
7     (let* ((months-elapsed  ; Since start of Hebrew calendar.
8            (quotient (- (* 235 h-year) 234) 19))
9           (parts-elapsed; Fractions of days since prior noon.
10           (+ 12084 (* 13753 months-elapsed)))
11          (day  ; Whole days since prior noon.
12           (+ (* 29 months-elapsed)
13             (quotient parts-elapsed 25920)))
14     ;; If (* 13753 months-elapsed) causes integers that
15     ;; are too large, use instead:
16     ;; (parts-elapsed
17     ;; (+ 204 (* 793 (mod months-elapsed 1080))))
18     ;; (hours-elapsed
19     ;; (+ 11 (* 12 months-elapsed)
20     ;;    (* 793 (quotient months-elapsed 1080))
21     ;;    (quotient parts-elapsed 1080)))
22     ;; (day
23     ;; (+ (* 29 months-elapsed)
24     ;;    (quotient hours-elapsed 24)))
25     )
26     (if (< (mod (* 3 (1+ day)) 7) 3); Sun, Wed, or Fri
27       (+ day 1)  ; Delay one day.
28       day)))
```

```
1   (defun hebrew-new-year (h-year)
2     ;; TYPE hebrew-year -> fixed-date
3     ;; Fixed date of Hebrew new year h-year.
4     (+ hebrew-epoch
5       (hebrew-calendar-elapsed-days h-year)
6       (hebrew-new-year-delay h-year)))
```

```
1   (defun hebrew-new-year-delay (h-year)
2     ;; TYPE hebrew-year -> {0,1,2}
3     ;; Delays to start of Hebrew year to keep ordinary year in
4     ;; range 353-356 and leap year in range 383-386.
5     (let* ((ny0 (hebrew-calendar-elapsed-days (1- h-year)))
6           (ny1 (hebrew-calendar-elapsed-days h-year))
7           (ny2 (hebrew-calendar-elapsed-days (1+ h-year))))
8     (cond
9       ((= (- ny2 ny1) 356)  ; Next year would be too long.
10        2)
11       ((= (- ny1 ny0) 382)  ; Previous year too short.
12        1)
13       (t 0))))
```

```
1   (defun short-kislev? (h-year)
2     ;; TYPE hebrew-year -> boolean
3     ;; True if Kislev is short in Hebrew year.
4     (member (days-in-hebrew-year h-year) (list 353 383)))
```

```
1   (defun last-day-of-hebrew-month (h-month h-year)
2     ;; TYPE (hebrew-month hebrew-year) -> hebrew-day
3     ;; Last day of month in Hebrew year.
4     (if (or (member h-month (list 2 4 6 10 13))
5             (and (= h-month 12)
6                  (not (hebrew-leap-year? h-year)))
7             (and (= h-month 8) (not (long-marheshvan? h-year)))
8             (and (= h-month 9) (short-kislev? h-year)))
9         29
10      30))
```

```
1   (defun days-in-hebrew-year (h-year)
2     ;; TYPE hebrew-year -> {353,354,355,383,384,385}
3     ;; Number of days in Hebrew year.
4     (- (hebrew-new-year (1+ h-year))
5        (hebrew-new-year h-year)))
```

```
1   (defun fixed-from-hebrew (h-date)
2     ;; TYPE hebrew-date -> fixed-date
3     ;; Fixed date of Hebrew date.
4     (let* ((month (standard-month h-date))
5            (day (standard-day h-date))
6            (year (standard-year h-date)))
7       (+ (hebrew-new-year year)
8          day -1                    ; Days so far this month.
9          (if ;; before Tishri
10             (< month tishri)
11             ;; Then add days in prior months this year before
12             ;; and after Nisan.
13             (+ (sum (last-day-of-hebrew-month m year)
14                     m tishri
15                     (<= m (last-month-of-hebrew-year year)))
16                (sum (last-day-of-hebrew-month m year)
17                     m nisan (< m month)))
18             ;; Else add days in prior months this year
19             (sum (last-day-of-hebrew-month m year)
20                  m tishri (< m month))))))
```

```
1   (defun hebrew-from-fixed (date)
2     ;; TYPE fixed-date -> hebrew-date
3     ;; Hebrew (year month day) corresponding to fixed date.
4     ;; The fraction can be approximated by 365.25.
5     (let* ((approx    ; Approximate year
6            (1+
7             (quotient (- date hebrew-epoch) 35975351/98496)))
8            ;; The value 35975351/98496, the average length of
9            ;; a Hebrew year, can be approximated by 365.25
10           (year     ; Search forward.
11           (final y (1- approx)
12                  (<= (hebrew-new-year y) date)))
13           (start    ; Starting month for search for month.
14           (if (< date (fixed-from-hebrew
15                        (hebrew-date year nisan 1)))
16               tishri
17             nisan))
18           (month ; Search forward from either Tishri or Nisan.
19           (next m start
20                 (<= date
21                     (fixed-from-hebrew
22                      (hebrew-date
23                       year
24                       m
```

```
25                           (last-day-of-hebrew-month m year))))))
26            (day   ; Calculate the day by subtraction.
27            (1+ (- date (fixed-from-hebrew
28                         (hebrew-date year month 1))))))
29      (hebrew-date year month day)))
```

We are using Common Lisp exact arithmetic for rationals here (and elsewhere). Without that facility, one must rephrase all quotient operations to work
with integers only.

The function hebrew-calendar-elapsed-days is called repeatedly during the calculations, often several times for the same year. A more efficient
algorithm could avoid such repetition.

```
1    (defun yom-kippur (g-year)
2      ;; TYPE gregorian-year -> fixed-date
3      ;; Fixed date of Yom Kippur occurring in Gregorian year.
4      (let* ((hebrew-year
5              (1+ (- g-year
6                     (gregorian-year-from-fixed
7                      hebrew-epoch)))))
8        (fixed-from-hebrew (hebrew-date hebrew-year tishri 10))))
```

```
1    (defun passover (g-year)
2      ;; TYPE gregorian-year -> fixed-date
3      ;; Fixed date of Passover occurring in Gregorian year.
4      (let* ((hebrew-year
5              (- g-year
6                 (gregorian-year-from-fixed hebrew-epoch))))
7        (fixed-from-hebrew (hebrew-date hebrew-year nisan 15))))
```

```
1    (defun omer (date)
2      ;; TYPE fixed-date -> omer-count
3      ;; Number of elapsed weeks and days in the omer at date.
4      ;; Returns bogus if that date does not fall during the
5      ;; omer.
6      (let* ((c (- date
7                   (passover
8                    (gregorian-year-from-fixed date)))))
9        (if (<= 1 c 49)
10           (list (quotient c 7) (mod c 7))
11         bogus)))
```

```
1    (defun purim (g-year)
2      ;; TYPE gregorian-year -> fixed-date
3      ;; Fixed date of Purim occurring in Gregorian year.
4      (let* ((hebrew-year
5              (- g-year
6                 (gregorian-year-from-fixed hebrew-epoch)))
7             (last-month   ; Adar or Adar II
8              (last-month-of-hebrew-year hebrew-year)))
9        (fixed-from-hebrew
10         (hebrew-date hebrew-year last-month 14))))
```

```
1    (defun ta-anit-esther (g-year)
2      ;; TYPE gregorian-year -> fixed-date
3      ;; Fixed date of Ta'anit Esther occurring in
4      ;; Gregorian year.
5      (let* ((purim-date (purim g-year)))
6        (if ; Purim is on Sunday
7            (= (day-of-week-from-fixed purim-date) sunday)
8            ;; Then prior Thursday
```

```
 9              (- purim-date 3)
10              ;; Else previous day
11              (1- purim-date)))))


 1  (defun tishah-be-av (g-year)
 2      ;; TYPE gregorian-year -> fixed-date
 3      ;; Fixed date of Tishah be-Av occurring in Gregorian year.
 4      (let* ((hebrew-year
 5              (- g-year
 6                 (gregorian-year-from-fixed hebrew-epoch)))
 7             (av9
 8              (fixed-from-hebrew
 9               (hebrew-date hebrew-year 5 9))))
10        (if ; Ninth of Av is Saturday
11            (= (day-of-week-from-fixed av9) saturday)
12            ;; Then the next day
13            (1+ av9)
14          av9)))


 1  (defun birkath-ha-hama (g-year)
 2      ;; TYPE gregorian-year -> list-of-fixed-dates
 3      ;; List of fixed date of Birkath ha-Hama occurring in
 4      ;; Gregorian year, if it occurs.
 5      (let* ((dates (coptic-in-gregorian 7 30 g-year)))
 6        (if (and (not (equal dates nil))
 7                 (= (mod (standard-year
 8                          (coptic-from-fixed (first dates)))
 9                         28)
10                    17))
11            dates
12          nil)))


 1  (defun yom-ha-zikkaron (g-year)
 2      ;; TYPE gregorian-year -> fixed-date
 3      ;; Fixed date of Yom ha-Zikkaron occurring in Gregorian
 4      ;; year.
 5      (let* ((hebrew-year
 6              (- g-year
 7                 (gregorian-year-from-fixed hebrew-epoch)))
 8             (iyyar4; Ordinarily Iyyar 4
 9              (fixed-from-hebrew
10               (hebrew-date hebrew-year 2 4))))
11        (if (< wednesday (day-of-week-from-fixed iyyar4))
12            ;; But prior Wednesday if Iyyar 5 is Friday or
13            ;; Saturday
14            (kday-before iyyar4 wednesday)
15          iyyar4)))


 1  (defun sh-ela (g-year)
 2      ;; TYPE gregorian-year -> list-of-fixed-dates
 3      ;; List of fixed dates of Sh'ela occurring in
 4      ;; Gregorian year.
 5      (coptic-in-gregorian 3 26 g-year))


 1  (defun hebrew-birthday (birthdate h-year)
 2      ;; TYPE (hebrew-date hebrew-year) -> fixed-date
 3      ;; Fixed date of the anniversary of Hebrew birthdate
 4      ;; occurring in Hebrew h-year.
 5      (let* ((birth-day (standard-day birthdate))
 6             (birth-month (standard-month birthdate))
 7             (birth-year (standard-year birthdate)))
 8        (if ; It's Adar in a normal Hebrew year or Adar II
 9            ; in a Hebrew leap year,
10            (= birth-month (last-month-of-hebrew-year birth-year))
```

```
11          ;; Then use the same day in last month of Hebrew year.
12          (fixed-from-hebrew
13           (hebrew-date h-year (last-month-of-hebrew-year h-year)
14                        birth-day))
15          ;; Else use the normal anniversary of the birth date,
16          ;; or the corresponding day in years without that date
17          (+ (fixed-from-hebrew
18              (hebrew-date h-year birth-month 1))
19             birth-day -1))))
```

```
1   (defun hebrew-birthday-in-gregorian (birthdate g-year)
2     ;; TYPE (hebrew-date gregorian-year)
3     ;; TYPE -> list-of-fixed-dates
4     ;; List of the fixed dates of Hebrew birthday
5     ;; that occur in Gregorian g-year.
6     (let* ((jan1 (fixed-from-gregorian
7                   (gregorian-date g-year january 1)))
8            (dec31 (fixed-from-gregorian
9                    (gregorian-date g-year december 31)))
10           (y (standard-year (hebrew-from-fixed jan1)))
11           ;; The possible occurrences in one year are
12           (date1 (hebrew-birthday birthdate y))
13           (date2 (hebrew-birthday birthdate (1+ y))))
14      ;; Combine in one list those that occur in current year.
15      (append
16       (if (<= jan1 date1)
17           (list date1) nil)
18       (if (<= date2 dec31)
19           (list date2) nil))))
```

```
1   (defun yahrzeit (death-date h-year)
2     ;; TYPE (hebrew-date hebrew-year) -> fixed-date
3     ;; Fixed date of the anniversary of Hebrew death-date
4     ;; occurring in Hebrew h-year.
5     (let* ((death-day (standard-day death-date))
6            (death-month (standard-month death-date))
7            (death-year (standard-year death-date)))
8       (cond
9        ;; If it's Marheshvan 30 it depends on the first
10       ;; anniversary; if that was not Marheshvan 30, use
11       ;; the day before Kislev 1.
12       ((and (= death-month 8)
13             (= death-day 30)
14             (not (long-marheshvan? (1+ death-year))))
15        (1- (fixed-from-hebrew
16             (hebrew-date h-year 9 1))))
17       ;; If it's Kislev 30 it depends on the first
18       ;; anniversary; if that was not Kislev 30, use
19       ;; the day before Tevet 1.
20       ((and (= death-month 9)
21             (= death-day 30)
22             (short-kislev? (1+ death-year)))
23        (1- (fixed-from-hebrew
24             (hebrew-date h-year 10 1))))
25       ;; If it's Adar II, use the same day in last
26       ;; month of Hebrew year (Adar or Adar II).
27       ((= death-month 13)
28        (fixed-from-hebrew
29         (hebrew-date
30              h-year (last-month-of-hebrew-year h-year)
31              death-day)))
32       ;; If it's the 30th in Adar I and Hebrew year is not a
33       ;; Hebrew leap year (so Adar has only 29 days), use the
34       ;; last day in Shevat.
35       ((and (= death-day 30)
36             (= death-month 12)
37             (not (hebrew-leap-year? h-year)))
```

```
38        (fixed-from-hebrew (hebrew-date h-year 11 30)))
39        ;; In all other cases, use the normal anniversary of
40        ;; the date of death.
41        (t (+ (fixed-from-hebrew
42              (hebrew-date h-year death-month 1))
43              death-day -1)))))
```

```
1   (defun yahrzeit-in-gregorian (death-date g-year)
2       ;; TYPE (hebrew-date gregorian-year)
3       ;; TYPE -> list-of-fixed-dates
4       ;; List of the fixed dates of yahrzeit
5       ;; that occur in Gregorian year.
6       (let* ((jan1 (fixed-from-gregorian
7                     (gregorian-date g-year january 1)))
8              (dec31 (fixed-from-gregorian
9                      (gregorian-date g-year december 31)))
10             (y (standard-year (hebrew-from-fixed jan1)))
11             ;; The possible occurrences in one year are
12             (date1 (yahrzeit death-date y))
13             (date2 (yahrzeit death-date (1+ y))))
14       ;; Combine in one list those that occur in current year
15       (append
16        (if (<= jan1 date1)
17            (list date1) nil)
18        (if (<= date2 dec31)
19            (list date2) nil))))
```

B.11 The Ecclesiastical Calendars

```
1   (defun eastern-orthodox-christmas (g-year)
2       ;; TYPE gregorian-year -> list-of-fixed-dates
3       ;; List of zero or one fixed dates of Eastern Orthodox
4       ;; Christmas in Gregorian year.
5       (julian-in-gregorian december 25 g-year))
```

```
1   (defun orthodox-easter (g-year)
2       ;; TYPE gregorian-year -> fixed-date
3       ;; Fixed date of Orthodox Easter in Gregorian year.
4       (let* ((shifted-epact  ; Age of moon for April 5.
5              (mod (+ 14 (* 11 (mod g-year 19)))
6                   30))
7              (j-year (if (> g-year 0); Julian year number.
8                          g-year
9                          (1- g-year)))
10             (paschal-moon  ; Day after full moon on
11                            ; or after March 21.
12              (- (fixed-from-julian (julian-date j-year april 19))
13                 shifted-epact)))
14       ;; Return the Sunday following the Paschal moon.
15       (kday-after paschal-moon sunday)))
```

```
1   (defun alt-orthodox-easter (g-year)
2       ;; TYPE gregorian-year -> fixed-date
3       ;; Alternate calculation of fixed date of Orthodox Easter
4       ;; in Gregorian year.
5       (let* ((paschal-moon  ; Day after full moon on
6                             ; or after March 21.
7              (+ (* 354 g-year)
8                 (* 30 (quotient (+ (* 7 g-year) 8) 19))
9                 (quotient g-year 4)
10                (- (quotient g-year 19))
11                -272)))
12       ;; Return the Sunday following the Paschal moon.
13       (kday-after paschal-moon sunday)))
```

```
 7              (+ (* 354 g-year)
 8                 (* 30 (quotient (+ (* 7 g-year) 8) 19))
 9                 (quotient g-year 4)
10                 (- (quotient g-year 19))
11                 -272)))
12           ;; Return the Sunday following the Paschal moon.
13           (kday-after paschal-moon sunday)))
```

```
 1    (defun easter (g-year)
 2      ;; TYPE gregorian-year -> fixed-date
 3      ;; Fixed date of Easter in Gregorian year.
 4      (let* ((century (1+ (quotient g-year 100)))
 5             (shifted-epact        ; Age of moon for April 5...
 6              (mod
 7               (+ 14 (* 11 (mod g-year 19));   ...by Nicaean rule
 8                  (- ;...corrected for the Gregorian century rule
 9                   (quotient (* 3 century) 4))
10                  (quotient; ...corrected for Metonic
11                   ; cycle inaccuracy.
12                   (+ 5 (* 8 century)) 25))
13               30))
14             (adjusted-epact        ; Adjust for 29.5 day month.
15              (if (or (= shifted-epact 0)
16                      (and (= shifted-epact 1)
17                           (< 10 (mod g-year 19))))
18                  (1+ shifted-epact)
19                shifted-epact))
20             (paschal-moon; Day after full moon on
21              ; or after March 21.
22              (- (fixed-from-gregorian
23                  (gregorian-date g-year april 19))
24                 adjusted-epact)))
25        ;; Return the Sunday following the Paschal moon.
26        (kday-after paschal-moon sunday)))
```

```
 1    (defun pentecost (g-year)
 2      ;; TYPE gregorian-year -> fixed-date
 3      ;; Fixed date of Pentecost in Gregorian year.
 4      (+ (easter g-year) 49))
```

B.12 The Old Hindu Calendars

```
 1    (defconstant hindu-epoch
 2      ;; TYPE fixed-date
 3      ;; Fixed date of start of the Hindu calendar (Kali Yuga).
 4      (fixed-from-julian (julian-date (bce 3102) february 18)))
```

```
 1    (defun hindu-day-count (date)
 2      ;; TYPE hindu-moment -> integer
 3      ;; Elapsed days (Ahargana) to date since Hindu epoch (KY).
 4      (- date hindu-epoch))
```

```
 1    (defconstant arya-jovian-period
 2      ;; TYPE rational
 3      ;; Number of days in one revolution of Jupiter around the
 4      ;; Sun.
 5      1577917500/364224)
```

```
 1    (defun jovian-year (date)
 2      ;; TYPE fixed-date -> {1-60}
 3      ;; Year of Jupiter cycle at fixed date.
 4      (1+ (mod (quotient (hindu-day-count date)
 5                         (/ arya-jovian-period 12))
 6               60)))
```

```
1   (defconstant arya-solar-year
2     ;; TYPE rational
3     ;; Length of Old Hindu solar year.
4     1577917500/4320000)
```

```
1   (defconstant arya-solar-month
2     ;; TYPE rational
3     ;; Length of Old Hindu solar month.
4     (/ arya-solar-year 12))
```

```
1    (defun old-hindu-solar-from-fixed (date)
2      ;; TYPE fixed-date -> hindu-solar-date
3      ;; Old Hindu solar date equivalent to fixed date.
4      (let* ((sun ; Sunrise on Hindu date.
5             (+ (hindu-day-count date) 1/4))
6            (year    ; Elapsed years.
7             (quotient sun arya-solar-year))
8            (month (1+ (mod (quotient sun arya-solar-month)
9                            12)))
10           (day (1+ (floor (mod sun arya-solar-month)))))
11      (hindu-solar-date year month day)))
```

```
1    (defun fixed-from-old-hindu-solar (s-date)
2      ;; TYPE hindu-solar-date -> fixed-date
3      ;; Fixed date corresponding to Old Hindu solar date.
4      (let* ((month (standard-month s-date))
5             (day (standard-day s-date))
6             (year (standard-year s-date)))
7        (ceiling
8         (+ hindu-epoch ; Since start of era.
9            (* year arya-solar-year) ; Days in elapsed years
10           (* (1- month) arya-solar-month) ; ...in months.
11           day -5/4)))) ; Midnight of day.
```

```
1    (defun old-hindu-lunar-date (year month leap day)
2      ;; TYPE (old-hindu-lunar-year old-hindu-lunar-month
3      ;; TYPE  old-hindu-lunar-leap old-hindu-lunar-day)
4      ;; TYPE -> old-hindu-lunar-date
5      (list year month leap day))
```

```
1    (defun old-hindu-lunar-month (date)
2      ;; TYPE old-hindu-lunar-date -> old-hindu-lunar-month
3      (second date))
```

```
1    (defun old-hindu-lunar-leap (date)
2      ;; TYPE old-hindu-lunar-date -> old-hindu-lunar-leap
3      (third date))
```

```
1    (defun old-hindu-lunar-day (date)
2      ;; TYPE old-hindu-lunar-date -> old-hindu-lunar-day
3      (fourth date))
```

```
1    (defun old-hindu-lunar-year (date)
2      ;; TYPE old-hindu-lunar-date -> old-hindu-lunar-year
3      (first date))
```

```
1   (defconstant arya-lunar-month
2     ;; TYPE rational
3     ;; Length of Old Hindu lunar month.
4     1577917500/53433336)
```

```
1  (defun old-hindu-lunar-leap-year? (l-year)
2    ;; TYPE old-hindu-lunar-year -> boolean
3    ;; True if l-year is a leap year on the
4    ;; old Hindu calendar.
5    (>= (mod (- (* l-year arya-solar-year)
6                arya-solar-month)
7             arya-lunar-month)
8        23902504679/1282400064))
```

```
1  (defun old-hindu-lunar-from-fixed (date)
2    ;; TYPE fixed-date -> old-hindu-lunar-date
3    ;; Old Hindu lunar date equivalent to fixed date.
4    (let* ((sun ; Sunrise on Hindu date.
5            (+ (hindu-day-count date) 1/4))
6           (new-moon ; Beginning of lunar month.
7            (- sun (mod sun arya-lunar-month)))
8           (leap ; If lunar contained in solar.
9            (and (>= (- arya-solar-month arya-lunar-month)
10                     (mod new-moon arya-solar-month))
11                 (> (mod new-moon arya-solar-month) 0)))
12           (month ; Next solar month's name.
13            (1+ (mod (ceiling (/ new-moon
14                                 arya-solar-month))
15                     12)))
16           (day ; Lunar days since beginning of lunar month.
17            (1+ (mod (quotient sun arya-lunar-day) 30)))
18           (year ; Solar year at end of lunar month(s).
19            (1- (ceiling (/ (+ new-moon arya-solar-month)
20                            arya-solar-year)))))
21      (old-hindu-lunar-date year month leap day)))
```

```
1  (defun fixed-from-old-hindu-lunar (l-date)
2    ;; TYPE old-hindu-lunar-date -> fixed-date
3    ;; Fixed date corresponding to Old Hindu lunar date.
4    (let* ((year (old-hindu-lunar-year l-date))
5           (month (old-hindu-lunar-month l-date))
6           (leap (old-hindu-lunar-leap l-date))
7           (day (old-hindu-lunar-day l-date))
8           (mina ; One solar month before solar new year.
9            (* (1- (* 12 year)) arya-solar-month))
10           (lunar-new-year ; New moon after mina.
11            (* arya-lunar-month
12               (1+ (quotient mina arya-lunar-month)))))
13      (floor
14       (+ hindu-epoch
15          lunar-new-year
16          (* arya-lunar-month
17             (if ; If there was a leap month this year.
18                 (and (not leap)
19                      (<= (ceiling (/ (- lunar-new-year mina)
20                                      (- arya-solar-month
21                                         arya-lunar-month)))
22                          month))
23                 month
24                 (1- month)))
25          (* (1- day) arya-lunar-day) ; Lunar days.
26          3/4)))) ; Add 1 if phase begins after sunrise.
```

B.13 The Mayan Calendars

```
1  (defun mayan-long-count-date (baktun katun tun uinal kin)
2    ;; TYPE (mayan-baktun mayan-katun mayan-tun mayan-uinal
3    ;; TYPE  mayan-kin) -> mayan-long-count-date
4    (list baktun katun tun uinal kin))
```

```
1    (defun mayan-baktun (date)
2      ;; TYPE mayan-long-count-date -> mayan-baktun
3      (first date))


1    (defun mayan-katun (date)
2      ;; TYPE mayan-long-count-date -> mayan-katun
3      (second date))


1    (defun mayan-tun (date)
2      ;; TYPE mayan-long-count-date -> mayan-tun
3      (third date))


1    (defun mayan-uinal (date)
2      ;; TYPE mayan-long-count-date -> mayan-uinal
3      (fourth date))


1    (defun mayan-kin (date)
2      ;; TYPE mayan-long-count-date -> mayan-kin
3      (fifth date))


1    (defconstant mayan-epoch
2      ;; TYPE fixed-date
3      ;; Fixed date of start of the Mayan calendar, according
4      ;; to the Goodman-Martinez-Thompson correlation.
5      ;; That is, August 11, -3113.
6      (fixed-from-jd 584283))


1    (defun fixed-from-mayan-long-count (count)
2      ;; TYPE mayan-long-count-date -> fixed-date
3      ;; Fixed date corresponding to the Mayan long count,
4      ;; which is a list (baktun katun tun uinal kin).
5      (let* ((baktun (mayan-baktun count))
6             (katun (mayan-katun count))
7             (tun (mayan-tun count))
8             (uinal (mayan-uinal count))
9             (kin (mayan-kin count)))
10       (+ mayan-epoch       ; Fixed date at Mayan 0.0.0.0.0
11          (* baktun 144000); Baktun.
12          (* katun 7200)   ; Katun.
13          (* tun 360)      ; Tun.
14          (* uinal 20)     ; Uinal.
15          kin)))           ; Kin (days).


1    (defun mayan-long-count-from-fixed (date)
2      ;; TYPE fixed-date -> mayan-long-count-date
3      ;; Mayan long count date of fixed date.
4      (let* ((long-count (- date mayan-epoch))
5             (baktun (quotient long-count 144000))
6             (day-of-baktun (mod long-count 144000))
7             (katun (quotient day-of-baktun 7200))
8             (day-of-katun (mod day-of-baktun 7200))
9             (tun (quotient day-of-katun 360))
10            (day-of-tun (mod day-of-katun 360))
11            (uinal (quotient day-of-tun 20))
12            (kin (mod day-of-tun 20)))
13       (mayan-long-count-date baktun katun tun uinal kin)))


1    (defun mayan-haab-date (month day)
2      ;; TYPE (mayan-haab-month mayan-haab-day) -> mayan-haab-date
3      (list month day))
```

```
1  (defun mayan-haab-day (date)
2    ;; TYPE mayan-haab-date -> mayan-haab-day
3    (second date))
```

```
1  (defun mayan-haab-month (date)
2    ;; TYPE mayan-haab-date -> mayan-haab-month
3    (first date))
```

```
1  (defun mayan-haab-ordinal (h-date)
2    ;; TYPE mayan-haab-date -> nonnegative-integer
3    ;; Number of days into cycle of Mayan haab date.
4    (let* ((day (mayan-haab-day h-date))
5           (month (mayan-haab-month h-date)))
6      (+ (* (1- month) 20) day)))
```

```
1  (defconstant mayan-haab-epoch
2    ;; TYPE fixed-date
3    ;; Fixed date of start of haab cycle.
4    (- mayan-epoch
5       (mayan-haab-ordinal (mayan-haab-date 18 8))))
```

```
1  (defun mayan-haab-from-fixed (date)
2    ;; TYPE fixed-date -> mayan-haab-date
3    ;; Mayan haab date of fixed date.
4    (let* ((count
5            (mod (- date mayan-haab-epoch) 365))
6           (day (mod count 20))
7           (month (1+ (quotient count 20))))
8      (mayan-haab-date month day)))
```

```
1  (defun mayan-haab-on-or-before (haab date)
2    ;; TYPE (mayan-haab-date fixed-date) -> fixed-date
3    ;; Fixed date of latest date on or before fixed date
4    ;; that is Mayan haab date haab.
5    (- date
6       (mod (- date mayan-haab-epoch
7               (mayan-haab-ordinal haab))
8            365)))
```

```
1  (defun mayan-tzolkin-date (number name)
2    ;; TYPE (mayan-tzolkin-number mayan-tzolkin-name)
3    ;; TYPE -> mayan-tzolkin-date
4    (list number name))
```

```
1  (defun mayan-tzolkin-number (date)
2    ;; TYPE mayan-tzolkin-date -> mayan-tzolkin-number
3    (first date))
```

```
1  (defun mayan-tzolkin-name (date)
2    ;; TYPE mayan-tzolkin-date -> mayan-tzolkin-name
3    (second date))
```

```
1  (defun mayan-tzolkin-ordinal (t-date)
2    ;; TYPE mayan-tzolkin-date -> nonnegative-integer
3    ;; Number of days into Mayan tzolkin cycle of t-date.
4    (let* ((number (mayan-tzolkin-number t-date))
5           (name (mayan-tzolkin-name t-date)))
6      (mod (+ number -1
7              (* 39 (- number name)))
8           260)))
```

```
1  (defconstant mayan-tzolkin-epoch
2    ;; TYPE fixed-date
3    ;; Start of tzolkin date cycle.
4    (- mayan-epoch
5       (mayan-tzolkin-ordinal (mayan-tzolkin-date 4 20))))
```

```
1  (defun mayan-tzolkin-from-fixed (date)
2    ;; TYPE fixed-date -> mayan-tzolkin-date
3    ;; Mayan tzolkin date of fixed date.
4    (let* ((count (- date mayan-tzolkin-epoch -1))
5           (number (adjusted-mod count 13))
6           (name (adjusted-mod count 20)))
7      (mayan-tzolkin-date number name)))
```

```
1  (defun mayan-tzolkin-on-or-before (tzolkin date)
2    ;; TYPE (mayan-tzolkin-date fixed-date) -> fixed-date
3    ;; Fixed date of latest date on or before fixed date
4    ;; that is Mayan tzolkin date tzolkin.
5    (- date
6       (mod (- date
7               mayan-tzolkin-epoch
8               (mayan-tzolkin-ordinal tzolkin))
9            260)))
```

```
1  (defun mayan-calendar-round-on-or-before (haab tzolkin date)
2    ;; TYPE (mayan-haab-date mayan-tzolkin-date fixed-date)
3    ;; TYPE -> fixed-date
4    ;; Fixed date of latest date on or before date, that is
5    ;; Mayan haab date haab and tzolkin date tzolkin.
6    (let* ((haab-count
7            (+ (mayan-haab-ordinal haab) mayan-haab-epoch))
8           (tzolkin-count
9            (+ (mayan-tzolkin-ordinal tzolkin)
10              mayan-tzolkin-epoch))
11          (diff (- tzolkin-count haab-count)))
12     (if (= (mod diff 5) 0)
13         (- date
14            (mod (- date haab-count (* 365 diff))
15                 18980))
16       bogus)))  ;  haab-tzolkin combination is impossible.
```

B.14 The Balinese Pawukon Calendar

```
1  (defun balinese-date (b1 b2 b3 b4 b5 b6 b7 b8 b9 b0)
2    ;; TYPE (boolean 1-2 1-3 1-4 1-5 1-6 1-7 1-8 1-9 0-9)
3    ;; TYPE -> balinese-date
4    (list b1 b2 b3 b4 b5 b6 b7 b8 b9 b0))
```

```
1  (defun bali-luang (b-date)
2    ;; TYPE balinese-date -> boolean
3    (first b-date))
```

```
1  (defun bali-dwiwara (b-date)
2    ;; TYPE balinese-date -> 1-2
3    (second b-date))
```

```
1  (defun bali-triwara (b-date)
2    ;; TYPE balinese-date -> 1-3
3    (third b-date))
```

```
1    (defun bali-caturwara (b-date)
2      ;; TYPE balinese-date -> 1-4
3      (fourth b-date))


1    (defun bali-pancawara (b-date)
2      ;; TYPE balinese-date -> 1-5
3      (fifth b-date))


1    (defun bali-sadwara (b-date)
2      ;; TYPE balinese-date -> 1-6
3      (sixth b-date))


1    (defun bali-saptawara (b-date)
2      ;; TYPE balinese-date -> 1-7
3      (seventh b-date))


1    (defun bali-asatawara (b-date)
2      ;; TYPE balinese-date -> 1-8
3      (eighth b-date))


1    (defun bali-sangawara (b-date)
2      ;; TYPE balinese-date -> 1-9
3      (ninth b-date))


1    (defun bali-dasawara (b-date)
2      ;; TYPE balinese-date -> 0-9
3      (tenth b-date))


1    (defconstant bali-epoch
2      ;; TYPE fixed-date
3      ;; Fixed date of start of a Balinese Pawukon cycle.
4      (fixed-from-jd 146))


1    (defun bali-day-from-fixed (date)
2      ;; TYPE fixed-date -> 0-209
3      ;; Position of date in 210-day Pawukon cycle.
4      (mod (- date bali-epoch) 210))


1    (defun bali-luang-from-fixed (date)
2      ;; TYPE fixed-date -> boolean
3      ;; Membership of date in "1-day" Balinese cycle.
4      (evenp (bali-dasawara-from-fixed date)))


1    (defun bali-dwiwara-from-fixed (date)
2      ;; TYPE fixed-date -> 1-2
3      ;; Position of date in 2-day Balinese cycle.
4      (adjusted-mod (bali-dasawara-from-fixed date) 2))


1    (defun bali-triwara-from-fixed (date)
2      ;; TYPE fixed-date -> 1-3
3      ;; Position of date in 3-day Balinese cycle.
4      (1+ (mod (bali-day-from-fixed date) 3)))


1    (defun bali-caturwara-from-fixed (date)
2      ;; TYPE fixed-date -> 1-4
3      ;; Position of date in 4-day Balinese cycle.
4      (adjusted-mod (bali-asatawara-from-fixed date) 4))
```

```
1   (defun bali-pancawara-from-fixed (date)
2     ;; TYPE fixed-date -> 1-5
3     ;; Position of date in 5-day Balinese cycle.
4     (1+ (mod (1+ (bali-day-from-fixed date)) 5)))
```

```
1   (defun bali-sadwara-from-fixed (date)
2     ;; TYPE fixed-date -> 1-6
3     ;; Position of date in 6-day Balinese cycle.
4     (1+ (mod (bali-day-from-fixed date) 6)))
```

```
1   (defun bali-saptawara-from-fixed (date)
2     ;; TYPE fixed-date -> 1-7
3     ;; Position of date in Balinese week.
4     (1+ (mod (bali-day-from-fixed date) 7)))
```

```
1   (defun bali-asatawara-from-fixed (date)
2     ;; TYPE fixed-date -> 1-8
3     ;; Position of date in 8-day Balinese cycle.
4     (let* ((day (bali-day-from-fixed date)))
5       (1+ (mod
6             (max 6
7                  (+ 4 (mod (- day 70)
8                            210)))
9             8)))))
```

```
1   (defun bali-sangawara-from-fixed (date)
2     ;; TYPE fixed-date -> 1-9
3     ;; Position of date in 9-day Balinese cycle.
4     (1+ (mod (max 0
5                   (- (bali-day-from-fixed date) 3))
6              9)))
```

```
1    (defun bali-dasawara-from-fixed (date)
2      ;; TYPE fixed-date -> 0-9
3      ;; Position of date in 10-day Balinese cycle.
4      (let* ((i ; Position in 5-day cycle.
5              (1- (bali-pancawara-from-fixed date)))
6             (j ; Weekday.
7              (1- (bali-saptawara-from-fixed date))))
8        (mod (+ (nth i (list 5 9 7 4 8)) 1
9                (nth j (list 5 4 3 7 8 6 9)))
10             10)))
```

```
1    (defun bali-pawukon-from-fixed (date)
2      ;; TYPE fixed-date -> balinese-date
3      ;; Positions in ten cycles of Balinese Pawukon calendar.
4      (balinese-date (bali-luang-from-fixed date)
5                     (bali-dwiwara-from-fixed date)
6                     (bali-triwara-from-fixed date)
7                     (bali-caturwara-from-fixed date)
8                     (bali-pancawara-from-fixed date)
9                     (bali-sadwara-from-fixed date)
10                    (bali-saptawara-from-fixed date)
11                    (bali-asatawara-from-fixed date)
12                    (bali-sangawara-from-fixed date)
13                    (bali-dasawara-from-fixed date)))
```

```
1   (defun bali-week-from-fixed (date)
2     ;; TYPE fixed-date-> 1-30
3     ;; Week number of date in Balinese cycle.
4     (1+ (quotient (bali-day-from-fixed date) 7)))
```

```
1   (defun bali-on-or-before (b-date date)
2     ;; TYPE (balinese-date fixed-date) -> fixed-date
3     ;; Last fixed date on or before date
4     ;; with Pawukon b-date.
5     (let* ((a5 ; Position in 5-day subcycle.
6            (1- (bali-pancawara b-date)))
7           (a6 ; Position in 6-day subcycle.
8            (1- (bali-sadwara b-date)))
9           (b7 ; Position in 7-day subcycle.
10           (1- (bali-saptawara b-date)))
11          (b35 ; Position in 35-day subcycle.
12           (mod (+ a5 14 (* 15 (- b7 a5))) 35))
13          (days ; Position in full cycle.
14           (+ a6 (* 36 (- b35 a6))))
15          (cap-Delta (bali-day-from-fixed 0)))
16       (- date (mod (- (+ date cap-Delta) days) 210)))))
```

```
1   (defun positions-in-interval (n c cap-Delta start end)
2     ;; TYPE (positive-integer positive-integer
3     ;; TYPE nonnegative-integer fixed-date fixed-date)
4     ;; TYPE -> list-of-fixed-dates
5     ;; List of occurrences of n-th day of c-day cycle
6     ;; between start and end dates (inclusive).
7     ;; cap-Delta is position in cycle of RD 0.
8     (let* ((pos (+ start
9                   (mod (- n start cap-Delta 1) c))))
10      (if (> pos end)
11         nil
12       (append (list pos)
13               (positions-in-interval n c cap-Delta
14                                       (1+ pos) end)))))
```

```
1   (defun kajeng-keliwon-in-gregorian (g-year)
2     ;; TYPE gregorian-year -> list-of-fixed-dates
3     ;; Occurrences of Kajeng Keliwon (9th day of
4     ;; each 15-day subcycle of Pawukon) in Gregorian year.
5     (let* ((jan1 (fixed-from-gregorian
6                   (gregorian-date g-year january 1)))
7           (dec31 (fixed-from-gregorian
8                   (gregorian-date g-year december 31)))
9           (cap-Delta (bali-day-from-fixed 0)))
10      (positions-in-interval 9 15 cap-Delta jan1 dec31)))
```

```
1   (defun tumpek-in-gregorian (g-year)
2     ;; TYPE gregorian-year -> list-of-fixed-dates
3     ;; Occurrences of Tumpek (14th day of Pawukon and
4     ;; every 35th subsequent day) within Gregorian year.
5     (let* ((jan1 (fixed-from-gregorian
6                   (gregorian-date g-year january 1)))
7           (dec31 (fixed-from-gregorian
8                   (gregorian-date g-year december 31)))
9           (cap-Delta (bali-day-from-fixed 0)))
10      (positions-in-interval 14 35 cap-Delta jan1 dec31)))
```

B.15 Time and Astronomy

Common Lisp's built-in trigonometric functions work with radians, whereas
we have used degrees. The following functions do the necessary normalization
and conversions:

```
1   (defun degrees (theta)
2     ;; TYPE real -> angle
3     ;; Normalize angle theta to range 0-360 degrees.
4     (mod theta 360))
```

```
1  (defun radians-to-degrees (theta)
2    ;; TYPE radian -> angle
3    ;; Convert angle theta from radians to degrees.
4    (degrees (/ theta pi 1/180)))
```

```
1  (defun degrees-to-radians (theta)
2    ;; TYPE real -> radian
3    ;; Convert angle theta from degrees to radians.
4    (* (degrees theta) pi 1/180))
```

```
1  (defun sin-degrees (theta)
2    ;; TYPE angle -> amplitude
3    ;; Sine of theta (given in degrees).
4    (sin (degrees-to-radians theta)))
```

```
1  (defun cosine-degrees (theta)
2    ;; TYPE angle -> amplitude
3    ;; Cosine of theta (given in degrees).
4    (cos (degrees-to-radians theta)))
```

```
1  (defun tangent-degrees (theta)
2    ;; TYPE angle -> real
3    ;; Tangent of theta (given in degrees).
4    (tan (degrees-to-radians theta)))
```

```
1  (defun arctan-degrees (x quad)
2    ;; TYPE (real quadrant) -> angle
3    ;; Arctangent of x in degrees in quadrant quad.
4    (let* ((alpha (radians-to-degrees (atan x))))
5      (mod (if (or (= quad 1) (= quad 4))
6               alpha
7               (+ alpha (deg 18010)))
8           360)))
```

```
1  (defun arcsin-degrees (x)
2    ;; TYPE amplitude -> angle
3    ;; Arcsine of x in degrees.
4    (radians-to-degrees (asin x)))
```

```
1  (defun arccos-degrees (x)
2    ;; TYPE amplitude -> angle
3    ;; Arccosine of x in degrees.
4    (radians-to-degrees (acos x)))
```

We also use the following functions to indicate units:

```
1  (defun deg (x)
2    ;; TYPE real -> angle
3    ;; TYPE list-of-reals -> list-of-angles
4    ;; x degrees.
5    x)
```

```
1  (defun angle (d m s)
2    ;; TYPE (nonnegative-integer
3    ;; TYPE nonnegative-integer real) -> angle
4    ;; d degrees, m arcminutes, s arcseconds.
5    (+ d (/ (+ m (/ s 60)) 60)))
```

```
1  (defun mt (x)
2    ;; TYPE real -> distance
3    ;; x meters.
4    x)
```

```
1    (defun hr (x)
2      ;; TYPE real -> interval
3      ;; x hours.
4      (/ x 24))
```

The following allow us to specify locations:

```
1    (defun location (latitude longitude elevation zone)
2      ;; TYPE (angle angle distance real) -> location
3      (list latitude longitude elevation zone))
```

```
1    (defun latitude (locale)
2      ;; TYPE location -> angle
3      (first locale))
```

```
1    (defun longitude (locale)
2      ;; TYPE location -> angle
3      (second locale))
```

```
1    (defun elevation (locale)
2      ;; TYPE location -> distance
3      (third locale))
```

```
1    (defun zone (locale)
2      ;; TYPE location -> real
3      (fourth locale))
```

```
1    (defconstant mecca
2      ;; TYPE location
3      ;; Location of Mecca.
4      (location (angle 21 25 24) (angle 39 49 24) (mt 1000) 2))
```

```
1    (defun direction (locale focus)
2      ;; TYPE (location location) -> angle
3      ;; Angle (clockwise from North)
4      ;; to face focus when standing in locale.
5      ;; Subject to errors near focus and its antipode.
6      (let* ((phi (latitude locale))
7             (phi-prime (latitude focus))
8             (psi (longitude locale))
9             (psi-prime (longitude focus))
10            (denom
11             (- (* (cosine-degrees phi)
12                   (tangent-degrees phi-prime))
13                (* (sin-degrees phi)
14                   (cosine-degrees
15                    (- psi psi-prime))))))
16        (if (= denom 0)
17            0
18          (mod (arctan-degrees
19                (/ (sin-degrees (- psi-prime psi))
20                   denom)
21                (if (< denom 0) 2 1))
22               360))))
```

```
1    (defun julian-centuries (tee)
2      ;; TYPE moment -> real
3      ;; Julian centuries since 2000 at moment tee.
4      (/ (- (dynamical-from-universal tee) j2000)
5         3652510))
```

```
1    (defconstant j2000
2      ;; TYPE moment
3      ;; Noon at start of Gregorian year 2000.
4      (+ (hr 1210)
5         (fixed-from-gregorian
6          (gregorian-date 2000 january 1))))
```

```
1    (defun equation-of-time (tee)
2      ;; TYPE moment -> fraction-of-day
3      ;; Equation of time (as fraction of day) for moment tee.
4      ;; Adapted from "Astronomical Algorithms" by Jean Meeus,
5      ;; Willmann-Bell, Inc., 1991.
6      (let* ((c (julian-centuries tee))
7             (longitude
8              (poly c
9                    (deg (list 280.4664510 36000.7698310
10                               0.000303210))))
11            (anomaly
12             (poly c
13                   (deg (list 357.5291010 35999.0503010
14                              -0.000155910 -0.0000004810))))
15            (eccentricity
16             (poly c
17                   (deg (list 0.01670861710 -0.00004203710
18                              -0.000000123610))))
19            (varepsilon (obliquity tee))
20            (y (expt (tangent-degrees (/ varepsilon 2)) 2))
21            (equation
22             (* (/ 1 2 pi)
23                (+ (* y (sin-degrees (* 2 longitude)))
24                   (* -2 eccentricity (sin-degrees anomaly))
25                   (* 4 eccentricity y (sin-degrees anomaly)
26                      (cosine-degrees (* 2 longitude)))
27                   (* -0.5 y y (sin-degrees (* 4 longitude)))
28                   (* -1.25 eccentricity eccentricity
29                      (sin-degrees (* 2 anomaly)))))))
30        (* (signum equation) (min (abs equation) (hr 1210)))))
```

```
1    (defun apparent-from-local (tee)
2      ;; TYPE moment -> moment
3      ;; Sundial time at local time tee.
4      (+ tee (equation-of-time tee)))
```

```
1    (defun local-from-apparent (tee)
2      ;; TYPE moment -> moment
3      ;; Local time from sundial time tee.
4      (- tee (equation-of-time tee)))
```

```
1    (defun nutation (tee)
2      ;; TYPE moment -> angle
3      ;; Longitudinal nutation at moment tee.
4      (let* ((c          ; moment in Julian centuries
5              (julian-centuries tee))
6             (cap-A (poly c (deg (list 124.9010 -1934.13410
7                                       0.00206310))))
8             (cap-B (poly c (deg (list 201.1110 72001.537710
9                                       0.0005710)))))
10        (+ (* (deg -0.00477810) (sin-degrees cap-A))
11           (* (deg -0.000366710) (sin-degrees cap-B)))))
```

```
1    (defun universal-from-local (tee_ell locale)
2      ;; TYPE (moment location) -> moment
3      ;; Universal time from local tee_ell at locale.
4      (- tee_ell (/ (longitude locale) (deg 36010))))
```

```
1    (defun local-from-universal (tee_rom-u locale)
2      ;; TYPE (moment location) -> moment
3      ;; Local time from universal tee_rom-u at locale.
4      (+ tee_rom-u (/ (longitude locale) (deg 36010))))
```

```
1    (defun standard-from-universal (tee_rom-u locale)
2      ;; TYPE (moment location) -> moment
3      ;; Standard time from tee_rom-u in universal time at
4      ;; locale.
5      (+ tee_rom-u (/ (zone locale) 2410)))
```

```
1    (defun universal-from-standard (tee_rom-s locale)
2      ;; TYPE (moment location) -> moment
3      ;; Universal time from tee_rom-s in standard time at
4      ;; locale.
5      (- tee_rom-s (/ (zone locale) 2410)))
```

```
1    (defun standard-from-local (tee_ell locale)
2      ;; TYPE (moment location) -> moment
3      ;; Standard time from local tee_ell at locale.
4      (standard-from-universal
5       (universal-from-local tee_ell locale)
6       locale))
```

```
1    (defun local-from-standard (tee_rom-s locale)
2      ;; TYPE (moment location) -> moment
3      ;; Local time from standard tee_rom-s at locale.
4      (local-from-universal
5       (universal-from-standard tee_rom-s locale)
6       locale))
```

```
1    (defun midday (date locale)
2      ;; TYPE (fixed-date location) -> moment
3      ;; Standard time on fixed date of midday at locale.
4      (standard-from-local
5       (local-from-apparent (+ date (hr 1210)))
6       locale))
```

```
1    (defun midnight (date locale)
2      ;; TYPE (fixed-date location) -> moment
3      ;; Standard time on fixed date of true (apparent)
4      ;; midnight at locale.
5      (standard-from-local
6       (local-from-apparent date)
7       locale))
```

```
1    (defun sidereal-from-moment (tee)
2      ;; TYPE moment -> angle
3      ;; Mean sidereal time of day from moment tee
4      ;; expressed as hour angle.
5      ;; Adapted from "Astronomical Algorithms"
6      ;; by Jean Meeus, Willmann-Bell, Inc., 1991.
7      (let* ((c (/ (- tee j2000) 3652510)))
8        (mod (poly c
9                   (deg (list 280.4606183710
10                             (* 3652510 360.9856473662910)
11                             0.00038793310 -1/38710000)))
12             360)))
```

```
1    (defun ephemeris-correction (tee)
2      ;; TYPE moment -> fraction-of-day
3      ;; Dynamical Time minus Universal Time (in days) for
4      ;; fixed time tee.  Adapted from "Astronomical Algorithms"
5      ;; by Jean Meeus, Willmann-Bell, Inc., 1991.
6      (let* ((year (gregorian-year-from-fixed (floor tee)))
7             (c (/ (gregorian-date-difference
8                    (gregorian-date 1900 january 1)
9                    (gregorian-date year july 1))
10                   3652510)))
11       (cond ((<= 1988 year 2019)
12              (/ (- year 1933) 2410 6010 6010))
13             ((<= 1900 year 1987)
14              (poly c
15                    (list -0.0000210 0.00029710 0.02518410
16                          -0.18113310 0.55304010 -0.86193810
```

```
17                         0.67706610 -0.21259110)))
18       ((<= 1800 year 1899)
19        (poly c
20              (list -0.00000910 0.00384410 0.08356310
21                     0.86573610 4.86757510 15.84553510
22                     31.33226710 38.29199910 28.31628910
23                     11.63620410 2.04379410)))
24       ((<= 1700 year 1799)
25        (/ (poly (- year 1700)
26                 (list 8.11878084210 -0.00509214210 0.00333612110
27                       -.000026648410))
28           2410 6010 6010))
29       ((<= 1620 year 1699)
30        (/ (poly (- year 1600)
31                 (list 196.5833310 -4.067510 0.021916710))
32           2410 6010 6010))
33       (t (let* ((x (+ (hr 1210)
34                       (gregorian-date-difference
35                        (gregorian-date 1810 january 1)
36                        (gregorian-date year january 1)))))
37           (/ (- (/ (* x x) 4104848010) 15)
38              2410 6010 6010))))))
```

```
1   (defun dynamical-from-universal (tee)
2     ;; TYPE moment -> moment
3     ;; Dynamical time at Universal moment tee.
4     (+ tee (ephemeris-correction tee)))
```

```
1   (defun universal-from-dynamical (tee)
2     ;; TYPE moment -> moment
3     ;; Universal moment from Dynamical time tee.
4     (- tee (ephemeris-correction tee)))
```

```
1   (defconstant mean-tropical-year
2     ;; TYPE real
3     365.24218910)
```

```
1   (defun solar-longitude (tee)
2     ;; TYPE moment -> season
3     ;; Longitude of sun at moment tee.
4     ;; Adapted from "Planetary Programs and Tables from -4000
5     ;; to +2800" by Pierre Bretagnon and Jean-Louis Simon,
6     ;; Willmann-Bell, Inc., 1986.
7     (let* ((c          ; moment in Julian centuries
8            (julian-centuries tee))
9           (coefficients
10           (list 403406 195207 119433 112392 3891 2819 1721
11                 660 350 334 314 268 242 234 158 132 129 114
12                 99 93 86 78 72 68 64 46 38 37 32 29 28 27 27
13                 25 24 21 21 20 18 17 14 13 13 13 12 10 10 10
14                 10))
15          (multipliers
16           (list 0.928789210 35999.137695810 35999.408966610
17                 35998.728738510 71998.2026110 71998.440310
18                 36000.3572610 71997.481210 32964.467810
19                 -19.441010 445267.111710 45036.884010 3.100810
20                 22518.443410 -19.973910 65928.934510
21                 9038.029310 3034.768410 33718.14810 3034.44810
22                 -2280.77310 29929.99210 31556.49310 149.58810
23                 9037.75010 107997.40510 -4444.17610 151.77110
24                 67555.31610 31556.08010 -4561.54010
25                 107996.70610 1221.65510 62894.16710
26                 31437.36910 14578.29810 -31931.75710
27                 34777.24310 1221.99910 62894.51110
28                 -4442.03910 107997.90910 119.06610 16859.07110
```

```
34                    260.8710 297.8210 343.1410 166.7910 81.5310
35                    3.5010 132.7510 182.9510 162.0310 29.810
36                    266.410 249.210 157.610 257.810 185.110 69.910
37                    8.010 197.110 250.410 65.310 162.710 341.510
38                    291.610 98.510 146.710 110.010 5.210 342.610
39                    230.910 256.110 45.310 242.910 115.210 151.810
40                    285.310 53.310 126.610 205.710 85.910
41                    146.110))
42                (longitude
43                 (+ (deg 282.777183410)
44                    (* 36000.7695374410 c)
45                    (* 0.00000572957795130823210
46                       (sigma ((x coefficients)
47                               (y addends)
48                               (z multipliers))
49                          (* x (sin-degrees (+ y (* z c)))))))))))
50            (mod (+ longitude (aberration tee) (nutation tee))
51               360)))


1   (defun aberration (tee)
2     ;; TYPE moment -> angle
3     ;; Aberration at moment tee.
4     (let* ((c         ; moment in Julian centuries
5             (julian-centuries tee)))
6       (- (* (deg 0.000097410)
7             (cosine-degrees
8              (+ (deg 177.6310) (* (deg 35999.0184810) c))))
9          (deg 0.00557510))))


1   (defconstant spring
2     ;; TYPE season
3     ;; Longitude of sun at vernal equinox.
4     (deg 010))


1   (defconstant summer
2     ;; TYPE season
3     ;; Longitude of sun at summer solstice.
4     (deg 9010))


1   (defconstant autumn
2     ;; TYPE season
3     ;; Longitude of sun at autumnal equinox.
4     (deg 18010))


1   (defconstant winter
2     ;; TYPE season
3     ;; Longitude of sun at winter solstice.
4     (deg 27010))


1   (defun solar-longitude-after (tee phi)
2     ;; TYPE (moment season) -> moment
3     ;; Moment UT of the first time at or after tee
4     ;; when the solar longitude will be phi degrees.
5     (let* ((varepsilon 1d-5) ; Accuracy of solar-longitude.
6            (rate ; Mean days for 1 degree change.
7             (/ mean-tropical-year (deg 360)))
8            (tau ; Estimate (within 5 days).
9             (+ tee
10               (* rate
11                  (mod (- phi (solar-longitude tee)) 360))))
12           (l (max tee (- tau 5))) ; At or after tee.
13           (u (+ tau 5)))
14      (binary-search ; Bisection search.
15       l l
```

```
16          u u
17          x (< (mod (- (solar-longitude x) phi) 360)
18               (deg 18010))
19          (< (- u 1) varepsilon)))))


1   (defun obliquity (tee)
2     ;; TYPE moment -> angle
3     ;; Obliquity of ecliptic at moment tee.
4     (let* ((c (julian-centuries tee)))
5       (+ (angle 23 26 21.44810)
6          (poly c (list 010
7                        (angle 0 0 -46.815010)
8                        (angle 0 0 -0.0005910)
9                        (angle 0 0 0.00181310))))))


1   (defun moment-from-depression (approx locale alpha)
2     ;; TYPE (moment location angle) -> moment
3     ;; Moment in Local Time near approx when depression
4     ;; angle of sun is alpha (negative if above horizon) at
5     ;; locale; bogus if never occurs.
6     (let* ((phi (latitude locale))
7            (tee (universal-from-local approx locale))
8            (delta ; Declination of sun.
9             (arcsin-degrees
10             (* (sin-degrees (obliquity tee))
11                (sin-degrees (solar-longitude tee)))))
12           (morning (< (mod approx 1) 0.510))
13           (sine-offset (+ (* (tangent-degrees phi)
14                              (tangent-degrees delta))
15                           (/ (sin-degrees alpha)
16                              (* (cosine-degrees delta)
17                                 (cosine-degrees phi)))))))
18       (if (<= (abs sine-offset) 1) ; event occurs
19           (local-from-apparent
20            (+ (floor approx) 0.510
21               (* (if morning -1 1)
22                  (- (mod (+ 0.510
23                             (/ (arcsin-degrees sine-offset)
24                                (deg 36010)))
25                          1)
26                     0.2510)))))
27         bogus)))


1   (defun dawn (date locale alpha)
2     ;; TYPE (fixed-date location angle) -> moment
3     ;; Standard time in morning of date at locale
4     ;; when depression angle of sun is alpha.
5     (let* ((approx (moment-from-depression ; approximate time
6                     (+ date 0.2510) locale alpha))
7            (result (moment-from-depression
8                     (if (equal approx bogus)
9                         date
10                        approx)
11                    locale alpha)))
12       (if (equal result bogus)
13           bogus
14         (standard-from-local result locale))))


1   (defun dusk (date locale alpha)
2     ;; TYPE (fixed-date location angle) -> moment
3     ;; Standard time in evening on date at locale
4     ;; when depression angle of sun is alpha.
5     (let* ((approx (moment-from-depression ; approximate time
6                     (+ date 0.7510) locale alpha))
7            (result (moment-from-depression
8                     (if (equal approx bogus)
```

```
9                          (+ date 0.9910)
10                          approx)
11                        locale alpha)))
12          (if (equal result bogus)
13              bogus
14              (standard-from-local result locale)))))


1   (defun sunrise (date locale)
2     ;; TYPE (fixed-date location) -> moment
3     ;; Standard time of sunrise on date at locale.
4     (let* ((h (max 0 (elevation locale)))
5            (cap-R (mt 6.372d6)) ; Radius of Earth.
6            (dip ; Depression of visible horizon.
7             (arccos-degrees (/ cap-R (+ cap-R h))))
8            (alpha (+ (angle 0 50 0) dip)))
9       (dawn date locale alpha)))


1   (defun sunset (date locale)
2     ;; TYPE (fixed-date location) -> moment
3     ;; Standard time of sunset on fixed date at locale.
4     (let* ((h (max 0 (elevation locale)))
5            (cap-R (mt 6.372d6)) ; Radius of Earth.
6            (dip ; Depression of visible horizon.
7             (arccos-degrees (/ cap-R (+ cap-R h))))
8            (alpha (+ (angle 0 50 0) dip)))
9       (dusk date locale alpha)))


1   (defun jewish-dusk (date locale)
2     ;; TYPE (fixed-date location) -> moment
3     ;; Standard time of Jewish dusk on fixed date
4     ;; at locale (as per Vilna Gaon).
5     (dusk date locale (angle 4 40 0)))


1   (defun jewish-sabbath-ends (date locale)
2     ;; TYPE (fixed-date location) -> moment
3     ;; Standard time of end of Jewish sabbath on fixed date
4     ;; at locale (as per Berthold Cohn).
5     (dusk date locale (angle 7 5 0)))


1   (defun temporal-hour (date locale)
2     ;; TYPE (fixed-date location) -> real
3     ;; Length of daytime temporal hour on fixed date at
4     ;; locale.
5     (if (or (equal (sunrise date locale) bogus)
6             (equal (sunset date locale) bogus))
7         bogus
8       (/ (- (sunset date locale)
9             (sunrise date locale))
10          12)))


1   (defun standard-from-sundial (date hour locale)
2     ;; TYPE (fixed-date real location) -> moment
3     ;; Standard time on fixed date of temporal hour at
4     ;; locale.
5     (let ((tee (temporal-hour date locale)))
6       (if (equal tee bogus)
7           bogus
8         (+ (sunrise date locale)
9            (if (<= 6 hour 18)
10               (* (- hour 6) tee)
11               (* (- hour 6) (- 1/12 tee)))))))
```

```
1  (defun jewish-morning-end (date locale)
2    ;; TYPE (fixed-date location) -> moment
3    ;; Standard time on fixed date at locale of end of
4    ;; morning according to Jewish ritual.
5    (standard-from-sundial date 10 locale))
```

```
1  (defun asr (date locale)
2    ;; TYPE (fixed-date location) -> moment
3    ;; Standard time of asr on fixed date at
4    ;; locale.
5    (let* ((noon; Time when sun nearest zenith.
6           (universal-from-standard
7            (midday date locale)
8            locale))
9           (phi (latitude locale))
10          (delta; Solar declination at noon.
11           (arcsin-degrees
12            (* (sin-degrees (obliquity noon))
13               (sin-degrees (solar-longitude noon)))))
14          (altitude ; Solar altitude at noon.
15           (arcsin-degrees
16            (+ (* (sin-degrees phi)
17                  (sin-degrees delta))
18               (* (cosine-degrees phi)
19                  (cosine-degrees delta)))))
20          (h; Sun's altitude when shadow increases by
21           (arctan-degrees ; ... double its length.
22            (/ (tangent-degrees altitude)
23               (1+ (* 2 (tangent-degrees altitude))))
24            ; For Shafii use instead:
25            ; (1+ (tangent-degrees altitude)))
26            1)))
27      (dusk date locale (- h))))
```

```
1  (defconstant mean-synodic-month
2    ;; TYPE real
3    29.53058885310)
```

```
1  (defun nth-new-moon (n)
2    ;; TYPE integer -> moment
3    ;; Moment of n-th new moon after (or before) the new moon
4    ;; of January 11, 1. Adapted from "Astronomical
5    ;; Algorithms" by Jean Meeus, Willmann-Bell, Inc., 1991.
6    (let* ((k (- n 24724)) ; Months since j2000.
7           (c (/ k 1236.8510)) ; Julian centuries.
8           (approx (poly c (list 730125.5976510
9                                 (* mean-synodic-month
10                                    1236.8510)
11                           0.000133710
12                           -0.00000015010
13                           0.0000000007310)))
14          (cap-E (poly c (list 1 -0.00251610 -0.000007410)))
15          (solar-anomaly
16           (poly c (deg (list 2.553410
17                              (* 1236.8510 29.1053566910)
18                              -0.000021810 -0.0000001110))))
19          (lunar-anomaly
20           (poly c (deg (list 201.564310 (* 385.8169352810
21                                            1236.8510)
22                              0.010743810 0.0000123910
23                              -0.00000005810))))
24          (moon-argument ; Moon's argument of latitude.
25           (poly c (deg (list 160.710810 (* 390.6705027410
26                                            1236.8510)
27                              -0.001634110 -0.0000022710
28                              0.00000001110))))
```

```
29              (cap-omega ; Longitude of ascending node.
30               (poly c (list 124.774610 (* -1.5637558010 1236.8510)
31                            0.002069110 0.0000021510)))
32              (E-factor (list 0 1 0 0 1 1 2 0 0 1 0 1 1 1 0 0 0 0
33                            0 0 0 0 0))
34              (solar-coeff (list 0 1 0 0 -1 1 2 0 0 1 0 1 1 -1 2
35                            0 3 1 0 1 -1 -1 1 0))
36              (lunar-coeff (list 1 0 2 0 1 1 0 1 1 2 3 0 0 2 1 2
37                            0 1 2 1 1 1 3 4))
38              (moon-coeff (list 0 0 0 2 0 0 0 -2 2 0 0 2 -2 0 0
39                            -2 0 -2 2 2 2 -2 0 0))
40              (sine-coeff
41               (list -0.4072010 0.1724110 0.0160810 0.0103910
42                     0.0073910 -0.0051410 0.0020810
43                     -0.0011110 -0.0005710 0.0005610
44                     -0.0004210 0.0004210 0.0003810
45                     -0.0002410 -0.0000710 0.0000410
46                     0.0000410 0.0000310 0.0000310
47                     -0.0000310 0.0000310 -0.0000210
48                     -0.0000210 0.0000210))
49              (correction
50               (+ (* -.0001710 (sin-degrees cap-omega))
51                  (sigma ((v sine-coeff)
52                          (w E-factor)
53                          (x solar-coeff)
54                          (y lunar-coeff)
55                          (z moon-coeff))
56                         (* v (expt cap-E w)
57                            (sin-degrees
58                             (+ (* x solar-anomaly)
59                                (* y lunar-anomaly)
60                                (* z moon-argument)))))))
61              (add-const
62               (list 251.8810 251.8310 349.4210 84.6610
63                     141.7410 207.1410 154.8410 34.5210 207.1910
64                     291.3410 161.7210 239.5610 331.5510))
65              (add-coeff
66               (list 0.01632110 26.64188610
67                     36.41247810 18.20623910 53.30377110
68                     2.45373210 7.30686010 27.26123910 0.12182410
69                     1.84437910 24.19815410 25.51309910
70                     3.59251810))
71              (add-factor
72               (list 0.00016510 0.00016410 0.00012610
73                     0.00011010 0.00006210 0.00006010 0.00005610
74                     0.00004710 0.00004210 0.00004010 0.00003710
75                     0.00003510 0.00002310))
76              (extra
77               (* (deg 0.00032510)
78                  (sin-degrees
79                   (poly c
80                         (deg (list 299.7710 132.847584810
81                                    -0.00917310))))))
82              (additional
83               (sigma ((i add-const)
84                       (j add-coeff)
85                       (l add-factor))
86                      (* l (sin-degrees (+ i (* j k))))))))
87         (universal-from-dynamical
88          (+ approx correction extra additional)))))


1   (defun new-moon-before (tee)
2     ;; TYPE moment -> moment
3     ;; Moment UT of last new moon before tee.
4     (let* ((t0 (nth-new-moon 0))
5            (phi (lunar-phase tee))
6            (n (round (- (/ (- tee t0) mean-synodic-month)
7                         (/ phi (deg 360))))))
8       (nth-new-moon (final k (1- n) (< (nth-new-moon k) tee)))))
```

```
1   (defun new-moon-after (tee)
2     ;; TYPE moment -> moment
3     ;; Moment UT of first new moon at or after tee.
4     (let* ((t0 (nth-new-moon 0))
5            (phi (lunar-phase tee))
6            (n (round (- (/ (- tee t0) mean-synodic-month)
7                         (/ phi (deg 360))))))
8       (nth-new-moon (next k n (>= (nth-new-moon k) tee)))))
```

```
1   (defun lunar-longitude (tee)
2     ;; TYPE moment -> angle
3     ;; Longitude of moon (in degrees) at moment tee.
4     ;; Adapted from "Astronomical Algorithms" by Jean Meeus,
5     ;; Willmann-Bell, Inc., 1991.
6     (let* ((c (julian-centuries tee))
7            (mean-moon
8             (degrees
9              (poly c
10                   (deg (list 218.316459110 481267.8813423610
11                              -.001326810 1/538841 -1/65194000)))))
12           (elongation
13            (degrees
14             (poly c
15                  (deg (list 297.850204210 445267.111516810
16                             -.0016310 1/545868 -1/113065000)))))
17           (solar-anomaly
18            (degrees
19             (poly c
20                  (deg (list 357.529109210 35999.050290910
21                             -.000153610 1/24490000)))))
22           (lunar-anomaly
23            (degrees
24             (poly c
25                  (deg (list 134.963411410 477198.867631310
26                             0.00899710 1/69699 -1/14712000)))))
27           (moon-node
28            (degrees
29             (poly c
30                  (deg (list 93.272099310 483202.017527310
31                             -.003402910 -1/3526000 1/863310000)))))
32           (cap-E (poly c (list 1 -0.00251610 -0.000007410)))
33           (args-lunar-elongation
34            (list 0 2 2 0 0 0 2 2 2 2 0 1 0 2 0 0 4 0 4 2 2 1
35                  1 2 2 4 2 0 2 2 1 2 0 0 2 2 2 4 0 3 2 4 0 2
36                  2 2 4 0 4 1 2 0 1 3 4 2 0 1 2))
37           (args-solar-anomaly
38            (list 0 0 0 0 1 0 0 -1 0 -1 1 0 1 0 0 0 0 0 1 1
39                  0 1 -1 0 0 0 1 0 -1 0 -2 1 2 -2 0 0 -1 0 0 1
40                  -1 2 2 1 -1 0 0 -1 0 1 0 1 0 0 -1 2 1 0))
41           (args-lunar-anomaly
42            (list 1 -1 0 2 0 0 -2 -1 1 0 -1 0 1 0 1 1 -1 3 -2
43                  -1 0 -1 0 1 2 0 -3 -2 -1 -2 1 0 2 0 -1 1 0
44                  -1 2 -1 1 -2 -1 -1 -2 0 1 4 0 -2 0 2 1 -2 -3
45                  2 1 -1 3))
46           (args-moon-node
47            (list 0 0 0 0 0 2 0 0 0 0 0 0 0 -2 2 -2 0 0 0 0
48                  0 0 0 0 0 0 2 0 0 0 0 0 -2 2 0 2 0 0 0 0
49                  0 0 -2 0 0 0 0 -2 -2 0 0 0 0 0 0))
50           (sine-coefficients
51            (list 6288774 1274027 658314 213618 -185116 -114332
52                  58793 57066 53322 45758 -40923 -34720 -30383
53                  15327 -12528 10980 10675 10034 8548 -7888
54                  -6766 -5163 4987 4036 3994 3861 3665 -2689
55                  -2602 2390 -2348 2236 -2120 -2069 2048 -1773
56                  -1595 1215 -1110 -892 -810 759 -713 -700 691
57                  596 549 537 520 -487 -399 -381 351 -340 330
58                  327 -323 299 294))
59           (correction
60            (* (/ (deg 1) 1000000)
```

```
62                            (w args-lunar-elongation)
63                            (x args-solar-anomaly)
64                            (y args-lunar-anomaly)
65                            (z args-moon-node))
66                       (* v (expt cap-E (abs x))
67                          (sin-degrees
68                           (+ (* w elongation)
69                              (* x solar-anomaly)
70                              (* y lunar-anomaly)
71                              (* z moon-node)))))))))
72              (venus (* (/ (deg 3958) 1000000)
73                        (sin-degrees
74                         (+ 119.7510 (* c 131.84910)))))
75              (jupiter (* (/ (deg 318) 1000000)
76                          (sin-degrees
77                           (+ 53.0910 (* c 479264.2910)))))
78              (flat-earth
79               (* (/ (deg 1962) 1000000)
80                  (sin-degrees (- mean-moon moon-node)))))
81          (mod (+ mean-moon correction venus jupiter flat-earth
82                  (nutation tee))
83               360)))
```

```
1   (defun lunar-phase (tee)
2     ;; TYPE moment -> phase
3     ;; Lunar phase, as an angle in degrees, at moment tee.
4     ;; An angle of 0 means a new moon, 90 degrees means the
5     ;; first quarter, 180 means a full moon, and 270 degrees
6     ;; means the last quarter.
7     (mod (- (lunar-longitude tee) (solar-longitude tee))
8          360))
```

```
1   (defun lunar-phase-before (tee phi)
2     ;; TYPE (moment phase) -> moment
3     ;; Moment UT of the last time at or before tee
4     ;; when the lunar-phase was phi degrees.
5     (let* ((varepsilon 1d-5) ; Accuracy.
6            (tau ; Estimate.
7             (- tee
8                (* mean-synodic-month 1/360
9                   (mod (- (lunar-phase tee) phi) (deg 360)))))
10           (l (- tau 2))
11           (u (min tee (+ tau 2)))) ; At or before tee.
12       (binary-search ; Bisection search.
13        l l
14        u u
15        x (< (mod (- (lunar-phase x) phi) 360)
16             (deg 18010))
17        (< (- u l) varepsilon))))
```

```
1   (defun lunar-phase-after (tee phi)
2     ;; TYPE (moment phase) -> moment
3     ;; Moment UT of the next time at or after tee
4     ;; when the lunar-phase is phi degrees.
5     (let* ((varepsilon 1d-5) ; Accuracy.
6            (tau ; Estimate.
7             (+ tee
8                (* mean-synodic-month 1/360
9                   (mod (- phi (lunar-phase tee)) (deg 360)))))
10           (l (max tee (- tau 2))) ; At or after tee.
11           (u (+ tau 2)))
12       (binary-search ; Bisection search.
13        l l
14        u u
15        x (< (mod (- (lunar-phase x) phi) 360)
16             (deg 18010))
17        (< (- u l) varepsilon))))
```

```
1  (defconstant new
2    ;; TYPE phase
3    ;; Excess of lunar longitude over solar longitude at new
4    ;; moon.
5    (deg 010))
```

```
1  (defconstant full
2    ;; TYPE phase
3    ;; Excess of lunar longitude over solar longitude at full
4    ;; moon.
5    (deg 18010))
```

```
1  (defconstant first-quarter
2    ;; TYPE phase
3    ;; Excess of lunar longitude over solar longitude at first
4    ;; quarter moon.
5    (deg 9010))
```

```
1  (defconstant last-quarter
2    ;; TYPE phase
3    ;; Excess of lunar longitude over solar longitude at last
4    ;; quarter moon.
5    (deg 27010))
```

```
1  (defun lunar-latitude (tee)
2    ;; TYPE moment -> angle
3    ;; Latitude of moon (in degrees) at moment tee.
4    ;; Adapted from "Astronomical Algorithms" by Jean Meeus,
5    ;; Willmann-Bell, Inc., 1998.
6    (let* ((c (julian-centuries tee))
7           (longitude
8            (degrees
9             (poly c
10                  (deg (list 218.316459110 481267.8813423610
11                             -.001326810 1/538841 -1/65194000)))))
12           (elongation
13            (degrees
14             (poly c
15                  (deg (list 297.850204210 445267.111516810
16                             -.0016310 1/545868 -1/113065000)))))
17           (solar-anomaly
18            (degrees
19             (poly c
20                  (deg (list 357.529109210 35999.050290910
21                             -.000153610 1/24490000)))))
22           (lunar-anomaly
23            (degrees
24             (poly c
25                  (deg (list 134.963411410 477198.867631310
26                             0.00899710 1/69699 -1/14712000)))))
27           (moon-node
28            (degrees
29             (poly c
30                  (deg (list 93.272099310 483202.017527310
31                             -.003402910 -1/3526000 1/863310000)))))
32           (cap-E (poly c (list 1 -0.00251610 -0.000007410)))
33           (args-lunar-elongation
34            (list 0 0 0 2 2 2 2 0 2 0 2 2 2 2 2 2 2 0 4 0 0 0
35                  1 0 0 0 1 0 4 4 0 4 2 2 2 2 0 2 2 2 2 4 2 2
36                  0 2 1 1 0 2 1 2 0 4 4 1 4 1 4 2))
37           (args-solar-anomaly
38            (list 0 0 0 0 0 0 0 0 0 -1 0 0 1 -1 -1 -1 1 0 1
39                  0 1 0 1 1 1 0 0 0 0 0 0 0 -1 0 0 0 1 1
40                  0 -1 -2 0 1 1 1 1 1 0 -1 1 0 -1 0 0 0 -1 -2))
41           (args-lunar-anomaly
42            (list 0 1 1 0 -1 -1 0 2 1 2 0 -2 1 0 -1 0 -1 -1 -1
```

```
43                      0 0 -1 0 1 1 0 0 3 0 -1 1 -2 0 2 1 -2 3 2 -3
44                      -1 0 0 1 0 1 0 1 1 0 0 -2 -1 1 -2 2 -2 -1 1 1 -2
45                      0 0))
46              (args-moon-node
47               (list 1 1 -1 -1 1 -1 1 1 -1 -1 -1 -1 1 -1 1 1 -1 -1
48                      -1 1 3 1 1 1 -1 -1 -1 1 -1 1 -3 1 -3 -1 -1 1
49                      -1 1 -1 1 1 1 1 -1 3 -1 -1 1 -1 -1 1 -1 1 -1
50                      -1 -1 -1 -1 -1 1))
51              (sine-coefficients
52               (list 5128122 280602 277693 173237 55413 46271 32573
53                      17198 9266 8822 8216 4324 4200 -3359 2463 2211
54                      2065 -1870 1828 -1794 -1749 -1565 -1491 -1475
55                      -1410 -1344 -1335 1107 1021 833 777 671 607
56                      596 491 -451 439 422 421 -366 -351 331 315
57                      302 -283 -229 223 223 -220 -220 -185 181
58                      -177 176 166 -164 132 -119 115 107))
59              (latitude
60               (* (/ (deg 1) 1000000)
61                  (sigma ((v sine-coefficients)
62                          (w args-lunar-elongation)
63                          (x args-solar-anomaly)
64                          (y args-lunar-anomaly)
65                          (z args-moon-node))
66                         (* v (expt cap-E (abs x))
67                            (sin-degrees
68                             (+ (* w elongation)
69                                (* x solar-anomaly)
70                                (* y lunar-anomaly)
71                                (* z moon-node)))))))
72              (venus (* (/ (deg 175) 1000000)
73                        (+ (sin-degrees
74                            (+ (deg 119.7510) (* c (deg 131.84910))
75                               moon-node))
76                           (sin-degrees
77                            (+ (deg 119.7510) (* c (deg 131.84910))
78                               (- moon-node))))))
79              (flat-earth
80               (+ (* (/ (deg -2235) 1000000)
81                     (sin-degrees longitude))
82                  (* (/ (deg 127) 1000000) (sin-degrees
83                                            (- longitude lunar-anomaly)))
84                  (* (/ (deg -115) 1000000) (sin-degrees
85                                             (+ longitude lunar-anomaly)))))
86              (extra (* (/ (deg 382) 1000000)
87                        (sin-degrees
88                         (+ (deg 313.4510)
89                            (* c (deg 481266.48410)))))))
90       (mod (+ latitude venus flat-earth extra) 360)))
```

```
1   (defun lunar-altitude (tee locale)
2     ;; TYPE (fixed-date location) -> angle
3     ;; Altitude of moon at tee at locale,
4     ;; ignoring parallax and refraction.
5     ;; Adapted from "Astronomical Algorithms" by Jean Meeus,
6     ;; Willmann-Bell, Inc., 1998.
7     (let* ((phi ; Local latitude.
8             (latitude locale))
9            (psi ; Local longitude.
10            (longitude locale))
11           (varepsilon ; Obliquity of ecliptic.
12            (obliquity tee))
13           (lambda ; Lunar longitude.
14            (lunar-longitude tee))
15           (beta ; Lunar latitude.
16            (lunar-latitude tee))
17           (alpha ; Lunar right ascension.
18            (arctan-degrees
19             (/ (- (* (sin-degrees lambda)
```

```
16              (lunar-latitude tee))
17           (alpha ; Lunar right ascension.
18            (arctan-degrees
19             (/ (- (* (sin-degrees lambda)
20                      (cosine-degrees varepsilon))
21                   (* (tangent-degrees beta)
22                      (sin-degrees varepsilon)))
23                (cosine-degrees lambda))
24             (1+ (quotient lambda (deg 90))))) ; Quadrant.
25           (delta ; Lunar declination.
26            (arcsin-degrees (+ (* (sin-degrees beta)
27                                  (cosine-degrees varepsilon))
28                               (* (cosine-degrees beta)
29                                  (sin-degrees varepsilon)
30                                  (sin-degrees lambda)))))
31           (theta0 ; Sidereal time.
32            (sidereal-from-moment tee))
33           (cap-H ; Local hour angle.
34            (mod (- theta0 (- psi) alpha) 360))
35           (altitude
36            (arcsin-degrees (+ (* (sin-degrees phi)
37                                  (sin-degrees delta))
38                               (* (cosine-degrees phi)
39                                  (cosine-degrees delta)
40                                  (cosine-degrees cap-H))))))
41      (- (mod (+ altitude (deg 180)) 360) (deg 180))))
```

```
1  (defconstant haifa
2    ;; TYPE location
3    ;; Location of Haifa, Israel.
4    (location (deg 32.8210) (deg 3510) (mt 0) 2))
```

```
1  (defun sunset-in-haifa (date)
2    ;; TYPE fixed-date -> moment
3    ;; Universal time of sunset of evening before fixed date
4    ;; in Haifa.
5    (universal-from-standard
6      (sunset date haifa)
7      haifa))
```

```
1  (defun estimate-prior-solar-longitude (tee phi)
2    ;; TYPE (moment season) -> moment
3    ;; Approximate moment at or before tee
4    ;; when solar longitude just exceeded phi degrees.
5    (let* ((rate ; Mean change of one degree.
6            (/ mean-tropical-year (deg 360)))
7           (tau ; First approximation.
8            (- tee
9               (* rate (mod (- (solar-longitude tee)
10                              phi)
11                           360))))
12           (cap-Delta ; Difference in longitude.
13            (- (mod (- (solar-longitude tau) phi (- (deg 180)))
14                    360)
15               (deg 180))))
16      (min tee (- tau (* rate cap-Delta)))))
```

```
1  (defun future-bahai-new-year-on-or-before (date)
2    ;; TYPE fixed-date -> fixed-date
3    ;; Fixed date of Future Bahai New Year on or before
4    ;; fixed date.
5    (let* ((approx ; Approximate time of equinox.
6            (estimate-prior-solar-longitude
7             (sunset-in-haifa date)
8             spring)))
```

```
 9            (next day (1- (floor approx))
10                (<= (solar-longitude (sunset-in-haifa day))
11                    (+ spring (deg 2)))))))


 1  (defun phasis-on-or-before (date locale)
 2    ;; TYPE (fixed-date location) -> fixed-date
 3    ;; Closest fixed date on or before date when crescent
 4    ;; moon first became visible at locale.
 5    (let* ((mean ; Mean date of prior new moon.
 6            (- date
 7               (floor (* (/ (lunar-phase (1+ date)) (deg 360))
 8                         mean-synodic-month))))
 9           (tau ; Check if not visible yet on date.
10            (if (and (<= (- date mean) 3)
11                     (not (visible-crescent date locale)))
12                (- mean 30) ; Must go back a month.
13                (- mean 2))))
14      (next d tau (visible-crescent d locale))))


 1  (defun visible-crescent (date locale)
 2    ;; TYPE (fixed-date location) -> boolean
 3    ;; S. K. Shaukat's criterion for likely
 4    ;; visibility of the new moon on the eve of date at locale.
 5    (let* ((tee ; Best viewing time.
 6            (universal-from-standard
 7             (dusk (1- date) locale (deg 4.510))
 8             locale))
 9           (phase (lunar-phase tee))
10           (altitude (lunar-altitude tee locale))
11           (arc-of-light ; Angular separation of ...
12            (arccos-degrees ; ... sun and moon.
13             (* (cosine-degrees (lunar-latitude tee))
14                (cosine-degrees phase)))))
15      (and (< new phase first-quarter)
16           (<= (deg 10.610) arc-of-light (deg 90))
17           (> altitude (deg 4.110)))))


 1  (defconstant islamic-locale
 2    ;; TYPE location
 3    ;; Sample location for Observational Islamic calendar
 4    ;; (Cairo, Egypt).
 5    (location (deg 30.110) (deg 31.310) (mt 200) 2))


 1  (defun fixed-from-observational-islamic (i-date)
 2    ;; TYPE islamic-date -> fixed-date
 3    ;; Fixed date equivalent to Observational Islamic date.
 4    (let* ((month (standard-month i-date))
 5           (day (standard-day i-date))
 6           (year (standard-year i-date))
 7           (midmonth ; Middle of given month.
 8            (+ islamic-epoch
 9               (floor (* (+ (* (1- year) 12)
10                            month -1/2)
11                         mean-synodic-month)))))
12      (+ (phasis-on-or-before ; First day of month.
13          midmonth islamic-locale)
14         day -1)))


 1  (defun observational-islamic-from-fixed (date)
 2    ;; TYPE fixed-date -> islamic-date
 3    ;; Observational Islamic date (year month day)
 4    ;; corresponding to fixed date.
 5    (let* ((crescent ; Most recent new moon.
 6            (phasis-on-or-before date islamic-locale))
```

```
12                    (day (1+ (- date crescent)))))
13             (islamic-date year month day)))


1    (defconstant jerusalem
2      ;; TYPE location
3      ;; Location of Jerusalem.
4      (location (deg 31.810) (deg 35.210) (mt 800) 2))


1    (defun astronomical-easter (g-year)
2      ;; TYPE gregorian-year -> fixed-date
3      ;; Date of (proposed) astronomical Easter in Gregorian
4      ;; year.
5      (let* ((jan1 ; Beginning of year.
6              (fixed-from-gregorian
7                (gregorian-date g-year january 1)))
8             (equinox ; Spring equinox.
9              (solar-longitude-after jan1 spring))
10            (paschal-moon ; Date of next full moon.
11             (floor (apparent-from-local
12                      (local-from-universal
13                        (lunar-phase-after equinox full)
14                        jerusalem)))))
15        ;; Return the Sunday following the Paschal moon.
16        (kday-after paschal-moon sunday)))


1    (defun classical-passover-eve (g-year)
2      ;; TYPE gregorian-year -> fixed-date
3      ;; Fixed date of Classical (observational) Passover Eve
4      ;; (Nisan 14) occurring in Gregorian year.
5      (let* ((jan1 (fixed-from-gregorian
6                     (gregorian-date g-year january 1)))
7             (equinox ; Date (UT) of spring of g-year.
8              (solar-longitude-after
9                jan1 spring))
10            (new-moon ; First possible new moon.
11             (phasis-on-or-before
12               (+ (floor equinox) 10)
13               jerusalem))
14            (set ; Time (UT) of sunset at end of 15th.
15             (universal-from-standard
16               (sunset (+ new-moon 14) jerusalem)
17               jerusalem))
18            (nisan1 ; First day of Nisan.
19             (if ; Spring starts before end of 15th.
20               (< equinox set)
21               new-moon
22               (phasis-on-or-before ; Otherwise next month.
23                 (+ new-moon 45)
24                 jerusalem))))
25        (+ nisan1 13)))
```

B.16 The Persian Calendar

```
1    (defun persian-date (year month day)
2      ;; TYPE (persian-year persian-month persian-day)
3      ;; TYPE -> persian-date
4      (list year month day))


1    (defconstant persian-epoch
2      ;; TYPE fixed-date
3      ;; Fixed date of start of the Persian calendar.
4      (fixed-from-julian (julian-date (ce 622) march 19)))
```

```
1    (defconstant tehran
2      ;; TYPE location
3      ;; Location of Tehran, Iran.
4      (location (deg 35.6810) (deg 51.4210) (mt 1100) 3.510))


1    (defun midday-in-tehran (date)
2      ;; TYPE fixed-date -> angle
3      ;; Universal time of midday on fixed date in Tehran.
4      (universal-from-standard
5        (midday date tehran)
6        tehran))


1    (defun persian-new-year-on-or-before (date)
2      ;; TYPE fixed-date -> fixed-date
3      ;; Fixed date of Astronomical Persian New Year on or
4      ;; before fixed date.
5      (let* ((approx ; Approximate time of equinox.
6              (estimate-prior-solar-longitude
7                (midday-in-tehran date)
8                spring)))
9        (next day (- (floor approx) 1)
10             (<= (solar-longitude (midday-in-tehran day))
11                 (+ spring (deg 2))))))


1    (defun fixed-from-persian (p-date)
2      ;; TYPE persian-date -> fixed-date
3      ;; Fixed date of Astronomical Persian date.
4      (let* ((month (standard-month p-date))
5             (day (standard-day p-date))
6             (year (standard-year p-date))
7             (new-year
8              (persian-new-year-on-or-before
9               (+ persian-epoch 180; Fall after epoch.
10                 (floor
11                  (* mean-tropical-year
12                     (if (< 0 year)
13                         (1- year)
14                         year)))))))); No year zero.
15        (+ (1- new-year)       ; Days in prior years.
16           (if (<= month 7)    ; Days in prior months this year.
17               (* 31 (1- month))
18               (+ (* 30 (1- month)) 6))
19           day)))              ; Days so far this month.


1    (defun persian-from-fixed (date)
2      ;; TYPE fixed-date -> persian-date
3      ;; Astronomical Persian date (year month day)
4      ;; corresponding to fixed date.
5      (let* ((new-year
6              (persian-new-year-on-or-before date))
7             (y (1+ (round (/ (- new-year persian-epoch)
8                              mean-tropical-year))))
9             (year (if (< 0 y)
10                      y
11                      (1- y))); No year zero.
12             (day-of-year (1+ (- date
13                                 (fixed-from-persian
14                                  (persian-date year 1 1)))))
15             (month (if (<= day-of-year 186)
16                        (ceiling (/ day-of-year 31))
17                        (ceiling (/ (- day-of-year 6) 30))))
18             (day                ; Calculate the day by subtraction
19              (- date (1- (fixed-from-persian
20                           (persian-date year month 1))))))
21        (persian-date year month day)))
```

```
1   (defun arithmetic-persian-leap-year? (p-year)
2     ;; TYPE persian-year -> boolean
3     ;; True if p-year is a leap year on the Persian calendar.
4     (let* ((y ; Years since start of 2820-year cycles
5             (if (< 0 p-year)
6                 (- p-year 474)
7                 (- p-year 473))); No year zero
8            (year ; Equivalent year in the range 474...3263
9             (+ (mod y 2820) 474)))
10      (< (mod (* (+ year 38)
11                 682)
12              2816)
13          682)))
```

```
1   (defun fixed-from-arithmetic-persian (p-date)
2     ;; TYPE persian-date -> fixed-date
3     ;; Fixed date equivalent to Persian date.
4     (let* ((day (standard-day p-date))
5            (month (standard-month p-date))
6            (p-year (standard-year p-date))
7            (y ; Years since start of 2820-year cycle
8             (if (< 0 p-year)
9                 (- p-year 474)
10                (- p-year 473))); No year zero
11           (year ; Equivalent year in the range 474...3263
12            (+ (mod y 2820) 474)))
13      (+ (1- persian-epoch); Days before epoch
14         (* 1029983          ; Days in 2820-year cycles
15                             ; before Persian year 474
16            (quotient y 2820))
17         (* 365 (1- year)) ; Nonleap days in prior years this
18                             ; 2820-year cycle
19         (quotient           ; Leap days in prior years this
20                             ; 2820-year cycle
21          (- (* 682 year) 110) 2816)
22         (if (<= month 7)    ; Days in prior months this year
23             (* 31 (1- month))
24             (+ (* 30 (1- month)) 6))
25         day)))              ; Days so far this month
```

```
1   (defun arithmetic-persian-year-from-fixed (date)
2     ;; TYPE fixed-date -> persian-year
3     ;; Persian year corresponding to the fixed date.
4     (let* ((d0        ; Prior days since start of 2820-year cycle
5                       ; beginning in Persian year 474
6            (- date (fixed-from-arithmetic-persian
7                     (persian-date 475 1 1))))
8           (n2820     ; Completed prior 2820-year cycles
9            (quotient d0 1029983))
10          (d1        ; Prior days not in n2820--that is, days
11                     ; since start of last 2820-year cycle
12           (mod d0 1029983))
13          (y2820 ; Years since start of last 2820-year cycle
14           (if (= d1 1029982)
15               ;; Last day of 2820-year cycle
16               2820
17               ;; Otherwise use cycle of years formula
18               (quotient (+ (* 2816 d1) 1031337)
19                         1028522)
20               ;; If (* 2816 d1) causes integers that are
21               ;; too large, use instead:
22               ;; (let ((a (floor d1 366))
23               ;;       (b (mod d1 366)))
24               ;;   (+ 1 a (quotient
25               ;;           (+ (* 2134 a) (* 2816 b) 2815)
26               ;;           1028522)))
27               ))
```

```
28          (year    ; Years since Persian epoch
29            (+ 474    ; Years before start of 2820-year cycles
30              (* 2820 n2820) ; Years in prior 2820-year cycles
31              y2820))); Years since start of last 2820-year
32                       ; cycle
33      (if (< 0 year)
34          year
35        (1- year)))); No year zero
```

```
1  (defun arithmetic-persian-from-fixed (date)
2    ;; TYPE fixed-date -> persian-date
3    ;; Persian date corresponding to fixed date.
4    (let* ((year (arithmetic-persian-year-from-fixed date))
5           (day-of-year (1+ (- date
6                               (fixed-from-arithmetic-persian
7                                (persian-date year 1 1)))))
8           (month (if (<= day-of-year 186)
9                      (ceiling (/ day-of-year 31))
10                     (ceiling (/ (- day-of-year 6) 30))))
11           (day           ; Calculate the day by subtraction
12            (- date (1- (fixed-from-arithmetic-persian
13                         (persian-date year month 1))))))
14      (persian-date year month day)))
```

```
1  (defun naw-ruz (g-year)
2    ;; TYPE gregorian-year -> fixed-date
3    ;; Fixed date of Persian New Year (Naw-Ruz) in Gregorian
4    ;; year.
5    (let* ((persian-year
6            (1+ (- g-year
7                   (gregorian-year-from-fixed
8                    persian-epoch)))))
9      (fixed-from-persian
10      (persian-date (if (<= persian-year 0)
11                        ;; No Persian year 0
12                        (1- persian-year)
13                        persian-year)
14                    1 1))))
```

B.17 The Bahá'í Calendar

```
1  (defun bahai-date (major cycle year month day)
2    ;; TYPE (bahai-major bahai-cycle bahai-year
3    ;; TYPE  bahai-month bahai-day) -> bahai-date
4    (list major cycle year month day))
```

```
1  (defun bahai-major (date)
2    ;; TYPE bahai-date -> bahai-major
3    (first date))
```

```
1  (defun bahai-cycle (date)
2    ;; TYPE bahai-date -> bahai-cycle
3    (second date))
```

```
1  (defun bahai-year (date)
2    ;; TYPE bahai-date -> bahai-year
3    (third date))
```

```
1  (defun bahai-month (date)
2    ;; TYPE bahai-date -> bahai-month
3    (fourth date))
```

```
1   (defun bahai-day (date)
2     ;; TYPE bahai-date -> bahai-day
3     (fifth date))
```

```
1   (defconstant ayyam-i-ha
2     ;; TYPE bahai-month
3     ;; Signifies intercalary period of 4 or 5 days.
4     0)
```

```
1   (defconstant bahai-epoch
2     ;; TYPE fixed-date
3     ;; Fixed date of start of Bahai calendar.
4     (fixed-from-gregorian (gregorian-date 1844 march 21)))
```

```
1   (defun fixed-from-bahai (b-date)
2     ;; TYPE bahai-date -> fixed-date
3     ;; Fixed date equivalent to the Bahai date.
4     (let* ((major (bahai-major b-date))
5            (cycle (bahai-cycle b-date))
6            (year (bahai-year b-date))
7            (month (bahai-month b-date))
8            (day (bahai-day b-date))
9            (g-year; Corresponding Gregorian year.
10            (+ (* 361 (1- major))
11               (* 19 (1- cycle)) year -1
12               (gregorian-year-from-fixed bahai-epoch))))
13       (+ (fixed-from-gregorian ; Prior years.
14          (gregorian-date g-year march 20))
15          (cond ((= month ayyam-i-ha) ; Intercalary period.
16                 342) ; 18 months have elapsed.
17                ((= month 19); Last month of year.
18                 (if (gregorian-leap-year? (1+ g-year))
19                     347  ; Long ayyam-i-ha.
20                     346)); Ordinary ayyam-i-ha.
21                (t (* 19 (1- month)))); Elapsed months.
22          day))) ; Days of current month.
```

```
1   (defun bahai-from-fixed (date)
2     ;; TYPE fixed-date -> bahai-date
3     ;; Bahai (major cycle year month day) corresponding to fixed
4     ;; date.
5     (let* ((g-year (gregorian-year-from-fixed date))
6            (start   ; 1844
7            (gregorian-year-from-fixed bahai-epoch))
8            (years ; Since start of Bahai calendar.
9            (- g-year start
10               (if (<= date
11                      (fixed-from-gregorian
12                       (gregorian-date g-year march 20)))
13                   1 0)))
14            (major (1+ (quotient years 361)))
15            (cycle (1+ (quotient (mod years 361) 19)))
16            (year (1+ (mod years 19)))
17            (days; Since start of year
18            (- date (fixed-from-bahai
19                     (bahai-date major cycle year 1 1))))
20            (month
21            (cond ((>= date
22                       (fixed-from-bahai
23                        (bahai-date major cycle year 19 1)))
24                   19) ; Last month of year.
25                  ((>= date ; Intercalary days.
26                       (fixed-from-bahai
27                        (bahai-date major cycle year
28                                    ayyam-i-ha 1)))
```

```
29                        ayyam-i-ha) ; Intercalary period.
30                       (t (1+ (quotient days 19)))))
31             (day (- date -1
32                    (fixed-from-bahai
33                        (bahai-date major cycle year month 1)))))
34        (bahai-date major cycle year month day)))


1     (defun fixed-from-future-bahai (b-date)
2       ;; TYPE bahai-date -> fixed-date
3       ;; Fixed date of Bahai date.
4       (let* ((major (bahai-major b-date))
5              (cycle (bahai-cycle b-date))
6              (year (bahai-year b-date))
7              (month (bahai-month b-date))
8              (day (bahai-day b-date))
9              (years; Years from epoch
10               (+ (* 361 (1- major))
11                  (* 19 (1- cycle))
12                  year)))
13        (cond ((= month 19); last month of year
14                (+ (future-bahai-new-year-on-or-before
15                     (+ bahai-epoch
16                        (floor (* mean-tropical-year
17                                  (+ years 1/2)))))
18                   -19 day -1))
19              ((= month ayyam-i-ha)
20                ; intercalary month, between 18th & 19th
21                (+ (future-bahai-new-year-on-or-before
22                     (+ bahai-epoch
23                        (floor (* mean-tropical-year
24                                  (- years 1/2)))))
25                   342 day -1))
26              (t (+ (future-bahai-new-year-on-or-before
27                       (+ bahai-epoch
28                          (floor (* mean-tropical-year
29                                    (- years 1/2)))))
30                    (* (1- month) 19)
31                    day -1)))))


1     (defun future-bahai-from-fixed (date)
2       ;; TYPE fixed-date -> bahai-date
3       ;; Future Bahai date corresponding to fixed date.
4       (let* ((new-year (future-bahai-new-year-on-or-before date))
5              (years (round (/ (- new-year bahai-epoch)
6                               mean-tropical-year)))
7              (major (1+ (quotient years 361)))
8              (cycle (1+ (quotient (mod years 361) 19)))
9              (year (1+ (mod years 19)))
10             (days; Since start of year
11              (- date new-year))
12             (month
13              (cond
14               ((>= date (fixed-from-future-bahai
15                           (bahai-date major cycle year 19 1)))
16                ; last month of year
17                19)
18               ((>= date
19                    (fixed-from-future-bahai
20                      (bahai-date major cycle year ayyam-i-ha 1)))
21                ; intercalary month
22                ayyam-i-ha)
23               (t (1+ (quotient days 19)))))
24             (day (- date -1
25                    (fixed-from-future-bahai
26                        (bahai-date major cycle year month 1)))))
27        (bahai-date major cycle year month day)))
```

```
21                  ; intercalary month
22                  ayyam-i-ha)
23               (t (1+ (quotient days 19)))))
24            (day (- date -1
25                    (fixed-from-future-bahai
26                      (bahai-date major cycle year month 1)))))
27        (bahai-date major cycle year month day)))
```

```
1   (defun bahai-new-year (g-year)
2     ;; TYPE gregorian-year -> fixed-date
3     ;; Fixed date of Bahai New Year in Gregorian year.
4     (fixed-from-gregorian
5      (gregorian-date g-year march 21)))
```

```
1   (defun feast-of-ridvan (g-year)
2     ;; TYPE gregorian-year -> fixed-date
3     ;; Fixed date of Feast of Ridvan in Gregorian year.
4     (let* ((years (- g-year
5                      (gregorian-year-from-fixed
6                       bahai-epoch)))
7            (major (1+ (quotient years 361)))
8            (cycle (1+ (quotient (mod years 361) 19)))
9            (year (1+ (mod years 19))))
10       (fixed-from-future-bahai
11        (bahai-date major cycle year 2 13))))
```

B.18 The French Revolutionary Calendar

```
1   (defun french-date (year month day)
2     ;; TYPE (french-year french-month french-day) -> french-date
3     (list year month day))
```

```
1   (defconstant french-epoch
2     ;; TYPE fixed-date
3     ;; Fixed date of start of the French Revolutionary
4     ;; calendar.
5     (fixed-from-gregorian (gregorian-date 1792 september 22)))
```

```
1   (defconstant paris
2     ;; TYPE location
3     ;; Location of Paris Observatory.  Longitude corresponds
4     ;; to difference of 9m 21s between Paris time zone and
5     ;; Universal Time.
6     (location (angle 48 50 11) (angle 2 20 15) (mt 27) 1))
```

```
1   (defun midnight-in-paris (date)
2     ;; TYPE fixed-date -> moment
3     ;; Universal time of true midnight at end of fixed date
4     ;; in Paris.
5     (universal-from-standard
6      (midnight (+ date 1) paris)
7      paris))
```

```
1   (defun french-new-year-on-or-before (date)
2     ;; TYPE fixed-date -> fixed-date
3     ;; Fixed date of French Revolutionary New Year on or
4     ;; before fixed date.
5     (let* ((approx ; Approximate time of solstice.
6             (estimate-prior-solar-longitude
7              (midnight-in-paris date)
8              autumn)))
9       (next day (- (floor approx) 1)
10           (<= autumn (solar-longitude
11                       (midnight-in-paris day))))))
```

```
1    (defun fixed-from-french (f-date)
2      ;; TYPE french-date -> fixed-date
3      ;; Fixed date of French Revolutionary date.
4      (let* ((month (standard-month f-date))
5             (day (standard-day f-date))
6             (year (standard-year f-date))
7             (new-year
8              (french-new-year-on-or-before
9               (floor (+ french-epoch 180; Spring after epoch.
10                        (* mean-tropical-year
11                           (1- year))))))))
12        (+ new-year -1      ; Days in prior years
13           (* 30 (1- month)); Days in prior months
14           day)))           ; Days this month
```

```
1    (defun french-from-fixed (date)
2      ;; TYPE fixed-date -> french-date
3      ;; French Revolutionary date of fixed date.
4      (let* ((new-year
5              (french-new-year-on-or-before date))
6             (year (1+ (round (/ (- new-year french-epoch)
7                                 mean-tropical-year))))
8             (month (1+ (quotient (- date new-year) 30)))
9             (day (1+ (mod (- date new-year) 30))))
10        (french-date year month day)))
```

```
1    (defun modified-french-leap-year? (f-year)
2      ;; TYPE french-year -> boolean
3      ;; True if f-year is a leap year on the French
4      ;; Revolutionary calendar.
5      (and (= (mod f-year 4) 0)
6           (not (member (mod f-year 400) (list 100 200 300)))
7           (not (= (mod f-year 4000) 0))))
```

```
1    (defun fixed-from-modified-french (f-date)
2      ;; TYPE french-date -> fixed-date
3      ;; Fixed date of French Revolutionary date.
4      (let* ((month (standard-month f-date))
5             (day (standard-day f-date))
6             (year (standard-year f-date)))
7        (+ french-epoch -1; Days before start of calendar.
8           (* 365 (1- year)); Ordinary days in prior years.
9           ; Leap days in prior years.
10          (quotient (1- year) 4)
11          (- (quotient (1- year) 100))
12          (quotient (1- year) 400)
13          (- (quotient (1- year) 4000))
14          (* 30 (1- month)); Days in prior months this year.
15          day))); Days this month.
```

```
1    (defun modified-french-from-fixed (date)
2      ;; TYPE fixed-date -> french-date
3      ;; French Revolutionary date (year month day) of fixed
4      ;; date.
5      (let* ((approx    ; Approximate year (may be off by 1).
6              (1+ (quotient (- date french-epoch -2)
7                            1460969/4000)))
8             (year (if (< date
9                          (fixed-from-modified-french
10                          (french-date approx 1 1)))
11                      (1- approx)
12                    approx))
13            (month    ; Calculate the month by division.
14             (1+ (quotient
15                  (- date (fixed-from-modified-french
16                           (french-date year 1 1)))
17                  30)))
```

B.19 The Chinese Calendar

```
1  (defun chinese-date (cycle year month leap day)
2    ;; TYPE (chinese-cycle chinese-year chinese-month
3    ;; TYPE  chinese-leap chinese-day) -> chinese-date
4    (list cycle year month leap day))
```

```
1  (defun chinese-cycle (date)
2    ;; TYPE chinese-date -> chinese-cycle
3    (first date))
```

```
1  (defun chinese-year (date)
2    ;; TYPE chinese-date -> chinese-year
3    (second date))
```

```
1  (defun chinese-month (date)
2    ;; TYPE chinese-date -> chinese-month
3    (third date))
```

```
1  (defun chinese-leap (date)
2    ;; TYPE chinese-date -> chinese-leap
3    (fourth date))
```

```
1  (defun chinese-day (date)
2    ;; TYPE chinese-date -> chinese-day
3    (fifth date))
```

```
1  (defun current-major-solar-term (date)
2    ;; TYPE fixed-date -> integer
3    ;; Last Chinese major solar term (zhongqi) before fixed
4    ;; date.
5    (let ((s (solar-longitude
6              (universal-from-standard
7               date
8               (chinese-location date)))))
9      (adjusted-mod (+ 2 (quotient s (deg 30))) 12)))
```

```
1  (defun chinese-location (tee)
2    ;; TYPE moment -> location
3    ;; Location of Beijing; time zone varies with tee.
4    (let* ((year (gregorian-year-from-fixed (floor tee))))
5      (if (< year 1929)
6          (location (deg 39.5510) (angle 116 25 0)
7                    (mt 43.5) 1397/180)
8        (location (deg 39.5510) (angle 116 25 0)
9                  (mt 43.5) 8)))))
```

```
1  (defun chinese-solar-longitude-on-or-after (date theta)
2    ;; TYPE (moment season) -> moment
3    ;; Moment (Beijing time) of the first date on or after
4    ;; fixed date (Beijing time) when the solar longitude
5    ;; will be theta degrees.
6    (let ((tee (solar-longitude-after
7               (universal-from-standard
8                date
9                (chinese-location date))
10               theta)))
11      (standard-from-universal
12       tee
13       (chinese-location tee))))
```

```
1   (defun major-solar-term-on-or-after (date)
2     ;; TYPE fixed-date -> moment
3     ;; Fixed date (in Beijing) of the first Chinese major
4     ;; solar term (zhongqi) on or after fixed date.  The
5     ;; major terms begin when the sun's longitude is a
6     ;; multiple of 30 degrees.
7     (let* ((l (mod (* 30
8                       (ceiling (/ (solar-longitude
9                                    (midnight-in-china date))
10                                  30)))
11                    360)))
12       (chinese-solar-longitude-on-or-after date l)))
```

```
1   (defun current-minor-solar-term (date)
2     ;; TYPE fixed-date -> integer
3     ;; Last Chinese minor solar term (jieqi) before date.
4     (let* ((s (solar-longitude
5                (midnight-in-china date))))
6       (adjusted-mod (+ 3 (quotient (- s (deg 15)) (deg 30)))
7                     12)))
```

```
1   (defun minor-solar-term-on-or-after (date)
2     ;; TYPE fixed-date -> moment
3     ;; Moment (in Beijing) of the first Chinese minor solar
4     ;; term (jieqi) on or after fixed date.  The minor terms
5     ;; begin when the sun's longitude is an odd multiple of 15
6     ;; degrees.
7     (let* ((l (mod
8                (+ (* 30
9                      (ceiling
10                      (/ (- (solar-longitude
11                             (midnight-in-china date))
12                         (deg 15))
13                        30)))
14                   (deg 15))
15                360)))
16       (chinese-solar-longitude-on-or-after date l)))
```

```
1   (defun chinese-new-moon-before (date)
2     ;; TYPE fixed-date -> fixed-date
3     ;; Fixed date (Beijing) of first new moon before
4     ;; fixed date.
5     (let ((tee (new-moon-before
6                 (midnight-in-china date))))
7       (floor
8        (standard-from-universal
9         tee
10        (chinese-location tee)))))
```

```
1   (defun chinese-new-moon-on-or-after (date)
2     ;; TYPE fixed-date -> fixed-date
3     ;; Fixed date (Beijing) of first new moon on or after
4     ;; fixed date.
5     (let ((tee (new-moon-after
6                 (midnight-in-china date))))
7       (floor
8        (standard-from-universal
9         tee
10        (chinese-location tee)))))
```

```
1   (defconstant chinese-epoch
2     ;; TYPE fixed-date
3     ;; Fixed date of start of the Chinese calendar.
4     (fixed-from-gregorian (gregorian-date -2636 february 15)))
```

```
1   (defun no-major-solar-term? (date)
2     ;; TYPE fixed-date -> boolean
3     ;; True if Chinese lunar month starting on date
4     ;; has no major solar term.
5     (= (current-major-solar-term date)
6        (current-major-solar-term
7         (chinese-new-moon-on-or-after (+ date 1)))))
```

```
1   (defun midnight-in-china (date)
2     ;; TYPE fixed-date -> moment
3     ;; Universal time of (clock) midnight at start of fixed
4     ;; date in China.
5     (universal-from-standard date
6                              (chinese-location date)))
```

```
1   (defun chinese-winter-solstice-on-or-before (date)
2     ;; TYPE fixed-date -> fixed-date
3     ;; Fixed date, in the Chinese zone, of winter solstice
4     ;; on or before fixed date.
5     (let* ((approx ; Approximate time of solstice.
6             (estimate-prior-solar-longitude
7              (midnight-in-china (+ date 1))
8              winter)))
9       (next day (1- (floor approx))
10             (<= winter (solar-longitude
11                         (midnight-in-china (1+ day)))))))
```

```
1   (defun chinese-new-year-in-sui (date)
2     ;; TYPE (fixed-date) -> fixed-date
3     ;; Fixed date of Chinese New Year in sui (period from
4     ;; solstice to solstice) containing date.
5     (let* ((s1; prior solstice
6             (chinese-winter-solstice-on-or-before date))
7            (s2; following solstice
8             (chinese-winter-solstice-on-or-before
9              (+ s1 370)))
10            (m12 ; month after 11th month--either 12 or leap 11
11             (chinese-new-moon-on-or-after (1+ s1)))
12            (m13 ; month after m12--either 12 (or leap 12) or 1
13             (chinese-new-moon-on-or-after (1+ m12)))
14            (next-m11 ; next 11th month
15             (chinese-new-moon-before (1+ s2))))
16       (if ; Either m12 or m13 is a leap month if there are
17           ; 13 new moons (12 full lunar months) and
18           ; either m12 or m13 has no major solar term
19           (and (= (round (/ (- next-m11 m12)
20                             mean-synodic-month))
21                   12)
22                (or (no-major-solar-term? m12)
23                    (no-major-solar-term? m13)))
24           (chinese-new-moon-on-or-after (1+ m13))
25           m13)))
```

```
1   (defun chinese-new-year-on-or-before (date)
2     ;; TYPE fixed-date -> fixed-date
3     ;; Fixed date of Chinese New Year on or before fixed date.
4     (let* ((new-year (chinese-new-year-in-sui date)))
5       (if (>= date new-year)
6           new-year
7         ; Got the New Year after--this happens if date is
8         ; after the solstice but before the new year.
9         ; So, go back half a year.
10         (chinese-new-year-in-sui (- date 180)))))
```

```
1   (defun chinese-new-year (g-year)
2     ;; TYPE gregorian-year -> fixed-date
```

```
3     ;; Fixed date of Chinese New Year in Gregorian year.
4     (chinese-new-year-on-or-before
5      (fixed-from-gregorian
6       (gregorian-date g-year july 1))))
```

```
1     (defun chinese-from-fixed (date)
2      ;; TYPE fixed-date -> chinese-date
3      ;; Chinese date (cycle year month leap day) of fixed
4      ;; date.
5      (let* ((s1; Prior solstice
6              (chinese-winter-solstice-on-or-before date))
7             (s2; Following solstice
8              (chinese-winter-solstice-on-or-before (+ s1 370)))
9             (m12     ; month after last 11th month
10             (chinese-new-moon-on-or-after (1+ s1)))
11            (next-m11; next 11th month
12             (chinese-new-moon-before (1+ s2)))
13            (m       ; start of month containing date
14             (chinese-new-moon-before (+ date 1)))
15            (leap-year; if there are 13 new moons (12 full
16                      ; lunar months)
17             (= (round (/ (- next-m11 m12)
18                          mean-synodic-month))
19                12))
20            (month   ; month number
21             (adjusted-mod
22              (-
23               ;; ordinal position of month in year
24               (round (/ (- m m12) mean-synodic-month))
25               ;; minus 1 during or after a leap month
26               (if (and leap-year (prior-leap-month? m12 m))
27                   1
28                   0))
29              12))
30            (leap-month    ; it's a leap month if...
31             (and leap-year; ...there are 13 months
32                  (no-major-solar-term? m); no major solar term
33                  (not (prior-leap-month?
34                                 ; month
35                        m12 (chinese-new-moon-before m)))))
36            (elapsed-years  ; Approximate since the epoch
37             (floor (+ 1.510   ; 18 months (because of truncation)
38                       (- (/ month 12)); after at start of year
39                       (/ (- date chinese-epoch)
40                          mean-tropical-year))))
41            (cycle (1+ (quotient (1- elapsed-years) 60)))
42            (year (adjusted-mod elapsed-years 60))
43            (day (1+ (- date m))))
44       (chinese-date cycle year month leap-month day)))
```

```
1     (defun fixed-from-chinese (c-date)
2      ;; TYPE chinese-date -> fixed-date
3      ;; Fixed date of Chinese date (cycle year month leap day).
4      (let* ((cycle (chinese-cycle c-date))
5             (year (chinese-year c-date))
6             (month (chinese-month c-date))
7             (leap (chinese-leap c-date))
8             (day (chinese-day c-date))
9             (mid-year     ; Middle of the Chinese year
10             (floor
11              (+ chinese-epoch
12                 (* (+ (* (1- cycle) 60); years in prior cycles
13                       (1- year)         ; prior years this cycle
14                       0.510)            ; half a year
15                    mean-tropical-year))))
16            (new-year (chinese-new-year-on-or-before mid-year))
17            (p; new moon before date--a month too early if
```

```
18                 ; there was prior leap month that year
19                 (chinese-new-moon-on-or-after
20                  (+ new-year (* (1- month) 29))))
21               (d (chinese-from-fixed p))
22               (prior-new-moon
23                (if  ; If the months match...
24                    (and (= month (chinese-month d))
25                         (equal leap (chinese-leap d)))
26                    p; ...that's the right month
27                    ;; otherwise, there was a prior leap month that
28                    ;; year, so we want the next month
29                    (chinese-new-moon-on-or-after (1+ p)))))
30          (+ prior-new-moon day -1)))
```

```
1   (defun prior-leap-month? (m-prime m)
2     ;; TYPE (fixed-date fixed-date) -> boolean
3     ;; True if there is a Chinese leap month on or after lunar
4     ;; month starting on fixed day m-prime and at or before
5     ;; lunar month starting at fixed date m.
6     (and (>= m m-prime)
7          (or (no-major-solar-term? m)
8              (prior-leap-month? m-prime
9                                 (chinese-new-moon-before m)))))
```

```
1   (defun chinese-name (stem branch)
2     ;; TYPE (chinese-stem chinese-branch) -> chinese-name
3     ;; Returns bogus if stem/branch combination is impossible.
4     (if (= (mod stem 2) (mod branch 2))
5         (list stem branch)
6       bogus))
```

```
1   (defun chinese-stem (name)
2     ;; TYPE chinese-name -> chinese-stem
3     (first name))
```

```
1   (defun chinese-branch (name)
2     ;; TYPE chinese-name -> chinese-branch
3     (second name))
```

```
1   (defun chinese-sexagesimal-name (n)
2     ;; TYPE integer -> chinese-name
3     ;; The n-th name of the Chinese sexagesimal cycle.
4     (chinese-name (adjusted-mod n 10)
5                   (adjusted-mod n 12)))
```

```
1   (defun chinese-name-difference (c-name1 c-name2)
2     ;; TYPE (chinese-name chinese-name) -> integer
3     ;; Number of names from Chinese name c-name1 to the
4     ;; next occurrence of Chinese name c-name2.
5     (let* ((stem1 (chinese-stem c-name1))
6            (stem2 (chinese-stem c-name2))
7            (branch1 (chinese-branch c-name1))
8            (branch2 (chinese-branch c-name2))
9            (stem-difference (- stem2 stem1))
10           (branch-difference (- branch2 branch1)))
11       (1+ (mod (+ (1- stem-difference)
12                   (* 25 (- branch-difference
13                            stem-difference)))
14                60))))
```

```
1   (defun chinese-name-of-year (year)
2     ;; TYPE chinese-year -> chinese-name
3     ;; Sexagesimal name for Chinese year year of any cycle.
4     (chinese-sexagesimal-name year))
```

```
1  (defconstant chinese-month-name-epoch
2    ;; TYPE integer
3    ;; Index of Chinese sexagesimal name of month 1 of Chinese
4    ;; year 1.
5    3)
```

```
1  (defun chinese-name-of-month (year month)
2    ;; TYPE (chinese-year chinese-month) -> chinese-name
3    ;; Sexagesimal name for month month of Chinese year year.
4    (let* ((elapsed-months (+ (* 12 (1- year))
5                              (1- month))))
6      (chinese-sexagesimal-name
7       (+ elapsed-months chinese-month-name-epoch))))
```

```
1  (defconstant chinese-day-name-epoch
2    ;; TYPE integer
3    ;; Index of Chinese sexagesimal name of RD 1.
4    15)
```

```
1  (defun chinese-name-of-day (date)
2    ;; TYPE fixed-date -> chinese-name
3    ;; Chinese sexagesimal name for date.
4    (chinese-sexagesimal-name
5     (+ date chinese-day-name-epoch)))
```

```
1  (defun chinese-day-name-on-or-before (name date)
2    ;; TYPE (chinese-name fixed-date) -> fixed-date
3    ;; Fixed date of latest date on or before fixed date
4    ;; that has Chinese name.
5    (- date
6       (mod (+ date
7               (chinese-name-difference
8                name
9                (chinese-sexagesimal-name
10                chinese-day-name-epoch)))
11            60)))
```

```
1  (defun dragon-festival (g-year)
2    ;; TYPE gregorian-year -> fixed-date
3    ;; Fixed date of the Dragon Festival occurring in
4    ;; Gregorian year.
5    (let* ((elapsed-years
6            (1+ (- g-year
7                   (gregorian-year-from-fixed
8                    chinese-epoch))))
9           (cycle (1+ (quotient (1- elapsed-years) 60)))
10          (year (adjusted-mod elapsed-years 60)))
11      (fixed-from-chinese (chinese-date cycle year 5 false 5))))
```

```
1  (defun qing-ming (g-year)
2    ;; TYPE gregorian-year -> fixed-date
3    ;; Fixed date of Qingming occurring in Gregorian year.
4    (floor
5     (minor-solar-term-on-or-after
6      (fixed-from-gregorian
7       (gregorian-date g-year march 30)))))
```

```
1  (defun chinese-age (birthdate date)
2    ;; TYPE (chinese-date fixed-date) -> nonnegative-integer
3    ;; Age at fixed date, given Chinese birthdate,
4    ;; according to the Chinese custom.
5    (let* ((today (chinese-from-fixed date)))
6      (if (>= date (fixed-from-chinese birthdate))
```

```
 7        (+ (* 60 (- (chinese-cycle today)
 8                    (chinese-cycle birthdate)))
 9            (- (chinese-year today)
10               (chinese-year birthdate))
11            1)
12        bogus)))
```

```
 1   (defun japanese-location (tee)
 2     ;; TYPE moment -> location
 3     ;; Location for Japanese calendar; varies with tee.
 4     (let* ((year (gregorian-year-from-fixed (floor tee))))
 5       (if (< year 1888)
 6           ; Tokyo (139 deg 46 min east) local time
 7           (location (deg 35.710) (angle 139 46 0)
 8                     (mt 24) (+ 9 143/450))
 9         ; Longitude 135 time zone
10         (location (deg 35) (deg 135)
11                   (mt 0) 9))))
```

B.20 The Modern Hindu Calendars

Common Lisp supplies arithmetic with arbitrary rational numbers, and we take advantage of it for implementing the Hindu calendars. With other languages, 64-bit arithmetic is required for many of the calculations.

```
 1   (defun hindu-sine-table (entry)
 2     ;; TYPE integer -> rational-amplitude
 3     ;; This simulates the Hindu sine table.
 4     ;; entry is an angle given as a multiplier of 225'.
 5     (let* ((exact (* 3438 (sin-degrees (* entry 225/60))))
 6            (error (* 0.215 (signum exact)
 7                      (signum (- (abs exact) 1716)))))
 8       (/ (round (+ exact error)) 3438)))
```

```
 1   (defun hindu-sine (theta)
 2     ;; TYPE angle -> rational-amplitude
 3     ;; Linear interpolation in Hindu table is used.
 4     (let* ((entry (* theta 60/225)) ; Interpolate in table.
 5            (fraction (mod entry 1)))
 6       (+ (* fraction
 7             (hindu-sine-table (ceiling entry)))
 8          (* (- 1 fraction)
 9             (hindu-sine-table (floor entry))))))
```

```
 1   (defun hindu-arcsin (amp)
 2     ;; TYPE rational-amplitude -> rational-angle
 3     ;; Inverse of Hindu sine function.
 4     (if (< amp 0) (- (hindu-arcsin (- amp)))
 5       (let* ((pos (next k 0 (<= amp (hindu-sine-table k))))
 6              (below ; Lower value in table.
 7               (hindu-sine-table (1- pos))))
 8         (* 225/60
 9            (+ pos -1  ; Interpolate.
10               (/ (- amp below)
11                  (- (hindu-sine-table pos) below)))))))
```

```
 1   (defconstant hindu-sidereal-year
 2     ;; TYPE rational
 3     ;; Mean length of Hindu sidereal year.
 4     (+ 365 279457/1080000))
```

```
1   (defconstant hindu-sidereal-year
2     ;; TYPE rational
3     ;; Mean length of Hindu sidereal year.
4     (+ 365 279457/1080000))


1   (defconstant hindu-creation
2     ;; TYPE fixed-date
3     ;; Fixed date of Hindu creation.
4     (- hindu-epoch (* 1955880000 hindu-sidereal-year)))


1   (defun mean-position (tee period)
2     ;; TYPE (rational-moment rational) -> rational-angle
3     ;; Position in degrees at moment tee in uniform circular
4     ;; orbit of period days.
5     (* (deg 360) (mod (/ (- tee hindu-creation) period) 1)))


1   (defun true-position (tee period size anomalistic change)
2     ;; TYPE (rational-moment rational rational rational
3     ;; TYPE  rational) -> rational-angle
4     ;; Longitudinal position at moment tee. period is
5     ;; period of mean motion in days. size is ratio of
6     ;; radii of epicycle and deferent. anomalistic is the
7     ;; period of retrograde revolution about epicycle.
8     ;; change is maximum decrease in epicycle size.
9     (let* ((long ; Position of epicycle center
10            (mean-position tee period))
11           (offset ; Sine of anomaly
12            (hindu-sine (mean-position tee anomalistic)))
13           (contraction (* (abs offset) change size))
14           (equation ; Equation of center
15            (hindu-arcsin (* offset (- size contraction)))))
16       (mod (- long equation) 360)))


1   (defconstant hindu-sidereal-month
2     ;; TYPE rational
3     ;; Mean length of Hindu sidereal month.
4     (+ 27 4644439/14438334))


1   (defconstant hindu-synodic-month
2     ;; TYPE rational
3     ;; Mean time from new moon to new moon.
4     (+ 29 7087771/13358334))


1   (defconstant hindu-anomalistic-year
2     ;; TYPE rational
3     ;; Time from aphelion to aphelion.
4     (/ 1577917828000 (- 4320000000 387)))


1   (defconstant hindu-anomalistic-month
2     ;; TYPE rational
3     ;; Time from apogee to apogee, with bija correction.
4     (/ 1577917828 (- 57753336 488199)))


1   (defun hindu-solar-longitude (tee)
2     ;; TYPE rational-moment -> rational-angle
3     ;; Solar longitude at moment tee.
4     (true-position tee hindu-sidereal-year
5                    14/360 hindu-anomalistic-year 1/42))


1   (defun hindu-zodiac (tee)
2     ;; TYPE rational-moment -> hindu-solar-month
3     ;; Zodiacal sign of the sun, as integer in range 1..12,
4     ;; at moment tee.
5     (1+ (quotient (hindu-solar-longitude tee) (deg 30))))
```

```
1   (defun hindu-lunar-longitude (tee)
2     ;; TYPE rational-moment -> rational-angle
3     ;; Lunar longitude at moment tee.
4     (true-position tee hindu-sidereal-month
5                    32/360 hindu-anomalistic-month 1/96))
```

```
1   (defun hindu-lunar-phase (tee)
2     ;; TYPE rational-moment -> rational-angle
3     ;; Longitudinal distance between the sun and moon
4     ;; at moment tee.
5     (mod (- (hindu-lunar-longitude tee)
6             (hindu-solar-longitude tee))
7          360))
```

```
1   (defun lunar-day (tee)
2     ;; TYPE rational-moment -> hindu-lunar-day
3     ;; Phase of moon (tithi) at moment tee, as an integer in
4     ;; the range 1..30.
5     (1+ (quotient (hindu-lunar-phase tee) (deg 12))))
```

```
1   (defun hindu-new-moon-before (tee)
2     ;; TYPE rational-moment -> rational-moment
3     ;; Approximate moment of last new moon preceding
4     ;; moment tee.
5     (let* ((varepsilon (expt 2 -1000)) ; Safety margin.
6            (tau   ; Can be off by almost a day.
7             (- tee (* (/ 1 (deg 360)) (hindu-lunar-phase tee)
8                       hindu-synodic-month))))
9       (binary-search ; Search for phase start.
10       l (1- tau)
11       u (min tee (1+ tau))
12       x (< (hindu-lunar-phase x) (deg 180))
13       (or (= (hindu-zodiac l)
14              (hindu-zodiac u))
15           (< (- u l) varepsilon)))))
```

```
1   (defun hindu-solar-date (year month day)
2     ;; TYPE (hindu-solar-year hindu-solar-month hindu-solar-day)
3     ;; TYPE -> hindu-solar-date
4     (list year month day))
```

```
1   (defconstant hindu-solar-era
2     ;; TYPE standard-year
3     ;; Years from Kali Yuga until Saka era.
4     3179)
```

```
1   (defun hindu-solar-from-fixed (date)
2     ;; TYPE fixed-date -> hindu-solar-date
3     ;; Hindu (Orissa) solar date equivalent to fixed date.
4     (let* ((critical    ; Sunrise on Hindu date.
5            (hindu-sunrise (1+ date)))
6           (month (hindu-zodiac critical))
7           (year (- (hindu-calendar-year critical)
8                    hindu-solar-era))
9           (approx ; 3 days before start of mean month.
10           (- date 3
11              (mod (floor (hindu-solar-longitude critical))
12                   (deg 30))))
13          (begin ; Search forward for beginning...
14           (next i approx ; ... of month.
15                 (= (hindu-zodiac (hindu-sunrise (1+ i)))
16                    month)))
17          (day (- date begin -1)))
18       (hindu-solar-date year month day)))
```

```
1    (defun hindu-solar-on-or-before? (s-date1 s-date2)
2      ;; TYPE (hindu-solar-date hindu-solar-date) -> boolean
3      ;; True if Hindu solar s-date1 is on or before s-date2.
4      (let* ((month1 (standard-month s-date1))
5             (month2 (standard-month s-date2))
6             (day1 (standard-day s-date1))
7             (day2 (standard-day s-date2))
8             (year1 (standard-year s-date1))
9             (year2 (standard-year s-date2)))
10       (or (< year1 year2)
11           (and (= year1 year2)
12                (or (< month1 month2)
13                    (and (= month1 month2)
14                         (<= day1 day2)))))))
```

```
1    (defun hindu-calendar-year (tee)
2      ;; TYPE rational-moment -> hindu-solar-year
3      ;; Determine solar year at given moment tee.
4      (round (- (/ (- tee hindu-epoch)
5                   hindu-sidereal-year)
6                (/ (hindu-solar-longitude tee)
7                   (deg 360)))))
```

```
1    (defun fixed-from-hindu-solar (s-date)
2      ;; TYPE hindu-solar-date -> fixed-date
3      ;; Fixed date corresponding to Hindu solar date (Saka era).
4      (let* ((month (standard-month s-date))
5             (day (standard-day s-date))
6             (year (standard-year s-date))
7             (approx; Approximate date from below
8                    ; by adding days...
9              (+ (floor (* (+ year hindu-solar-era
10                              (/ (1- month) 12))    ; in months...
11                           hindu-sidereal-year))    ; ... and years
12                hindu-epoch    ; and days before RD 0.
13                day -1))
14             (rate (/ (deg 360) hindu-sidereal-year))
15             (phi ; Estimated longitude.
16              (+ (* (1- month) (deg 30)) (* (1- day) rate)))
17             (cap-Delta ; Difference in longitude.
18              (- (mod (- (hindu-solar-longitude
19                          (+ approx 1/4))
20                         phi (- (deg 180)))
21                      360)
22                 (deg 180)))
23             (tau ; Better approximation.
24              (- approx (ceiling (/ cap-Delta rate)))))
25        ;; Search forward to correct date or just past.
26        (next d (- tau 2)
27              (hindu-solar-on-or-before?
28               s-date
29               (hindu-solar-from-fixed d)))))
```

```
1    (defun hindu-lunar-date (year month leap-month day leap-day)
2      ;; TYPE (hindu-lunar-year hindu-lunar-month
3      ;; TYPE  hindu-lunar-leap-month hindu-lunar-day
4      ;; TYPE  hindu-lunar-leap-day) -> hindu-lunar-date
5      (list year month leap-month day leap-day))
```

```
1    (defun hindu-lunar-month (date)
2      ;; TYPE hindu-lunar-date -> hindu-lunar-month
3      (second date))
```

```
1    (defun hindu-lunar-leap-month (date)
2      ;; TYPE hindu-lunar-date -> hindu-lunar-leap-month
3      (third date))
```

```
1  (defun hindu-lunar-day (date)
2    ;; TYPE hindu-lunar-date -> hindu-lunar-day
3    (fourth date))
```

```
1  (defun hindu-lunar-leap-day (date)
2    ;; TYPE hindu-lunar-date -> hindu-lunar-leap-day
3    (fifth date))
```

```
1  (defun hindu-lunar-year (date)
2    ;; TYPE hindu-lunar-date -> hindu-lunar-year
3    (first date))
```

```
1  (defconstant hindu-lunar-era
2    ;; TYPE standard-year
3    ;; Years from Kali Yuga until Vikrama era.
4    3044)
```

```
1  (defun hindu-lunar-from-fixed (date)
2    ;; TYPE fixed-date -> hindu-lunar-date
3    ;; Hindu lunar date equivalent to fixed date.
4    (let* ((critical (hindu-sunrise date)) ; Sunrise that day.
5           (day (lunar-day critical)); Day of month.
6           (leapday                  ; If previous day the same.
7            (= day (lunar-day (hindu-sunrise (- date 1)))))
8           (last-new-moon
9            (hindu-new-moon-before critical))
10          (next-new-moon
11           (hindu-new-moon-before
12            (+ (floor last-new-moon) 35)))
13          (solar-month         ; Solar month name.
14           (hindu-zodiac last-new-moon))
15          (leapmonth          ; If begins and ends in same sign.
16           (= solar-month (hindu-zodiac next-new-moon)))
17          (month                   ; Month of lunar year.
18           (adjusted-mod (1+ solar-month) 12))
19          (year ; Solar year at next new moon.
20           (- (hindu-calendar-year next-new-moon)
21              hindu-lunar-era ; Era
22              ;; If month is leap, it belongs to next month's
23              ;; year.
24              (if (and leapmonth (= month 1)) -1 0))))
25     (hindu-lunar-date year month leapmonth day leapday)))
```

```
1  (defun hindu-lunar-on-or-before? (l-date1 l-date2)
2    ;; TYPE (hindu-lunar-date hindu-lunar-date) -> boolean
3    ;; True if Hindu lunar date l-date1 is on or before
4    ;; Hindu lunar date l-date2.
5    (let* ((month1 (hindu-lunar-month l-date1))
6           (month2 (hindu-lunar-month l-date2))
7           (leap1 (hindu-lunar-leap-month l-date1))
8           (leap2 (hindu-lunar-leap-month l-date2))
9           (day1 (hindu-lunar-day l-date1))
10          (day2 (hindu-lunar-day l-date2))
11          (leapday1 (hindu-lunar-leap-day l-date1))
12          (leapday2 (hindu-lunar-leap-day l-date2))
13          (year1 (hindu-lunar-year l-date1))
14          (year2 (hindu-lunar-year l-date2)))
15     (or (< year1 year2)
16         (and (= year1 year2)
17              (or (< month1 month2)
18                  (and (= month1 month2)
19                       (or (and leap1 (not leap2))
20                           (and (equal leap1 leap2)
21                                (or (< day1 day2)
```

```
22                                        (and (= day1 day2)
23                                             (or (not leapday1)
24                                                 leapday2)))))
25                          ))))))


 1   (defun fixed-from-hindu-lunar (l-date)
 2     ;; TYPE hindu-lunar-date -> fixed-date
 3     ;; Fixed date corresponding to Hindu lunar date l-date.
 4     (let* ((year (hindu-lunar-year l-date))
 5            (month (hindu-lunar-month l-date))
 6            (leap (hindu-lunar-leap-month l-date))
 7            (day (hindu-lunar-day l-date))
 8            (approx
 9             (+ hindu-epoch
10                (* hindu-sidereal-year
11                   (+ year hindu-lunar-era
12                      (/ (1- month) 12)))))
13            (s (floor
14                (- approx
15                   (* (/ 1 (deg 360)) hindu-sidereal-year
16                      (- (mod (- (hindu-solar-longitude approx)
17                                 (* (1- month) (deg 30))
18                                 (- (deg 180)))
19                              (deg 360))
20                         180)))))
21            (k (lunar-day (+ s 1/4)))
22            (est
23             (- s (- day)
24                (cond
25                 ((< 3 k 27) ; Not borderline case.
26                  k)
27                 ((let* ((mid ; Middle of preceding solar month.
28                          (hindu-lunar-from-fixed
29                           (- s 15))))
30                    (or ; In month starting near s.
31                     (< (hindu-lunar-month mid) month)
32                     (and (hindu-lunar-leap-month mid)
33                          (not leap))))
34                  (- (mod (+ k 15) 30) 15))
35                 (t ; In preceding month.
36                  (+ (mod (- k 15) 30) 15)))))
37            (tau ; Refined estimate.
38             (- est (mod (- (lunar-day (+ est 1/4))
39                            day -15)
40                         30)
41                -15)))
42       (next d (1- tau)
43             (hindu-lunar-on-or-before?
44              l-date
45              (hindu-lunar-from-fixed d)))))


 1   (defun ascensional-difference (date locale)
 2     ;; TYPE (fixed-date location) -> rational-angle
 3     ;; Difference between right and oblique ascension
 4     ;; of sun on date at locale.
 5     (let* ((sin-decl
 6             (* 1397/3438 ; Sine of inclination.
 7                (hindu-sine (hindu-tropical-longitude date))))
 8            (lat (latitude locale))
 9            (diurnal-radius
10             (hindu-sine (+ (deg 90) (hindu-arcsin sin-decl))))
11            (tan-lat ; Tangent of latitude as rational number.
12             (/ (hindu-sine lat)
13                (hindu-sine (+ (deg 90) lat))))
14            (earth-sine (* sin-decl tan-lat)))
15       (hindu-arcsin (- (/ earth-sine diurnal-radius)))))
```

```
1   (defun solar-sidereal-difference (date)
2     ;; TYPE fixed-date -> rational-angle
3     ;; Difference between solar and sidereal day on date.
4     (* (daily-motion date) (rising-sign date)))
```

```
1   (defun hindu-tropical-longitude (date)
2     ;; TYPE fixed-date -> rational-angle
3     ;; Hindu tropical longitude on fixed date.
4     ;; Assumes precession with maximum of 27 degrees
5     ;; and period of 7200 sidereal years
6     ;; (= 1577917828/600 days).
7     (let* ((days (floor (- date hindu-epoch))) ; Whole days.
8            (precession
9             (- (deg 27)
10              (abs
11               (- (deg 54)
12                (mod (+ (deg 27)
13                       (* (deg 108) 600/1577917828 days))
14                     108))))))
15      (mod (- (hindu-solar-longitude date) precession)
16           360)))
```

```
1   (defun rising-sign (date)
2     ;; TYPE fixed-date -> rational-amplitude
3     ;; Tabulated speed of rising of current zodiacal sign on
4     ;; date.
5     (let* ((i  ; Index.
6            (quotient (hindu-tropical-longitude date)
7                      (deg 30))))
8       (nth (mod i 6)
9            (list 1670/1800 1795/1800 1935/1800 1935/1800
10                 1795/1800 1670/1800))))
```

```
1   (defun daily-motion (date)
2     ;; TYPE fixed-date -> rational-angle
3     ;; Sidereal daily motion of sun on date.
4     (let* ((mean-motion ; Mean daily motion in degrees.
5            (/ (deg 360) hindu-sidereal-year))
6           (anomaly
7            (mean-position date hindu-anomalistic-year))
8           (epicycle ; Current size of epicycle.
9            (- 14/360 (/ (abs (hindu-sine anomaly)) 1080)))
10          (entry (quotient anomaly (/ (deg 225) 60)))
11          (sine-table-step ; Marginal change in anomaly
12           (- (hindu-sine-table (1+ entry))
13              (hindu-sine-table entry)))
14          (factor
15           (* sine-table-step -3438/225 epicycle)))
16      (* mean-motion (1+ factor))))
```

```
1   (defun hindu-equation-of-time (date)
2     ;; TYPE fixed-date -> rational-moment
3     ;; Time from mean to true midnight of date.
4     ;; (This is a gross approximation to the correct value.)
5     (let* ((offset (hindu-sine
6                     (mean-position date
7                                    hindu-anomalistic-year)))
8            (equation-sun ; Sun's equation of center
9             ; Arcsin is not needed since small
10            (* offset (/ (deg 3438) 60)
11               (- (/ (abs offset) 1080) 14/360))))
12      (* (daily-motion date) (/ 1 (deg 360))
13         equation-sun (/ 1 (deg 360))
14         hindu-sidereal-year)))
```

```
1   (defconstant ujjain
2     ;; TYPE location
3     ;; Location of Ujjain.
4     (location (angle 23 9 0) (angle 75 46 6)
5               (mt 0) (+ 5 461/9000)))


1   (defconstant hindu-locale
2     ;; TYPE location
3     ;; Location (Ujjain) for determining Hindu calendar.
4     ujjain)


1   (defun hindu-sunrise (date)
2     ;; TYPE fixed-date -> rational-moment
3     ;; Sunrise at hindu-locale on date.
4     (+ date 1/4 ; Mean sunrise.
5        (/ (- (longitude ujjain) (longitude hindu-locale))
6           (deg 360)) ; Difference from longitude.
7        (hindu-equation-of-time date) ; Apparent midnight.
8        (* ; Convert sidereal angle to fraction of civil day.
9           (/ 1577917828/1582237828 (deg 360))
10          (+ (ascensional-difference date hindu-locale)
11             (* 1/4 (solar-sidereal-difference date)))))))


1   (defun alt-hindu-sunrise (date)
2     ;; TYPE fixed-date -> rational-moment
3     ;; Astronomical sunrise at Hindu locale on date,
4     ;; rounded to nearest minute, as a rational number.
5     (let* ((rise (sunrise date hindu-locale)))
6       (* 1/24 1/60 (round (* rise 24 60)))))


1   (defun lunar-day-after (tee k)
2     ;; TYPE (rational-moment rational) -> rational-moment
3     ;; Time lunar-day (tithi) number k begins at or after
4     ;; moment tee. k can be fractional (for karanas).
5     (let* ((varepsilon (expt 2 -17))
6            (phase ; Degrees corresponding to k.
7             (* (1- k) 12))
8            (tau ; Mean occurrence of lunar-day.
9             (+ tee (* 1/360
10                      (mod (- phase (hindu-lunar-phase tee))
11                           (deg 360))
12                      hindu-synodic-month))))
13      (binary-search ; Search for phase start.
14       l (max tee (- tau 2))
15       u (+ tau 2)
16       x (< (mod (- (hindu-lunar-phase x) phase) 360)
17            (deg 180))
18       (< (- u l) varepsilon))))


1   (defun lunar-station (date)
2     ;; TYPE fixed-date -> nakshatra
3     ;; Hindu lunar station (nakshatra) at sunrise on date.
4     (let* ((critical (hindu-sunrise date)))
5       (1+ (quotient (hindu-lunar-longitude critical)
6                     (/ (deg 800) 60)))))


1   (defun hindu-solar-longitude-after (tee phi)
2     ;; TYPE (moment season) -> moment
3     ;; Moment UT of the first time at or after tee
4     ;; when Hindu solar longitude will be phi degrees.
5     (let* ((varepsilon 1/1000000) ; Accuracy.
6            (tau ; Estimate (within 5 days).
7             (+ tee
8                (* hindu-sidereal-year 1/360
```

```
9                   (mod (- phi (hindu-solar-longitude tee))
10                       (deg 360)))))
11             (1 (max tee (- tau 5))) ; At or after tee.
12             (u (+ tau 5)))
13         (binary-search ; Bisection search.
14          l l
15          u u
16          x (< (mod (- (hindu-solar-longitude x) phi) 360)
17              (deg 180))
18          (< (- u l) varepsilon)))))
```

```
1   (defun mesha-samkranti (g-year)
2     ;; TYPE gregorian-year -> rational-moment
3     ;; Fixed moment of Mesha samkranti (Vernal equinox)
4     ;; in Gregorian g-year.
5     (let* ((jan1 (fixed-from-gregorian
6                   (gregorian-date g-year january 1))))
7       (hindu-solar-longitude-after jan1 (deg 0))))
```

```
1   (defun hindu-lunar-new-year (g-year)
2     ;; TYPE gregorian-year -> fixed-date
3     ;; Fixed date of Hindu lunisolar new year
4     ;; in Gregorian g-year.
5     (let* ((jan1 (fixed-from-gregorian
6                   (gregorian-date g-year january 1)))
7            (mina ; Fixed moment of solar longitude 330.
8             (hindu-solar-longitude-after jan1 (deg 330)))
9            (new-moon ; Next new moon.
10            (lunar-day-after mina 1))
11           (h-day (floor new-moon))
12           (critical ; Sunrise that day.
13            (hindu-sunrise h-day)))
14      (+ h-day
15         ;; Next day if new moon after sunrise,
16         ;; unless lunar day ends before next sunrise.
17         (if (or (< new-moon critical)
18                 (= (lunar-day
19                     (hindu-sunrise (1+ h-day))) 2))
20             0 1))))
```

```
1   (defun karana (n)
2     ;; TYPE {1-60} -> {0-10}
3     ;; Number (0-10) of the name of the n-th (1-60)
4     ;; Hindu karana.
5     (cond ((= n 1) 0)
6           ((> n 57) (- n 50))
7           (t (adjusted-mod (1- n) 7))))
```

```
1   (defun yoga (date)
2     ;; TYPE fixed-date -> {1-27}
3     ;; Hindu yoga on date.
4     (1+ (floor (mod (* (+ (hindu-solar-longitude date)
5                           (hindu-lunar-longitude date))
6                        60/800)
7                     (deg 27)))))
```

```
1   (defun sacred-wednesdays-in-gregorian (g-year)
2     ;; TYPE gregorian-year -> list-of-fixed-dates
3     ;; List of Wednesdays in Gregorian year g-year
4     ;; that are day 8 of Hindu lunar months.
5     (sacred-wednesdays
6      (fixed-from-gregorian ; From beginning of year.
7       (gregorian-date g-year january 1))
8      (fixed-from-gregorian ; To end.
9       (gregorian-date g-year december 31))))
```

```
1   (defun sacred-wednesdays (start end)
2     ;; TYPE gregorian-year -> list-of-fixed-dates
3     ;; List of Wednesdays between fixed dates start and
4     ;; end (inclusive) that are day 8 of Hindu lunar months.
5     (if (> start end)
6         nil
7       (let* ((wed (kday-on-or-after start wednesday))
8              (h-date (hindu-lunar-from-fixed wed)))
9         (append
10          (if (= (hindu-lunar-day h-date) 8)
11              (list wed)
12            nil)
13          (sacred-wednesdays (1+ wed) end)))))
```

Reference

[1] G. L. Steele, Jr., *Common LISP: The Language*, 2nd ed. Digital Press, Bedford, MA, 1990.

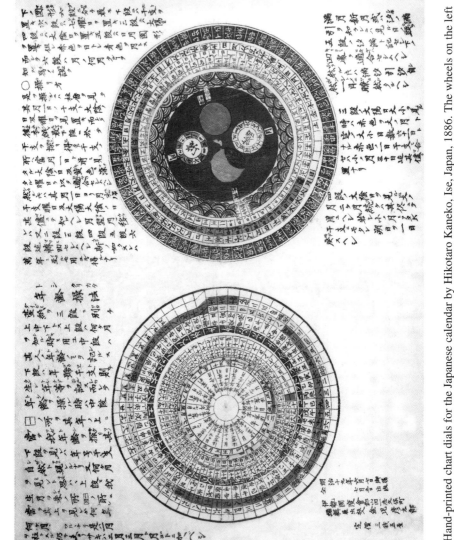

Hand-printed chart dials for the Japanese calendar by Hikotaro Kaneko, Ise, Japan, 1886. The wheels on the left calculate one's age; those on the right show lunar and solar months, tides, and so on.

Appendix C

Sample Data

המבין יבין
—Abraham ben David of Posquieres: *Strictures to
Maimonides' Mishneh Torah, Gifts to the Poor 5:11*

To aid the reader interested in translating our functions into other programming languages, we give a table of 33 dates from years −1000 to 2100 with their equivalents on all the calendars discussed in the book. For each date we also give the solar longitude at 12:00:00 U.T., the fixed date of the next summer solstice (U.T.), the lunar longitude at 00:00:00 U.T., the fixed date of the next new moon (U.T.), the standard time of astronomical dawn in Paris, and the standard time of sunset for Jerusalem. All dates and values given are as computed by our functions and hence may not represent historical reality; furthermore, some of these dates are not meaningful for all calendars.

But go thou thy way till the end be; and thou shalt rest, and
shalt stand up to thy lot, at the end of the days.
—Daniel 12:13

R.D.	Weekday	Julian Day	Modified Julian Day	Gregorian	ISO	Julian[1] Date	Roman Name	Egyptian	Armenian	Coptic
-214193	Sunday	1507231.5	-892769	-586 7 24	-586 29 7	-587 7 30	-587 8 1 3 f	161 7 15	-1138 4 10	-870 12 6
-61387	Wednesday	1660037.5	-739963	-168 12 5	-168 49 3	-169 12 8	-169 12 3 6 f	580 3 6	-720 12 6	-451 4 12
25469	Wednesday	1746893.5	-653107	70 9 24	70 39 3	70 10 2	70 10 1 6 f	818 2 22	-482 11 22	-213 1 29
49217	Sunday	1770641.5	-629359	135 10 2	135 39 7	135 10 3	135 10 2 5 f	883 3 15	-417 12 15	-148 2 5
171307	Wednesday	1892731.5	-507269	470 1 8	470 2 3	470 1 7	470 1 3 7 f	1217 9 15	-82 6 10	186 5 12
210155	Monday	1931579.5	-468421	576 5 20	576 21 1	576 5 18	576 6 1 15 f	1324 2 18	24 11 18	292 9 23
253427	Saturday	1974851.5	-425149	694 11 10	694 45 6	694 11 7	694 11 3 7 f	1442 9 10	143 6 5	411 3 11
369740	Sunday	2091164.5	-308836	1013 4 25	1013 16 7	1013 4 19	1013 5 1 13 f	1761 5 8	462 2 3	729 8 24
400085	Sunday	2121509.5	-278491	1096 5 24	1096 21 7	1096 5 18	1096 6 1 15 f	1844 6 28	545 3 23	812 9 23
434355	Friday	2155779.5	-244221	1190 3 23	1190 12 5	1190 3 16	1190 4 1 17 f	1938 5 18	639 2 13	906 7 20
452605	Saturday	2174029.5	-225971	1240 3 10	1240 10 6	1240 3 3	1240 3 2 5 f	1988 5 18	689 2 13	956 7 7
470160	Friday	2191584.5	-208416	1288 4 2	1288 14 5	1288 3 26	1288 4 1 7 f	2036 6 23	737 3 18	1004 7 30
473837	Sunday	2195261.5	-204739	1298 4 27	1298 17 7	1298 4 20	1298 5 1 12 f	2046 7 20	747 4 15	1014 8 25
507850	Sunday	2229274.5	-170726	1391 6 12	1391 23 7	1391 6 4	1391 6 2 2 f	2139 9 28	840 6 23	1107 10 10
524156	Wednesday	2245580.5	-154420	1436 2 3	1436 5 3	1436 1 25	1436 2 1 8 f	2184 5 29	885 2 24	1152 5 29
544676	Saturday	2266100.5	-133900	1492 4 9	1492 14 6	1492 3 31	1492 4 1 2 f	2240 8 19	941 5 14	1208 8 5
567118	Saturday	2288542.5	-111458	1553 9 19	1553 38 6	1553 9 9	1553 9 3 5 f	2302 2 11	1002 11 11	1270 1 12
569477	Saturday	2290901.5	-109099	1560 3 5	1560 9 6	1560 2 24	1560 3 1 6 f	2308 7 30	1009 4 25	1276 6 29
601716	Wednesday	2323140.5	-76860	1648 6 10	1648 24 3	1648 5 31	1648 6 1 2 f	2396 11 29	1097 8 24	1364 10 6
613424	Sunday	2334848.5	-65152	1680 6 30	1680 26 7	1680 6 20	1680 7 1 12 f	2428 12 27	1129 9 22	1396 10 26
626596	Friday	2348020.5	-51980	1716 7 24	1716 30 5	1716 7 13	1716 7 3 6 f	2465 1 24	1165 10 24	1432 11 19
645554	Monday	2366978.5	-33022	1768 6 19	1768 24 7	1768 6 8	1768 6 3 6 f	2517 1 2	1217 10 2	1484 10 14
664224	Monday	2385648.5	-14352	1819 8 2	1819 31 1	1819 7 21	1819 8 1 12 f	2568 2 27	1268 11 27	1535 11 27
671401	Wednesday	2392825.5	-7175	1839 3 27	1839 13 3	1839 3 15	1839 3 3 1 f	2587 10 29	1288 7 24	1555 7 19
694799	Sunday	2416223.5	16223	1903 4 19	1903 16 7	1903 4 6	1903 4 3 8 f	2651 12 7	1352 9 2	1619 8 11
704424	Sunday	2425848.5	25848	1929 8 25	1929 34 7	1929 8 12	1929 8 3 2 f	2678 4 17	1379 1 12	1645 12 19
708842	Monday	2430266.5	30266	1941 9 29	1941 40 1	1941 9 16	1941 10 1 16 f	2690 5 25	1391 2 20	1658 1 19
709409	Monday	2430833.5	30833	1943 4 19	1943 16 1	1943 4 6	1943 4 3 8 f	2691 12 17	1392 9 12	1659 8 11
709580	Thursday	2431004.5	31004	1943 10 7	1943 40 4	1943 9 24	1943 10 1 8 f	2692 6 3	1393 2 28	1660 1 26
727274	Tuesday	2448698.5	48698	1992 3 17	1992 12 2	1992 3 4	1992 3 2 4 f	2740 11 27	1441 8 22	1708 7 8
728714	Sunday	2450138.5	50138	1996 2 25	1996 8 7	1996 2 12	1996 2 3 2 f	2744 11 7	1445 8 2	1712 6 17
744313	Wednesday	2465737.5	65737	2038 11 10	2038 45 3	2038 10 28	2038 11 1 5 f	2787 8 1	1488 4 26	1755 3 1
764652	Sunday	2486076.5	86076	2094 7 18	2094 28 7	2094 7 5	2094 7 2 3 f	2843 4 20	1544 1 15	1810 11 11

[1] As mentioned in Section 1.3, the negative years in the first two lines of the columns for Julian date and the Roman name are B.C.E. years: 587 B.C.E. and 169 B.C.E., respectively. They appear as negative numbers because the table consists of raw output from the functions.

R.D.	Ethiopic			Islamic Arithmetic			Islamic Observational			Bahá'í (Western)					Bahá'í (Future)					Mayan Long Count					Haab		Tzolkin	
-214193	-594	12	6	-1245	12	9	-1245	12	11	-6	6	3	7	12	-6	6	3	7	11	6	8	3	13	9	11	12	5	9
-61387	-175	4	12	-813	2	23	-813	2	25	-5	9	3	14	13	-5	9	3	14	13	7	9	8	3	15	5	3	9	15
25469	63	1	29	-568	4	1	-568	4	2	-4	2	13	10	17	-4	2	13	10	18	8	1	9	8	11	4	9	12	11
49217	128	2	5	-501	4	6	-501	4	7	-4	6	2	11	6	-4	6	2	13	6	8	4	15	7	19	5	12	9	19
171307	462	5	12	-157	10	17	-157	10	18	-3	4	13	16	9	-3	4	13	16	10	9	1	14	10	9	14	12	3	9
210155	568	9	23	-47	6	3	-47	6	3	-3	10	6	4	4	-3	10	6	4	5	9	7	2	12	17	4	5	7	17
253427	687	3	11	75	7	13	75	7	13	-3	16	10	13	7	-3	16	10	13	7	9	13	2	8	17	14	7	2	9
369740	1005	8	24	403	10	5	403	10	22	-2	14	6	10	17	-2	14	6	2	17	10	9	5	14	2	8	5	4	2
400085	1088	9	23	489	5	22	489	5	22	-2	18	13	4	8	-2	18	13	4	9	10	13	10	1	7	10	15	7	7
434355	1182	7	20	586	2	7	586	2	7	-1	4	12	1	3	-1	4	12	1	3	10	18	5	4	17	8	15	9	17
452605	1232	7	7	637	8	7	637	8	7	-1	7	4	19	13	-1	7	4	19	14	11	0	15	17	7	8	15	7	7
470160	1280	7	30	687	2	20	687	2	21	-1	9	15	1	13	-1	9	15	1	1	11	3	14	13	2	10	10	12	2
473837	1290	8	25	697	7	7	697	7	7	-1	10	6	2	19	-1	10	6	3	19	11	3	14	16	19	11	17	10	19
507850	1383	10	10	793	7	1	793	6	30	-1	15	4	5	8	-1	15	4	5	8	11	8	9	7	12	15	5	2	12
524156	1428	5	29	839	7	6	839	7	6	-1	17	10	17	16	-1	17	10	14	12	11	10	14	12	18	9	6	6	18
544676	1484	8	5	897	6	1	897	6	2	0	1	10	2	12	0	1	10	2	12	11	13	11	12	18	13	6	6	18
567118	1546	1	12	960	9	30	960	9	30	0	4	14	10	12	0	4	14	1	0	11	16	14	1	0	3	18	3	20
569477	1552	6	29	967	5	27	967	5	27	0	5	1	19	4	0	5	1	19	4	11	17	0	10	19	12	7	9	19
601716	1640	10	6	1058	5	18	1058	5	18	0	9	14	5	6	0	9	14	5	5	12	1	10	2	18	18	6	8	18
613424	1672	10	26	1091	6	2	1091	6	3	0	11	8	6	8	0	11	8	6	8	12	3	2	12	6	1	9	3	6
626596	1708	11	19	1128	8	4	1128	8	4	0	13	6	7	12	0	13	6	7	13	12	4	19	4	18	3	1	6	18
645554	1760	10	14	1182	2	3	1182	2	4	0	16	1	5	15	0	16	1	5	16	12	7	11	16	16	1	19	10	16
664224	1811	11	27	1234	10	10	1234	10	10	0	18	14	8	2	0	18	14	8	2	12	10	3	14	6	4	14	12	6
671401	1831	7	19	1255	1	11	1255	1	11	0	19	15	1	7	0	19	15	1	7	12	11	8	13	3	16	16	13	3
694799	1895	8	11	1321	1	21	1321	1	20	1	4	3	2	11	1	4	3	2	10	12	14	8	13	1	18	14	11	1
704424	1921	12	19	1348	3	19	1348	3	19	1	5	10	9	6	1	5	10	9	6	12	15	15	8	6	7	4	3	6
708842	1934	1	19	1360	9	8	1360	9	7	1	6	3	11	3	1	6	3	11	3	12	16	7	13	4	9	2	1	4
709409	1935	8	11	1362	4	13	1362	4	14	1	6	5	2	11	1	6	5	2	11	12	16	9	5	11	19	4	9	11
709580	1936	1	26	1362	10	7	1362	10	7	1	6	5	11	11	1	6	5	11	11	12	16	9	14	2	9	10	11	2
727274	1984	7	8	1412	9	13	1412	9	12	1	8	15	19	16	1	8	15	19	16	12	18	18	16	16	18	4	12	16
728714	1988	6	17	1416	10	5	1416	10	5	1	8	19	18	19	1	8	19	18	19	12	19	2	16	16	17	4	9	16
744313	2031	3	1	1460	10	12	1460	10	12	1	11	5	13	7	1	11	5	13	8	13	1	6	4	15	12	8	8	15
764652	2086	11	11	1518	3	5	1518	3	5	1	14	4	7	6	1	14	4	7	7	13	4	2	13	14	7	7	2	14

Table of sample calendar dates. The table is printed rotated on the page; columns are: R.D., Hebrew (year, month, day), Balinese Pawukon, Persian (Astronomical, Arithmetic — each year, month, day), and French Revolutionary (Original, Modified — each year, month, day).

R.D.	Hebrew			Balinese Pawukon											Persian Astronomical			Persian Arithmetic			French Rev. Original			French Rev. Modified		
−214193	3174	5	10	f	1	1	1	1	3	1	1	5	7	3	−1208	5	1	−1208	5	1	−2378	11	5	−2378	11	4
−61387	3593	9	25	t	2	2	1	4	5	4	5	5	5	2	−790	9	14	−790	9	14	−1959	3	14	−1959	3	13
25469	3831	7	3	t	2	2	1	5	5	4	1	3	5	6	−552	7	2	−552	7	2	−1721	1	2	−1721	1	2
49217	3896	7	9	f	1	2	3	3	5	1	3	5	3	3	−487	7	9	−487	7	9	−1656	1	10	−1656	1	10
171307	4230	10	18	f	1	1	3	3	1	4	3	1	4	5	−153	10	19	−153	10	18	−1322	4	19	−1322	4	18
210155	4336	3	4	t	2	2	1	3	3	5	7	3	8	0	−46	2	31	−46	2	30	−1216	9	1	−1216	9	1
253427	4455	8	13	t	2	3	3	5	7	3	2	7	2	7	73	8	19	73	8	19	−1097	2	19	−1097	2	19
369740	4773	2	6	f	1	2	1	2	1	2	1	2	1	1	392	2	5	392	2	5	−779	8	5	−779	8	4
400085	4856	2	23	f	1	2	1	2	5	1	1	8	1	1	475	3	4	475	3	3	−696	9	5	−696	9	5
434355	4950	1	7	t	2	3	1	1	3	6	1	3	2	2	569	1	3	569	1	3	−602	7	2	−602	7	1
452605	5000	13	8	f	1	1	1	1	7	5	1	5	5	5	618	12	20	618	12	20	−552	6	20	−552	6	20
470160	5048	1	21	t	2	3	4	1	6	6	8	6	2	2	667	1	14	667	1	14	−504	7	13	−504	7	13
473837	5058	2	7	f	1	2	3	5	1	3	5	3	3	3	677	2	8	677	2	8	−494	8	8	−494	8	8
507850	5151	4	1	f	1	1	4	1	4	7	1	4	7	1	770	3	22	770	3	22	−401	9	23	−401	9	23
524156	5196	11	7	f	1	1	4	1	4	2	5	7	5	7	814	11	13	814	11	13	−356	5	14	−356	5	13
544676	5252	1	3	f	1	2	4	2	4	2	7	8	8	9	871	1	21	871	1	21	−300	7	20	−300	7	19
567118	5314	7	1	t	2	1	4	4	4	7	4	7	4	4	932	6	28	932	6	28	−239	13	2	−239	13	1
569477	5320	12	27	f	1	2	3	3	5	7	3	2	7	2	938	12	14	938	12	14	−232	6	15	−232	6	14
601716	5408	3	20	f	1	3	4	2	6	4	8	3	7	7	1027	3	21	1027	3	21	−144	9	22	−144	9	22
613424	5440	4	3	t	2	2	2	4	5	2	1	1	4	10	1059	4	10	1059	4	10	−112	10	12	−112	10	12
626596	5476	5	5	t	2	2	4	6	2	1	2	4	1	6	1095	5	2	1095	5	2	−76	11	6	−76	11	6
645554	5528	4	4	t	2	2	2	5	1	4	5	5	4	4	1147	3	30	1147	3	30	−24	10	1	−24	10	1
664224	5579	5	11	f	1	3	4	5	6	2	8	3	3	3	1198	5	10	1198	5	10	27	11	14	27	11	14
671401	5599	1	12	f	1	2	1	2	2	5	4	5	4	7	1218	1	7	1218	1	7	47	7	6	47	7	6
694799	5663	1	22	t	2	1	5	5	1	5	8	4	1	4	1282	1	29	1282	1	29	111	7	28	111	7	29
704424	5689	5	19	t	2	3	5	6	1	2	3	2	3	8	1308	6	3	1308	6	3	137	12	7	137	12	7
708842	5702	7	8	t	2	2	5	2	2	1	4	1	2	7	1320	7	7	1320	7	7	150	1	7	150	1	7
709409	5703	1	14	f	1	2	2	5	3	2	5	1	1	29	1322	1	29	1322	1	29	151	7	29	151	7	29
709580	5704	7	8	t	2	2	4	1	2	5	4	8	4	4	1322	7	14	1322	7	14	152	1	15	152	1	15
727274	5752	13	12	t	2	2	4	4	5	2	3	8	2	27	1370	12	27	1370	12	27	200	6	27	200	6	27
728714	5756	12	5	t	2	2	2	5	4	1	4	5	4	6	1374	12	6	1374	12	6	204	6	6	204	6	7
744313	5799	8	12	t	2	1	1	4	4	1	7	1	2	19	1417	8	19	1417	8	19	247	2	20	247	2	20
764652	5854	5	5	f	1	3	4	3	6	1	8	6	3	28	1473	4	28	1473	4	28	302	10	30	302	11	1

R.D.	Chinese Date					Chinese Name		Next Zhongqi	Hindu Solar Old			Hindu Solar Modern			Hindu Lunisolar Old				Hindu Lunisolar Modern			
-214193	35	11	6	f	12	2	10	-214191.634729	2515	5	19	-664	5	19	2515	6	f	11	-529	6	f	11
-61387	42	9	10	f	27	8	8	-61370.733038	2933	5	26	-246	9	26	2933	9	f	26	-111	9	f	27
25469	46	7	8	f	4	4	8	25498.215830	3171	7	11	-8	7	9	3171	8	f	3	127	8	f	3
49217	47	12	8	f	9	2	8	49239.006687	3236	7	17	57	7	16	3236	8	f	9	192	8	f	9
171307	52	46	11	f	20	2	10	171318.590237	3570	10	19	391	10	21	3570	11	t	19	526	11	t	19
210155	54	33	4	f	5	10	2	210156.746118	3677	2	28	498	2	31	3677	3	f	5	633	3	f	5
253427	56	31	10	f	15	2	2	253439.316510	3795	8	17	616	8	16	3795	9	f	15	751	9	f	15
369740	61	50	3	f	7	5	11	369767.417293	4114	1	26	935	1	28	4114	2	f	7	1070	2	f	7
400085	63	13	4	f	24	10	8	400113.935688	4197	2	24	1018	2	26	4197	2	f	24	1153	3	t	24
434355	64	47	2	f	9	10	6	434384.030321	4291	12	20	1111	12	23	4291	1	f	9	1247	1	f	9
452605	65	37	2	f	9	10	4	452615.453447	4340	12	7	1161	12	10	4340	12	f	9	1297	1	f	8
470160	66	25	2	f	23	5	3	470177.755730	4389	1	30	1210	1	2	4389	1	f	23	1345	1	f	23
473837	66	35	3	f	9	2	8	473861.320341	4399	1	24	1220	1	27	4399	2	f	8	1355	2	f	8
507850	68	8	5	f	2	5	1	507860.232802	4492	3	7	1313	3	8	4492	4	f	2	1448	4	f	1
524156	68	53	1	f	11	1	11	524172.834565	4536	10	3	1357	10	30	4536	11	f	7	1492	11	f	7
544676	69	49	3	f	4	8	4	544687.133715	4593	1	5	1414	1	5	4593	1	f	3	1549	2	f	3
567118	70	50	8	f	2	4	2	567122.834963	4654	6	12	1475	6	10	4654	7	f	2	1610	7	f	2
569477	70	57	1	f	29	2	3	569492.996118	4660	11	27	1481	11	29	4660	11	f	29	1616	11	f	29
601716	72	25	6	t	20	1	1	601727.342116	4749	3	1	1570	3	3	4749	3	f	20	1705	3	f	20
613424	72	57	5	f	5	9	1	613446.520888	4781	3	21	1602	3	22	4781	4	f	4	1737	4	f	4
626596	73	33	6	f	6	5	7	626626.467423	4817	4	13	1638	4	13	4817	5	f	6	1773	5	f	6
645554	74	25	5	f	5	9	5	645556.325334	4869	3	8	1690	3	10	4869	4	f	5	1825	4	f	5
664224	75	16	6	f	12	9	3	664246.376294	4920	4	20	1741	4	20	4920	5	f	12	1876	5	f	11
671401	75	36	2	f	13	6	4	671426.124336	4939	12	13	1760	12	16	4940	1	t	13	1896	1	f	13
694799	76	40	3	f	22	4	2	694801.614263	5004	1	4	1825	1	7	5004	1	f	23	1960	2	f	22
704424	77	6	7	f	21	9	3	704453.869488	5030	5	11	1851	5	10	5030	5	f	21	1986	5	f	20
708842	77	18	8	f	9	7	5	708867.143728	5042	6	15	1863	6	14	5042	7	f	9	1998	7	f	9
709409	77	20	3	f	15	4	8	709411.313395	5044	1	7	1865	1	7	5044	1	f	15	2000	1	f	14
709580	77	20	9	f	9	5	11	709597.630491	5044	6	23	1865	6	21	5044	7	f	9	2000	7	f	8
727274	78	9	2	f	14	9	5	727277.699907	5092	12	2	1913	12	4	5092	12	f	14	2048	12	f	14
728714	78	13	1	f	7	7	9	728738.668667	5096	11	11	1917	11	13	5096	12	f	7	2052	12	f	7
744313	78	55	10	f	14	8	4	744325.562389	5139	7	26	1960	7	24	5139	8	f	14	2095	8	f	14
764652	79	51	6	f	7	7	3	764656.564424	5195	4	2	2016	4	2	5195	4	f	6	2151	4	f	6

R.D.	Solar Longitude at 12:00:00 U.T. (degrees)	Next Solstice/Equinox (U.T.)	Lunar Longitude at 00:00:00 U.T. (degrees)	Next New Moon (U.T.)	Dawn in Paris 48.84° N, 2.34° E, 27m (Standard Time)	Sunset in Jerusalem 31.8° N, 35.2° E, 800m (Standard Time)
-214193	119.474975	-213857.885383	245.036581	-214174.621008	0.095291 = 02:17:13	0.780311 = 18:43:39
-61387	254.252390	-61094.447554	209.009373	-61383.008248	0.277377 = 06:39:25	0.697040 = 16:43:44
25469	181.435260	25833.305203	213.821493	25495.802668	0.203567 = 04:53:08	0.734627 = 17:37:52
49217	188.662093	49574.080827	292.104807	49238.497566	0.212228 = 05:05:36	0.728250 = 17:28:41
171307	289.089403	171653.984713	156.851211	171318.433031	0.286372 = 06:52:23	0.708501 = 17:00:15
210155	59.119357	210459.464587	108.104381	210180.687915	0.096282 = 02:18:39	0.773952 = 18:34:29
253427	228.316498	253744.632597	39.417290	253442.854298	0.253733 = 06:05:23	0.700597 = 16:48:52
369740	34.466872	370070.362106	98.661798	369763.737893	0.149459 = 03:35:13	0.762484 = 18:17:59
400085	63.193926	400385.467959	333.062297	400091.570277	0.088475 = 02:07:24	0.776532 = 18:38:12
434355	2.462920	434718.238937	92.338110	434376.571202	0.209207 = 05:01:15	0.747826 = 17:56:52
452605	350.480679	452891.033496	78.211911	452627.186209	0.228544 = 05:29:06	0.742269 = 17:48:52
470160	13.502229	470512.003485	275.018078	470167.573455	0.189851 = 04:33:23	0.752843 = 18:04:06
473837	37.407733	474164.418920	128.420669	473858.848230	0.143912 = 03:27:14	0.764151 = 18:20:23
507850	81.030567	508131.957615	89.563254	507878.663442	bogus	0.783796 = 18:48:40
524156	313.862451	524478.621610	24.636880	524179.244329	0.272360 = 06:32:12	0.722257 = 17:20:03
544676	19.955639	545021.433864	53.507927	544702.752301	0.178064 = 04:16:25	0.755877 = 18:08:28
567118	176.060000	567394.307115	187.910712	567146.512283	0.196839 = 04:43:27	0.739393 = 17:44:44
569477	344.923458	569768.743350	320.182580	569479.202529	0.236577 = 05:40:40	0.739394 = 17:44:44
601716	79.964907	601999.244898	314.044964	601727.033423	0.045754 = 01:05:53	0.783812 = 18:48:41
613424	99.302275	613779.989199	145.475718	613449.761986	bogus	0.786840 = 18:53:03
626596	121.535304	626928.688049	185.032179	626620.369647	0.105596 = 02:32:04	0.781720 = 18:45:41
645554	88.567429	645828.317248	142.190205	645579.076668	bogus	0.786063 = 18:51:56
664224	129.289884	664548.570941	253.744068	664242.886600	0.122463 = 02:56:21	0.777882 = 18:40:09
671401	6.146911	671760.527969	151.649135	671418.970437	0.202855 = 04:52:07	0.749426 = 17:59:10
694799	28.251993	695136.040368	287.987873	694807.563367	0.162578 = 03:54:07	0.759976 = 18:14:22
704424	151.780633	704725.161646	25.626767	704433.491161	0.163288 = 03:55:08	0.761652 = 18:16:47
708842	185.945867	709201.678015	290.288335	708863.596972	0.208697 = 05:00:31	0.730378 = 17:31:45
709409	28.555608	709745.741746	189.913174	709424.404926	0.162019 = 03:53:18	0.760136 = 18:14:36
709580	193.347892	709932.167421	284.931761	709602.082675	0.216911 = 05:12:21	0.723741 = 17:22:11
727274	357.151263	727553.613128	152.339165	727291.209381	0.217686 = 05:13:28	0.745097 = 17:52:56
728714	336.170709	729014.587352	51.662475	728737.447666	0.247980 = 05:57:05	0.734479 = 17:37:39
744313	228.185702	744630.158285	26.691872	744329.573169	0.251892 = 06:02:43	0.699539 = 16:47:20
764652	116.439301	764990.025958	175.500487	764676.191300	0.094957 = 02:16:44	0.784233 = 18:49:18

References

[1] A. P. Bloch, *Day by Day in Jewish History: A Chronology and Calendar of Historic Events*, Ktav Publishing House, New York, 1983.

[2] M. Gilbert, *Atlas of the Holocaust*, Pergamon Press, New York, 1988.

[3] H. H. Graetz, *History of the Jews*, Jewish Publication Society, Philadelphia, 1891.

[4] C. Roth, ed., *Encyclopædia Judaica*, Macmillan, New York, 1971.

[5] C. Roth, *A Jewish Book of Days*, Goldston Ltd., London, 1931.

[6] F. E. Peters, *Jerusalem: The Holy City in the Eyes of Chroniclers, Visitors, Pilgrims, and Prophets from the Days of Abraham to the Beginnings of Modern Times*, Princeton University Press, Princeton, NJ, 1985.

[7] I. Singer, ed., *The Jewish Encyclopedia*, Funk and Wagnalls, New York, 1906.

In octo libros De emendatione temporum Index.

A

O●

Index

. . . there will be few who will consider the industry, labor, vigils which we have bestowed upon [the index], or the profit and utility that may be gathered from our labors. For it is the equivalent of a whole book.
—Joseph Scaliger: Letter to Isaac Casaubon (January 7, 1604)

It requires more scholarship to make a good index than to write the book that is indexed.
—George Foote Moore: Address at a reception of the Harvard Graduate School of Arts and Sciences (1925)

Function and constant names are given in **boldface**, and page numbers for a function are of four types: The page with the function definition is shown in **boldface**. The page with the type description is shown underlined. The page with the corresponding Lisp code is shown in *italics*. Pages of other occurrences are given in roman.

Names of people are indexed according to the guidelines of *The Chicago Manual of Style: The Essential Guide for Writers, Editors, and Publishers*, 14th Edition, The University of Chicago Press, Chicago, 1993.

function definition   function type   *Lisp code*

function definition   function type   *Lisp code*

function definition   function type   *Lisp code*

function definition   function type   *Lisp code*

function definition   function type   *Lisp code*

function definition   function type   *Lisp code*

function definition   <u>function type</u>   *Lisp code*

---

function definition   function type   *Lisp code*

function definition   function type   *Lisp code*

function definition   function type   *Lisp code*

---

function definition   function type   *Lisp code*

---

function definition   function type   *Lisp code*

function definition   function type   *Lisp code*

function definition   function type   *Lisp code*

Envoi

Ohe, iam satis est, ohe, libelle,
Iam pervenimus usque ad umbilicos.
Tu procedere adhuc et ire quæris,
Nec summa potes in schida teneri,
Sic tamquam tibi res peracta non sit,
Quae prima quoque pagina peracta est.
Iam lector queriturque deficitque,
Iam librarius hoc et ipse dicit
"Ohe, iam satis est, ohe, libelle."

Martial: *Epigrams*, IV, 89 (circa 90 C.E.)